IN LOVE WITH A HANDSOME SAILOR: THE EMERGENCE OF
GAY IDENTITY AND THE NOVELS OF PIERRE LOTI

RICHARD M. BERRONG

In Love with a Handsome Sailor: The Emergence of Gay Identity and the Novels of Pierre Loti

UNIVERSITY OF TORONTO PRESS
Toronto Buffalo London

© University of Toronto Press Incorporated 2003
Toronto Buffalo London
Printed in Canada

ISBN 0-8020-3695-3

Printed on acid-free paper

National Library of Canada Cataloguing in Publication

Berrong, Richard M., 1951–
    In love with a handsome sailor : the emergence of gay identity and
    the novels of Pierre Loti / Richard Berrong.

    Includes bibliographical references and index.
    ISBN 0-8020-3695-3

    1. Loti, Pierre, 1850–1923 – Criticism and interpretation.
    2. Homosexuality, male, in literature.   3. Gay men in literature.
    I. Title.

    PQ2472.Z8B47 2003   843'.8   C2002-904738-2

University of Toronto Press acknowledges the financial assistance to its
publishing program of the Canada Council for the Arts and the Ontario
Arts Council.

University of Toronto Press acknowledges the financial support for
its publishing activities of the Government of Canada through the
Book Publishing Industry Development Program (BPIDP).

Contents

Acknowledgments

This book was a long time in the making, but it was very much a labour of love, so I never tired of working on it. While I did not have the pleasure of being able to trade ideas with others who also knew and loved Loti's texts, I did benefit greatly from the ideas of several friends in different fields who read parts of the manuscript at various stages. My colleague Manuel da Costa Fontes was generous enough to take time from his own very busy research agenda to read the entire manuscript for general coherence and logic, a fresh perspective that I very much needed and appreciated after having mulled over my work, writing and revising, for several years. Bob Candage was good enough to read *The Story of a Child* and then my chapter on it, offering me helpful insight from his years as a social worker dealing with gay men. Brian Baer, another of my colleagues, read the introduction in one of its last versions and helped me keep on track. To these three I give my thanks.

A Note on References and Translations

All of Loti's novels are available in English, most of them in several translations. Even those that were translated only once have been republished by other houses, with different pagination. Since readers will therefore encounter different editions and paginations for any of the works examined here, it seemed futile to key my study to any one. Instead, I took advantage of the fact that Loti used very short chapters and referenced all citations of his works with chapter numbers, making them easy to locate in any edition. In some of the novels the chapters are grouped into parts; in those cases, my references include part and chapter number: I:II; III:VI; etc.

Because the English translations of Loti's works have often had various titles, some very different from the French originals, I list them in the bibliography, so readers can track them down more easily. Since there was no way of knowing which translation, if any, a given reader might use, I decided to translate all the quotations myself. I also translated the passages from secondary sources not available in English.

Introduction

During the last two decades of the nineteenth century and the first several of the twentieth, Julien Viaud (1850–1923), writing under the pseudonym Pierre Loti, was one of France's most widely read and admired authors. His popular works went through hundreds of editions in his homeland and were translated regularly into many languages, including English. The French Academy, election to which was France's highest honour for men of letters, chose him as a member in 1891 at the unusually young age of forty-one. In the English-speaking world no less a critic than Henry James declared him to be a 'remarkable genius,'[1] and Willa Cather confessed that 'she would swoon with joy if anyone saw traces of Loti in her work.'[2] At his death in 1923, the French government accorded him a state funeral.

Viaud's novels continue to be published and read in France, but in the United States they no longer enjoy their former popularity. Perhaps this is because they were viewed here largely as travelogues about exotic lands and travelogues began to lose their appeal around the time of his death.[3] Perhaps there were other reasons. Many other authors once equally popular have similarly faded from view.

In the case of Viaud's works, however, this is particularly unfortunate. The result has been that his fiction has not been familiar to the mostly American and British literary critics who since around 1970 have been developing what is now called gay or queer studies. His significance as a gay novelist has long been recognized in continental Europe: in the early 1930s, before the Nazis shut it down, his works figured in the Berlin library of Magnus Hirschfeld's Institute for Sexual Research along with those of Wilde, Gide, and Proust;[4] Dominique Fernandez, one of contemporary France's major gay writers, has cited Viaud along with

Verlaine, Rimbaud, Wilde, Gide, Proust, and Forster as one of the founders of what he calls 'homosexual culture';[5] Renaud Camus, another contemporary French gay author, even wrote in one of his columns for *Gai pied* about a gay Frenchman who named his hound Loti;[6] on a more serious note, in 1980, when conservative deputies tried to reinstate discriminatory legislation against gays in France, socialist senator Cécile Goldat announced on the floor of the French senate: 'Homosexuality is not a crime, even if those who commit it are neither Gide, nor Pierre Loti, nor Cocteau.'[7] But Viaud has been overlooked by those here in North America who have spent the last several decades attempting to define and establish a canon of gay literature. English-language surveys of French gay literature generally start with *In Search of Lost Time* (1913–27), the mammoth novel by Viaud's younger contemporary and admirer, Marcel Proust (1871–1922), which that author did not begin to conceptualize until several years after the appearance of Viaud's last novel, *The Awakened*, in 1906. They generally ignore Viaud and suggest, as did J.E. Rivers, that 'Proust is the first major [French] novelist to deal with homosexuality.'[8]

This is, in part, because, unlike Proust, Viaud does not deal openly with homosexuality in his works, though his treatment of it is often less covert than that of Oscar Wilde in *The Picture of Dorian Gray* (1890), which is regularly cited as the first gay novel in English literature.[9] During the era when he wrote Viaud could not have presented the issue positively in an open fashion.[10] Instead, he developed strategies that allowed him to treat homosexuality in various indirect fashions, which his 'unknown friends,' as he called them, could detect if they read his works in the order in which they were written, but which eluded the general reading public of his day. The great commercial success of his novels shows the extent to which Viaud's presentation of these themes succeeded in eluding that public, as does the fact that several of his texts, *My Brother Yves, Iceland Fisherman*, and *Ramuntcho*, were regularly edited by American publishers for use by high school students of French.[11] At the same time, however, Viaud's indirect treatment of homosexuality explains why his work was not known to those outside the French tradition who began the study of gay literature.

Still, when Viaud's narratives were familiar to Anglo-American audiences, those among them who had an interest in this topic detected the homoerotic subject matter behind his coding and judged his work to be an important part of gay literary discourse. E.M. Forster read Viaud in 1907 as part of his search for 'a homosexual literary tradition.'[12] John P.

Anders has argued that Willa Cather's great interest in Viaud had its roots in her appreciation of 'the erotic subtleties of Loti's male romances.'[13] Xavier Mayne, in his history of 'similisexualism,' *The Intersexes* (1908), included Viaud in his catalogue of 'French novelists and poets, who have concerned themselves distinctly with uranism and its various *nuances*,'[14] having remarked earlier that 'something of the influence elemental to sailor-homosexuality is admirably expressed in the novels of "Pierre Loti" ... "My Brother Yves", for instance, is manifestly uranistic, the passional affection for young Yves on the part of the narrator going beyond mere friendship; a strong note of sexual relationship at times sounded in the tale.'[15] Much more recently, the distinguished American scholar of gay literature Michael Moon described Viaud's most popular novel, *Iceland Fisherman*, as 'perhaps the most pungently male homoerotic novel about a sailor before Jean Genet's *Querelle de Brest.*'[16]

That gay studies has so far overlooked Viaud is unfortunate, as we shall see, but not simply because his texts can be shown to depict male same-sex desire; many texts, often of little or no quality, do that. It is important to make their historical precedence known, since they are probably the first significant gay novels in French literature,[17] and therefore can play a major role in the important undertaking of establishing what Claude J. Summers has called 'the gay and lesbian literary heritage.'[18] As already noted, Forster saw Viaud's works as key elements in his own efforts along these lines. It is most important that we become aware of Viaud's work, however, because, as gay novels, his narratives are valuable and, in fact, unique in several ways that make them worth studying and that give them the potential of being of real interest to modern readers, in particular readers of gay literature but also any reader who appreciates the intelligent crafting of a literary text.

One of the ways in which Viaud's novels are unique for their time and appealing to our own is that they are remarkably free of the internalized homophobia that marks so much earlier gay literature. If Wilde's *Dorian Gray* actually deals with homosexuality – the text never states that the title character has sexual dealings with or even erotic feelings for other men, and repeatedly talks of his affairs with women – it does so not only in a very ambiguous way, which is understandable given the English laws of the time against homosexuality, but also in a very negative fashion. Dorian's 'secret,' whatever it is, is repeatedly equated with sin, shame, corruption, and degradation. In E.M. Forster's *Maurice* (1913–14), not intended for publication and therefore not limited by any need to mollify the general public or government censors, the title character does come to accept his homosexuality, but both he and the text still continue to speak of it as abnormal and perverse.

Similar internalized homophobia characterizes most early French gay fiction. As Christopher Robinson remarked of French gay writing, 'the immediate legacy of the generation which came to maturity in the final decades of the nineteenth century was, in its main lines ... a gay male literature of guilt.'[19] Belgian writer Georges Eekhoud did offer a remarkably positive depiction of homosexual characters in his 1899 novel *Escal-Vigor*, and Joris-Karl Huysmans included a brief non-negative homosexual relationship for his protagonist, Des Esseintes, in chapter 9 of his 1884 novel *Against the Grain*, which became the handbook of the Decadent movement. As Robinson notes, however, most gay male French authors of the first half of the twentieth century who chose to deal with homosexuality in their fiction included strong doses of internalized homophobia.

This is certainly true of Viaud's younger contemporary, Proust. As Rivers remarked, there are 'numerous passages in *In Search of Lost Time* that give ... wholesale endorsement to the most negative stereotypes about homosexuality.'[20] Proust may have incorporated these negative ideas into his work in order to make it clear that he could not be gay himself. As Rivers remarked: 'Proust was extremely defensive on the subject of homosexuality and always officially posed as heterosexually inclined.'[21] Robert A. Nye reports that Proust even went to the extent of fighting duels to deny charges of homosexuality.[22] Whatever his reason, Proust offers an often negative or at best ambiguous depiction of homosexuals in his great novel.[23]

André Gide (1869–1951), in his polemical work *Corydon* (1924), glorified pedophilia but distanced himself from men attracted to other adult men, grouping them with inverts and the effeminate;[24] in his fictional works dealing with male same-sex desire, such as *The Immoralist* (1902) and *The Counterfeiters* (1926), he also focused on pedophilia. Julien Green (1900–98), when he dealt with homosexuality in his fiction, as in *The Transgressor* (1956; 1973), evinced a great deal of shame and internalized homophobia. In the novels that he published in the 1940s and 1950s, Jean Genet (1910–86) glorified certain of his gay characters but still accepted some of society's negative images of homosexuals. As Robinson observed, in French literature until as late as 1950 'adult male homosexuality had been more or less exclusively represented, however defiantly, as a defective condition.'[25]

The absence of internalized homophobia in Viaud's work is all the more remarkable given the scientific thinking on homosexuality current in France when he wrote. Western culture has often discriminated against men who are attracted to other men. During the second half of the nineteenth century, however, starting in 1857 with Ambroise Tardieu's *Medical-Legal Study of Assaults on Morals*, French psychiatrists and physicians began a detailed and often widely read study of the newly named homosexual.[26] Their descriptions, at least until the publication of Marc-André Raffalovich's *Uranism and Unisexuality* in 1895, were generally quite negative and hostile, linking homosexuality with criminality, physical degeneracy, the dissolution of social order, and other horrors.[27] Such writing, backed with all the authority of science, not only reinforced general society's negative view of homosexuality, it also undermined the often already poor self-images of contemporary gay authors. Rivers, in a passage already quoted, maintained that Proust accepted much of this negative pseudo-science,[28] and Dominique Fernandez, in his survey of the writing that he had been able to find on homosexuality when he was young, emphasized that these works had long had a strong negative influence on his image of himself as a gay man.[29]

Why Viaud, unlike other gay writers of his and several succeeding generations, did not incorporate contemporary negative thinking about gay men into his work would be hard to say. As a career naval officer he spent much of his life in non-Western cultures with different, non-Western standards and mores, some of which clearly appealed to him.[30] He had ample occasion to see, both among French sailors and in those non-Western countries, a far wider variety of male-male interaction and attitudes toward it than other French authors of gay fiction encountered. Whatever the reason, however, Viaud presented homosexual desire in a positive fashion during an era when such a presentation was particularly in opposition to generally received wisdom backed by all the authority of 'scientific' thought. The purpose of this book, in part, is to demonstrate not simply that he did so, but how he did so before the eyes of a general audience who would not have found such a positive presentation acceptable. In the process, this study shows how to read Viaud's texts as gay.

Since 'gay,' when used to refer to persons attracted to others of the same sex, does not have one generally accepted meaning, I need to explain what I mean by it in this text. For some, like Stanton and other writers in *The Gay and Lesbian Literary Heritage*, it is synonymous with male homosexual and designates men primarily attracted to other men.[31] By and large, this is the definition of the word that I have chosen to use.

For others, however, 'gay' does not mean all male homosexuals. Instead, it has a more limited definition, denoting only those male homosexuals who participate in and identify with the subculture more or less specific to homosexuals (dress, language, mannerisms, etc.). Of course, no two gay men will agree on what constitutes that subculture and to what extent one has to participate in it to be gay in this sense. Still others maintain that a gay man is one who has come to accept his homosexuality and, perhaps, to become involved with other gay men and this culture.

While I find these narrower definitions to be appealing in certain respects, as they allow distinctions between sexual orientation ('homosexual') and not uniquely sexual behaviour ('gay') – some who do not care for the subculture argue that while they consider themselves to be homosexual, they do not consider themselves to be gay – accepting them would mean that I could not apply 'gay' to the novels that I am about to present, since they do not depict what we now term gay subculture. That would leave me with an unacceptable contortion like 'male same-sex-attracted novels,' or 'homosexual novels.' The former I rejected for aesthetic reasons; the latter takes more explanation.

'Homosexual,' at least to some gay men, is clinical or even pejorative. For these individuals, 'homosexual' is a negative term heterosexuals use to describe individuals who are attracted to others of their own sex, while 'gay' is the term that at least some homosexuals have chosen to describe themselves. As a journalist in the *Gay People's Chronicle* wrote:

> There is no question that the terms *gay* and *lesbian* are preferred over *homosexual* by the lesbian and gay community. *Homosexual* is a clinical term, and in fact puts the focus on sexuality. Being gay is much more than sexual activity and terms like *gay* and *lesbian* suggest the depth of individual identity. Referring to the gay and lesbian community as *homosexual* is akin to referring to the African-American community as *colored* or other antiquated terms. *Homosexual* is a word used by clinicians to label us as sick, by fundamentalists to call us immoral, and by extreme conservatives to deny us our civil rights. As the word *homosexual* has been used as a weapon against us, it is understandable why the community demands the use of terms of empowerment, like *gay* and *lesbian*.[32]

This is ironic, since 'homosexual' was coined in 1869 by Karoly Maria Benkert, one of the early proponents of homosexual/gay rights. Nevertheless, because I did not want to drive away any of my potential audience, I chose to use 'gay' in my title and elsewhere in this study in the more general sense given above, simply as a synonym for homosexual.

Some will not be happy with this decision, but I hope that they will understand my choice, which in no way invalidates any other uses of the term. In the body of this study, I use 'gay' quite sparingly, and rely more on homosexual.

'Homosexual' is not a simple term either, however, and this is where the second of the central issues of this book lies. It does not just mean a man who is sexually attracted to other men. As David M. Halperin has pointed out, 'The very concept of homosexuality implies that there is a specifically sexual dimension to the human personality, a characterological seat within the individual of sex acts, desires, and pleasures ... It posits sexuality as a constitutive principle of the self,' as something that 'serves to interpret and to organize human experience.'[33] In other words, homosexuals are understood as being essentially different from men attracted to women because they have a distinct, different sexuality.

While this notion that everyone has a specific sexuality, be it homo-, hetero-, bi-, or whatever, that determines one's desires and is not the same for everyone is widely accepted in contemporary Western culture today, it is, Halperin and others have argued, relatively recent; many historians link the origin of the idea of distinct sexualities to the scientific discourse on the topic that began in the mid-nineteenth century.[34] In other words, whereas today many people in Western society, including many gays, believe that men who are attracted to other men have a distinct, gay sexuality that makes them fundamentally different from other men who do not, scholars have convincingly argued that this is a relatively recent understanding.[35] As Michel Foucault, in his highly influential *History of Sexuality*, wrote:

> As defined by the ancient civil or canonical codes, sodomy was a category of forbidden acts; their perpetrator was nothing more than the juridical subject of them. The nineteenth-century homosexual became a personage, a past, a case history, and a childhood, in addition to being a type of life, a life form, and a morphology, with an indiscreet anatomy and possibly a mysterious physiology. Nothing that went into his total composition was unaffected by his sexuality ... The sodomite had been a temporary aberration; the homosexual was now a species.[36]

Or in Halperin's words:

> It never occurred to pre-modern cultures to ascribe a person's sexual tastes to some positive, structural, or constitutive feature of his or her personality

> ... So most pre-modern and non-Western cultures, despite an awareness of the range of possible variations in human sexual behavior, refuse to individuate human beings at the level of sexual preference and assume, instead, that we all share the same fundamental set of sexual appetites, the same 'sexuality.'[37]

When Halperin wrote that 'although there have been, in many different times and places ... persons who sought sexual contact with other persons of the same sex as themselves, it is only within the last hundred years or so that such persons (or some portion of them, at any rate) have been homosexuals,'[38] he therefore meant that a homosexual is not simply someone who desires to have sex with another individual of the same sex, but more specifically someone who experiences this desire and believes, as does his or her society, that he or she does so because they are significantly different from the majority of humankind.[39] As Claude J. Summers wrote in his Introduction to *The Gay and Lesbian Literary Heritage*, homosexual identity includes 'a subjective awareness of difference and a sense of alienation from society.'[40]

Readers may have noticed that there has been a slippage in the meaning of 'homosexual' here. When Benkert first coined it in 1869, it meant, as it still does today for many, a man whose attraction to other men is the result of an essential difference. When Halperin, on the other hand, writes that 'it is only within the last hundred years or so that [persons who sought sexual contact with other persons of the same sex as themselves] ... have been homosexuals,' he makes it clear that, for him at least, homosexuality depends on the existence of a common belief in distinct sexualities in general and such a sexuality in particular, and so is a socially constructed mindset rather than a psychological or biological essence. Benkert and other essentialists could conceive of homosexuals throughout history; like other constructionists, Halperin, as the title of his book, *One Hundred Years of Homosexuality*, announces, cannot. This is an important difference; it stresses that the significant issue, at least for the constructionists, is not the possible existence of a distinct gay sexuality, but rather how society views men who experience same-sex desire and causes them, as members of society, to view themselves.[41] In a literary study such as this, it is the second issue that counts, not whether men who experience desire for other men do so because they are essentially different, but how a given text or texts presents them as a result of this desire.

As we have already seen, some scholars, such as Foucault and Halperin, have maintained that a distinct homosexual identity did not exist before the second half of the nineteenth century, when the medical and legal communities began defining and describing the men whom they were including in their newly created category. Similarly, Christopher Robinson asserts that, 'in France prior to the 1870s at the earliest, there is almost no concept of the homosexual which defines who or what he is; there is only terminology describing what he does,'[42] and Fernandez, in his history of homosexuality in France, wrote that 'before 1869 ... no homosexual thought of telling his story, because none of them felt "different."'[43] Other scholars have argued that individual men attracted to other men, if not necessarily their society as a whole, had already developed a notion of a distinct, (homo)sex-based identity some time before.[44] Whoever is right, because men attracted to other men have not always been seen as fundamentally different and thus have not always seen themselves as such, literary works from previous eras that describe same-sex desire may, after an initial appeal, fail to awake any real feelings of identification in contemporary Western gay readers. Many of these readers see themselves, consciously or not, not simply as individuals attracted to others of their sex, but as men who are essentially different from the majority because of this, as homosexuals. They will, therefore, identify only so far with men who feel the same desire but do not feel the same sense of difference and alienation. Conversely, they may see same-sex desire and assume that the other feelings that they have as a result of this desire and contemporary Western civilization's understanding of it must also be present, even when they are in fact not in the literary work itself.[45] It is for this reason that Summers issued a warning for those dealing with authors before our time:

> Homoerotic desire and behavior have been documented in every conceivable kind of society. What varies are the meanings that they are accorded from era to era and place to place ... Thus, any transhistorical and transcultural exploration of the gay and lesbian literary heritage must guard against the risk of anachronism, of inappropriately imposing contemporary culture-bound conceptions of homosexuality on earlier ages and different societies.[46]

James Creech, for example, in his study of *Pierre* (1852), a novel by Herman Melville (1819–91), wanted to reveal what he claimed to be the 'homosexual subtext' of the work,[47] but recognized that, given the dates of its composition, he faced a problem in trying to argue that Melville could have conceived of a homosexual. (He finally simply declared that Melville was a gay writer based on his own feelings of identity with the text, but nonetheless described him as 'a "prehomosexuality" homosexual.')[48] Christopher Marlowe's *Edward the Second*, written at the end of the sixteenth century and dealing with the English king's open love for Gaveston and his nobles' reaction to it, never suggests either that Edward is different from the majority of men because of his homosexual attraction or that his court rebels against him because he is attracted to another man. Reading his English king as a homosexual would therefore falsify the text.

Since Viaud came of age after the general public formulation of the notion of homosexuality and thus sexuality, I do not see a historical problem with asserting that he developed homosexual characters. In fact, the second of the ways in which his novels are so unique and therefore fascinating is that, reading them chronologically, one can observe the development of the modern idea of the male homosexual and his sense of a separate identity that parallels its formation in contemporary Western thought as summarized above.[49] One reason for my summary of the constructionist argument concerning the historical limitations of the idea of homosexuality is to show that I am aware of the danger of misconstruing same-sex attraction in literature from previous eras. I also want to show, however, how remarkable it is to find our modern idea of homosexuality in a writer as 'old' as Viaud, and how significant it is to be able to watch that idea take shape through his pages and characters.

Part of the modern scientific understanding of homosexuality is, as Halperin paraphrases Benkert, the creator of the word, that 'homosexuality simply referred to sexual drive directed toward persons of the same sex as the sex of the person who was driven by it.'[50] Whereas, with previous conceptions such as inversion, 'sexual preference for a member of one's own sex was not clearly distinguished from other sorts of nonconformity to one's gender identity,'[51] 'one effect of the concept of homosexuality is to detach sexual object choice from any necessary connection with gender identity, making it possible to ascribe homosexuality to women and to men whose gender styles and outward appearance are perfectly normative.'[52] As Halperin goes on to note, and as one can still find readily in the media and on the street, 'this conceptual transformation has not been either total or absolute.' Homosexual men are still regularly portrayed as necessarily effeminate, given to cross-dressing, etc. Proust, Gide, and Green, each in different ways, all had problems accepting this conceptual transformation, which is why the works of the first two, in particular, can sometimes be problematic for modern readers who have accepted it. In this way as well, however, Viaud's novels were unique for their time and for much of the half-century that followed them. They adhere to an understanding of homosexuality based strictly on sexual object choice and not on gender deviation; their male same-sex attracted characters, in other words, are 'normative.' At the same time, however, through their pages Viaud plays with the socially defined conceptualizations of 'masculine' and 'feminine,' conceptualizations that the France of his era, in the wake of its humiliating defeat during the Franco-Prussian War, was making particularly rigid, exclusionary, and finally dehumanizing, especially for men.

Over the years that I have developed this gay reading of Viaud's novels, I have often been met by questions regarding the author's own sexuality. Some critics, in providing gay readings of literary texts, have replied to such questions with variations on the stance taken by Gregory Woods in his recent *History of Gay Literature: The Male Tradition.*

> It may be completely beside the point whether William Shakespeare was 'gay' or 'queer' or a 'homosexual' or a 'sodomite'; or if he and the male addressee of his sonnets were 'just good friends'; or even if no such friend ever existed and the sonnets in question were – as so many heterosexually identified critics have claimed – mere poetic exercises, common to their time. All of this is irrelevant if any of the sonnets are amenable to being read by a gay reader *as if they were* 'gay poems.' If they work as if they were, they *are*. The reader's pleasure is paramount.[53]

In many cases, this is a perfectly valid response. If, without doing violence to it, a text can be read as expressing gay themes in a manner that makes it attractive to those interested in such themes, why should its author's sexuality be a concern? There are, for example, fine gay novels by women, such as Marguerite Yourcenar and Mary Renault.

This issue is more complex with the reading that we are about to undertake of Viaud's works, however. First, and as already noted, we will show the possibility of seeing not simply gay themes in Viaud's novels, but the development of the modern idea of distinct gay identity that arose during Viaud's lifetime. It would be difficult to imagine that so complex an issue could figure in Viaud's narratives if the author, whatever his sexuality, had not had some interest in the subject and some intention of incorporating it into his work.

Second, as we shall see, the protagonist in most of Viaud's novels, the character through whom the development of the idea of gay identity is expressed, bears a striking resemblance to the author. Rather than try to distance himself from these protagonists, as Proust sometimes did with his Marcel, Viaud took one of their names, Pierre Loti, as his pseudonym, and in other ways stressed the similarities between himself and them. It is therefore necessary to turn to Viaud's biography as another context against which to read his works and, as a result, to consider the question of his sexuality, if we are to do justice to the texts as Viaud presents them. This is not to say that we will read the novels as keys to Viaud's life, however, as unmediated refractions of their author. They are intentionally crafted works of art, not transcriptions of an individual's sessions with his therapist while under hypnosis. Rather, as Viaud makes repeatedly clear, they are his conscious working out of issues in his own life, and can therefore be read against that context. In chapter 1 I therefore survey that context.

In chapter 2 I examine Viaud's first novel, *Aziyadé*. Though certain of the homoerotic aspects of the work have already been touched on, most notably by Roland Barthes, no one has examined the complex strategies that the author develops to suggest indirectly the protagonist Loti's attraction to his boatman, Samuel, something that Viaud could not have expressed openly in a positive fashion in 1879. He does not yet formulate the conception of a distinct gay sexuality: Loti is attracted to Aziyadé as well as to Samuel, and the text never suggests that his interest in the boatman makes him different from other men. With his presentation of Samuel Viaud also begins to break down contemporary society's constructions of 'masculine' and 'feminine,' offering as an object of Loti's attraction a man who is normatively masculine yet also endowed with feminine traits.

Chapters 3 and 4 show how Viaud composed his next two novels, *The Marriage of Loti* and *The Story of a Spahi*, as what we now call prequels to explain and justify how Loti could have become involved with Samuel. *The Marriage of Loti* presents the title character's previous adventures in Tahiti, where he had fallen in love with a young Polynesian woman, as a first attraction to someone different from those with whom Western society expected men such as him to become involved. It also suggests, circumspectly, that Loti had experienced at least some attraction to men before his arrival in the Middle East. *The Story of a Spahi*, recounting the relationship between a white European soldier and a black African woman, argues that the human need for affection justifies non-traditional involvements, very much unlike most colonialist literature of the era.

Chapter 5, dealing with *My Brother Yves*, shows how Viaud returned to dealing with Loti in the present and moved beyond the approach of *Aziyadé*. This text describes Loti's feelings for another man, the sailor Yves Kermadec, directly, rather than using parallels with heterosexual desire, which Viaud had done in *Aziyadé*. Though there is still no indication of a separate homosexual identity, Viaud now endows Loti with a 'gay gaze' that focuses uniquely on men, as well as writing Aziyadé out of his past. The author also pursues the undermining of gender differentiation, while suggesting, long before contemporary gender theorists, that heterosexuality itself might be an artificial social construction not found in primitive man. (Gide would argue this two decades later in *Corydon*, and even modern French gay theorists, such as Fernandez, continue to propound it today.)[54]

Iceland Fisherman, Viaud's next novel, recounts the love of a woman, Gaud Mével, for a man, Yann Gaos. In chapter 6, I explain how, with this text, Viaud turned to parallels of a different sort to convey and universalize one man's love for another, linking Gaud to the Loti of *My Brother Yves* so that perceptive readers would recall the earlier novel while reading the later one and see Gaud's clearly expressed desire for Yann as an elucidation of Loti's more circumspectly described love for Yves. In this chapter I also trace Viaud's continued blurring of gender distinctions, not simply his linking Gaud to Loti, but also his giving the very masculine Yann traits that Western society has classified as feminine.

Chapter 7 explains how the author, in *Madame Chrysanthemum*, returned again to a direct description of Loti's feelings for Yves, thereby establishing a gay element in the legend of the Western sailor who takes and then leaves a young Japanese bride. Though ignored by the composer and librettists of *Madame Butterfly*, this element has been developed in our own time in David Henry Hwang's successful play *M. Butterfly* and in a recent movie version of the opera by French director Frédéric Mitterand.

In chapter 8, devoted to *The Story of a Child*, I demonstrate how Viaud next undertook a recovery of Loti's childhood, the classic gay man's attempt to make sense of his present self by looking to his youth.[55] (The similarities with Proust's subsequent efforts to recapture the past are presented at length.) There the narrator finds early incidences of his attraction to men, to which the adult Loti gives homoerotic connotations. In the process, Viaud for the first time presents Loti as experiencing a sense of being different because of this attraction. He also explores the role of literature in the coming out process and in awakening understanding among the homophobic.

Chapter 9 illustrates how, for a moment, Viaud seemed to hesitate, composing two works, *A Phantom from the East* and *Sailor*, that appear to be attempts to write homosexual desire out of Loti's past and Viaud's present literary production. In chapter 10, I explain how the author incorporated this hesitation into the narrative of his next novel, *Ramuntcho*, but not directly, building a system of interconnected symbols that allowed him to present the conflict allegorically. In the process, pursuing ideas first suggested in *The Story of a Child*, Viaud develops his protagonist's feelings of difference and isolation arising from desires that he perceives to be inherited, and distinguishes between those who cross boundaries simply out of a sense of adventure and those like Ramuntcho who feel themselves to be essentially different because of these desires. This novel is the first to express a longing to find and join others who experience these different desires in order better to understand one's difference, a first tentative call for gay community.

Chapter 11 focuses on Viaud's last novel, *The Awakened*. Viewed from a gay perspective, this is not only his most interesting and positive work, it is one of the most remarkable novels of the first half of the twentieth century. Working with French women's rights activist Marc Hélys in a way that prefigures the modern alliance between feminism and gay liberation, Viaud created a work that argues for the rights of both women and homosexual men. Gone is the hesitation of the immediately preceding works. In its stead is not simply an acceptance of gay identity and a presentation of the feelings of one gay man, but an awareness of and concern for others and even a declaration of the necessity of forming and maintaining community for mutual support against the repression imposed by society and its traditions, something that Proust, fifteen years later in *Sodom and Gomorrah*, would declare to be impossible for gays. (Gide, though he called for an awareness and rejection of such repression, as in *The Immoralist*, did not envision a communal response to it.) Far from the hesitant protagonist of *Ramuntcho*, the courageous activist of *The Awakened* dares to speak out, even in a hostile environment, for the rights and dignity of the repressed, in particular for the right to take a partner of one's own choosing rather than someone imposed by society. Pursuing the lead set forth by *The Story of a Child*, *The Awakened* also examines the role of literature not only to inform the repressed about the worlds and experiences of which they have been kept ignorant at the cost of understanding themselves, but also to assist them in consciousness raising that can give them a sense of dignity and their own potential denied them by their culture.

In providing these keys to a gay reading of Viaud's novels, I show how they hold an interest and importance both as gay literature and simply as literature that should regain for them a substantial modern audience as well as a significant place in the canon of gay literature that is now taking shape.[56]

This analysis of Viaud's work also provides a demonstration of the purposes and validity of gay reading itself. First, it offers an example of how gay reading can enrich everyone's experience of literary texts. Viaud's novels have sometimes been viewed, by those who do not know them well, as secondary works. A gay reading of his narratives shows how rich they actually are, thereby enhancing every reader's encounter with them. Second, a gay reading of texts as popular and respected as those under examination here serves the polemical and empowering function of demonstrating yet again the extent to which the gay experience has played a role in mainstream Western culture. Third, a gay reading such as this makes yet another body of literature available for direct experience by gay readers. This is not to suggest that gays cannot appreciate literature that does not deal with gay issues. One of the functions of great literature is that it makes a given experience accessible to readers who have not personally encountered it, and gays are as open to the power of such greatness as anyone else.[57] It remains true, however, that much of the pleasure readers derive from literature comes from identification. Just as heterosexual readers delight in the heterosexual love stories that fill so much literature, so gay readers take particular pleasure in well-told tales dealing with the experiences of other gay men. In pointing out the gay content of literary works, gay reading adds to the corpus from which gays can derive such pleasure.

It is also because Viaud's novels, once seen as gay, provide this pleasure in abundance that they merit the following study.

IN LOVE WITH A HANDSOME SAILOR

CHAPTER ONE

Was Julien Viaud Gay?
An Examination of the Evidence

In his interesting but often homophobic *L'Oeuvre de Pierre Loti et l'Esprit 'fin de siècle'* (1955), Keith G. Millward admitted that he could not pronounce on Viaud's sexuality for lack of written proof.[1] That is the only honest answer that can be offered. Many writers on Viaud have not stopped there, however, preferring to cross the boundary between speculation and unverified assertion. Lesley Blanch, in the most widely available biography of Viaud in English, *Pierre Loti: The Legendary Romantic* (1983), declared that 'Loti was heterosexual, loving women passionately, and while he loved some men with *equal* fervour ... it is clear that Pierre Le Cor [a sailor Viaud knew] was, before all else, a *companion.*'[2] She offered no proof for her declaration, however, and her own words actually undermine what she wanted to assert: if Viaud loved some men with a fervour equal to that which he experienced for women, how could he have been heterosexual? Irene L. Szyliowicz, in *Pierre Loti and the Oriental Woman* (1988), declared that 'ample proof exists that Loti was bisexual.'[3] She substantiated this claim only by citing unnamed 'recent English biographers,' however. If her 'recent English biographers' are Blanch – her bibliography lists no others – she based her assertion on an unreliable and unobjective source. Many other examples of this sort could be cited. In the end, none of the writers on Viaud seems to have any proof one way or the other regarding his sexuality.

But then, what would constitute proof? The author's words? Authors are like other men or women: they sometimes tell lies, especially when they feel a need to protect themselves or a desire to enhance their self-image. Others' words? Others are men and women, too. It is therefore often hard to prove that a figure in the past experienced or acted on homosexual desires and basically impossible to prove that he or she did not. This caveat understood, we can proceed to a review of what evidence exists.

Our major window onto Viaud's actions and thoughts is his diary, which he evidently began around the age of thirteen and kept regularly, with one significant break, from 1873, when he was twenty-two, until 1918, when he was sixty-eight, five years before his death.[4] Diarists are not always truthful, of course, nor do they always record everything that we might like to know. Viaud's diary is particularly problematic, moreover. As the editors of the latest edition point out, the author several times late in his life went back through and 'purified' it. After his death, his son and literary executor, Samuel Viaud, and his daughter-in-law Elise also went through and deleted passages that they found 'unpleasant.'[5] What was in these passages? We don't know. According to Blanch, Viaud and his son destroyed most of the author's papers that dealt with his relationships with other men,[6] but she provides no indication of how she knew what was in documents that she could not have seen. The diary as it remains contains no clear references to homosexual contact or thought, but given what has been said, this absence cannot be used to adduce anything. As we will see, there are passages in it and Viaud's non-fiction writings that show a definite physical interest in men, but they are too general to be conclusive – and the non-fiction is usually signed Pierre Loti, which means that it may have been written to develop Loti's character.[7]

We have nothing from other men claiming to have had a romantic or sexual involvement with Viaud. Not all such involvements are documented, however, and a person can experience homosexual desires without acting on them. We do have remarks by several of Viaud's acquaintances, but these, too, are inconclusive. Some assert that the author did not have homosexual tendencies. Loti scholar Raymonde Lefèvre, for example, in her effort to deny allegations that Viaud was homosexual, cites the assertion by Louis de Robert, a friend of the novelist, that the author 'was the most normal, most mentally healthy person I have known. There was nothing dubious about him.'[8] What de Robert meant here is not as clear as Lefèvre wants her readers to believe, however. They can see that de Robert was trying to defend Viaud; he had been the recipient of the novelist's generosity and was very devoted to him and to what he understood to be the positive preservation of his memory. As a result, there is no way of knowing if he was telling the truth here, or if he even knew the truth. We do know, however, that he evidently did not, himself, have problems dealing with gay men, as he was also a friend of Proust.[9] His statement regarding Viaud proves nothing, therefore, whatever it may mean.

There were also contemporaries who asserted the opposite. Edmond de Goncourt, a distinguished contemporary novelist, wrote in his diary on 3 November 1895, after an encounter with Viaud at a social function: 'Loti ... is or ... does everything that one could do to be thought to be a *pédéraste.*'[10] On 21 February 1888, describing a dinner at the home of novelist Alphonse Daudet to which Viaud had brought a handsome sailor whose attire revealed much of his chest, Goncourt had already indicated that, at least in his view, the author seemed to be trying to show that he was homosexual: 'Is this *pédérastie* that he presents really sincere?' Goncourt wondered.

Neither of these passages proves that Viaud was gay, however; in fact, both indicate that Goncourt himself was uncertain. They do, however, indicate that Viaud, rather than trying to deny a homosexual orientation in public like Proust, did things openly that suggested it. Michel Desbruères, in his preface to Viaud's gay love story, *My Brother Yves*, quoted a remark by the author's son that seems to indicate the same partial openness: 'Loti probably wanted to be figured out under his mask and was aggravated by others' failure to do so. Did he not express himself more openly out of timidity? Modesty? This need to be figured out tormented Loti throughout his life.'[12] The vague wording of Viaud's son does not permit us to say exactly what is meant here, however.

The preceding excerpts from the Goncourt diary show his most famous remark concerning Viaud to be much less authoritative than it has sometimes been taken to be. On 7 April 1892, furious at him for having criticized the Naturalists in his acceptance speech at the French Academy and for having condemned their work as immoral, Goncourt referred to Viaud as 'this author, whose female lover, in his first novel, is a man.'[13] He gave no indication of how he knew such a thing, and the assertion is patently false. As we will see in the chapter devoted to that first novel, *Aziyadé*, the male protagonist's female lover, Aziyadé, is described as a woman, behaves as such, and was based on Hakidjé, a woman whom Viaud had known while he was stationed in the Middle East. There is a homoerotic relationship between the protagonist and a man, the boatman Samuel, but there is no reason to argue that the female lover in the novel is a disguised male. In all probability, what Goncourt meant to say is that the female lover in the novel was based on a man in real life, which was evidently not the case, and not that the character was actually a man described as a woman, which is a literary impossibility.[14] In an entry for 21 September 1890, which does not appear in earlier editions of the diary and which is not indexed under 'Pierre Loti' in the 1956 edition, Goncourt wrote: 'Is it true? The princess [Napoleon III's sister] declared that an admiral and a sub-admiral had confirmed to her that Loti had been surprised in the act of pederasty and that a prosecution had been begun against him, but that it had been abandoned for I know not what reason.'[15] None of Viaud's biographers mentions this episode, so we have no way of knowing if it actually took place, or if Goncourt was just spreading rumours as a result of his dislike of Viaud.

Lacking any irrefutable proof from Viaud's contemporaries one way or the other, all we can do is summarize the relevant facts of his biography and allow readers to draw their own conclusions.

Louis Marie Julien Viaud was born in 1850 in the small southwestern French city of Rochefort. The household in which he grew up consisted mostly of women: his mother, sister, grandmothers, and various aunts and great-aunts. There were only two male presences. Viaud's father, Théodore, evidently a weak man, very seldom figures in the author's published reminiscences. He died when Viaud was twenty. As Pierre Brodin wrote: 'Mr. Viaud did not have the unique place in his existence and his development that his mother occupied.'[16] On the other hand, Viaud's brother, Gustave, twelve years older than Viaud, was idolized by the young boy. Many years later, in a volume of memoirs entitled *First Youth*, the author not only recalled his great love for his brother and grief at his loss – Gustave died at sea in 1865, when Viaud was fifteen – but also remarked that Gustave had been the one person to whom he had turned for advice and counsel (293). Gustave left to join the navy when the future author was only eight, however, and returned home only infrequently.[17]

Viaud's mother, Nadine, was evidently a strong-willed woman, and it was she, her daughter, Marie, twenty years older than Viaud, and various female relatives who raised Julien. Since he was educated mostly at home until he was twelve, he therefore grew up in an almost exclusively female environment. According to the author, Gustave worried that the family would make a little girl out of Julien (*First Youth* 310).[18]

In a piece entitled 'Fragments from a Private Diary' that he first published in 1916 in the *Revue des deux mondes* and later republished in *Some Aspects of the World's Madness*, Viaud wrote that, starting at age eight or ten, he had had 'visions' of a man in a black coat who signaled Viaud to follow him 'with a discreet and confidential gesture' (23). Viaud termed this and subsequent visions, all of whom beckoned to him to join them, as 'a disturbance that must have come from the Great Mystery underneath,' a phrase to which, as we shall see in chapter 8, the author had given homoerotic connotations in his 1890 autobiographical novel, *The Story of a Child*. He offered no analysis of these visions in the piece that he published in *Some Aspects*, however.

According to *First Youth*, at sixteen Viaud had his first (hetero)sexual experience. A band of gypsies had moved into the area, and Julien several times noticed a very attractive woman in their group. One day while he was out in the woods, where he knew their camp to be, he encountered her and they had sex. Viaud blames the gypsy, claiming that she seduced him (345). He also presents the episode as very traumatic, calling it 'the most troubling scene of my adolescent life' (320), and asserts that it marked the end of his childhood (344). The young Julien gave up on her rather quickly.[19]

It is tempting to dismiss this episode as a clichéd literary fabrication. The thirty-some volumes that Viaud had published before *First Youth* contain many recollections of childhood but not one mention of this incident. Moreover, the chapters devoted to the incident read very much like a literary invention. Gypsies were seen by many nineteenth-century Western Europeans rather like African-Americans have been seen by some white Americans, as the incarnation of uncontrolled sexuality; the scenario of a gypsy woman seducing an innocent young boy was a racialized commonplace in Western European culture, and at least one Viaud scholar, Szyliowicz, has maintained that the episode with the gypsy is 'little more than a pastiche of commonplaces.'[20] Viaud may have created this scene to add some spice to his narrative, and perhaps to imply that he had always been unambiguously heterosexual.[21] Émile Vedel, a friend and collaborator who wrote a preface to the next volume of Viaud's memoirs, *Notes of My Youth*, read the scene as a significant declaration of heterosexuality, or at least wanted others to read it that way. Focusing on it and one later brief scene also involving a woman, both of which comprise only a small part of *First Youth*, he declared that they indicate 'what the future writer's existence would be.'[22]

One detail is particularly striking, however, in light of the often sexually ambiguous content of many of Viaud's previous works. Before the troubling encounter with the gypsy woman, young Julien, looking out his window one night at the forest where the gypsy band is camped, imagines her 'in the tawny arms of a member of her tribe' (341). Suddenly attention moves from the woman to an eroticized aspect of a man.

Is it the elderly Viaud shifting focus, or the young Julien? The text is not clear.[23]

It was about this time that Viaud decided to enter the navy, as his brother had before him. His family was unhappy with this decision, quite understandably, as they had just lost Gustave to the sea and were now faced with the absence and possible loss of their remaining son. Viaud persisted, though, and finally left to spend several months in Paris preparing for the entrance exam.

In part, Viaud chose the navy out of a desire to escape from his family's, and in particular his mother's, control – a feeling that many teenagers, gay and not gay, experience at that age. Viaud's family was evidently particularly possessive with him, moreover. Even as an adult, he repeatedly mentioned it. In 1881, at the age of thirty-one, when he was posted to Rochefort, he remarked, speaking of his mother and aunt: 'Those two good old ladies are so happy to think that they will be able to keep me for a long time, like a bird in a cage!' (*Private Diary 1878–1881* 238). The year before, when Viaud had recounted to her some of his adventures in Eastern Europe, his mother had written him not to endanger his life, 'which does not belong to you' (198). Since at that time there was far less mobility than today, life in the navy offered one of the few means for a man to find employment away from home.[24]

Viaud felt restricted by his family, and in particular his mother, not simply because of their possessiveness, however. As repeated passages in his diary make clear, he also felt that he could not be himself when he was with her, whatever that entailed, because it would have displeased her. In 1880, when he was about to turn thirty, he wrote that his mother's death would be the 'milestone that will probably also signal, for me, the end of the role that I am still playing only for her' (114). A year later he repeated this idea, writing to his friend Emile Pouvillon that when his mother died 'people will see this character that I play for her whose name is Monsieur Julien Viaud, naval officer, an orderly and sufficiently proper young man, disappear' (246). Later that same year, when he took her to see Paris, he confessed in his diary that, as much pleasure as that gave him, he also wanted to 'lead my own life, the life of *Pierre Loti*' (*Cette éternelle nostalgie* 85).[25] Obviously Viaud felt a need to hide some aspect of his life from his mother, but these passages do not specify what it was.[26]

In part, however, Viaud seems to have chosen the navy because he was fascinated by sailors. In a diary entry recollecting how, as a young adolescent, he used to walk by the Saint-Maurice naval barracks in his home town with his father, he remarked: 'I loved those sailors, I felt drawn to them, to the life of seafolk, to adventures and the unknown ...' (60). In some of Viaud's literary works, Pierre Loti recalls similar, even more potentially erotic childhood thoughts about seamen. In *Blossoms of Boredom* he states: 'I remember that, when I was in bed, comfortably tucked in in my white bed, it used to disturb me to hear the sailors' noisy gaiety and songs in the streets in the evening ... I was taken with extraordinary dreams, dreaming about the countries from which these tanned men had returned, about that life and those adventures. – Who would have suspected, at that time, what was going through my head! ... For me, all of that had the appeal of forbidden, impossible things; at that period, it was understood, and accepted even by me, that I would never leave the family aegis ... Who could have told me that, later, I would direct and share in their fatigue, their adventures and their pleasures, those of these men who had the presumption to sing at night, and not to go to bed in order to make a racket.' (168). In *The Story of a Child*, the young Pierre imagines a cake seller moving from his neighbourhood to those same sailors' quarters, and continues: 'What could have been going on there? What were those animalistic joys that were expressed in shouts like? What were those people up to, who had returned from the sea and from distant countries where the sun burns? What rougher, simpler, and freer life did they have? ... the seed of an uneasiness, of an aspiration toward something different and unknown, was already planted in my little head' (XXIII). In these cases, however, it bears remembering that these are the recollections of a middle-aged adult, so they may or may not accurately reflect the feelings of the teen-aged Julien Viaud. It is certainly true that the sea was, then as now, one of the few fields that allowed a man to have close, continuous, and often very intimate contact with other men, some of whom had chosen to live away from women. It is equally true, however, that many men go to sea for reasons that have nothing to do with this.[27]

While in Paris to prepare for his exams, Viaud evidently did not go out looking for women on his own. According to *First Youth*, he had to be led by fellow students (371). Indeed, that book describes him as avoiding women while there (382–3). The only exception was an unnamed woman portrayed as 'already too ripe for my age' (371), whom he saw on Thursdays, though apparently only for drinks and conversation. Viaud dropped her as soon as she started to ask him questions about his family. In *Notes of My Youth*, on the other hand, he declared that he did not become involved in the bohemian life while he was in

Paris, seeking instead 'the love of a sad young girl who was richly kept' (26 March 1875). Although both of these brief episodes are very much literary clichés, that does not mean that they could not have had a counterpart in reality.

In *Notes of My Youth* Viaud also mentions, quite obliquely, that while in Paris he often spent time in the hidden corners of the Luxembourg Gardens, during what was 'an era of transition in my life' (Paris, June 1878). That recollection could have nothing to do with any kind of sex, or it could refer to homosexual cruising. The classic cruising park in Paris was evidently the Tuilleries, but as a Parisian friend remarked, where there are parks with hidden areas homosexual cruising is always a possibility. The fact that this mention comes immediately after an apparently unrelated recollection of Pierre Le Cor's quarters in Toulon may be significant or may not. In the part of his diary covering his sojourn in Paris, Viaud wrote: 'I have already fallen morally and I no longer have any esteem for myself.'[28] What he meant we cannot say. In October 1867, having passed his exam, Viaud entered naval training.

While in naval school, the future author became very attached to handsome fellow student Joseph Bernard.[29] In a letter of 26 March 1873, contained in *Notes of My Youth*, he addressed him as 'Dear little brother,' introducing the ambiguous use of the word 'brother' that will recur in so much of his literary creation, and recalled wistfully the room that they had shared while in training in Toulon.[30] The letter is full of the pronouns 'we' and 'our,' linking Viaud to Bernard in every small detail of their lives. In a letter of 27 June of the same year, Viaud wrote his 'dear brother' that he was about to leave the latter's former hotel room in Cherbourg 'with sorrow, because it is still full of your memory ... I became attached to all of that because of you.' Once they entered the navy, the two made several apprentice voyages together, including one on *La Flore* around the globe during which Viaud went about 'creating a home for the two of us' in Tahiti.[31] When Bernard was subsequently sent to the French outpost of Dakar in what is today Senegal, Viaud arranged to be assigned there as well. According to Viaud, this was at Bernard's request.[32]

What followed was, for the future author at least, a magical time; the description of it even in the published version of his diaries can easily be read as a gay idyll. The two shared a house – 'our big house in Dakar, that I had taken such care to make beautiful' (*Notes of My Youth*, March 1874) – and, according to *Notes of My Youth*, they did everything together. The pages recounting those months are filled with constant references to 'we' and 'our,' a rhetorical trait that will reappear in several of Viaud's novels when the first-person narrator describes his relationship with another man. In May 1874, Bernard left Africa, however, and the relationship seems to have come to an abrupt, unexplained end. Suddenly everything is 'I' and 'my' rather than 'we' and 'our': the giraffe skin that 'we had brought back from Podor' (March 1874) becomes 'my giraffe skin brought back from Podor' (20 June 1874), etc.

None of Viaud's autobiographical volumes explains what happened. His son Samuel, who edited and published *Notes of My Youth* after his father's death, remarked that his father had ripped up a substantial portion of the diary entries that he had made at that point (note to entry for May 1874). A reference four years later to 'the dark mystery that has irremediably distanced him from me' (Cherbourg, May 1878) suggests that Viaud himself did not understand the cause of the rift. The author kept recalling Bernard, however, often in sad dreams, and some of those recollections appear in the published form of the diaries covering the next several years.[33] Viaud also used Bernard as the primary model for the character John B., who figures prominently in *The Marriage of Loti* (1880) and is mentioned on occasion in other works. On 8 October 1881, the author travelled to Lille to see Bernard and 'make a clean breast of things.' Bernard received him in his home, 'clasped me in his arms, kissed me and cried. The explanation didn't take long. Six years of my life vanished, and I found once again, more or less, my friend from the past' (*Cette éternelle nostalgie* 86). What this 'explanation' involved Viaud did not write. According to Blanch, who again provides no source, in later life Bernard did not want to hear mention of Viaud.[34] In 1898, when Viaud revised his original description of the time that he and Bernard had spent on Easter Island in 1872 while sailing around the globe, he removed all mention of his companion's name.[35]

What the exact nature of the relationship between Viaud and Bernard was we do not know. It could have been very emotional but completely unsexual. Perhaps there was an emotional and sexual element on Viaud's part but not Bernard's. At one point Viaud wrote his sister that 'we are not at all in love [*amoureux*] as you might suppose' (Loti, *Correspondance inédite* 125), which would suggest that Viaud's sister had reasons to believe the contrary. Blanch's assertion that 'the relationship between the two young men was typical of those romantic attachments which were so particularly remarked between men in the middle years of the nineteenth century'[36] has a basis in her efforts to deny that Viaud might have had homosexual tendencies and nothing else. Millward described Viaud's affection for Bernard as a form of masochism, another reason to feel miserable,[37] but nothing in Viaud's writings suggests that there was anything masochistic about the relationship. Wake maintained that Viaud's 'affair' with Bernard led him to confront his bisexuality,[38] which may well have been the case, but again, there is no documentation.

At the same time that it recounts Bernard's departure from Africa, *Notes of My Youth* also mentions the return to Europe of a previously unmentioned unnamed married woman with whom Viaud had evidently had an affair and over whose loss he expresses great grief. It would be easy to see this as a literary fabrication to metaphorize the break-up with Bernard in a way that would allow the author to express his sorrow in a more conventionally acceptable fashion – in some of the passages there are times when it is unclear whether he is speaking about his fellow officer or about the married woman – but it appears that the events involving the woman had a basis in reality. Viaud describes his subsequent efforts to get in touch with her back in Europe as a matter of life and death: 'I had come to play for my life' (28 October 1874). When things do not work out, he refers to her as 'the one who broke my life' (1 February 1875). This notion that a woman who refuses to have a relationship with him is destroying his very life runs throughout Viaud's published diaries. It could suggest that he saw such relationships as attempts to establish his heterosexuality in the face of significant homosexual tendencies.[39] Then again, it might not indicate anything of the sort. The woman gave birth to a child that Viaud always believed to have been his, and he thought about it repeatedly during the years to come.

The diary passage that recounts Viaud's last attempt to resume relations with this unknown woman is immediately followed by a description of his return to Annecy to see a male friend. 'I was in a hurry to return there and get back together with the friend whom I had left ...' (28 October 1874). Elsewhere Viaud describes this friend, a steel worker named François Eminet, as having been a 'very handsome sailor' (23 June 1875). 'I love him with all my heart,' he wrote to a friend (ibid). With that handsome, loved friend, Viaud proceeded to spend 'five beautiful days ... in the mountains, and I have a good memory of those few days' (28 October 1874; this scenario will be repeated two years later when, having finally given up on bringing Hakidjé to France, Viaud spends the night with another handsome sailor, Pierre Le Cor [*Cette éternelle nostalgie* 56]). A year and a half later, when he was about to sail for Turkey, Viaud respected Eminet's mother's plea not to take his friend with him, though Eminet evidently wanted to go very much. Viaud described this decision at the time as 'a great sacrifice,' one that cost him real feelings (*Notes of My Youth* 10 April 1876). Viaud saw Eminet one last time in 1881, two days after his reunion with Bernard, and that time he linked the two, writing that, when he arrived at Eminet's home, 'I was again afraid that someone would say: he's gone away on the spur of the moment, and we don't know where he is' (*Cette éternelle nostalgie* 87). 'Again' refers back to a similar fear two days before when he had arrived at Bernard's home (86).

In Turkey Viaud had a relationship with a young Circassian woman named Hakidjé, as well as relationships of some sort with a handsome Spanish Jew named Daniel and a Herculean Armenian named Mehmed. This episode he immortalized, and fictionalized, several years later in his first novel, *Aziyadé*. I will discuss what might have happened in the East in chapter 2. In the novel, as well as in several of his subsequent works, Viaud presents his liaison with Hakidjé as a great love story. Years later, however, his own son wrote that the author 'began to caress this Oriental dream and gild it with love' only after he had returned to France and started reading over his diary notes.[40] It is also true that, two years after his return from Turkey, when he became involved with a woman in Rochefort, Viaud wrote in the published version of his diary: 'I know in advance that I will love her to such a point that I could say that I did not know what love was before' (*Private Diary 1878–1881*, 2). Whatever his real feelings for Hakidjé may have been, after returning home Viaud tried to bring her to France and even spoke of marrying her there (*Notes of My Youth* 8 March 1878; *Cette éternelle nostalgie* 56). He could not work it out, however, and, as already noted, went to spend the evening with his sailor friend Pierre Le Cor after accepting that fact. In his diary entries over the next four decades Viaud occasionally mentioned Hakidjé and Mehmed, speaking of his love for them, but rarely did he mention Daniel.

After his return from Turkey Viaud got to know the Breton sailor Pierre Le Cor, whom he used as the model for the character Yves Kermadec in several of his books. Alain Quella-Villéger maintained that Yves was the 'double' of Le Cor,[41] and in many instances, if not all, he was. Le Cor first appears in Viaud's published diaries at the end of 1877 (*Notes of My Youth* 5 January 1878; *Cette éternelle nostalgie* 30), and is quickly described as Viaud's favourite companion. Viaud often depicted him as childlike and wrote that he found that to be one of Le Cor's most appealing qualities.[42] For the next fourteen years, the author made repeated efforts to spend time with the Breton sailor. As with the descriptions of his time together, with Joseph Bernard, these episodes are often thick with repeated 'we' and 'our.' At one point, Viaud wrote to his friend Lucien Jousselin that only Le Cor, 'this simple brother,' had reached the author's deepest layer (*Private Diary 1878–1881*, 174).

Without supporting documentation, Blanch declared that Le Cor was 'before all else, a *companion*' for Viaud.[43] Does 'before all else' mean that he was something else, such as a lover, in addition to being a companion? The suggestive nature of Blanch's phrasing is, I suspect, unintentional, and as Desbruères mentioned, there is no documentation to prove that this was anything other than a non-sexual friendship.[44] Then again, there is no documentation to prove that it was not sexual, or to prove that it did not at least have an erotic if never fulfilled aspect for Viaud. Several passages in the most recent edition of Viaud's diary certainly suggest something other than even the most devoted friendship. In February 1878, when the two of them stop in Paimpol, Viaud literally rejoices when his companion decides to spend the night with him at his hotel, in which, he notes, his room had only one bed (*Cette éternelle nostalgie* 38). Later, when Pierre changes his mind and insists on walking to Kergrist to see his mother, the author, after accompanying him part-way, 'returns to the hotel sadly, going to bed alone' (39). When, subsequently, Viaud stays with Pierre at the latter's mother's house, they share a bunk bed. It collapses, and Viaud lands on top of the sailor. Pierre asks his commanding officer if he's uncomfortable but, Viaud recalled, 'In fact, no, I was not significantly more uncomfortable; I even felt less cold on that living mattress,' so they spend the rest of the night as they are (46). By the end of 1883, Viaud refers to Le Cor, 'my poor, beloved Pierre,' as 'my dominant preoccupation for so many years' (111). It is not surprising that, in November 1881, Viaud's sister wrote to him with regard to Le Cor: 'Maybe I would appreciate him better if you told me what he did to you to make you love him so much.'[45]

After 1890, Le Cor and Viaud go their separate ways, but the author formed intimate friendships with several other large, handsome sailors, some of whom he took into his household as domestics. Christian Genet and Daniel Hervé's lavishly illustrated *Pierre Loti l'enchanteur*, which provides photographic documentation for Viaud's life, contains pictures of some of these men. Attractiveness is subjective, of course, but any reader will note that these men were all attractive in the same way: large, masculine, and friendly. The published diaries also contain references to encounters and affairs with various often unnamed women. Since these women were usually married, any relationship would have been doomed from the start. Millward might have spoken of masochism at this point.

Being a middle-class man in nineteenth century France, the author was under certain pressure to take a wife, an idea to which he reacted in different ways at different times. In 1879, on his twenty-ninth birthday, he wrote to Lucien Jousselin that he had looked into becoming a Trappist monk only to be disillusioned by the members of the order whom he had met; now, he says, 'all my plans for the future are contained in two capsules of concentrated prussic acid that I am going to try to obtain' (*Private Diary 1878–1881*, 48). Three sentences later he closed the letter with: 'They [his family, no doubt, and primarily his mother] are busy trying to get me married.' He did not explain directly why he was so desperate to leave this world, but it would appear to have been related to the prospect of having to marry.

On the other hand, but in keeping with the extreme nature of the preceding reaction, four years later, at the end of 1882, in recounting to his diary how he was paying court to a young Breton peasant girl (marriage to whom would no doubt have mortified his middle-class family and hindered his career as a naval officer), he confided: 'I desired this marriage, which others found to be insane, as a form of salvation' (*Private Diary 1882–1885*, 5). Salvation from what? He did not say. One could speculate that, like more than one other gay man before and since, Viaud hoped that marriage to a woman would keep him from becoming involved with other men and help him 'become' heterosexual. The tone of the passage recalls his life and death reaction to the end of certain previous heterosexual affairs mentioned earlier.

Finally, in 1886, after many unsuccessful candidates, Viaud's mother came up with Jean-Blanche Blanc de Ferrière, a diminutive and evidently shy Protestant whom Viaud married on 17 October of that year. The marriage was not a particularly happy one for either party. Michael G. Lerner remarked on 'the noticeable increase in his traveling abroad after it,'[46] and Viaud wrote: 'I hope that I have found a little peace in life, for lack of happiness, which is impossible.'[47] In 1906, Blanche Viaud separated from her husband permanently and retired to a family estate in Bertranet.[48]

In 1894, while he was married, Viaud brought to Rochefort a young Basque woman, Crucita Gainza, set her up in a household not far from his own, and subsequently had three sons with her, two of whom grew to maturity. We know that he did this because he wanted sons, at least in part to keep from being left alone in his old age. In his diary he at first speaks of loving her, though later this love seems to fade.[49]

One could mention various character traits of Viaud's that, while not unique to or universal among gay men, are nonetheless common to a significant number of them. As Millward remarked and as Viaud's diary makes clear, the author was terrified of getting old and wanted to remain and appear young.[50] So obsessed was he by this that he even resorted to using rouge.[51] In addition, Viaud had a great fondness for costumes, Arab especially but others as well. He staged elaborate costume parties at his home in Rochefort and sometimes appeared at others' homes in Arab or other exotic attire.

Some further comments in the published versions of the diary are interesting and suggestive, if not conclusive. *Notes of My Youth* records a letter to his sister from February 1878, in which Viaud says: 'I deserve indulgence, because I have had more temptations than others and because I suffer strangely.' A diary entry from 2 March of the same year contains the remark: 'My existence is becoming more and more compli-cated because of impossibilities and contradictions.' Later he wrote of the 'inextricable complications between which my life moves' (*Private Diary 1882–1885*, 81).

There is no clear indication of when Viaud began to feel these 'contradictions' within himself or acted on them, if he ever did. The published version of the diary mentions 'the agitation, the anxiety, the terrible jolts that spoiled my adolescence' (*Private Diary 1878–1881*, 207). There is also one remarkable passage in a letter to his friend Émile Pouvillon, from June 1881: 'The savage within me ... was turned loose very young, in contact with other savages, real ones, without control, in countries where the thousand restraints of our policed societies do not exist and where the sun beats down hard on the passions' (*Private Diary 1878–1881*, 256–7). What exactly does this mean and which countries was Viaud referring to? Tahiti? Africa? Greece and Turkey?[52] His first three novels are set in these countries and will all raise this issue.

Perhaps the single most remarkable and striking phrase concerning Viaud's sexuality appears in *First Youth,* where, describing an incident that occurred when J., as Viaud refers to himself in that book, was four-teen, the text, signed Pierre Loti, reads: 'No, I did not like myself, I was not at all "my type"' (285).[53] It seems hard to imagine a heterosexual man making such a statement about himself.

In short, given the evidence we have, we cannot prove that Julien Viaud had homosexual tendencies or thought of himself as gay. Nor, of course, can anyone prove that he did not. His emotional attachment to Joseph Bernard, Pierre Le Cor, and several other men is certainly suggestive, as is his preoccupation with male physical attractiveness. His desire to sleep with Le Cor and other men is particularly striking. Given all the biographical evidence, it would seem safe to say that the homosexual elements I am about to point out in his novels are not there solely by chance or as the result of a dispassionate interest. If Viaud devotes his novelistic output to examining questions of gay desire and identity, it would seem to be because that was an issue of central interest to him. As we shall see, when he dealt with gay issues in his novels, he would seem to have been using his narratives as a way of working out some of his own feelings.

That said, it is now time to examine the novels in question.

CHAPTER TWO

Contextualized Suggestion and Ambiguity: *Aziyadé*

For the general reading public, Viaud's first novel, *Aziyadé* (1879), has been the story of a young British naval officer, Harry Grant, referred to as Loti, who, during a tour of duty in Salonika and Constantinople, falls in love with a young Circassian odalisque.[1] The view of Pierre Loti as an author of exotic heterosexual love stories that developed as a result may explain why the gay elements in this and subsequent narratives were not generally noticed. Even predisposed readers do not always see what they are not expecting to encounter. Nor were there any public scandals in Viaud's life, as there were, for example, in Oscar Wilde's, to cause readers to search such elements out.

Those who have written on *Aziyadé* have also, by and large, treated the work as an unproblematic heterosexual romance. In 1971, Roland Barthes published a preface to an Italian translation of the novel, republished subsequently in various locations, in which he hailed the work as 'a little Sodomitic epic.'[2] His actual discussion of the topic in the narrative is very disappointing, however. Rather than focus on how Viaud presents homosexual desire in the text, Barthes devoted much of his essay to accusing Loti – and, by extension, Viaud – of bad faith for participating in and then denying several homosexual adventures that, in fact, are not what Barthes claimed them to be. Given the celebrity of Barthes's essay, it is perhaps a good idea to start this analysis of *Aziyadé* by showing how it is not a 'Sodomitic epic' in the way that he claimed.

First, Barthes claimed that the 'imprudent adventure' (II:V) Loti describes himself as pursuing while awaiting Aziyadé's arrival in Istanbul is one of several 'experiences that certainly mask "the vices of Sodom."'[3] Not true: In the novel, Loti explains that these adventures involved 'beautiful creatures.' 'Nothing else ever bound me to any of them [*'aucune d'elles,'* a pronoun that refers only to women], and they [*'elles'* again] were quickly forgotten' (II:V).

Barthes also claimed that 'the poetical descriptions [of Istanbul and Salonika] cover for ... persistent cruising of young Asiatic boys.'[4] Not true again: As we will see, while roaming the underworld of Istanbul Loti does encounter 'young Asiatic boys' hired for an evening of dancing and pleasure. Far from having searched for this 'saturnalia of sickening novelty,' as he describes it, however, Loti 'asked to be spared the end of this performance, which was worthy of the finest moments of Sodom' (II:XVI). As we will see, one interdiction that is not transgressed in *Aziyadé*, even in the most ambiguous fashion, is pederasty.

Barthes claimed that Loti 'provokes [Kaïroullah, a pimp] into offering his twelve-year-old son,' only to send him away 'ignominiously' at dawn. Not true in the sense Barthes gives it: As we will see, again, the procurer at one point brings Loti 'six young Jewish boys' (II:XXVII). Understanding that these boys are being offered to him as prostitutes, Loti terms this an example of 'human abjection' and, to humiliate the procurer for having made him this offer, tells Kaïroullah that the latter's son is better looking than the boys, implying, of course, that he would be interested in having sex with the procurer's offspring. When Kaïroullah replies 'we can talk again tomorrow ...' perhaps suggesting that he might consider selling his son, Loti chases him and the dancing boys from his house 'like a troop of mangy animals.' It is true that, when the procurer reappears, asking if he can stay the night so that he will not be robbed on his way home, Loti consents, even providing him with a rug to cover himself. 'As soon as the sky seemed to lighten,' however, 'I gave him the order to disappear, with the advice that he never cross the threshold of my door again, and that he never even appear anywhere on my path.' There is no further mention of Kaïroullah's son – contrary to Barthes's implication, the procurer never offers him to Loti – and every indication that Loti would refuse to see either of them again, since he had already made his abhorrence of pederasty clear earlier in Part II in the passage cited previously.

Finally, Barthes asserted that Loti 'accepts' the 'advances' of the cemetery night-watchman before he pushes him over a precipice.[5] Not true again: One night while pursuing an 'imprudent adventure' in the fields of Pera, Loti encounters a nightwatchman: 'He was armed with a long iron stick, two pistols and a dagger; – and I was without arms' (II:V). 'I understood right away what that man wanted,' Loti continues, leaving room for ambiguity here. 'He would have made an attack on my life rather than give up on his plan ... I consented to follow him: I had my plan.' When they arrive at a precipice, Loti pushes the night-watchman over it and flees, noting that his victim 'must have had accomplices.' Barthes neglected to mention both the night-watchman's weapons, which left Loti no choice but to follow his orders (so 'accepts' is not the right verb; nor is there any indication of sexual 'advances' by the night-watchman), and the accomplices, who, along with the weapons, suggest that the night-watchman did not intend to have sex with Loti, but to rob him. Later in Part II Loti notes that Istanbul cemeteries are 'haunted by these bands of evil doers who, after having robbed you, bury you on the spot, without the Turkish police ever getting involved' (II:XXII).

Though Barthes hailed *Aziyadé* at the end of his essay as modern because it dared to treat a variety of forbidden topics, among them male same-sex desire, rather than analysing how the text presents such desire despite the constraints of the day, which is part of what makes it so interesting, he instead decried what he termed Loti's 'bad faith' in denying participation in encounters that were not homosexual or did not take place.[6] Just as it is hard to understand why, in a novel full of homoeroticism, Barthes tried to impose it where it did not exist, so it is difficult to forgive him for condemning Viaud for not being more open, given what we now know about Barthes's own homosexuality and his coyness in speaking of it.[7] In short, Barthes's essay, which could have been insightful, offers little of value on this topic, other than focusing attention on the presence of male same-sex desire in the novel.

Since the publication of Barthes's essay, a few other writers on the novel have mentioned the topic, but only in passing. Alain Buisine, for example, asserted, rather along Barthes's exaggerated lines: '*Aziyadé* is above all the narration of fundamentally homosexual debauchery.'[8] Even in the wake of Barthes, however, most critics still prefer either to ignore or to deny the implied male same-sex desire in Viaud's narrative. Marie-Paule de Saint-Leger, in a doctoral dissertation devoted to *Aziyadé* that appeared as recently as 1996, wrote at the outset that 'it is difficult for us, however, to share [Barthes's] approach [to the novel], which is essentially centered around homosexuality,'[9] and proceeded to devote over three hundred pages to the work without ever mentioning the subject again. Others who touch on the issue usually do so only to speculate on what it might say about the author and not how it is dealt with in the work itself. Blanch, for example, in her 1983 study of the author and his work, passes back and forth between the novel and Viaud's diary entries for the period to 'refute the legend of Loti's [Viaud's] *exclusive* homosexuality. This aspect of his nature was clearly only one side of his ardent sensuality, which, at that moment, was centered around Aziyadé: but Samuel was the way to Aziyadé.'[10] She shortly thereafter arrives at the ringing affirmation: 'Loti [Viaud, again] was heterosexual, loving women passionately.'[11] Setting aside the question of the validity of reconstructing an author's biography from his literary texts, one can see that Blanch does not, finally, focus on what happens in the novel, but rather on what she hopes happened, or did not happen, in Viaud's life. It is time, then, to focus once more on the text itself, to show, as even Barthes did not, the strategies that Viaud developed to present indirectly a topic that would have been unacceptable to a large part of the general reading public in 1879.

First, Viaud creates a setting that invites gay reading. 'In the old East everything is possible!' (I:XIV), Loti exclaims early in the text when describing Salonika. The officer speaks from first-hand knowledge:

> My evenings were spent in the company of Samuel. I saw strange things with him, in the taverns frequented by the boatmen; I was able to do studies of morals that few people have been able to do, in the *courts of miracles* [thieves' meeting places] and the *dens* of the Turkish Jews ... But I saw strange things at night with this vagabond, a strange prostitution, in the cellars where mastic and raki are consumed until one reaches complete inebriation ... (I:XIII)

Could the 'strange things' that happen here, the 'strange prostitution,' not include sexual encounters between men?[12]

Viaud presents Istanbul as similarly open. 'Each person lives as he chooses and without control' (III:IV), Loti explains, having just spoken admiringly of 'the sensual nonchalance of the peoples of the East' (II:XXV). There he can enjoy 'my Eastern life, my free life' (III:VII), in part because 'they have not yet imported in Turkey the French police commissioner, who tracks you down in three hours; you are free to live there peacefully and anonymously' (IV:XI). All this freedom is contrasted very clearly to Europe. Loti explains to Achmet: 'There are laws about everything and rules for everyone [in Europe] ... For a fourth of what we do in Istanbul daily, in my country you would have hour-long discussions with the police commissioner!' (IV:XXV). The text is sending signals to the predisposed reader that a gay interpretation of events in these settings would not do violence to the realm of possibility, and might coincide with the truth.[13]

Speaking of Flaubert and other nineteenth-century writers, Edward Said, in his landmark study of orientalism, remarked that 'the association is clearly made between the Orient and the freedom of licentious sex.'[14] As critics concerned with racial and colonial perspectives on literature have been noting ever since, Western authors often depict other cultures as immoral and highly sexed in order to denigrate them. Some of the passages already cited and many others show, however, that in *Aziyadé* Viaud celebrates what he depicts as the sexual openness of the Middle East and holds it up as superior to the West, which he presents as repressive but no more moral. He is quick to assert that Muslims are not sexually depraved (II:XVII).

Viaud's second strategy for presenting homosexuality indirectly in *Aziyadé* is to portray his protagonist as someone who might act on same-sex tendencies. To begin with, he presents Loti as being unconcerned with conventional morality. On the first page, Plumkett's preface declares that 'this book is not a novel at all, or, at least, is a novel that was no better conducted than the life of its hero ... In good as in bad, he always went far.'[15] Plumkett also recalls Victor Hugo's verse: 'In more than one soul we see two things at the same time: / Heaven ... / And *muck* – a sad, terrible, somber and sleeping base' (emphasis added). One might argue that with the apparently pejorative noun 'muck' (*vase* in the original French), Viaud was situating Plumkett in the conventional morality of his general reader and thereby providing a protective, familiar frame for the work to follow, rendering it more appealing to that general reader however immoral its contents might turn out to be.

Loti himself is open about his indifference to conventional morality. Early in the novel he writes to his friend William Brown: 'I have come to believe that everything I like is worth doing and that we should always spice up life's flavourless meal as much as we can' (I:X). Shortly afterward he confesses that during this expedition 'my last beliefs have vanished, and there is no bridle restraining me any longer' (I:XI). Later, when Brown despairs over his own misfortune in love, Loti becomes even bolder: 'There is no morality,' he proclaims. 'There is life that moves toward its end, from which it is logical to ask the greatest possible enjoyment ... My rule of conduct is always to do what I like, despite any morality, any social convention. I do not believe in anything or anybody' (II:X).[16]

Loti's epistolary exchange with Plumkett even makes clear his indifference to conventional morality's stance specifically on male same-sex desire. In his preface the latter speaks of 'this Loti whom we loved ... we loved him better than that egotistical Hassan [a character in Alfred de Musset's poetry].' Plumkett must have harboured warm feelings for his fellow officer, because Loti, commenting early in the novel on a letter from Plumkett to him that we never see, remarks: 'I also see that I was fortunate to awaken some affection in you; I thank you for that' (I:XV). Loti even suggests that Plumkett must have been quite effusive in his expression of affection: 'Your hand was moving rather hastily, no doubt, when you wrote: "an unlimited affection and devotion."'

Plumkett picks up on the out that Loti provides him with 'your hand was moving rather hastily, no doubt,' spending much of the first part of his next letter distancing himself from the effusiveness of the unseen epistle.

> I have a vague recollection of having sent you a formless, senseless letter last month. One of those letters that one's first impulse dictates, where the imagination bolts, followed by the pen, which only trots, and even that while often stumbling like an old rented nag ... One never rereads such letters before sealing them, because otherwise one would never send them ... My conclusion: that was all quite ridiculous. And the protestations of devotion! – Oh! indeed, that is where the old nag took the bit and ran! (I:XVIII)

Christian Gundermann went too far, however, in asserting that this is an example of what Eve Sedgwick has called 'homosexual panic,' a fear that one might be seen as gay.[17] In an important passage that Gundermann omitted from his citation of the text, Plumkett makes it clear that he does not regret what he said, however embarrassed he might be by the effusiveness with which he said it. 'It was one of those good impulses, one of those fortunate illuminations thanks to which one is better than oneself,' he asserts. 'Believe me when I say that one is sincere when one writes like that.' Later in the letter he even makes the flat declaration: 'It is, therefore, understood, that I love you a great deal. There is no need to repeat that.' Plumkett repeats his offer of 'an unlimited affection and devotion' in a subsequent letter (III:XXIII).[18]

Whatever the precise nature of Plumkett's feelings for him, none of his fellow officer's ambiguously emotional outpourings bother Loti. He prefaces his reply to the unseen letter with: 'You can, without ever boring me, tell me all the sad or absurd, or even gay things that pass through your head.'[19] If anything Loti seems disappointed that his fellow officer distances himself from the possible implications of his remarks. Having thanked Plumkett for his affection, for example, Loti adds: 'We will have, if that is what you want, what you call an *intellectual friendship.*' The 'if that is what you want' seems to suggest a certain disappointment on Loti's part that Plumkett wants to keep their relationship on a strictly non-emotional level. Earlier he had written, noting that Plumkett is a 'strange sort of person': 'That is not the only thing that I uncovered in your long letter, I assure you.' Is the reader to imagine that Loti thought he had detected the possibility of an other than intellectual fervour on Plumkett's part? The latter makes it clear in his next epistle that he does not want to get into the actual manifestation of human emotion, however: 'I like to have general views on people and things, I like to figure out their major features; as for the details, I have always been horrified by them' (I:XVIII). Later he defines friendship as 'the purely intellectual part of ourselves' (III:XL). Whatever his feelings for Loti, Plumkett wants them to be understood as having only an intellectual quality.[20] Loti shows no negative reaction to his friend's ambiguous declarations, however.

Nor is Loti's amorality all words. In one of his letters to Plumkett he recalls that, when he first went to London at the age of sixteen, 'I tasted a little of all pleasures' (I:XV). Elsewhere he admits that 'this boy with such a young face had already taken advantage of all the things in life, and he brought to it only an indifferent heart, looking for something different and new' (III:L). There are no specifics. In both cases, however, the adjective 'all' (forms of *tout* in the original French) suggests that no reading of Loti's past is outside the realm of possibility. It also suggests that the Middle East is not unique in offering opportunities for homosexual activity and that the Orient was not responsible for introducing Loti to it. Gundermann ignored these passages when, in his effort to turn Viaud into another evil Orientalist, he asserted: 'The Orient is clearly set up as the space where homosexuality is tolerated and practiced.'[21] Again, it is important to note that, unlike Gide in *The Immoralist* or *If it die*, Viaud never presents the Orient as a licentious culture that is responsible for Loti's involvement in homosexual activity.

The text does mark one limitation on Loti's present amorality, however. When, during Aziyadé's absence, the naval officer asks Kaïroullah to bring him women, the procurer, complaining that women are very expensive at the moment, shows up with six young boys instead. As already noted, Loti refers to this as 'human abjection,' chases them from his house like a 'troop of mangy animals,' and tells Kaïroullah never to appear before him again (II:XXVII). Earlier, having spent a night roaming through Istanbul with Izeddin-Ali, Loti and his Turkish friend had ended up in a suburban tavern where 'young Asiatic boys, dressed as *almées* [female Oriental dancers and singers], performed lascivious dances.' Loti had qualified that scene as 'disgustingly new' and had asked to leave before the end of the performance (II:XVI).

This rejection of pederasty by a man not indifferent, as we shall see, to other men contrasts, perhaps intentionally, with the contemporary French scientific writing on male homosexuality discussed in the Introduction. As Vernon A. Rosario has noted, those writers attempted 'to collect all the sexual perversions under the same diagnostic rubric [homosexuality] rather than to develop increasingly fine, phenomenological categories.'[22] Following these scientific contemporaries, Proust would later depict a link between male homosexuality and pederasty,[23] and Gide, after hinting at pederasty in *The Immoralist* (1902), would attempt to glorify it to the exclusion of all other male-male relationships in *Corydon* (1924). Viaud's text is careful to distinguish between adult homosexual desire and pederasty, however, and to condemn the latter.

There are also ambiguous passages that raise questions in the mind of a reader who has begun to notice these signs. Early in the novel Loti asks his sister to abandon her search for a spouse for him, writing: 'I would make the wife I married unhappy, I prefer to continue with a life of pleasure ...' (II:XXIV). In a different sense, he also informs his sibling: 'As long as I have my dear old mother, I will remain *publicly* what I am today. When she is no longer with us, I will say good-bye to you, and then I will disappear without leaving any trace of myself ...' This suggests that Loti maintains an appearance different from his true nature. Readers will recall similar statements from Viaud's diaries quoted in the presentation of his sexual biography, indicating, once again, that he was using Loti to work out some of his own issues.

Other aspects of Loti's nature, though not unique to gay men nor typical of all of them, are nonetheless common to a significant portion. Though only in his mid-twenties, Loti is already preoccupied with appearing young. He describes himself early on as 'a very young man' (I:V), and later as 'this boy with such a young face' (III:L); he assures himself that he is 'still very young' (III:LX), and to Plumkett he speaks of his 'extreme physical youth' (I:XV). Loti is also pleased to hear that he is regarded as handsome: he reports to William Brown that the three old women who dress him in Turkish attire 'express, with gestures, that Loti is very handsome like this' (I:X). Elsewhere he tells Brown that 'real misery is sickness, ugliness, and old age' (II:X). Therapists who deal with gay men usually attribute their preoccupation with appearing young to the difficulty, at least until relatively recently, that gays have had in maintaining relationships in a world that condemns them and therefore their feeling that they need to appear perpetually attractive because they will always be in the process of seeking a new partner.

Linked to his preoccupation with his physical appearance is Loti's fascination with exotic attire and the possibility that it affords him of appearing to be something other than what he actually is. To Brown he recalls that even in England he had been in the habit of changing clothes as a means of disguise: 'I am accustomed to these changes of setting' (I:X). In Greece and Turkey he constantly alternates between Western and Oriental dress, to the point that, as he admits to Brown, 'I am maintaining only in appearance two different personalities' (III:XXIV). In part, of course, this disguise is necessary to carry on his various escapades. As he confesses at one point, however, it also appeals to his dissatisfaction with himself as he is and his desire to become something else: 'I am so tired of myself, after these twenty-seven years that I have known myself, that I very much like being able to mistake myself a little for someone else' (III:XXXVIII).[24] Therapists accustomed to dealing with gay men explain this fascination with costumes as a compensatory mechanism developed to deal with the feelings of inferiority that general culture instils in those attracted to others of the same sex.

The most striking of Viaud's strategies to indicate the possibility of same-sex desire in his protagonist is his use of parallels in his presentation of Loti's relationships with Samuel and Aziyadé. These allow Viaud to suggest aspects of his protagonist's feelings for Samuel that he cannot express directly. To begin with, he concludes the chapter in which the officer recounts his first sighting of the odalisque with the line: 'This young woman was Aziyadé' (I:IV). Two pages later he concludes the chapter in which Loti first meets the Spanish boatman with the line: 'This character was Samuel' (I:VII). The parallel construction and placement of these two lines, highlighted by their position at the ends of chapters, link the young boatman early on with the young Circassian. If Loti is 'slightly captivated' (I:VI) by the latter, the parallel construction suggests the possibility of a similar attraction to the former.

The parallel construction also highlights a significant difference. All Loti sees of Aziyadé at their first meeting is her forehead and eyes – he speaks of 'a white veil carefully enveloping her head, allowing only the forehead and the large eyes to appear' – and this one unconcealed part of her anatomy has a definite effect on him: 'The green eyes had slightly captivated me, even though the exquisite face hidden by the white veil was still unknown to me' (I:VI). On the other hand, he is able to see quite a bit of Samuel, and he shares it with his diary. 'I noticed a man who had a strange beard, divided into tiny curls like the oldest statues of this country.[25] ... In addition, he had a very handsome head, a great sweetness in his eyes, which shone with honesty and intelligence. He was all in rags, his feet bare, his legs bare, his shirt in tatters' (I: VII). If 'two large green eyes' could leave Loti 'slightly captivated,' what is the reader to make of the potential effect of all this male beauty and exposed flesh in someone paralleled to the possessor of those two green eyes?[26]

The passage in I:VII is revealing in more ways than one, however, especially given its location near the beginning of the work and therefore at the beginning of Viaud's writing as a whole. First, Loti has no problems talking about male beauty: he describes Samuel as having 'a very handsome head,' etc.[27] Second, whereas very little of Aziyadé's body is exposed to the reader – this will be true of the entire novel; though Loti later has intimate moments with her, her body is never presented to the reader's gaze – the reader is allowed to run his or her eyes over much of Samuel's physique. The parallel of these two adjacent scenes makes clear from the beginning that this text, and thus the character whose diary excerpts compose most of it, Loti, are both sensitive to the attractions of the male body. Third, there is an attempt to justify the attractiveness of the male object of interest – 'He had ... a great sweetness in his eyes, which shone with honesty and intelligence' – that goes beyond mere physical appearance. Samuel is declared early on, even before Loti gets to know him, to be sweet, honest, and intelligent, qualities of character and intellect that make this simple boatman worthy of a naval officer. Later he is noted as having a 'frank and honest face' (II:II). The qualities ascribed to Aziyadé on first viewing – her expression is 'a mixture of energy and naivety; one might say a child's look, so great was its freshness and youth' (I:VI) – have nothing to do with either character or intellect, but rather suggest that, as a 'child,' she would not be capable of functioning with Loti at his level.

Viaud links Samuel to Aziyadé with parallel structures several more times. After much planning, Loti is finally able to spend his first night alone with Aziyadé, floating around the port in a small boat. All we glimpse of her is 'a woman so veiled that you can see nothing of her but a shapeless white mass' (I:XIX). Loti informs his diary: 'I tremble when I touch her, this first contact penetrates me with a mortal languor ... she is firm and cold to the touch,' but of actual love-making, or even of her body, which Loti would presumably have seen, he says nothing.

It is interesting to note how Loti phrases this description of his first erotic encounter with Aziyadé: 'This first contact penetrates me.' Though he is the male, *he* experiences penetration.[28] Furthermore, 'she is firm and cold to the touch,' two adjectives traditionally used to describe a man rather than a woman. Though the evidence is slight, one can see here the beginning of a breakdown of traditional gender constructions.

The chapter concludes with Loti's rather disorienting comment: 'I loved another woman more than she, a woman whom, now, I no longer have the right to see; but my senses never knew such intoxication.' His attraction to Aziyadé is portrayed at this point as physical. As he writes to William Brown: 'To begin with it was only an intoxication of the imagination and the senses' (I:X; cf. also: I:XVII; I:XX).

Once Aziyadé has departed Loti is left alone in his boat with Samuel. 'I was barely dressed' (I:XXI), he explains, the night on the sea grows deadly cold, and sleep begins to overtake him. 'Then, with infinite precautions, I raised the cover that enveloped Samuel, so as to be able to stretch out next to this chance friend without waking him.' There is a limiting passage immediately following – 'And, without being conscious of it, in less than a second, we fell asleep, both of us, an overwhelming sleep against which there is no possible resistance' – that would seem to be inserted to deny the possibility of any sexual activity. The force of the denial – 'in less than a second,' 'an overwhelming sleep against which there is no possible resistance' – only calls attention to the situation and what the limiting passage could be meant to deny, however.

The denial's effect is further undone by the words 'we fell asleep, both of us.' If Samuel were still asleep when Loti crawled under the cover with him, it would make no sense to state: 'We fell asleep, both of us,' rather than 'I fell asleep.' Obviously Samuel awakens when Loti joins him; what happens between that moment and the two of them falling sleep Viaud leaves to the alerted reader's imagination. The imagery in this scene is certainly suggestive and highly erotic, however. Loti recounts how 'a deadly cold *slid* up the length of my arms, and *penetrated* my chest little by little' (emphasis added). Having introduced the idea of physical contact and penetration and so of sexual activity, he then speaks of 'an overwhelming sleep against which there is no possible resistance.' In so erotically charged an atmosphere, it is hard not to read 'sleep' as a metaphor for either an overwhelming and irresistible desire or even an overwhelming and irresistible embodiment of such desire, i.e., Samuel. Another parallel emphasizes this suggestion. In describing his rendezvous with Aziyadé, Loti had spoken of 'this bed [their boat], which wanders without direction on the deep sea' (I:XX) while they perhaps made love. Immediately after describing how he and Samuel fell asleep under his cover, Loti notes: 'the boat wandered off' (I:XXI). While nothing is described as happening between Loti and Samuel, the parallels and imagery are suggestive.

This scene is a development of one in Viaud's life in which something did happen. In his unpublished diary account of an incident that occurred between himself and Daniel, a boatman he knew in Greece who became the model for Samuel, he wrote:

> [Daniel's] head was of an antique beauty. Sleep had imposed on it a tranquil, chaste, severe expression. I forgot [Hakidjé (Aziyadé)], thinking of this curious tie that had united me to this man ... [Daniel] opened his eyes wide, and took me in his arms with the unthinking embrace of one just waking, pressing his lips on mine. 'Is it you, *effendi* (my lord), he said, – I love you ...' (*Aziyadé*, ed. Vercier 250)

It does not take a therapist to spot the self-justificatory games Viaud was playing – with whom? – here: Daniel's head is 'chaste,' therefore not sensual and therefore not automatically to be avoided, etc. This leads one to wonder how honest the diary is on this episode.

Part of this passage survived into an early manuscript version of the novel:

> Samuel's sleeping head was at my feet; sleep had stamped it with a tranquil and serious expression; it was the beauty of antiquity in all its noble purity and perfection ... And I forgot Aziyadé while dreaming about the strange tie that attached me to this man. Was it an anomaly, a dark perversion? Where does this feeling, which can develop with such a terrible power, come from? ... It is comparable to those deformities, those monstrous errors of nature that make one doubt the existence of God the creator; it inspires, when one thinks about it, the same disgust and the same fear ... This charm, exerted on Samuel, plunges me into thoughts that are full of trouble, of vague uneasiness, and of mysterious horror ...[29]

Quella-Villéger's excerpt does not let us see whether Viaud retained Daniel's kiss in the early manuscript version of the novel. On the other hand, it does allow us to see that someone subsequently suppressed not only the forthright declaration of Loti's erotic interest in Samuel, but also the negative comments on that interest before the text was published. In the published version, Viaud settled for simple suggestion, not daring his diary's forthright depiction of male same-sex desire and love, perhaps because he did not want to include the subsequent negative commentary that the society of his time would have required as an antidote and that someone, he or one of the friends that helped him transform his diary into a publishable novel, had dutifully inserted when first transforming his non-judgmental diary into a for-the-public text.

The parallels continue. Having been ordered to leave Salonika for Istanbul, Loti remarks:

> I did, however, spend intoxicating hours on the tranquil water of. this great bay [with Aziyadé], nights that many men would pay greatly for, and I almost loved this young woman, who was so singularly delicious!
>
> I will soon forget those warm nights, when the first light of dawn found us stretched out in a boat, drunk with love, and completely soaked with the morning dew.
>
> I also miss Samuel ... It is in this way that I still let myself go, let myself be seized by every ardent affection, by everything that resembles it, no matter what the self-serving or shadowy motive for it may be; closing my eyes, I accept everything that can, for an hour, fill the terrifying emptiness of life, everything that has an appearance of friendship or love. (I:XXIV)

Loti's recollection of the nights that he spent with Aziyadé in their boat leads immediately to thoughts of Samuel and is linked to the latter with the equating adverb 'also.' Viaud underlines the implications of this parallel with Loti's immediately subsequent declaration that he has allowed himself to become caught up in 'every ardent affection,' etc. The repeated use of the all-inclusive 'every(thing),' in each case some form of *tout* in the original French, noted earlier in Loti's descriptions of his amoral youth, suggests that the 'ardent affection' in which he allowed himself to become involved with Samuel went beyond the bounds of conventional Western morality. He recounts all this not only in a vague manner, but also in a way that denies active effort or responsibility on his part: 'I let myself ... be seized by ...' etc. Nevertheless, he recounts it.

The adjective 'shadowy' recalls an earlier and highly significant scene. One warm June night while awaiting the hour to meet Aziyadé, Loti and Samuel had been together, 'stretched out, both of us, on the ground in the countryside' (I:XIV). When Samuel, not in a good mood, refused to answer Loti, the latter took his hand for the first time, as a sign of friendship, and made more or less this speech to him in Spanish:

– My good Samuel, each night you sleep on the hard earth or on boards; the grass that is here is better and smells good, like wild thyme. Sleep, and you will be in a better mood afterward. Aren't you happy with me? What can I have done to you?

His hand trembled in mine and clasped it tighter than was necessary.

– *Che volete,* he said in a somber and troubled voice, *che volete mî* (What do you want of me?) ...

Something unheard of and shadowy had passed through poor Samuel's head for a moment; – in the old East everything is possible! – and then he covered his face with his arms, and remained there, terrified of himself, motionless and trembling.

Almost every line in this passage is loaded with suggestion, some of it complex. Loti begins by noting that this is the first time that he has taken Samuel's hand. In so doing, he indicates both that there were subsequent times – he says 'first' and not 'only' – and that this event was of sufficient importance to him that he kept track of it. He then modifies or limits the suggestiveness of that act with the phrase 'as a sign of friendship.' The words would seem to have been inserted to dispel any sexual or romantic overtones that the earlier part of the sentence and more particularly the subsequent speech could evoke, especially given the context already established by this point in the novel.

What follows those cautionary words quickly undermines their limiting powers for any alerted reader, however, giving an ambiguous significance to 'friendship': Loti asks Samuel to sleep beside him on the grass. His subsequent questions – 'Aren't you happy with me? What can I have done to you?' – sound very much like those of a rejected lover. The implications of these words would seem to be fairly clear, especially given what has come before. Moreover, Samuel's extreme reaction, both physical and verbal, strongly reinforces them. Why would he tremble, why would his voice be 'troubled,' if he perceived no sexual subtext in Loti's invitation to sleep beside him? Is he terrified at the thought of having sex with another man, or rather overwhelmed at the unexpected joy and honour of being with Loti? The text is not and could not be specific, of course, though the parallel passage in Viaud's journal that served as the model for this scene makes things quite clear: 'And then he took me in his arms, and holding me against his chest pressed his lips ardently against mine ... This time the goal had been reached, and even terribly surpassed; I should have foreseen this outcome.'[30] Whatever Viaud meant by 'the goal,' it is clear that greater intimacy with Daniel was *his* idea.

Even in the novel, the scene's concluding paragraph is very suggestive.

> But, from that strange moment, [Samuel] is at my service, *body* and soul; every night he risks his freedom and his life by entering the house where Aziyadé lives; he crosses, in the darkness, in order to get her, the cemetery that, for him, is full of visions and mortal terrors; he rows until morning in his boat in order to watch over ours, or he waits for me all night, stretched out among fifty vagabonds, on the fifth paving stone of the Salonika dock. It is as if his personality is absorbed into mine, and I find him everywhere in my shadow, whatever the place and the outfit that I have chosen, ready to defend my life at the risk of losing his. (emphasis added)

As Barthes quite correctly remarked, Samuel is henceforth 'infatuated with Loti.'[31] This much one might expect from any Orientalist writer. More interesting, however, is the fact that Loti – and the text – does not condemn Samuel's infatuation or do anything to discourage it; in fact, the English officer goes on living – and sleeping – in close proximity to him.[32] Moreover, it would certainly seem that the reader is being led to believe that Loti feels something for Samuel as well. After all, it is Loti who takes Samuel's hand and asks Samuel to sleep beside him.

If Viaud had written in our own time, one might speak of bad faith here. Remembering when and under what constraints he did write, however, one can only marvel at the author's insistence on treating so difficult an issue, however oblique the approach. It is also worth noting that 'unheard of' and 'shadowy,' whether they are meant to reflect Samuel's opinion or Loti's, are actually non-judgmental. One has only to recall Proust's treatment of homosexuality in *In Search of Lost Time*, published several decades later and full of blatantly homophobic remarks, to appreciate Viaud's relative 'good faith.'

Those given to colonial or racial approaches to literature might want to argue that in portraying Samuel's affection for Loti as 'shadowy' Viaud was using the boatman's homosexual desire to suggest racial inferiority. Samuel is Jewish, and some contemporary anti-Semitic rhetoric had depicted Jews as homosexuals.[33] Viaud seldom mentions Samuel's ethnicity, however, and makes no effort to link it to the boatman's affection for him. Furthermore, the fact that Viaud structured the novel to suggest Loti's love and desire for Samuel should make it clear that in *Aziyadé* male same-sex desire is not used as a means of racial disparagement or even racial differentiation. Early on, Loti describes Samuel as intelligent and honest (I:IX), qualities that many Western writers have denied members of cultures other than our own, and the boatman is never subsequently depicted negatively. On the other hand, as already demonstrated, this novel suggests that more than one Westerner also experiences and perhaps acts on homosexual desire.[34]

Viaud continues with the parallel constructions. Having been transferred to Istanbul, Loti awaits Aziyadé's promised arrival. When Samuel leaves to take care of his own business, the officer exclaims:

> I counted on my poor Samuel being with me this evening, and no doubt I will never see him again. My heart is saddened at the thought of that and my solitude weighs on me ...
>
> My poor Samuel was the only person there who knew my name and my existence, and I sincerely started to love him.
>
> Did he abandon me, he *too* ...? (II:VII; emphasis added)

In the diary, this passage went on in a more direct fashion: 'Come back, beloved Daniel, I love you, my friend, my brother, now I feel it; I will probably never see you again, but when I return to my empty house in the evening, my heart is torn because you are no longer there ...' (*Aziyadé*, ed. Vercier 251). Again, Viaud or one of his editors evidently felt that this would have been too direct for the public of the time.

When Loti writes his friend William Brown, he recalls: 'There I met a young, strangely charming woman, by the name of Aziyadé, who helped me to spend my time as an exile in Salonika – and a vagabond, Samuel, whom I took as a friend' (II:X). Still later, describing his house in Istanbul to Plumkett, Loti explains that there are three rooms, one for himself, one for Aziyadé, and one for Samuel. Just as Aziyadé's is empty, awaiting her arrival from Salonika, so 'another small room, near mine, is also empty: it's Samuel's ... And he doesn't seem to be returning any more than she' (II:XXV). He later writes to his sister: 'Aziyadé ... has arrived. – She loves me with all her soul, and does not believe that I will ever be able to convince myself to leave her. – Samuel has come back as well; both of them surround me with so much love ...' (III:V).

Having used parallel construction repeatedly to suggest Loti's feelings for Samuel, Viaud can rely on the context that he has created to evoke a gay reading of otherwise ambiguous or apparently insignificant passages. He has the dervish Hassan-effendi say that the protagonist lives 'in singularly chosen close contact with a Jewish vagabond' (II:XX; the original French is *intimité*, which can denote sexual intimacy). Loti himself writes to Plumkett: 'I have very much attached myself to this tramp picked up on the docks of Salonika, whose name is Samuel' (II:XXV). When, in that same letter, he tells his friend that he has set up his house in Eyoub with one room for Aziyadé and one for Samuel, and that, speaking of the former, 'I almost loved her,' we recall that he had already written of the latter, 'I began to love him' (II:VII) some time before, without the limiting adverb 'almost.'

Thereafter Samuel begins to lose his parity with the title character. When Aziyadé finally arrives in Istanbul, Loti leads her toward their new house, 'forgetting about poor Samuel, who remained outside ...' (III:I). The boatman still has powerful feelings for his English friend: Loti informs his sister that 'both of them [Aziyadé and Samuel] surround me with so much love' (III:V); Samuel sleeps in Loti's bed when a cat infects his own with her scent (III:XXX); he sleeps in Loti's room when bothered by the memory of a drowned man whom he saw earlier in the day (III:XXXVIII). Indeed, his feelings seem to have become too powerful to suit Loti: the latter explains that this is why he has decided not to take Samuel back to England with him. 'Poor Samuel, he did not understand that there was an abyss between his affection for me, which was so tormented, and Mihran-Achmet's limpid and brotherly affection; that he, Samuel, was a hot-house plant, which it was impossible to transplant there, under my peaceful roof' (IV:IV). Still, the officer admits: 'I did love him a lot, though, my poor Samuel ... His tears broke my heart a little,' and the scene of his farewell to Samuel (IV:IV) is remarkably moving.

In part, the fading of Loti's interest in Samuel seems to result from this discomfort with the Spaniard's emotionalism. There is also a hint that something happened to disillusion Loti with regard to the boatman. After having described Samuel as 'a faithful friend' (II:II), the officer subsequently cites an old Oriental poem to the effect that 'one can find a companion, but not a faithful friend' (II:XXIII). In the next chapter he writes to his sister: 'Samuel ... is perhaps still, out of everyone, the one who values me most.[35] I have no illusions, though; it is a childish enthusiasm on his part. One fine day, everything will go up in smoke, and I will find myself alone again' (II:XXIV). Thereafter he no longer refers to Samuel as his friend.

In part, however, Samuel's fall from favour seems to be related to the contemporaneous arrival of the above-mentioned Achmet as Loti's new domestic. 'Built like Hercules' (III:VIII; physical strength is an important trait in the male objects of desire in Viaud's works), this young man one day offers Loti his services and asks to be 'taken into his household' (the original French is: *reçu dans l'intimité,*' which does not translate easily but again contains the French word that can denote sexual intimacy). He is soon featured in a scene that parallels the dramatic one in the countryside between Samuel and Loti (I:XIV) described earlier, but with important differences. Again, the two men are 'both stretched out' (III:XIX), but this time it is the middle of the day rather than a warm June night, both sit rather than lie on the ground, and they are in a public place, in front of the Mehmed-fatih mosque, rather than alone in the countryside. 'Both stretched out' suggests a certain intimacy, but 'both stretched out in the sun' certainly does not have the suggestiveness that 'both stretched out on the ground in the countryside' (I:XIV) did. Achmet demonstrates the same devotion to Loti that the Spanish boatman offered – he is 'devoted unto death!' (III:VII), Loti says of him – but there is nothing to suggest erotic overtones. Whereas Samuel and Loti had roamed the streets of Salonika and Istanbul together in search of unspecified sexual adventures (II:XV), there is no indication that Achmet and Loti do anything of the sort. Twice Achmet offers to take care of the children he is sure that Loti will have by his English wife (III:XL; IV:XXV), and repeatedly he defends Aziyadé (III:XLV; IV:XIX; Samuel had seemed quite jealous of Aziyadé and had refused to help Loti obtain her [I:XIII, I:XIV]). While Samuel's 'affection' for Loti is 'shadowy,' Achmet's is 'clear.' The closest Achmet gets to expressing anything like desire is in the letter that he writes to Loti after the Englishman's departure from Istanbul: 'Do you think that I can be happy in Istanbul one single moment without you? I can't, and, when you left, my heart broke with pain' (IV:XXIX).

For Loti's part, as he sails away he thinks back to Achmet via a parallel with Aziyadé that is as suggestive as it is rare. (Whereas, as already seen, Viaud often parallels Samuel and Aziyadé, he almost never parallels Achmet and the odalisque.)

> At this hour my beloved is in her harem, in one of the apartments in that dwelling, which is so somber and whose windows are barred. She is stretched out, without words and without tears, devastated, as night approaches.
> Achmet has stayed, following us with his eyes, seated on the Foundoucli

dock; I lost sight of him at the same time as that familiar spot in Istanbul, where, every evening, he or Samuel came to wait for me.

He also thinks that I will not come back.

Poor little friend Achmet, I will continue to love him, too; his friendship was sweet and beneficial to me. (IV:XXVII)

The reference to Samuel, rare in the second half of the novel, underlines the significance of the parallel linking Achmet to Aziyadé. The noun 'friendship' limits the ambiguous verb 'love,' however, and there are no outpourings about 'every ardent affection,' etc., such as followed earlier comments on Loti's relationship to the Spaniard. Achmet is physically attractive – though never, unlike Samuel, described as 'handsome' or 'beautiful' – and devoted, but not demanding. He is sufficiently restrained that Loti can even consider taking him back to England, though in fact he does not.[36] When the officer returns to Istanbul a month later, it is Achmet whom he asks about and not Samuel (V:I). As Loti, about to leave Istanbul, had explained: 'Achmet ... had taken his [Samuel's] place' (IV:IV).[37] Unlike Samuel, Achmet does not seem to understand Loti's sexuality or to share it; while this precludes fulfilment for the officer, it also precludes involvement or exposure.

There are a fair number of scenes with Loti and Achmet in the second half of the novel and almost none with Loti and Samuel, but none of the former are suggestive of any relationship beyond friendship, with one inconclusive exception. When Loti's house in Istanbul burns down he goes in search of Achmet, 'a boy of good council, whose friendly presence would have been precious to me in the middle of all that confusion' (III:LII; is the adjective 'friendly' meant to serve as a limiter, such as Viaud had used in previously discussed scenes between Loti and Samuel?). Unable to find his domestic, 'I had to return home to sleep alone.' Perhaps this line is meant to suggest that Loti had hoped to sleep with Achmet.[38]

The decline of Loti's interest in Samuel also seems linked to his changing feelings for Aziyadé, a different-sex relationship that metamorphoses considerably during the course of the narrative and provokes important reflections on the nature of sexual desire in general. As noted earlier, Viaud initially portrays Loti's feelings for the young Circassian as a simple stirring of his senses. During their first month they are 'linked by the intoxication of the senses' (I:XVII).[39] For Loti this is not all there is to love, however, as he is quick to point out: 'I loved another young woman more than she, whom, at present, I no longer have the right to see, but my senses have never known such intoxication' (I:XIX). After the tentative 'I almost loved her' mentioned earlier, Loti writes to William Brown: 'I am not far at all from loving' Aziyadé (III:XXIV). Then, finally, after a momentary infidelity with Séniha, another odalisque, and reconciliation with the Circassian, he declares unreservedly: 'I love her ... From the deepest part of my soul, I love her and I adore her ...' (III:LI).[40]

The failed dalliance with Séniha provides Loti with an opportunity to clarify his definition of love. 'I did not love that Séniha at all,' he explains as he prepares for their rendezvous; 'It was just that my senses were fevered and carried me off to this unknown full of intoxications' (III:XLV). Physical desire can be so strong for Viaud's protagonists that it leads them to jeopardize their own happiness, but Loti does not confuse that with love. As he sits across from the beautiful Séniha, he continues:

An unexpected battle began within me; my senses fought against something less definite that people have agreed to call the soul, and my soul fought against my senses. At that moment, I adored the dear little one whom I had chased away [Aziyadé]; my heart overflowed for her with tenderness and remorse for her. The beautiful creature seated near me awakened disgust in me more than love; I had desired her, she had come; it was up to me now if I wanted to have her; I didn't want any more of it and her presence was odious to me. (III:XLVI)

Desire is not all there is to love and can indeed get in the way of it, so powerful is its sway over Loti.[41]

But even Loti's love for Aziyadé is called into question. No sooner does he reconcile with her after his failed dalliance than Loti speculates: 'Who could ever determine, in these unexplained ecstasies, in these devouring intoxications, who could ever determine what comes from the senses and what comes from the heart? Is it the supreme effort of the soul toward heaven, or the blind power of nature, which wants to recreate itself and live again?' (III:LX).

All this provides an interesting perspective from which to view Loti's final comments on his relationship with Aziyadé, which gave rise to the perception of Julien Viaud as an author of exotic heterosexual romances. After her death the officer recalls: 'She loved me, with the deepest and purest love' (V:IV). Similarly, as he sailed away from Istanbul to return to England, Loti had remarked: 'And I adore her, however.

Beyond all intoxication, I love her, with the most tender and pure affection; I love her soul and her heart, which belong to me; I will love her still past ... the charm of the senses' (IV:XXVII). 'Soul' and 'heart,' previously presented as the opposites of 'senses' and 'desire,' are lined up with purity, leading the reader to wonder just what Loti meant by all this.

Perhaps it is tied to Aziyadé's remarkable offer, made when Loti, preparing to sail for England, promises to return to her. '"If you are married, Loti," she said, "that doesn't make any difference. I will no longer be your mistress, I will be your sister. Get married, Loti; that's secondary! I love your soul better. All that I ask of Allah is to see you again"' (IV:X). Aziyadé is willing to sacrifice sex altogether. If this is what makes her love for Loti pure, then by implication there is something impure about sexual desire, that 'blind power of nature' that Loti does not seem to be able to control. Of course, many heterosexual writers have been uncomfortable with sex and castigated it as impure; Viaud's austere Protestant upbringing no doubt did much to inculcate such views in him. Still, given Loti's complex sexuality and the power that he describes sexual desire as having over him, it is interesting that he idealizes a heterosexual relationship from which such activity could be excluded. At one point, when he considers leaving the English navy and going off to live with Aziyadé, he fantasizes about 'being a boatman in a golden vest, somewhere in the south of Turkey where the sky is always pure and the sun always warm' (III:XXII). In the course of the novel, Loti's relationship with Aziyadé develops from the purely physical to a point where the physical almost seems to disappear. It is tempting to speculate on the extent to which Viaud idealized this relationship because it allowed freedom from heterosexual activity. Years later, in *Supreme Visions of the East*, he would publish extracts from his 1910 diary in which he had written that his memory of Hakidjé (the real-life model for Aziyadé) 'has become so purified that it is, so to speak, without any physical attributes [*dématérialisé*]' (10 September 1910). By the end of *Aziyadé*, Loti has replaced the demanding – and knowing – Samuel with the undemanding and unknowing Aziyadé and Achmet.

In his attempt to present *Aziyadé* as an uncomplicatedly homosexual work, Barthes argued that 'Aziyadé is the neutral term, the zero term of this major paradigm: discursively, she occupies the front rank; structurally, she is absent, she is the place of an absence, she is a fact of discourse, not a fact of desire.'[42] Clive Wake found her to be 'sexless and unreal, a mere abstraction.'[43] Irene Szyliowicz asserted that the allusions to all-male gatherings in *Aziyadé* 'belie the strong heterosexual attachment Loti presumably professes, and point, minimally, to a yearning for another kind of love.'[44] According to Szyliowicz, Loti's affair with Aziyadé was used to cover other, same-sex interests. Gundermann declared that 'innumerable passages confirm that Aziyadé is hardly even the "cover-up" that Barthes sees in her,'[45] not specifying any of these 'innumerable passages' and misrepresenting Barthes, who, unlike Szyliowicz, never presents Aziyadé as a cover-up. In making such statements, these critics missed a major structural element of this not so simple novel: Aziyadé is and indeed must be 'a fact of desire,' albeit a changing one; since Viaud cannot express Loti's feelings for Samuel directly, at least in a positive fashion, it is important that the officer's desire for the title character seem real so that the parallels between her and Samuel can imply similar emotions for the Spanish boatman.

This is why I would not argue that *Aziyadé* is a homosexual tale. Samuel is certainly presented as attracted to Loti, but given the very different culture in which he lives he would have little in common with our modern Western homosexual as that term was developed in the nineteenth century. As the novel makes clear repeatedly, same-sex activity was not a cause for exclusion in 'the old East,' at least among men. Loti certainly seems as taken with Aziyadé as with Samuel and so does not, in this novel, qualify as a homosexual.[46] Nor is there any indication in *Aziyadé* that Loti sees himself as different because of his feelings for Samuel (and perhaps Achmet), that he has what we now call a homosexual or gay identity. That would not occur in a Viaud novel until *The Story of a Child*, a dozen years later.

Aziyadé could disappoint readers interested in gay literature for other reasons as well. Loti leaves Samuel as well as the title character but makes no effort to rejoin the boatman, much less to declare his feelings for him openly. While he portrayed same-sex desire here and did so without condemnation, Viaud did not portray its happy fulfilment. But then, neither did any of his contemporaries or immediate successors, including those we know to have been gay. Four decades later, Proust would flatly declare such fulfilment impossible.[47]

Rather than fault Viaud for what he did not do, it is more worthwhile to appreciate *Aziyadé* for its assets. The novel depicts the love of one man, albeit a Jew of Spanish extraction and therefore an 'other,' for another man. It also suggests none too obliquely a similar erotic and romantic interest on the part of the English protagonist himself, which was far more daring, since, as Christopher Robinson noted, 'male homosexuality is acceptable to the nineteenth-century French hetero-sexual only in so far as it is distant from him.'[48] Most importantly, it does all this without any of the homophobia that sours similar depictions in the novel before Viaud and even for some time after him.[49] Oscar Wilde's *Picture of Dorian Gray*, which did not appear until 1890, eleven years later, and which is so often cited as a pioneering work of gay fiction, is much more circumspect. As Eve Kosofsky Sedgwick has remarked, 'Reading *Dorian Gray* from our twentieth-century vantage point where the name Oscar Wilde virtually *means* "homosexual," it is worth reemphasizing how thoroughly the elements of even this novel can be read doubly or equivocally.'[50] E.M. Forster's *Maurice* (1913–14), though more open because not intended for publication, is, as noted in the Introduction, homophobic, as is *In Search of Lost Time*, which Proust began to publish in 1913. The fact that Viaud speaks without disparage-ment about male same-sex love and desire in a work written for publica-tion, despite the constraints of what his general public, his profession, and his personal world would allow, cannot help but make his novel seem not only modern but remarkably sympathetic.

The nature of the often first-person narrative suggests the confession-ality of autobiography, and the absence of a different name on the title page did nothing to dispel that. This suggestiveness is well demon-strated by the remarks of various critics. Raymonde Lefèvre asserted that Viaud wrote *Aziyadé* out of 'the need to express himself, to tell his story.'[51] Pierre Brodin believed that 'Loti [Viaud, again] ... takes ... the reader as his confessor. He opens to him entirely his doubts, his battles, his distress. He calls to him for help, he hides nothing from him ... We must see this as an effort toward absolute, total sincerity.'[52] In speaking of *The Awakened*, Viaud's last novel, Clive Wake asserted that 'all of Loti's previous novels were the product of his own most intimate preoccupa-tions.'[53] Before anyone mistakes *Aziyadé* for a public coming out, how-ever, it is only fair to remember that, though we now read the novel as being by 'Pierre Loti,' see that the protagonist is called Loti, and know that Viaud, like Loti, spent time in Salonika and Istanbul as a naval officer, all of which suggest an association between the protagonist and the author, most of the original readers of the text, his audience as Viaud imagined it, saw a novel published without any author's name and knew nothing about the similarities between the lives of Harry Grant/ Loti and Julien Viaud. Since, furthermore, Loti is English and dies at the end of the novel, these original readers would have had no reason to assume that whoever brought the work to publication in French was the individual whose life it recounts. In *A Phantom from the East* (1892), Viaud referred to his first novel as a work that he wrote 'not thinking that I would continue to write and that later people would know who the anonymous author of *Aziyadé* was' (I). In *The Awakened* (1906), he referred to it as 'a too intimate book, that should never have been published' (V).[54] Nonetheless, once his anonymity was lost, Viaud did nothing to disown the novel and went on to present Loti as attracted to other men in subsequent narratives, even taking his name as his pseudonym.[55]

In the end, however, the major achievement of *Aziyadé* is that, regardless of whatever confessional quality some readers may choose to ascribe to it, it dared, even if anonymously, to depict male same-sex desire in a non-homophobic and even sympathetic fashion to a general public, despite the homophobic assertions being fed to that public by the French scientific community in particular and Western culture in general. It would be several years before Viaud would equal and surpass such daring and far longer than that before any other French or English writer would repeat it.

CHAPTER THREE

Discovering a Fuller Range of Sexuality: *The Marriage of Loti*

The Marriage of Loti (1880), Julien Viaud's second novel, was his first literary and commercial success.[1] Indeed, eighteen years later Reynaldo Hahn turned it into an opéra-comique, making it the first of Viaud's works to be adapted for the lyric theatre. It repeats the formula that Viaud was in the process of making famous: a Western European sailor has an affair with a young woman in an exotic locale, only to sail away at the end. As with *Aziyadé*, however, such a summary does not do justice to the full range of sexual desire depicted in the text. *The Marriage of Loti* does not feature anything as central as the Loti-Samuel relationship in *Aziyadé*, but it does include some elements of implied male same-sex desire.

The circumstances of the work's creation may explain the reduced attention accorded this issue in what is not altogether Viaud's second novel. Though the narrative was published a year after *Aziyadé*, it recounts events in the life of the same protagonist, English midshipman Harry Grant/Loti, from 1872–6, the years preceding his arrival in the Middle East and encounters with Samuel and male same-sex desire there. Furthermore, to the extent that this novel, like *Aziyadé*, was based on Viaud's diary, parts of it were written, at least in the initial version, before Viaud himself had the experiences on which *Aziyadé* was based.[2] Both the protagonist and the foundation of the text therefore predate the Loti who encounters same-sex desire in the underworld of Salonika and ends up living in 'singularly chosen close contact' with Samuel (*Aziyadé* II:XX).

Male same-sex desire, or at least the possibility of it, is not altogether absent from Viaud's second novel, however. Though everything is more understated here, the title-page reminder that the text, which, like

Aziyadé, was originally published anonymously, is 'by the author of *Aziyadé*' signals the reader to recall the previous narrative while reading this one, thereby evoking the validity of a gay reading of *The Marriage of Loti* and making otherwise possibly unremarkable passages take on homoerotic connotations. From this perspective, two of the relationships described in the work acquire particular significance.

The first of these relationships involves the protagonist and his fellow shipmate aboard the *Rendeer* [*sic*], John B., a character based on Viaud's naval school friend, Joseph Bernard. John does not play as important a role in this novel as Samuel did in the first. He never actually appears; he is only talked about. Still, the few mentions of his relationship with Loti are presented as significant and, given the events of the preceding narrative, catch the attention of the alerted reader.

To begin with, Loti describes John to his sister as a 'faithful friend' (I:IV). This normally anodyne term is connotation-laden in a text presented as being by 'the author of *Aziyadé*,' since, as we have seen, Loti had used it in that work to describe Samuel during the most intense period of their relationship (*Aziyadé* II:II). If Loti uses this term in *The Marriage of Loti* to describe John, he signals the alerted reader that he has a special relationship with his fellow shipmate, one somehow similar to the one that he will develop with Samuel once he gets to the Middle East. It comes as no surprise that just as Samuel was described as having 'affection' for Loti (*Aziyadé* IV:IV), so Loti says of John that the latter's 'sweet and deep affection had for a long time been my great recourse in the sorrows of life' (II:XLVII). As this last passage, like the paraphrase of the Oriental poem cited in *Aziyadé* (II:XXVIII), makes quite clear, Loti feels a great need for a male friend who can offer him loyalty and affection, and finds this in John for a time, as he will later, for a time, in Samuel.[3]

While John, unlike Samuel, never appears on the stage of the story, his reported reactions to Loti's involvement with various Tahitian women suggest that his 'affection' for the protagonist can be subject to a jealousy that one might not expect from a non-erotic friendship. Early in the narrative Loti remarks that 'John himself, my beloved brother John ... experienced a sorrowful surprise when they told him about my nocturnal strolls with Faïmana in the queen's gardens' (I:XV).[4] Why is John surprised to learn that his friend goes for nocturnal strolls with a young Tahitian woman, and why does this surprise cause him sorrow? It could be that he is particularly moral and regrets that his friend does not share his morality. It could, on the other hand, be jealousy. By not specifying the cause of John's sorrow, Viaud leaves it open to interpretation.

This is also the case with Loti's subsequent remark: 'John was full of indulgence for this little girl [Rarahu, a young Tahitian woman with whom Loti has become involved] ... he was inclined to forgive his brother Harry everything, when it was a question of her.' This notion of John pardoning Loti for his involvement with Tahitian women returns somewhat later when Loti, having gone to Taravao on the other side of Tahiti for a few days, writes to his friend and, asking him to convey greetings to Rarahu, adds: 'You are too good not to forgive both of us' (I:XLII). What is there to forgive in each case? A breach of morality, or a betrayal of something more than friendship? As in *Aziyadé*, Viaud here leaves a great deal unspecified, allowing the reader to derive the interpretation that he or she chooses from the only somewhat determining context.

While John is bothered and even hurt by Loti's consorting with Tahitian women, he, unlike the stereotypical sailor, does not become involved with them at all. This behaviour is singled out as unusual: 'John ... passed through the festivities there like a beautiful mystic figure, impossible to explain for the Tahitian women who never found the path to his heart, or the vulnerable side of his neophyte's purity' (II:VIII). John's abstention does not prove that he is homosexual. Nevertheless, given the context established by the title-page reference to *Aziyadé*, a gay interpretation of John's lack of interest in the Tahitian women is not outside the realm of possibility.

Loti describes John here as possessing 'purity,' having earlier portrayed him, in a scene already cited, as someone 'who saw everything with his astonishingly pure eyes' (I:XV). For a sensualist like Loti who so easily succumbs to the desires of the flesh, anyone who can abstain from such activity becomes remarkable. In addition, however, and again recalling the context established by the title-page reference to *Aziyadé*, the reader might also remember the last pages in that novel, in which Loti had praised the title character for loving him 'with the deepest and purist love' (*Aziyadé* V:IV; cf. also IV:XXVII). In that instance, as we saw, the purity of the Loti-Aziyadé relationship was related to the latter's offer to forego sex in order to maintain contact with her beloved (*Aziyadé* IV:X). Is John's purity to be seen as a willingness to abstain from all sexual activity, or just from the different-sex activity whose absence seems to have made the Loti-Aziyadé relationship 'pure'?[5] The vagueness of the narrative leaves this open to only somewhat determined interpretation. One could note that John, like Samuel, is never presented as having any erotic involvement with women, his only noted 'affection' being for Loti.

John is also presented in a way that played no part in the portrayal of Samuel and that will be very significant in subsequent Viaud narratives. Seven times in the course of *The Marriage of Loti* Loti describes his ship-mate as his 'brother.'[6] This term should qualify the Loti-John relation-ship as non-erotic. It is used early in the novel to suggest an absence of the erotic when Loti says of his initial relationship with Rarahu: 'We used to sleep one beside the other, more or less like two brothers' (I:XV). Loti had used the term in a similar fashion near the end of *Aziyadé*. There he had explained that 'there was an abyss between his affection [Samuel's for Loti], which was so tormented, and the clear and brotherly affection of Mihran-Achmet' (IV:IV). Brotherly affection is 'clear,' free of passion, the opposite of 'tormented.'[7]

The use of 'brother' in some of these circumstances, rather than restricting the connotations of the relationships so described, ends up undermining the limiting power of the term, however. As noted in chap-ter 2, Loti's relationship with Achmet, though contrasted with that between Loti and Samuel as devoid of eroticism, had a certain ambigu-ity (cf. *Aziyadé* III:LII). At what point Loti starts having sex with Rarahu, in addition to just sleeping with her, is never specified, so what is going on between the two when they are described as lying together 'more or less like two brothers' is not clear. 'More or less' adds further suggestive-ness, of course.

There are also the direct declarations of affection between Loti and John, presented in the protecting shadow of that term. On Loti's feel-ings for John we have the former's description of the latter as 'this same good and tender brother, who watches over me like a guardian angel and whom I love with all the strength of my heart' (I:IV), as 'John ... my beloved brother John' (I:XV), and, once he returns to England, Loti's suggestive longing: 'Where is this beloved brother John, who shared with me those first vibrant, strange, enchanting impressions of youth? ... Where is all the indefinable charm of that country, all the freshness of our shared impressions, the joys we had together?' (IV:VIII). On John's feelings for his shipmate we have the already quoted mention of 'John B ... my dear brother John, whose sweet and deep affection had for a long time been my great recourse in the sorrows of life' (II:XLVII). Granted that the expression of affection between men was often stronger in the nineteenth century than Americans are accustomed to today, these passages, given the context in which they are presented, do as much to eroticize 'brother' as that word does to de-eroticize them.[8]

Context also plays a role in how we read other passages. Twice Loti expresses his regret at John's absence, once when he spends several days away from him at Taravao – 'I only need your presence, brother, to be absolutely charmed by my stay at Taravao' (I:XLII) – and then, when back in England, in the passage quoted just above. The passage in IV:VIII is particularly suggestive. Since we know that John did not become involved with Tahitian women, we are left to wonder what the erotic-sounding 'first vibrant, strange, enchanting impressions of youth,' the 'joys we had together' were. Loti never specifies, forcing the reader once again to provide his or her own interpretation.[9]

The same is true regarding Loti's own sexual orientation. He has feelings for Rarahu, yet he marries her at the queen's suggestion, not on his own impulse (I:XIII). Indeed, he sounds remarkably indifferent: 'I had no serious reason to resist the queen's desire, and little Rarahu from the Apiré district was very charming ...' (ibid). Later he explains:

I had hesitated for a long time. – I had resisted with all my strength – and that strange situation had gone on, past all likelihood, for several days: when we stretched out on the grass to take the noon meal together, and Rarahu surrounded my body with her arms, we used to fall asleep near each other, more or less like two brothers.

The two of us were playing a very childish comedy in that respect ... Feeling the emotion *that made Faust hesitate on Marguerite's threshold* for a Tahitian girl might have made me smile myself, if I had been a few years older. (I:XV)

It would appear, especially given the allusion to the scene in Goethe's *Faust* that ends with Faust entering Marguerite's house and making love to her for the first time, that Loti is hesitant not simply to marry Rarahu but to have sex with her. As usual, however, this passage remains ambiguous, but it does suggest a discomfort with different-sex activity that is not only new to Viaud's work with this novel, but also an indication of the development in Loti of something like a homosexual identity. (We need to remember that while the real-life episodes on which *The Marriage of Loti* was based occurred before those that inspired *Aziyadé*, Viaud composed his Tahitian tale after the Middle Eastern one and what it may have taught him about himself.) Loti also hesitates when Rarahu, having lost her parents, asks him if he would like to live together with her in Papeete (II:VI). It can also appear significant that the Tahitian name he retains for himself, Loti, is the one given to him by the members of Queen Pomaré's court (I:I), not Mata reva, the name given him by Rarahu (I:XXXI).

The partner in the novel's other erotically charged male-male relationship is even less physically present than John and yet even more important. He becomes a finally successful rival to Rarahu herself, winning Loti's attention away from his Tahitian consort at an important moment. This partner is none other than Loti's deceased older brother and fellow naval officer, Georges. All the originally envisioned readers of *The Marriage of Loti* knew about this character (as opposed to what we know about the individual on whom he was modeled, Viaud's brother Gustave) is that Georges spent some time on Tahiti prior to Loti's arrival, had a relationship there with a native woman, Taïmaha, and then died at sea after leaving the island. Still, the power that his memory exerts over his younger brother is immense. In fact, Loti's first words in the novel, in a letter to his sister back in England, begin:

> Here I am facing this distant island that our brother cherished, a mysterious point that was for a long time the place of dreams of my childhood. A strange desire to come here played no small part in pushing me toward the profession of sailor ... Here I am finally facing the dreamed-of island ... It is indeed about this corner of the world that our brother who is no longer spoke to us with love. (I:IV)

This is a clear example of what René Girard has called mediated desire.[10] Loti's fascination with the island has been determined by his brother's association with it. As Girard showed, such triangulated desire, though it appears directed at the third party (Tahiti, in this case), is actually the manifestation of a desire for the second party (Georges).

The same can be said, at least in part, of Loti's desire to see the two children that the Tahitian woman Taïmaha claims to have had by Georges. He makes it clear that he envisions them as manifestations of his deceased sibling, declaring, as he thinks about one of them, Taamari: 'At least everything that was Georges is not finished, did not die with him ...' (III:XLVII). He seeks them, as he sought Tahiti itself, in order to be close to his brother. Loti himself notes the strange power of this desire: 'I was strangely obsessed with the thought of Taïmaha, who had been the wife of my brother Rouéri. It was very difficult for me to leave without knowing her, I don't know why' (II:XXXVI). 'I waited with an unexplainable anxiety; I would have given a great deal at that moment to see that creature ... who was linked to the distant and poetic memory of Rouéri' (II:XXXVII).

When Loti discovers that Taïmaha lied and that Georges was not the father of her two children, his reaction follows the same lines:

> This emptiness that was forming there [in my heart] made me feel *a mysterious and profound sorrow*; it was as if my lost brother had been plunged further and forever into nothingness; everything that was him sank into the night, it was is if he had died a second time. – And it seemed that these islands had suddenly become deserted – that all of Oceania's charm had died from the same blow, and that nothing attached me to this country any longer.[11] (III:XIX)

Once the mediator (Georges) disappears, so does the desire for the only apparently loved third party (Tahiti).

All this becomes particularly significant during the last hours of Loti's sojourn on the exotic island. Having failed in previous attempts to locate both of Taïmaha's sons, he finally goes on an expedition to another island, sacrificing in the process what could have been final hours spent with Rarahu. His comment, 'And yet I was very parsimonious about these last several days spent in Papeete, very jealous of these last hours of love and strange happiness ...' (IV:X), makes it clear that Loti is making a conscious choice here between his brother and Rarahu. At this juncture in his own life, Viaud chose between a visit to his brother's former consort and Bernard, not a Tahitian woman.[12] As Bruno Vercier maintained in the preface to his edition of the novel, 'finding that nephew is more important than spending these last days with [Rarahu].'[13] Indeed, when he is with Taïmaha, Loti says: 'I had forgotten even Rarahu for the moment ...' (II:XL).

Nothing so far indicates that this preference is sexual, but several passages suggest that Viaud was using the novel to work out his feelings for his brother.[14] The fact that he named his protagonist's fictional paramour Rarahu when his brother Gustave's consort on the island had been named Tarahu suggests that he might have been trying, by having Loti become involved with (R)arahu, to imagine himself entering into some sort of relationship with (T)arahu and hence Gustave. As Vercier wrote in his 'Préface': 'Through Rarahu, it is indeed the brother who is desired,'[15] another case of mediated desire. It is also true that Loti hesitates to learn about Georges's past heterosexual activity. Writing to his sister about Taïmaha, he explains: 'I have often wanted to search out whatever remained of him – and then, at the last minute I hesitate; an undefinable feeling, like a scruple, stops me just when I am about to stir up these ashes and rummage through my brother's intimate past' (I:XXII). One could argue that Loti did not want to be confronted with evidence that a homosexual love for Georges would have been unlikely to have been reciprocated. Immediately after Loti confesses for the first time that he might be falling in love with Rarahu, the text continues: 'He recalled his brother Georges ... and he felt that things would go the same for him' (I:XXXVIII). In part he is recalling that Georges also became involved with a Tahitian woman. Given the context, however, the fact that the first mention of romantic love immediately triggers a recollection of Georges suggests that eroticism may also be involved in Loti's feelings for his brother.

Loti's relationship with his deceased brother is particularly complex. Later in the novel, during his efforts to see the children he believes to be his brother's, he remarks: 'These memories of my brother, which I had come there to invoke, came back to life like those of my childhood, through the night of the past ...' (IV:XIV). Loti, like Viaud, had still been a child when his older brother had gone to sea, so it is understandable that his memories of the latter are linked to those of his childhood. Nonetheless, as this passage makes clear, in searching for his lost brother Loti is also searching for his childhood, which generally is associated with the innocence that precedes the awakening of sexuality. He is particularly thrilled when Taïmaha recalls for him episodes in his childhood that Georges had recounted to her: 'I cannot describe the effect that that name and those memories had on me' (II:XLIII). One might go so far as to argue that in this novel Georges signifies both the original object of same-sex desire and a prelapsarian freedom from the troubles that such desire brings. Loti's preoccupation with this freedom is evidenced throughout the novel by his repeated references to the Tahitians as children.[16] This contrast is not, in the novel, a strict opposition, however, for as will be seen later, both with the descriptions of the Tahitians and, perhaps, of the young Loti himself, in Viaud's work childhood is not devoid of sexuality. As we will see, this is an issue to which Viaud would return at great length in *The Story of a Child* ten years later.

Viaud's depiction of Loti's relationship with his brother further complicates the connotations of the already highly charged term 'brother.' It therefore enhances the ambiguity of the relationship between Loti and John, since Loti repeatedly refers to the latter with that same term.

It adds further resonance to an already striking passage describing Loti as he sails away from Tahiti for a brief trip to California. After having noted that the last thing on the island that he can see, even after the Tahitian women have disappeared from sight, is the house where his brother lived (II:XLVI),[17] Loti descends to his cabin and there spends 'the whole day, sunk in this sort of sad meditation that is neither being awake nor sleep, and where images of Oceania and distant memories of my childhood become mixed together' (II:XLVI). He is already deeply affected by having to leave this contact with his brother. Yet when he takes the watch at sunset he notes that 'the person whom I replaced for the night watch was John B. ... my dear brother John, whose sweet and deep affection had for a long time been my great recourse in the sorrows of life' (II:XLVII). One 'brother' is linked to the other, comforting Loti for the renewed loss of the original.

Loti's relationship to Georges is rendered still more ambiguous by the already quoted mention of Loti and Rarahu sleeping together 'more or less like two brothers' (I:XV). In *The Marriage of Loti* there are no outpourings of male same-sex desire, as with Samuel and, by implication, Loti himself in *Aziyadé*, but there is still a great deal of homoeroticism in the air.[18]

For that matter, there is a great deal of eroticism in this novel, because Viaud presents Tahiti as a land of constant sensual stimulation. At one point he simply describes it as 'the most voluptuous island on earth ...' (III:XLVII). There one lives a 'soft existence' (I:XI), a 'sweetly enervating existence' (I:XXII) that offers 'this all-powerful charm of voluptuousness and nonchalance' (II:VI). Even the immaterial becomes erotic. Loti at one point remarks on how 'the warm and voluptuous darkness redescended on the wild island; as in the time when the first explorers named it the new Cythera, everything had once again become seduction, sensual uneasiness, and unrestrained desires' (III:XXX). Sunrise is equally erotic, 'that particularly voluptuous hour of the morning' (III:XXXII).

In addition to these generalities, there are also lots of specifics. The atmosphere plays a major role in creating this state of almost perpetual eroticism. Plumket begins the novel by speaking of 'the calm, the enervating languor of a summer night,' with its 'warm and perfumed atmosphere' (I:I). Loti himself also remarks on 'the air ... laden with enervating and unknown smells' (I:XI) and elsewhere describes how 'a warm breeze passed softly over the tops of the trees' (I:XXIV), 'a breath full of seduction and sensual uneasiness passed over this country'

(III:XL). 'The breeze brings ... Tahitian perfumes, puffs of orange trees and gardenias in flower,' so 'it is as if one is made drunk by this Tahitian perfume which condenses in the evening under the thick foliage' (III:VI).

Tahiti's flora also participates in this constant sensuality. Near the end of the novel Loti remarks on how, one evening, as he strolled with Rarahu, 'the air was laden with the odor of ripe guavas; all the plants were enervated' (III:XXVII). The fauna participate, too. Early in the narrative Loti describes how 'large butterflies of a velvety black, marked with large scabious-coloured eyes, flew slowly, or rested on us, as if their silky wings were too heavy to carry them away' (I:XI).

The two-legged fauna are also remarkably sensual. In speaking of the women at Queen Pomaré's court, Loti describes their 'black eyes, laden with languor' (I:VI). Elsewhere he refers to them as 'the voluptuous band of the female court attendants' (III:VIII). Nowhere is the inhabitants' erotic nature clearer than at the dances held during certain evenings. These 'demented and lascivious dances often lasted until morning' (III:XIII), one dancer surpassing the next 'in shamelessness and frenzy.' Even from aboard the *Rendeer* Loti can hear the 'raw and lustful songs' (II:XXXI) of the participants at what he terms 'this saturnalia.' Though he seldom does so directly, Loti at one point actually mentions 'the loose morals' of the inhabitants (I:XIII).

The most visibly sensual of all the Tahitians is Loti's 'wife,' Rarahu. Early on Loti mentions that her eyes are 'full of an exotic languor' and her 'hair perfumed with sandal' (I:V). She is a 'passionate little girl of fifteen' (II:XLIV), with a 'strangely ardent and passionate nature' (II:XXXV) that makes it impossible for her to be satisfied with only one lover: 'her Maori blood burned in her veins; she had days marked by fever and uneasiness.' Rarahu demonstrates this most clearly at the *upa-upa*, the wild evening dance. 'These displays ... made her blood burn' (II:XIII), Loti explains. Indeed, 'on those evenings it seemed that Rarahu was another creature. The *upa-upa* awakened in the depth of her uncultivated soul feverish voluptuousness and wildness ... Under the influence of a religious or passionate exaltation, she performed her most fantastic variations in a frenzied manner' (II:XXVIII). Though, as with Aziyadé, Loti never discusses the sex that he has with Rarahu or any other Tahitian women, these remarks about Rarahu and Tahitian women in general convey the notion that they are uninhibited sexually and that there is the potential for wild and uninhibited sex here.

Nothing suggests this more clearly than the frequent use of the

French word *sauvage* and its derivatives to describe the island and its inhabitants. As in French in general, so in this novel the word has several connotations, all interlocked and inter-referring. It indicates the natural that has not been controlled by man: Loti explains that 'the interior zones [of Tahiti] are uninhabited and covered with deep forests. These are *sauvages* regions' (II:XIX). It makes sense that this word is also used as the opposite of civilized, that is, pertaining to European culture: when in Papéuriri, Loti reflects on 'the solitude and the *sauvagerie* of this hidden corner of the earth. At night, when you could hear in the distance the plaintive sound of reed flutes, or the lugubrious sound of shell trumpets, I became aware of the terrifying distance of my homeland' (II:XII). He also makes this opposition earlier, lamenting that 'civilization, our stupid colonial civilization, all our customs, all our habits, all our vices, have come here as well, in excess, and the *sauvage* poetry has departed, with the customs and the traditions of the past' (I:IV). There is also Loti's comment on Taïmaha's lie about her children: 'It isn't possible for us, who were born on the other side of the world, to judge or even to understand these incomplete natures, so different from ours, in whom the depths remain mysterious and *sauvage*' (III:XXVII). A third connotation of *sauvage* here is wild and uninhibited sensuality. In a passage already quoted, Loti describes how 'the *upa-upa* awakened in the depths of [Rarahu's] uninstructed soul feverish voluptuousness and *sauvagerie*,' linking 'feverish voluptuousness' and *sauvagerie*. When he prepares to leave her, 'I felt that her heart was filling with bitterness, disenchantment, quiet irritation, and with all the unbridled passions of *sauvages* children' (III:XXVI).

The three connotations interconnect quite well within the context of *The Marriage of Loti*. The Tahitians are *sauvage* because they are not controlled by a limiting civilization, which makes them different from Europeans, and which allows them to be sexually uninhibited and passionate (which also makes them different from Europeans). Each connotation explains and reinforces the others.[19]

All this explains why Loti sets Rarahu up as quite different from his fellow English, and probably from Europeans in general. This difference, moreover, is one of the things that he finds attractive about her. 'A large and rapid transformation took place in her on the moral level,' he remarks. 'She was civilized enough already to like it when I called her "little *sauvage*" – to understand that that charmed me, and that she would gain nothing by copying the ways of white women' (II:XIV). Rarahu is morally different from Europeans, and that is how Loti wants her to remain.

All this fascination with uninhibited eroticism, to which Loti, unlike John, succumbs so easily, can be seen in the context of *Aziyadé* as an explanatory early step toward the sexual open-mindedness that just a few years later will allow Loti to deal with Samuel's homoerotic responses in such a non-judgmental, non-hostile, and even non-homophobic fashion. Exposure and capitulation to *savage* sensuality unleash the madness within human nature in Joseph Conrad's *Heart of Darkness* (1902). In this work by a French sailor-author, however, it seems only to dispel the limitations imposed by Western civilization to prevent men from exploring erotic adventure. In this respect *The Marriage of Loti* is the depiction of Loti's sexual 'coming out,' his first significant break with a Marcusian Western culture's repressive restrictions on man's erotic potential.

Along these lines, it is interesting to note how Viaud toned down the description of Loti's adolescent activities from *Aziyadé*. In the first novel, as we saw, Loti had proudly boasted that at the age of sixteen, while still in London: 'I tasted a little of all pleasures' (I:XV); 'this boy with such a young face had already taken advantage of everything in life' (III:I), with a use of the all-inclusive adjective *toutes* (all, everything) that was particularly suggestive. In the second novel, however, the description of that period in his life is far less open: 'When he was still very young, Loti had been thrown into the hubbub of European existence; he had raised the veil that hides the stage of the world from children early on; – thrown brusquely, at sixteen, into the whirlwind of London and Paris, he had suffered at an age when, ordinarily, one just begins to think ...' (I:XXXVIII). All the implications that Loti first experimented with all kinds of sex before ever leaving England are gone, which shifts his sexual liberation to the period six years later when he arrives in Tahiti.

With the possible exception of one very ambiguous passage. The multiple connotations of *sauvage* in this novel make it possible to believe that Loti at one point suggests that even as a child he had had a strongly erotic nature: 'He, too, had been a little *sauvage*, in whose heart a throng of fresh ideas and radiant illusions were engraved in isolation' (I:XXXVIII). This is very circumspect if it is meant to suggest that Loti engaged in erotic fantasies as a child, but then, Marcel is not much more direct in Proust's *Swann's Way* when describing what he did as a child when locked in the upstairs bathroom. Viaud will explore the young Loti's mental states in *The Story of a Child*.

It is significant that Viaud ends this novel with a description of Loti sailing for the East (IV:IX), where, as his readers knew, the naval officer would encounter Samuel and the underworld to which the boatman introduced him. *The Marriage of Loti* thus becomes an explanation of how an Englishman with a proper Englishman's moral code, albeit with the tendencies suggested by his ambiguous relationships with two 'brothers,' can arrive at the point of behaving like the almost totally amoral Loti of *Aziyadé*.

Note: Thirteen years after *The Marriage of Loti*, in *Carmen Sylva and Sketches From the Orient* (1893), Viaud published something entitled, 'A Few Forgotten Pages of "Madame Chrysanthemum,"' which, given the date on the episode, 16 September 1885, would make it a missing part of chapter 50 of that novel, which he had published in 1887 and which recounts Pierre Loti's first sojourn in Japan. At one point, while describing himself and his friend Yves climbing up a forest-covered mountain, Loti remarks:

> I feel very incapable of expressing the unexpected, poignant emotion of a memory that comes to me all of a sudden on these paths full of shadow. This green night under immense trees, these too large ferns, these mossy odours, and, in front of me, these men whose skin is copper coloured, all that suddenly transports me across the years and distances, to Oceania, in the great woods of Fata-hua, once familiar ... In different countries of the world, where I have led my life since my departure from the *delicious island* [Tahiti], I have already felt these painful recollections often, striking me like a flash of lightening and then disappearing as fast, leaving me only a vague anguish – itself fleeting ...
> But the trouble that occurs inside me, at the memory of this inexpressible Polynesian charm, is localized in deep layers, possibly pre-dating my present existence. When I try to talk about it, I feel that I am touching on an order of things that is barely comprehensible, shadowy even for me.

This very Proustian passage will make much more sense after we have examined *The Story of a Child*, which Viaud published in 1890 and which contains the key to much of the imagery here. Even now, however, we can see that in a later work Viaud further developed the earlier *Marriage of Loti*, suggesting that some signal event happened to Loti on Tahiti involving men with copper-coloured skin, something with which even years later his memory had difficulties coping.

CHAPTER FOUR

A Plea for Sexual Understanding:
The Story of a Spahi

Unlike his first two novels, Viaud's *The Story of a Spahi* (1881) does not feature the character Harry Grant/Loti, nor does it depict its protagonist, French spahi Jean Peyral, as involved in any sort of homoerotic relationship. Even more than the two preceding works, however, it seems to have been written intentionally to explain – and, unlike the first two novels, to justify – how a man, such as the Loti of *Aziyadé*, could become involved in a homosexual relationship. If anything, it is surprising that it took Viaud this long to do so. Gay writers, like gay men in general until not so long ago, often demonstrated a need to explain the way they were in order to counter society's, and sometimes their own, disapproval. What is remarkable about *The Story of a Spahi*, once again, like the two novels that precede it, is how free of homophobia and self-hatred Viaud's explanation is.

The Story of a Spahi recounts the life of French infantryman Jean Peyral during his tours of duty in Africa. As already mentioned, it does not deal to any significant extent with male same-sex relationships or desire; the slight indices of it would probably pass unnoticed were it not for the context established by the two preceding narratives. The black African spahi Nyaor-fall is likened to a 'faithful friend,' the term given such significance in *Aziyadé* and *The Marriage of Loti*. Near the end of the work the narrator describes him as 'the black spahi to whom [Jean Peyral] had confided his sorrow [at the loss of his fiancée] as if to his most faithful friend' (III:X),[1] just as the title character of *The Marriage of Loti* had found solace for his sorrows in his 'faithful friend' John (II:XLVII). The term here is the narrator's, however, and not Jean's; the narrator may see the relationship between Jean and Nyaor-fall as having similarities to those between Loti and John and Samuel, but there is nothing to indicate that Jean shares this viewpoint. Jean never refers to Nyaor-fall as a 'faithful friend' himself, and never as a brother, so there is no basis to assume that he envisions his relationship with the African as anything other than a non-erotic friendship.

Nor, unlike with the descriptions of Loti in the first two novels, is there any suggestion that Jean ever had sexual relationships with other men. The only possibly relevant remark comes after the failure of his affair with Cora, a woman of mixed race whom he meets in Africa, when the narrator divulges that Jean 'had traversed a terrible period during this month of suffering. He had devoured novels in which everything was new for his imagination, and he had assimilated their unhealthy extravagances' (I:XXI). What these 'unhealthy extravagances' are the narrator does not specify, but if Jean found them in the novels of his day it is unlikely that they included male same-sex activities.

Other remarks about Jean are even less substantial. It is true that, like Loti in *Aziyadé* (I:X), he enjoys the effect of an outfit that transforms him. The narrator notes that when Jean had first arrived in Africa, 'he had felt very vividly the happiness ... of wearing an Arab hat, a red vest and a large saber. He had found himself handsome, and that had pleased him' (I:III). In moments of homesickness, however, this costume loses its appeal; he thinks to himself: 'This red outfit and this Arab fez in which they had dressed him up, and which had, indeed, given him quite an air, – what a disguise it was for him, this poor little peasant from Cévennes!' (I:VIII).

Jean is also particularly devoted to his mother – 'But perhaps the most tender spot in his heart was still for his mother' (II:XII; cf. also I:V, I:XIII, I:XIV, III:II, III:XXVI) – but some gay men are not and some heterosexual men are. He occasionally whips Fatou-gaye, his black mistress, with his crop (Introduction:IX; II:XXXII), and doing so augments his anger against her – 'his rage was stimulated as he struck her' (II:XXXIII) – but there is no indication that such violence arouses him, and sadism is no more common to gay men than to straights.[2] He enjoys 'the freer life' (III:III) that his foreign posting allows him, as Loti had especially in the Middle East (*Aziyadé* III:VII), but many men reacted this way to military life in the nineteenth century. None of this makes Jean look same-sex oriented, even in the context of the two previous novels, even to the predisposed but still objective reader.

Almost the same is true of the world in which he functions. There is no equivalent of Samuel or John B., much less the underworld Loti encountered in Salonika and Istanbul. During one of the several episodes that take place in Virginie-Scholastique's ill-famed cabaret, the narrator notes: 'A small, stinking lamp lit a jumbled heap of things that swarmed painfully in the thick atmosphere; red vests and naked black flesh, strange embraces' (I:XXI). He goes on to note that 'the whole Virginie-Scholastique group was there: little twelve-year-old negresses, and also little boys!' There is pederasty here, but it never confronts Jean as it did Loti in *Aziyadé* (II:XXVII), where, as already noted, it had been presented as an alternative for men interested in women. There is no indication that adult male homosexuality is present in the cabaret.

Later, when explaining that Jean has not been promoted because of his affair with Fatou-gaye, the narrator or Jean, it is not clear which, exclaims indignantly:

Getting drunk, making a racket, getting carried off with one's head split open, striking passers-by in the street at night with your saber, wandering through all the dives, making use of *all* types of prostitution, that's all very well. – But leading astray from the path of virtue, for oneself alone, a little female captive from a good house who has been equipped with the sacrament of baptism is not permissible ... (II:I; emphasis added)

The inclusive adjective 'all' (*toutes* in the original French) would necessarily suggest sex with men as well as boys (remember the similar usage of all/every in the description of Loti's adolescence in *Aziyadé* [III:L]), but not only does Jean not become involved in 'all types of prostitution,' it is not even clear whether this passage asserts that 'all types of prostitution' actually occur in Jean's unit, or simply in military life in general. The setting of this novel, far different from that of *Aziyadé*, does not create a homoerotic atmosphere.

With one possible exception. Near the end of the novel Jean wanders by mistake into the camp of the Bambaras. (He is day-dreaming; again, as in *Aziyadé*, it is made clear here that the protagonist does not seek out this encounter of his own will.) There he stumbles upon a group of black spahis, among them Nyaor-fall, who are dancing in a circle. Though he smiles at them,

Jean nonetheless hurried, so as to leave these long chains of white dancers [they are dressed in white], which kept breaking apart and then reforming around him ... This made an impression on him, the night, this dance – and that music, which seemed not to be a music of this world. And, still saying 'Tjean! Enter the circle!' they continued to move around him like visions, taking pleasure in surrounding the spahi, purposely enlarging their turning chain to keep him from leaving it ... (III:XX)

This passage could be homoerotic. The black spahis want to draw Jean into their group and there is something strange about them ('that music, which seemed not to be a music of this world'). Are they trying to draw Jean into a sexual encounter? Jean is both bothered by them and interested: he hurries to get away, but 'this made an impression on him, the night, this dance.' Someone, Jean or the narrator, notes that Nyaor-fall is 'one of the largest and handsomest' of the black spahis, but that same person also twice refers to the 'chains' of spahis, suggesting a negative view of them and their intentions. Are these men trying to seduce Jean? Does he perceive their actions, whatever the intent, in this way? He had already been struck by the fact that Nyaor-fall did not seem to love his wives, buying and selling them without emotion (III:X). Jean thinks back on this strange scene twice (III:XXI, III:XXVI) and the narrator alludes to it one last time when describing how the various carnivores arrive to begin work on the corpses of the spahis, Jean among them, who have been left in the desert after the surprise attack by Boubakar-Ségou's army (III:XXXI). This association of the carnivores with the dancing men reinforces the negative feelings Jean had about the group.

The association also links the dancing, beckoning black spahis to the first mention of carnivores earlier in the novel. One night Jean hears terrible animal cries in the distance; Nyaor-fall explains that they are the sounds of wandering carnivores looking for corpses.

Jean understood and trembled. Since then, every time he heard the lugubrious concerts during the night, he recalled the explanation that Nyaor had so clearly given with his mimicry, and he who, during the day, was not afraid of much of anything, shuddered and felt himself grow cold as a result of one of those vague and somber terrors that superstitious mountainfolk experience. (I:XXIV)

Jean, a brave soldier, is terrified by the thought of these beasts. Does the narrator associate them with the dancing black spahis at the end of the novel to suggest that he, the narrator, has an inordinate terror of men who have sex with other men, or just of black men who do this? (Jean never associates the carnivores with the dancers himself.) How far should the reader go along these lines? None of the recollections of the dancers does anything to pin down the connotations of the dance scene for either Jean or the narrator. It is a fascinating note on which to end the novel, but also an ambiguous one.[3]

Here we might recall Brodin's unsupported report that, during Viaud's first sojourn in Africa, 'Julien allowed himself to be tempted by Corydonesque experiments. They were probably experiments, but nothing more. In any case, they would not leave any deep marks on Julien's moral makeup.'[4] Whether this scene is related to those alleged experiments I would not venture to guess. One might note, however, that the image of being surrounded by hostile individuals while in the African desert returns several times in Viaud's subsequent writings (see *The Book of Pity and of Death*, 'Land Without Name'; *The Desert*, III). Though the relation between the carnivores and the black spahis never occurs to Jean, Viaud evidently included it in the novel as one of his metaphors for some sort of menacing sexuality.

Directly related to this incident is the very revised account of Viaud's sojourn on Easter Island that he included eighteen years later in *On Life's By-ways* (1899). It is worth quoting in full because it resembles the passage in *The Story of a Spahi* and because it seems to contribute to a reading of it. Recounting his first landing on Easter Island in 1872, Viaud explains that the other two seamen who accompanied him took off in search of rabbit for their commanding officer. He himself

> remains alone, encircled tighter and tighter by my new hosts [a group of island men who appeared when the three Frenchmen put ashore] ... Their circle closed on all sides, and, each one offering me his spear or his idol, they sing to me, quickly at first, a sort of plaintive, lugubrious melopea, accompanying it with a swaying of their heads and their hips such as large upright bears might make ... I know that they are inoffensive and besides, their faces, which the tattoos make ferocious at first, are of a childlike sweetness; they inspire no reasoned fear in me; but all the same, for me who, the first time in my life, am penetrating into an island of the Great Ocean, there is a shiver of surprise and instinctive fear at feeling all these eyes and all these breaths so near, before daylight, on a deserted shore and under a black sky ...
>
> Now the rhythm of the song rushes forward, the movement of the heads and the hips accelerates, the voices become harsh and deep; it becomes, in the wind and the noise of the sea, a great wild clamour leading a furious dance.
>
> And then, suddenly, it quiets down. It's over. The circle opens and the

dancers disperse ... What did all of them want of me? Was it some childishness on their part, or a conspiracy, or wishes of welcome? ... Who can know? (*On Life's By-ways*, 'Easter Island,' V)

What is remarkable about this passage is not only how closely it resembles the one in *The Story of a Spahi*, but also the fact that most of this resemblance was a result of revision that Viaud did for the publication of *On Life's By-ways*. What he had written in 1872 at the time of the incident is very different and among other things makes no mention of a circle:

I remained alone in the middle of my new hosts.

It was something so strange that the most insensitive people would have been struck by it; as for me, I felt penetrated [note that this verb is used passively here and not actively, as in the revision] with sadness and terror – irrational terror, because all these faces to which the tattooing gave an initially ferocious appearance were, however, full of sweetness and goodness, all of them stamped with that air of terrified sadness that *savage* men have, that Pétéro [one of the islanders] had to such a high degree ... I would have abandoned myself to one of them without worry, but the group had too fantastic an appearance.

They sang a sort of plaintive and lugubrious melopea around me. It was the same notes repeated indefinitely without stopping; the harmony, the rhythm, the voices had nothing comparable to the bizarrest things that we hear in Europe, and the most daring passages in [Meyerbeer's exotic opera] *L'Africaine* are still far from this ideal of wildness [*sauvagerie*].

All these men examined me with curiosity, accompanying their song with a monotonous swaying of their heads and their hips; each of them offered me an idol, shapeless and grimacing, to which, more than to me, their speech seemed to be addressed. Then suddenly the rhythm became animated, the voices gave out harsh, hurried notes and the dance became furious, frenetic.

Their chorus had been organized spontaneously, without my being able to grasp its goal or its motive, and Pétéro did not understand me when I asked him for an explanation of it.

Nevertheless, Pétéro took me by my right hand, an old, tattooed chief took me by the left hand, the two of them led me, running, and the group of men followed. (Loti, *L'Île de Pâques* 27–30)

Viaud then recounts his visit to a native hut.

As a comparison of the two versions shows, much of the fear and all of the image of being surrounded by a threatening circle of men – note the addition of the spears – comes in the revision. This does not necessarily mean that the additions had no basis in the events of 1872, of course. Viaud could have been adding elements that remained in his memory. Nevertheless, the revision makes it clear that these additions, so similar to the passage in *The Story of a Spahi*, play upon and in turn reinforce the negative depiction of homoeroticism in the passage in the novel. The original version, with the line 'I would have abandoned myself to one of them' and the repeated descriptions elsewhere of how handsome Viaud found some of the male Easter Islanders to be, instead suggests a much more willing attitude on Viaud's part with regard to the homosexual possibilities of the encounter. Put most simply, it is as if, in revising his text, Viaud shifted the initiative, or at least the homosexual interest, from himself to the islanders. At the same time, the similarities between the revision and the novel suggest that Viaud recalled the passage in *The Story of a Spahi* in revising a homoerotic episode in his own past because the passage had had homoerotic connotations for him when he wrote it in 1881.

Those involved in colonialist studies might want to view the passage in *The Story of a Spahi* and the revision of the Easter Island text as examples of an imperialist white Western author trying to shift the blame for his own desires onto the Third World and men of colour. Here they would have some justification.

The preceding remarks should have made it clear that while there is little suggestion of male same-sex desire in the events of this narrative, there is considerably more in the narrating voice, which in this novel is not just an objective describer but rather the voice of an individual with his own personality. That individual has a name, Pierre Loti, because, after publishing *Aziyadé* and *The Marriage of Loti* anonymously, Viaud gave his third novel to the public with the pen name that he would make so famous.[5] Previous critics have made little of this change, but it is definitely significant, particularly given the perspective from which we are examining Viaud's works.

As we explained in chapter 1, unlike some other famous literary pseudonyms, such as Voltaire, George Sand, or Mark Twain, 'Pierre Loti' was not an empty term with no connotations in itself. Loti was already, for Viaud's readers, an individual whose character had been developed in great detail in the first two novels. In signing *The Story of a Spahi* (and subsequent books) 'Pierre Loti,' Viaud therefore presented

it as the work of someone other than himself; its peculiarities and preoccupations could be explained as manifestations of the personality of
Pierre Loti, a character Viaud was in the process of elaborating, and not
necessarily as Julien Viaud's. This presentation would not have posed
difficulties for Viaud's readers. The first two narratives had depicted
Loti as a diarist, so Viaud's readers already knew him as someone
who was in the habit of writing. That character had only been known as
Loti, however. *Pierre* Loti was something new, and calls for further
explanation.

To begin with, we can assume that the Pierre Loti who wrote *The Story
of a Spahi* is the Loti/Harry Grant encountered in *Aziyadé* and *The Marriage of Loti*. Near the end of the latter novel Plumket informs his readers
that, after having left Tahiti, Loti travelled 'a little everywhere, – princi-
pally in Africa' (IV:VIII). Had the name been Dupont or Smith one
might have to make allowance for coincidence; given the artificiality of
'Loti,' however, the fact that Loti/Harry Grant spent time in Africa
seems sufficient evidence to ground an assertion that he must be identical with the Pierre Loti who writes about Africa in *The Story of a Spahi*.
Furthermore, nothing in that novel contradicts what we know about
Loti from the first two narratives to invalidate such an assertion.

What about 'Pierre,' though? Why would the English sailor Harry
Grant/Loti have taken that fictitious French first name? He could, after
all, simply have signed 'his' books 'Loti.' Whatever other connotations
'Pierre' may have, it definitely screams French. In adding it to Loti,
Viaud was therefore signaling that Harry Grant was choosing to be a
French author, just as Teodor Jozef Konrad Korzeniowski, a Polish naval
officer, would do when he wanted to establish himself as an English
writer – Joseph Conrad – just a few years later. Admittedly, the pretence
of Grant being English had not always been maintained: in *The Marriage
of Loti* he had suggested that he and the other officers on his ship spoke
French (II:XXIV).[6] Still, in giving Loti a French first name, Viaud clarified that this character would be taking on a French persona, writing in
French, and aiming for a French readership.[7] In fact, Pierre Loti will be
presented in subsequent works as a Frenchman in the French navy, but
that is not relevant here. *The Story of a Spahi* does not treat Loti's nationality at all, as he never appears in the work itself.[8]

Other, from our perspective, more important issues are at stake here
as well, however. As already noted, in presenting *The Story of a Spahi* as
the work of the already developed individual Loti, Julien Viaud separated himself from it, declaring that elements in the novel were not nec-

essarily reflections of himself but might be part of his efforts to develop the characterization of the fictional Harry Grant, now Pierre Loti. It is true that Viaud could have written gay-themed literature under his own name, which would have suggested more directly that he was gay or at least had gay tendencies. That was not a realistic option for a career naval officer in nineteenth-century France, however, or for someone who wanted to have his works read by the general public. A generation later Proust, who did not have a career to defend or a need to earn money from his writings, did not do so; in fact, as we noted in the Introduction, he was very emphatic about denying his homosexuality publicly and presented his eponymous narrator from the beginning as heterosexual. Gide, a generation later still, spent years toying with *Corydon*, his defence of pederasty, before allowing it to be generally published in 1924, forty-three years after *The Story of a Spahi*.[9]

Instead Viaud chose a position that, for its time, is remarkably daring: by maintaining and developing the character of Pierre Loti as the author of *The Story of a Spahi* and subsequent tomes, Viaud made it possible for himself to deal with male same-sex desire – which he did, as we shall see – because there was now the possibility of asserting that any such elements in this and subsequent works were reflections not of himself but of the fictitious character that he had created. Pierre Loti let Viaud publish about things that he himself would not have been able to treat and that no other widely read novelist of his time discussed in a positive fashion. At the same time, by using as his pseudonym the name of one of his protagonists, Viaud would seem to have been inviting his readers to see links between the two of them.

Given what the reader knows about Loti from the two previous novels, the personality suggested by the narrating voice in *The Story of a Spahi* will come as no surprise, except, perhaps, in its development. Unlike in those two previous texts, however, this is the first time that Loti is not visible in the narrative, so the reader has to intuit his nature from the perspective of his words alone.

To begin with, Pierre Loti's narrating voice is particularly preoccupied with physical qualities that constitute for some – and, it would appear, for him – male attractiveness. He remarks on Jean Peyral's handsomeness no less than fourteen times, his strength eight times, his imposing size, linked to strength, four times.[10] These remarks indicate the physical aspect of Pierre Loti's concept of the ideal man, since he says of Jean Peyral at one point that 'a painter would have chosen him as the finished type ... of virile perfection' (III:I), and they match up with the physical features that Loti had admired in Samuel and Achmet. The difference, however, is the much greater frequency with which these qualities are noted in the third novel, constituting something of a 'gay gaze.'[11]

Pierre Loti's gaze also repeatedly finds an Arab quality in Jean. Though the spahi is from rural France, the narrator in his first description of him says that Jean has 'large, clear eyes, elongated like Arab eyes' (Introduction:IV). Later he remarks that the spahi 'has an indefinable proud nonchalance, a counterfeit air of an Arab prince' (II:I), and twice he describes Jean's hat as Arab in style (Introduction:III; III:III). To what extent this is simply part of Pierre Loti's 'type' and to what extent it is meant to be seen as a link with Samuel in *Aziyadé* it would be difficult to say. It could be that Samuel also matched this 'type.' One might notice, however, that just as Samuel on his first appearance 'stretched with ... the expression of a large angora cat, and yawning showed two rows of very small teeth, as brilliant as pearls' (I:VII), so Jean's initial portrait includes mention of 'a feline grace and ... teeth of a rare whiteness' (Introduction:IV). In fact, Viaud had originally written that Jean's teeth had a 'pearly whiteness,' but changed the wording on the advice of his friend Lucien-Hervé Jousselin.[12] The mention of Jean's 'feline grace' is also one of the few examples of gender bending in this novel. Later the narrator remarks on the care that the spahi takes in dressing (I:VIII) and speaks at one point about his 'coquetry' (III:I).

While the gay aspect of the narrator's gaze focuses primarily on Jean, it notices some of the same qualities in other men as well. In the first chapter, Pierre Loti remarks that the long canoes that greet ships arriving in Saint-Louis are rowed by 'tall, thin Hercules, admirable for their shape and muscles ... the sweat and the sea water trickle down their naked skin, which is like varnished ebony' (I:I). Later, during a celebration, the griots, wandering historians, perform 'with their muscles taut, their bodies streaming with sweat ...' (II:XXXIII). As Jean and his companions sail up the Senegal River they spot 'groups of men of pure white race – tawny and tanned, it is true – but handsome in the standard sense' (III:XII). Whether this last judgment is the narrator's or Jean's is not clear.

Above all, however, Pierre Loti is unabashed about describing the attractiveness of the other spahis. There is 'handsome Muller, a large Alsatian lad' (I:VI), whose good looks are noted again several times (I:VII, III:XXIV), and Nyaor-fall, 'a giant African ... with a refined Arab profile ... a handsome statue of black marble' (I:VI), described later, as already noted, as 'one of the largest and most handsome ...' (II:XX).[13] Even at Virginie-Scholastique's cabaret the narrator takes note of the spahis' 'handsome faces with energetic traits' (I:XXI), and at the end of the novel he exclaims, speaking of the spahis who have made the trip to fight Boubakar-Ségou: 'They are all handsome, with their red vests, their blue pants, their large white hats pulled down over their tanned faces' (III:XXIV). Pierre Loti is susceptible to male beauty and he knows what he likes. The comment with which this chapter opened, that *The Story of a Spahi* does not deal to any significant extent with male same-sex desire, is true at the level of plot. The persona of the narrator that Viaud created in this novel, to which the pseudonym he put on it draws further attention, definitely keeps such desire present, however.

Regardless of their apparently different sexualities, Pierre Loti and Jean Peyral both have problems with women and heterosexual desire. Both Cora, the woman of mixed race with whom Jean falls in love shortly after he arrives in Saint-Louis, and the feelings that he develops for her come between him and his memories of his family and childhood, memories that, in Viaud's novels, are an essential element in maintaining both happiness and morality. The narrator remarks that 'now there was a thick veil over [Jean's] childhood and family affections; this veil was Cora, his despair, and his passions' (I:XXII). Loti had used the image of a veil in much the same way in *The Marriage of Loti*: half-way through that novel, during his affair with Rarahu, he had remarked that

> time moved on, and very softly there began to weave around me those thousands of little inextricable threads, made of all the charms of Oceania, which finally form dangerous webs, veils over one's past, one's country, and one's family – and end up enveloping you so well that you can no longer escape ... (II:IX)

The passage in *The Story of a Spahi*, however, is more specific about the nature of the veil. It is no longer something general like 'all the charms of Oceania,' among which were Rarahu and the heterosexual eroticism described in that novel. Now it is very specifically 'Cora, his despair [at losing her] and his passions [for her].' Women, or at least women who awaken strong desire, cut men off from everything that keeps them good and are therefore bad.

The same is true of Fatou-gaye, the young African woman with whom Jean becomes involved after he breaks off with Cora. Early in the novel she steals money from Jean to buy jewelry – not insignificantly, in a

Viaud text, money that Jean was to send to his needy parents back in Cévennes (Introduction:IX). Later it is made clear that Jean fails to be promoted because of his affair with her (II:I). In the world of *The Story of a Spahi*, this failure is Fatou-gaye's fault: the narrator explains that 'Fatou-gaye ... had thrown over [Jean] an indefinable sensual and impure seduction, the unknown charm of some amulet' (I:I; cf. also II:IX; II:XX). It is not surprising that, when Jean first contemplates setting aside his scruples and having sex with her, the narrator describes Fatou-gaye as a 'savoury fruit of the Sudan ... filled with unhealthy, feverish, unknown pleasures ...' (I:XXXV). An element of racism certainly enters here, but if we recall the positive words said about Nyaor-fall we must also consider that part of this condemnation of Fatou-gaye is a function not of her race but of her being a desire-inciting woman.[14]

There are certainly many gay men who do not see women as threats.[15] In *The Story of a Spahi*, neither Jean's mother nor his fiancée, Jeanne, is ever presented in a negative fashion. Granted, Jean knows Jeanne not as a sexual woman but only as a child: at one point the spahi 'tried to imagine her face as a woman, by working from the traits of the fifteen-year-old child whom he had left behind' (II:XII). When she becomes a woman, she 'denies' Jean and marries Prosper Suirot (III:VII). Still, it is the strong desire that certain women arouse in men, and the women who make use of this desire, that come off poorly in this text. It does not take a feminist to see that there is shifting of responsibility here.

From the perspective of this study – and perhaps from any perspective – the most interesting thing about this novel is not how it treats male same-sex desire, but rather how it develops an explanation/justification for non-standard desire and relationships in general that serves as a context not only for the Loti-Samuel relationship already portrayed in *Aziyadé*, but also the Loti-Yves relationship that will be described in works to be written subsequently. *The Story of a Spahi* is, as remarked at the beginning of this chapter, in a careful and non-specific way Pierre Loti's (and no doubt Julien Viaud's) *apologia pro sexualita sua*. This he accomplishes by elaborating a detailed explanation of why Jean Peyral, a 'pure' young man from uncorrupted rural Cévennes (I:I), changed so much as to become involved with a black woman. The explanation/justification for his 'transformation,' to use the novel's term (I:I), is in a sense the real subject of the story.

To begin with, there are the reasons that first appeared in a less intense form in *The Marriage of Loti*, where there had been no attempt and evidently no perceived need to justify Loti's involvement with

Rarahu.[16] Perhaps the most obvious among these reasons is the repeated emphasis on the wild eroticism of the Africans. Even more than the Tahitians, Pierre Loti depicts many of the black Africans whom Jean encounters as almost constantly bursting with uncontrolled sexuality, likened often to animals in both the force of their desire and their lack of restraint. In the evening, for example, Jean observes repeated marriage processions. Pierre Loti remarks: 'These chants, this negro gaiety were somehow heavily voluptuous and bestially sensual' (I:XXXI). In his digression on the griots the narrator mentions that they perform 'dance tunes full of frenzy; – songs of love that seem to be the transports of amorous rage, the howls of delirious animals' (II:IV). Not surprisingly, when a griot performs, 'women flock ... and intone one of those obscene songs that fill them with passion' (II:V). Soon one of the women begins to dance, making 'horribly licentious gestures,' until she arrives at 'frenzy; you would think that you saw the shaking of a mad ape, the contortions of a possessed woman.'[17] 'The old women' who watch her 'stand out because of their more cynical and enraged indecency.'

The most striking presentation of the black Africans' unrestrained sexuality occurs during the description of the celebrations known as *bamboulas*. Readers familiar with *The Marriage of Loti* will recall Loti's depiction of the *upa-upa*, but the narrator of *The Story of a Spahi* portrays the *bamboula* as far more sexually charged. He paints the griots who lead the festivities as having 'their eyes filled with fire, their muscles taut, their torso streaming with sweat ...' (I:XXXIII). The gathered crowd repeats their words 'in a frenzied fashion,' words whose 'translation would burn these pages.' This is 'a devilish chant, drunk with ardour and licentiousness,' a 'howling of unbridled desire, of black blood over-heated by the sun, and of torrid hysteria ... a hallelujah of negro love, a hymn of seduction,' 'a mad rhythm on mad notes.' Just as Loti had noted hearing from his ship the 'raw and lustful songs' of the Tahitian festivity (*Marriage* II:XXXI), so the narrator of *The Story of a Spahi* notes that 'you could already hear the tam-tam of the griots and the chant of the unbridled desires that were beginning in the distance' (I:XXXVI).

As Loti presented Rarahu as the most visibly sexual of the Tahitians, so Pierre Loti focuses on Fatou-gaye. Summarizing his description of the latter, the narrator of *The Story of a Spahi* explains that she has 'a sensual charm, a power of material seduction, something undefinable, that seemed related at the same time to the ape, the young maiden, and the female tiger, – and that made unknown intoxications run through the spahi's veins' (II:XII). Fatou-gaye's sexuality is different from Rarahu's, however, as the sexuality of the black Africans is different from that of the Tahitians. The narrator describes the young African woman as a 'fruit ... swollen with poisonous juices, filled with unhealthy, feverish, unknown pleasures ...' (I:XXXV). She is not simply extremely sexual; her sexuality is unhealthy and a threat to anyone who falls under its spell. As Clive Wake wrote: 'Throughout the novel, [hetero]sexual love is portrayed as evil, dangerous, and destructive.'[18] Again, to what extent this difference between Rarahu and Fatou-gaye should be read as the result of racism and to what extent a growing discomfort with female sexuality it is difficult to say.

(Hetero)sexual desire is portrayed as a particularly powerful force in white Jean Peyral as well. Jean first encounters it when, having entered the service, he leaves home and spends a few days in some unspecified port city before being shipped off to Africa. There

> he had learned to know love amid everything that big-city prostitution can offer of the most abject and revolting nature. The surprise, the disgust – and also the devouring attraction of this new discovery that had just been revealed to him had thrown his young mind into great disorder. (I:II)[19]

When, having arrived in Saint-Louis, he falls in love with Cora, the married woman of mixed race, the narrator remarks that 'love ... now intoxicated him' to the point that 'when he was with her, he was completely drunk with love' (I:VIII). Later, when he meets Fatou-gaye and begins to be attracted to her, he at first fights to resist 'the terrible manner in which his senses pulled him along' (I:XXXVI).[20] If (heterosexual) desire is so powerful, how, the text would seem to suggest, could Jean not have succumbed to Fatou-gaye's particularly powerful attraction and enticements?

The use of 'intoxicated' and 'drunk' in the passage just cited is but one of several linkings of intoxication with (heterosexual) desire in this text, a linking that, while significant in itself as yet another way of expressing the power of (heterosexual) desire and the extent to which it can dominate a man, also foreshadows the much more significant role that literal drunkenness will play in Viaud's next novel, *My Brother Yves*. In *The Story of a Spahi* there is also the already cited description of the crowd at the *bamboula* as being 'drunk with ardour and licentiousness' (I:XXXIII). When Jean finally abandons his scruples and gives in to his desire for Fatou-gaye, spending his first night with her under the desert sky, the narrator speaks of his 'intoxicated delirium' (I:XXXVI), and in another already quoted passage the young woman subsequently 'made unknown intoxications course through the spahi's veins' (II:XII). Later, when Jean finally breaks off with her, Pierre Loti remarks that 'these past intoxications ... now awakened in him only a profound disgust, when he looked back' (III:I). It is not surprising that Jean himself associates literal intoxication with (heterosexual) desire: after going on a drinking binge as a way of dealing with his discovery that Cora has been unfaithful to him, the young spahi decides to give up both alcohol and sexual activity, linking the two in the same thought: 'He had sworn to himself not only not to drink absinthe anymore, but also to remain faithful to his fiancée to the blessed day of their marriage' (I:XXVII).[21]

The repeated linking of intoxication and (heterosexual) desire in *The Story of a Spahi* gives added resonance to one of the novel's already most striking passages. Having informed his readers that Jean took to drink as a way of dealing with his despair at Cora's unfaithfulness, Pierre Loti apostrophizes them:

> Oh! you who live a regular, family life, peacefully seated every day at the hearth, never judge sailors, spahis, those whom their destiny has cast with passionate natures on the great sea or in the distant lands of the sun, under abnormal conditions of existence, with unheard-of privations, desires, and influences you know nothing about. Do not judge these exiles or these wanderers, whose sufferings, joys, and tormented impressions are unknown to you. (I:XXI)

We will return to this passage later, since there is much to say about it, but as it stands now it calls for understanding and a suspension of judgment from the reader for Jean's drinking. Given the links made elsewhere between intoxication and the indulgence of non-standard desire, the narrator may mean his call for understanding to extend to the latter as well.

If Jean changes morally in part because of the extremes of the black Africans' eroticism and the power of his own sexual desires, the narrator also makes it clear that the spahi's ability to resist is undermined, in part, by his physical surroundings. As in *The Marriage of Loti* but not to as great an extent, Pierre Loti depicts the atmosphere of sub-Saharan Africa as being itself erotic. When spring arrives, he says, the air is filled with 'enervating smells' (I:XXIX), helping to create 'those enervating June nights' (I:XXXI). In his description of the *bamboula* the narrator speaks, as already noted, of a 'chanted hymn of seduction'; he then goes on to add that this hymn is sung 'by nature, the air, the earth, the planets, the perfumes as well!' (I:XXXIII). When he writes shortly afterwards that 'Jean felt that this negro spring was burning his blood' (I:XXXIV), the phrase 'negro spring' seems to blur any distinctions between the atmosphere and the people. As in *The Marriage of Loti,* so here they both contribute to the climate of constant, extreme eroticism.

As with the sexuality of Fatou-gaye, so the eroticism of the setting in *The Story of a Spahi* has an unhealthy, dangerous element lacking in the depiction of the erotic atmosphere of Tahiti in the previous novel. Here, 'in the plants, the sap that rose was poisoned; the flowers had dangerous scents, and the animals were swollen with poison ...' Elsewhere the narrator describes how 'everywhere ... datura plants ... make the air heavy with an unhealthy perfume, the air is laden with noxious scents of belladonna' (II:XX).

New to the depiction of the setting's effect on the protagonist is the attention devoted to conveying the overpowering nature of the heat. The text mentions the heat of the African setting no less than seventy-nine times in the novel's less than 200 small pages, not all of which describe Africa. There is no point in citing all those instances, but some are particularly significant, especially given the perspective of this study. To begin with, and it is not unique to this novel, heat is linked to sexual desire: in describing the *bamboula* Pierre Loti remarks that 'the translation [of the words being sung] would burn these pages' (I:XXXIII). Heat also intensifies such desire: later in the novel the narrator speaks of 'this fever of the senses that the climate of Africa stimulated to excess' (III:I). Not only does heat intensify desire, it also undermines reason and therefore a man's ability to refrain from giving in to manifestations of desire in conflict with conventional morality: the narrator remarks of the temperature in Virginie-Scholastique's cabaret that it was 'a heat that would drive you mad' (I:XXI).

Perhaps most striking, however, are the linkings in this novel of excessive heat to a breakdown of differentiation. Early in the text the narrator, in describing Saint-Louis, says of some of the taverns: 'Strange odours of negroes and alcohol came out of there, the whole thing mixed together and enhanced by the torrid heat' (I:VI). Nowhere is this linking more striking, however, than in the two equations of the African climate with that which existed during the primal chaos at the beginning of the world. As Jean sets off for Gadiangué, the narrator compares one of the first nights to the earliest geological ages, before the light was separated from the shadows ... to the eras when the planets were not yet condensed, when light was diffuse and undefined in the air, when the hanging clouds were of uncreated lead and iron, when all of eternal matter was sublimated by the intense heat of primitive chaos. (II:XXII)

When the spahi and his companions arrive at Dialdé, another evening evokes the following description:

The sky had those heavy and motionless aspects that the imagination uses to depict antediluvian sunsets – eras when the atmosphere, hotter and more laden with vital substances, incubated those monstrous seeds of mammoths and plesiosaurs on the primitive earth ... (III:XVIII)

Heat not only undoes modern distinctions, it takes one back to primordial, chaotic times that produced monsters, long a metaphor for the mixture of distinct categories.[22] More than the perfumes in the air, Pierre Loti portrays the African heat as playing a major role in undoing Jean's ability to maintain standard moral distinctions.

Once Jean becomes involved with Fatou-gaye, habit also plays a role in deadening any concern with conventional morality. Though Peyral is at first frightened by how different, indeed 'not human' the young African woman is – her hands, for example, remind him of those of a monkey (II:XXVIII) – 'over time, however, Jean became accustomed to it and didn't worry about it anymore' (II:VIII). Later in the novel the narrator will explain that 'having grown accustomed to physical possession had tied strong and very enduring bonds between them that being apart can hardly destroy' (III:XV).

The text offers other explanations/justifications for Jean's transformation that do not have predecessors in Viaud's two previous novels. In Africa the young spahi feels completely cut off from his homeland: the narrator describes at the very beginning of the work how, after Jean had entered the army, a ship took him away from France 'to deposit him, confused and out of his element, on the coast of Senegal' (I:II). (*Dépaysé* is a difficult word to translate. It suggests removal from homeland and therefore native culture.) Loti had never complained about being out of his element in the Middle East and had alluded to it only slightly in Tahiti. This distance from his home and family cuts Jean off from those things that instil and reinforce society's standard moral code, depriving him of the constant reinforcement that adhesion to that code requires.

Robert de Troy remarked that the goal of *The Story of a Spahi* was 'to show the mental disorder of, a European torn from his natural conditions.'[23] It is not surprising, therefore, that after Jean gives in to his desire for Fatou-gaye the narrator announces: 'He had no strength to separate himself from her. The veils thickened little by little over his past and his memories; he let himself be led now without resistance where his heart, troubled, undecided, and led astray by separation and exile, was leading him ...' (II:I). The image of the veil separating him from the home and family that constitute his link with morality, already discussed with regard to his affair with Cora, returns, here associated with distance from home ('separation,' 'exile'). Being so far from home and from his native culture is yet another factor offered as an explanation for Jean's alleged inability to adhere to conventional morality ('he had no strength ...' etc.).

The most interesting of all the arguments presented to explain Jean's moral transformation is the declaration that the spahi's moral strength is also undermined by the fact that he does not have a significant other, something that this text, unlike its two predecessors, presents as an absolute human need. During his visits to Nyaor-fall's home Jean sees his fellow spahi in the midst of family life with his wives.

> These scenes in a Yolof household of family life disturbed him as well ... How alone he felt, isolated from those like him on this cursed earth! ... He thought about the woman whom he loved with a chaste, childhood love, Jeanne Méry ... Alas! ... To have to wait more than four years more to see her again! ... He began to tell himself that he might lack the courage to continue to live alone, that soon no matter what the cost he would need someone to help him pass his time as an exile. But who? (I:XXXI)

The force of 'he would need' suggests that Jean cannot survive without someone in his life. 'Someone,' as opposed to 'a woman,' is, given the context, remarkably non-sex-specific, but the choice of words is indicative less of Jean's nature than of the speaker's, Pierre Loti.

This needed 'someone' is clearly more than just a sexual partner. The women and boys who frequent Virginie-Scholastique's cabaret can supply that. What Jean needs is someone to love and be loved by. When the spahi gives in to Fatou-gaye, the text remarks that he does so 'out of a need to love someone – out of a need for tenderness' (II:XXX). Later he leaves her, but she follows him with the child she has had by him and, when she finally catches up with him, Jean takes her back, 'moved to discover someone who loved him in Dialdé in Galam' (III:XIX). In addition to all the other reasons already examined, Jean cannot refrain from becoming involved with Fatou-gaye because, according to Pierre Loti, he cannot go without love.[24]

This is certainly the most remarkable of all the explanations/justifications put forth by the narrator. It provides Jean's non-standard, socially unacceptable relationship with Fatou-gaye with a legitimacy and a decency, and not just an excuse, that is truly remarkable given the time of the novel's creation. More generally, by positing as a given that man needs to love and be loved, it suggests that this need validates the choice of an object for that love even if the choice is socially unacceptable (Samuel, Fatou-gaye, and later Yves). While this is not a strictly gay issue, it does make *The Story of a Spahi* remarkably gay-supportive.[25]

With all the elements of the explanation/justification specified, it is worth rereading Pierre Loti's plea to his readers cited above.

> Oh! you who live a regular, family life, peacefully seated every day at the hearth, never judge sailors, spahis, those whom their destiny has cast with passionate natures on the great sea or in the distant lands of the sun, under abnormal conditions of existence, with unheard-of privations, desires, and influences you know nothing about. Do not judge these exiles or these wanderers, whose sufferings, joys, and tormented impressions are unknown to you. (I:XXI)

The narrator makes a clear contrast between 'you who live a regular, family life, peacefully seated every day at the hearth,' those who remain in continual contact with the source and reinforcement of conventional morality, and 'these exiles' whose behaviour must be understood as the forgivable result of the fact that they do not.[26]

While detailing all the factors in Jean's enlisted life that make it impossible in the eyes of the narrator for him not to give in to his multi-faceted desire for Fatou-gaye, Pierre Loti emphasizes the power of these factors by depicting the spahi as an initially very moral individual: 'He had a sort of instinctive dignity, an instinctive modesty' (I:XXXI). In this respect as in others Jean is unlike Loti in the first two novels, and especially in *Aziyadé*, which had presented that character as having indulged in 'all pleasures' by the time he was sixteen (*Aziyadé* I:XV). Arriving in Saint-Louis, Jean finds that his fellow spahis 'indulged in ... pleasures that he found extremely repugnant' (I:V). While they engage in drink and 'the ignoble prostitution of mulattoes' in what the narrator refers to as 'dives' (*bouges* in the original French), 'Jean avoided these pleasure spots with horror' (I:VI). (Recall that Loti felt no such horror when Samuel led him through various dives in *Aziyadé*.) Not surprisingly, then, Jean also rejects the seductions of Virginie-Scholastique's offerings: 'He could not get used to the ignoble black prostitution' (I:XXI). He is even shocked by the married Cora's willingness to take him as her lover: 'This woman's avowal, her lack of modesty made him somewhat indignant when he thought about them' (I:VIII). If so moral a person can change under the circumstances described in the novel, can any other man be expected to resist?

The Story of a Spahi is not about male same-sex desire to any significant extent. It is, however, about why some men move away from standard morality. Because Pierre Loti pleads the cause not just of Jean but, in the twice quoted passage, more generally of 'sailors and spahis' (I:XXI), this explanation can be read as applying to the naval officer Loti of *Aziyadé*, as well as, perhaps, to the naval officer Pierre Loti who will appear in Viaud's next novel, *My Brother Yves*. Julien Viaud may have been writing an *apologia pro sexualita sua*. He phrased it more generally, however, as an *apologia* (explanation, not apology) for 'transformation' from general society's moral standard regarding sexuality that calls upon society to refrain from judging what it cannot understand from experience. More remarkable still, the narrator's call for understanding suggests that a man's need for love is so important that it justifies his choice of a partner for that love, even if the choice is not conventional. *The Story of a Spahi*'s racism makes it difficult reading today, but since we continue to read some works of literature despite their bigotry, we should not altogether dismiss Viaud's third novel. Amid its lack of understanding for black women it calls out for tolerance for unconventional desire.[27]

CHAPTER FIVE

Man (Men?) in Love:
My Brother Yves

My Brother Yves (1883), Julien Viaud's fourth novel, must have been greeted with more than routine expectation by a portion of its original reading public. Four years before, with *Aziyadé*, a non-homophobic, accepting depiction of Samuel's love for Loti and Loti's tolerance and even sharing of such emotions and desires, Viaud must have left some readers hoping for a follow-up. *The Marriage of Loti* had gone back in time, showing the title character's earlier predisposition for same-sex relationships. *The Story of a Spahi* had developed narrator Pierre Loti as a character with an erotic interest in other men and proposed an argument in defence of non-conventional romantic relationships. With *My Brother Yves*, however, Viaud came to grips with the expectations that his first novel had aroused. Within the constraints imposed by his era and his situation he proceeded to write what is arguably the first novel in modern French literature to centre around a positively presented male homosexual love story, the relationship between French naval officer Pierre Loti and sailor Yves Kermadec.[1]

This is not a simple love story, however. Among the questions that it raises is whether the love is reciprocal. Since Loti is again the narrator, everything we know comes through him. As a result, we are faced with the question of whether Yves loves Loti – we know, as we shall see, that the officer loves Yves – or whether Loti only wishes and imagines that. This becomes the real intrigue of the novel, in fact. Before approaching *My Brother Yves*, however, we must first consider Yves's previous, initial appearance in Viaud's writing, since it created the image of Yves Kermadec and, to some extent, suggested the nature of Loti's relationship with him.

Between *The Story of a Spahi* and *My Brother Yves*, Viaud published a collection of four disparate pieces entitled *Blossoms of Boredom* (1882).[2] The first, 'Blossoms of Boredom,' is a dialogue between Loti and Plumkett, a discussion of various issues, including several personal anecdotes. The second, 'Pasquala Ivanovitch,' and the fourth, 'Suleïma,' recount Loti's erotic escapades in Bosnia and Algeria. The third, 'Trip to Montenegro,' is Viaud's first travelogue and has no plot. Yves is mentioned only in the first piece. From his initial appearance he is clearly presented as an object of homosexual desire: Loti starts the dialogue by recounting to Plumkett a dream in which 'I was on the very top of the Creizker bell tower; Yves was seated near me, on the head of a granite gargoyle,' a potentially phallic image.[3] The subsequent description of the sailor recalls the perspective of the 'gay gaze' in *The Story of a Spahi*: 'Yves seemed larger than usual to me, his shoulders even larger and more athletic.' Tall, broad-shouldered, and powerful: three of the qualities on which narrator Pierre Loti had focused with Jean Peyral in particular, and more generally with other spahis.

Loti also presents Yves as a simple person, as he had Jean, but now he conveys that simplicity with an image that reinforces the notion of Yves's physical power. At one point Loti says of him: 'He was larger than normal, and now he was dressed like a Celt, with wolf skins tossed over his shoulders.' Yves appears like a Celtic Hercules, animal skins tossed over his broad, muscular frame. Modern readers might think of Arnold Schwarzenegger as Conan the Barbarian, but Loti's own original readers were already familiar with depictions of primitive men that stressed their physical strength: Charles Leconte de Lisle's *Poèmes barbares* (1862–72), which evokes primitive men of great force, and most notably Gustave Flaubert's very successful novel, *Salammbô* (1862), which recounts the exploits of Mathô, the Herculean Numidian who defied Hamilcar's Carthage. This work is cited several times in *My Brother Yves* and according to Millward was one of Viaud's favourite books.[4]

Plumkett does a little philosophizing on Yves's simplicity. Remarking that 'there are all sorts of different individuals in us,' he assures Loti that Yves,

> very simple, very well balanced, at the same time lively and very intense in his personality ... responds to the most lively and constant aspect of you under all your layers: the primitive man.
>
> The primitive man, the pre-historic wild man [*sauvage* in the original French]; my dear Loti, that is what is in the very deepest part of you.[5]
>
> What is fairly unique to you, what gives your books that strangeness that

attracts the curious, is the contempt that you seem to feel for modern things; it is the easy independence with which you seem to divest yourself of everything that thirty centuries have brought to humanity, to return to the simple feelings of primitive man ...[6]

Plumkett provides a non-homoerotic explanation for Loti's interest in Yves (as of 'Blossoms of Boredom' it is no more than an interest): since the two men are one of a kind, both primitives, Loti is drawn to Yves because they are kindred spirits. What Plumkett is referring to in Loti's behaviour when he says that his friend has managed to 'divest [him]self of everything that thirty centuries have brought to humanity, to return to the simple feelings of primitive man' neither he nor Loti (nor Viaud) makes clear, however. No stranger to possible homoerotic feelings, as we saw in chapter 2, Plumkett may be suggesting that male same-sex attraction is one of 'the simple feelings of primitive man,' covered over by 'thirty centuries' of civilization.[7]

What is clear is that in this text Loti is realigning the connotations of primitivism from *The Story of a Spahi*. At one point he assures Plumkett that

at present, I am hoping to live among extraordinarily simple friends – those people who grow like healthy plants, produce their fruit, and know, afterward, how to die tranquilly when the hour for it arrives. – Simple people, simple things, that gives me renewed strength and soothes me; after having been the most complicated young man on earth [perhaps a reference to the description of Loti's wild adolescence in *Aziyadé* (I:XV; III:I)], I am returning very quietly to the most primitive means of living.

Primitivism is now aligned with good simplicity, health, and nature. If Loti's feelings for Yves are part of his primitive nature, are they not also good?[8]

The opening scene in 'Blossoms of Boredom' is also notable for a rhetorical strategy that Loti employs quite often in *My Brother Yves*. In his description, Loti repeatedly links himself and Yves by use of first-person plural pronouns:

We recalled the time when *we* used to sail, Yves and I, on the 'foggy sea' ... often, in the gray clouds, *we* saw from a distance the two bell-towers of the church of Saint-Pol and the Creizker ... *we* used to love seeing that ancient lookout over the sea, which seemed to watch over *us* from the height of the

Breton cliff. Now, that's over, and *we* will never see it again. (emphasis added)

As the highlighted pronouns make clear, this rhetorical strategy allows Loti to suggest that he and Yves shared their most intimate thoughts: *we* dreamed, *we* loved. If he can speak for Yves on such issues, must not Yves have confided in him entirely? Since Loti is the narrator, however, we have no way of knowing how accurate a depiction of reality this rhetorical strategy provides. There are many other examples of this use of first-person plural pronouns throughout 'Blossoms of Boredom.'

Our perception of Yves's feelings for Loti is not entirely a function of the narrator's words, however. The young sailor does call his companion 'my good brother,' a surprising term for a subordinate to use in addressing his superior officer. (The story behind Yves's use of the term will not be presented until *My Brother Yves*.) While readers may recall the word's homoerotic connotations in *The Marriage of Loti*, which Yves, of course, would not have known, Loti recounts later in this text an anecdote that suggests the word's non-standard significance for the Breton sailor.

Having passed up a chance to join their Basque cohorts in an evening with three Algerian prostitutes, Yves and two of his Breton shipmates, Kerboul and Le Hello, happen across a dive where soldiers and sailors are dancing with each other: 'About a dozen couples, zouaves and sailors, danced together, holding each other by the waist, seriously – zouaves who had put on sailor shirts, sailors who had put on zouave hats.' The fact that the men hold each other by the waist and exchange such intimate garments as shirts does not put Yves and his companions off. They join in; according to the narrator, 'they, too, wanted to dress a zouave, in order to make a *brother* out of him. A large blond went along with it good-heartedly, and each of the three Bretons gave him a piece of his outfit in order to transform him ... Now they were four, with this new recruit.' They wander off across the city together.

Coming after the suggestive use of 'brother' in *The Marriage of Loti*, this passage will not surprise alerted readers of Viaud. A 'brother' is now also a man with whom another man exchanges clothing, with whom he may dance. This exchange leads to a 'transformation,' a word associated with changing sexual attitudes in *The Story of a Spahi*. Though the exchange of apparel here is not cross-dressing, the use of the feminine French noun *recrue* (recruit) to describe the big blond infantryman after the transformation heightens the homoerotic atmosphere of the scene. In turn, the scene projects homoerotic connotations back on Yves's earlier use of 'brother' in addressing Pierre Loti.

A later scene in 'Blossoms of Boredom' reinforces those connotations. Loti recounts an event of which he appears to be ashamed, the moment he sent away 'an Israelite vagabond ... who had gambled his life and left his homeland to follow me.' 'One day, when I was feeling nasty, – I don't know why anymore – I had sent him away.' This vagabond, as readers of *Aziyadé* are not surprised to learn several pages later, was none other than Samuel. Suddenly the very moving scene in Viaud's first novel depicting Samuel's farewell to Loti as the latter prepares to sail back to England (IV:IV) appears to disintegrate. Which passage, we now wonder, tells the truth?

In this new version of his departure, Samuel, 'remembering that the cloak that covered him was mine, had taken it off and left it on the ground, before leaving my door.' Again, an exchange of clothing is presented as significant in a relationship between two men – Loti had given Samuel his coat – and when he sees the relationship as over, Samuel acknowledges it by returning the article. Our memories of the nature of Loti's relationship with Samuel colour our understanding both of the nature of the 'recruit' who had received a similar exchange of clothing and of the term 'brother' used to describe the recruit after his transformation. This is turn colours our understanding of Yves's attitude toward Loti in the opening scene.

Loti's reaction to Samuel's departure is also worth noting, for future reference: 'When he was gone, I felt that I was alone in Istanbul, and that that dismissed servant was, in this country, my only friend. Above all, remorse for this bad act gripped my heart.'[9] 'Only friend' here becomes a synonym for 'faithful friend,' the heavily charged term used in *Aziyadé* and *The Marriage of Loti*. When Loti later speaks of 'heart-rending regrets that I felt for others, and that have passed as well,' the reader can only wonder if Samuel is among those sexless 'others.' Plumkett, who hears all this and who would have remembered Samuel and Loti's original depiction of their parting in the first novel, since he prefaced it, makes no comment on any of this but also explains why: 'I fell asleep during your story, Loti,' he jibes. 'Therefore I am sorry that I cannot express to you all the interest that I would no doubt have taken in it.'

There is one negative element in the depiction of the relationship between Yves and Loti in the first scene of 'Blossoms of Boredom.' The officer explains to Plumkett that in his dream the spire of Creizker started to disintegrate beneath the two men. They finally fell to the ground, unharmed, 'but we felt anguish, because the Creizker no longer existed.' For Loti, the tower's destruction 'seemed to me to be a fatal sign of the times; the end of that giant of Breton bell-towers seemed to me to be the beginning of the end of all things – and I resigned myself to seeing everything end; it was as if I had drawn back in an apocalyptic expectation of chaos.' A dream of falling is open to any number of interpretations. What one can say confidently, though, is that, if nothing else, it indicates that Loti has fears regarding the stability and longevity of his relationship with Yves.[10]

The text continues with a justification for a homoerotic reading of this first scene. Having heard Loti recount his dream, Plumkett remarks:

My dear Loti, I believe I have found the explanation for your dream. You were asleep with your brother Yvon [Yves's Breton name] on the table of some cabaret in Lower Brittany; you had drunk cider and grain alcohol; you were completely drunk, and you had rolled under the table. That was your soft fall, in which, very fortunately, you didn't break anything. Yvon had, perhaps, fallen first and you on top of him.

Plumkett imagines the two men sleeping together on a table, and then Loti on top of Yves on the floor.[11] Given what we know of him from *Aziyadé*, it would not be too far-fetched to assume that Plumkett is suggesting some sort of sexual relationship between the two.

Loti's reaction to Plumkett's interpretation of the dream is interesting. 'My dear Plumkett, your explanation of my dream is idiotic. You know very well that ... I have only been drunk once in my life.' He does not deny that he may have slept next to Yves or lain on top of him, but only that his actions have ever been the unthinking result of an alcoholic stupor. If the events Plumkett describes did take place, the intimacy was therefore the result of something other than mindless drunkenness. Again, open-ended ambiguity is allowed to enter into play. (This is also true at the end of 'Suleïma,' where Loti talks of the day 'when my great-great grand nieces and nephews will look at Suleïma the tortoise,' as if, even though still young, he cannot imagine himself having direct descendants.) When Plumkett announces his marriage, Loti replies: 'Ah! traitor ... What have you done?'

As noted earlier, Plumkett at one point tries to explain Loti, and more particularly his attraction to Yves, by stating that 'there are all sorts of different individuals in us ... All these people, or all these beasts, appear, each in turn, according to the situation, speak, act, in place of the intimate and profound being who remains crouched behind them, not moving or making a sound, in a sort of disheartened weariness.' Reflecting on his adventures around the world, Loti himself remarks: 'What a foolish and devouring thing it is, to scatter oneself across the world, to get acclimated everywhere, to become attached to everything, to live five or six human existences, instead of one good one, the way the simple do who stay and die in the always beloved corner of the world where their eyes opened.' Both seem to recognize that, for some men at least, the 'real self,' that 'intimate and profound being,' the 'one good one,' gets obscured in the maintenance of all these others; both seem to regret this, especially Loti, who associates the ability to live as one's one true self with those good, simple people he is now in the process of idealizing through Yves. Plumkett says of Yves that 'he is himself, not someone else,' as if Yves, a simple man, did not bother to create all these other, extraneous existences. Both these more complicated souls clearly regret and envy Yves's ability to live just as himself. Given the context established for both characters in this work and Viaud's preceding ones, it is tempting to suggest that this regret and envy are a desire to be able to live as a gay man without any need to create other 'human existences' as covers.[12]

All this should make clear that Yves brought with him very considerable baggage by the time he appeared as the title character in Viaud's fourth novel. This determined, at least in part, how the reader perceived him and his relationship with Loti and also how he helped redefine the changing depiction of Pierre Loti himself who, with *Blossoms of Boredom*, appears for the first time as an almost uniquely homosexually oriented individual.

If readers approached *My Brother Yves* with ideas and expectations regarding Yves Kermadec triggered by a knowledge of 'Blossoms of Boredom,' this was also true regarding Loti, who had figured in all of Viaud's previous texts. Following the creation of 'Pierre Loti' in *The Story of a Spahi* and his actual appearance in *Blossoms of Boredom*, the Loti who figures in and narrates *My Brother Yves* is definitely a Frenchman, an officer in the French navy, and not the Englishman Harry Grant of the first two novels. Nor is there any possibility that this Frenchman is just the Englishman after a change of allegiance. Pierre Loti appears in *My Brother Yves* as early as December 1875 (III), at which point Harry Grant had already completed his adventures in Tahiti but had not yet started those in Salonika and Istanbul. Pierre Loti is still alive as of the last chapters of *My Brother Yves*, which take place in 1883, though Harry Grant/ Loti died in 1877 (*Aziyadé*).

If Pierre Loti is not the Loti of Viaud's first two novels, he is not someone altogether different, either. He still has Plumkett as a friend and also mentions sailing to the Middle East in early 1876 (XXIV), which Harry Grant/Loti had done in *Aziyadé* (I:I) and *The Marriage of Loti* (IV:IX); Pierre Loti's next appearance in *My Brother Yves* is dated May 1877 (ibid), by which time all of *Aziyadé* except Harry Grant/Loti's return to Istanbul and death, the events covered in Part V of that novel, is over. Some of Pierre Loti is therefore the same as the Harry Grant/ Loti encountered in the first two novels and some is not.

The most obvious difference is that Pierre Loti does not die for love of a woman (Aziyadé). *My Brother Yves* and several of Viaud's subsequent novels make it almost equally obvious that if Pierre Loti leaves behind much of Harry Grant/Loti's fascination with women, he retains from his predecessor the erotic interest in men first seen in Harry Grant/ Loti's relationship with Samuel and later developed with that character's relationship to John and his own brother in *The Marriage of Loti*. The transformation of the Englishman Harry Grant/Loti into the Frenchman Pierre Loti as of *The Story of a Spahi, Blossoms of Boredom,* and *My Brother Yves* was not, therefore, a case of carelessness on Viaud's part. It underlines that Pierre Loti, while not altogether different from the sexually ambivalent protagonist of the first two novels, is not altogether the same. As we have seen and will continue to see, he is far more unambiguously homosexual.

To begin with, Loti's gay gaze is even more developed in *My Brother Yves* than it had been in Viaud's third novel. In the early scenes it is fairly wide-ranging, lighting on various sailors whom Loti encounters. The officer describes Kerboul as 'large and strong' (IV). He notes that the group of sailors he sees on deck one morning stand 'with their torsos naked' (XI) and that their handkerchiefs dry 'on the bare backs of the young men.'[13] Among them is Barrada, with 'his handsome head' thrown back. Besides finding Barrada 'still handsome' (XXV), Loti later describes how that sailor, very drunk, danced 'completely naked ... looking like a Greek statue' (Viaud's metaphor for male beauty) and outshone some Siamese women dancers. Still later he describes how the enlisted men prepare for bed aboard ship: 'They got undressed, hanging up their caps, hanging up their large knives on leather chains, their soaked clothing, hanging up *everything*, and hanging themselves up as well; and when they were naked, they used their hands to flick

off a little water that was still streaming down their hard chests'
(XXVIII).[14]

From the beginning of the novel, however, Loti's gaze focuses primarily on Yves. Even before he meets him, he imagines the young topman
'with his chest exposed to the wind, living half-naked at the top of those
large rocking stems that are the masts of a ship' (I).[15] Once he meets
him, Loti focuses immediately on Yves's body: 'Large, thin with the thin-
ness of the ancient Greeks, with muscular arms, the neck and the shoulders of an athlete, the over-all impression of the man giving the feeling
of quiet and unconcernedly disdainful strength' (III). It is interesting to
note that Loti describes Yves's face as having 'an Arab colouring' (III),
a strange remark to make about a Breton. As we noted in the discussion
of *The Story of a Spahi*, however, he had found the same quality in Jean
Peyral, also a Frenchman. Again, whether this indicates Loti's 'type,' or
a nostalgia for Samuel, or both it would be difficult to say.

Thereafter Loti remarks repeatedly on Yves's physique. He notes his
'muscular arms' (VI), his 'large and slender silhouette' (XI), his 'athlete's build' (XLVIII), 'his considerable height' (LXXXI), the fact that
'his silence and the breadth of his shoulders were imposing' (LXVIII),
and describes him as 'big Yves' several times (XLVII, L, XCIII). In particular, he focuses on instances when Yves is partially naked. Loti reports
that Yves arrives on board after a scuffle with several drunken officers,
'his chest entirely naked' (XXXI). Similarly, he describes how he saw
Yves 'with his torso naked, as sailors aboard ship are when they do the
morning cleaning' (XLVIII) when Yves gets drunk at his son's baptism. Later he says that Yves lives in the crow's nest 'barely clothed'
(LXXXII).[16]

It is only near the end of the novel, when, as we shall see, Loti begins
to realize that he is losing Yves, that his gaze again begins to roam. He
notes that the sailors who obey his orders to return to the rigging are
'half-naked' (LXXXIV), describes how, in the early morning, they prepare for the day 'naked, like the ancient Greeks with their strong arms'
(XC), and then wash down the ship itself 'completely naked' (XCII),
something of an exaggeration, as the sailors in question actually have on
'a hat with a pompon, or [are] well attired in a *combat jersey*.' 'In this
trade,' Loti observes, 'arms became strong and chests developed.' He
even goes back to noting that Barrada is 'still as perfectly handsome'
and remarks on 'his great strength' (XCVII). The attention that Pierre
Loti the narrator devoted to the bodies of the men in *The Story of a Spahi*
justified, as we saw, talk of a gay gaze in that novel. The far greater atten-

tion he devotes to the male physique in Viaud's fourth novel confirms our earlier analysis.[17]

In *My Brother Yves* Pierre Loti does more than just look appreciatively at other men, however. New with this novel is the fact that Loti experiences very real feelings for another man, not just desire but also concern for the object of his affection. Furthermore, this affection is expressed not indirectly, through parallels with affection for a woman, as in *Aziyadé*, but directly – if carefully – without any female love interest to balance or disguise it. It is this breadth and depth of Loti's feelings for Yves, as well as their more direct presentation, that make *My Brother Yves* a major development in Viaud's work and in modern gay literature as a whole. There are many examples of this, but a few should make the point.

Once he becomes a midshipman, Loti chooses Yves to be his personal '*hammock topman*' (VIII). As he gets to know the sailor whom he has chosen to work in such intimacy with him, Loti's emotions go beyond simple physical attraction: 'That Kermadec was so devoted, he seemed to have such a good heart, that I had ended up becoming attached to that often drunk sort of pirate ... Oh! then, it became almost affection' (ibid). There is hedging with the adjective 'almost,' but 'affection' is here nonetheless, charged with the importance given to that term in *The Story of a Spahi*.

Thereafter Loti continues to demonstrate his more than simply professional interest in Yves. Having visited Yves with the latter's family in Brittany, he notes as he crosses the square in nearby Paimpol that of the sailors walking there

> none of these men was alone. They strolled back and forth, singing, in the streets with young women on their arms, sisters, fiancées, mistresses. And these images of joy and life gave me the feeling of my deep loneliness. *I* was walking alone, sad and unknown to all of them, in my borrowed outfit similar to theirs. People stared at me. 'Who is he? A sailor from somewhere else, looking for a ship? We haven't ever seen him among us.'
>
> I felt a chill in my heart, and suddenly I set off on the road to Plouherzel [where Yves was staying with his family]. After all, I probably wouldn't bother my simple friends there much by going to warm myself a little at their place. (XVII)

He speaks here of wanting to see 'them' (Yves's family) and not just Yves, but the fact that observing other men out with those to whom they are romantically attached makes him decide to return to the house where Yves is staying is telling.

When Loti returns to Yves's family's dwelling he sees more than he had bargained for: 'Two men, one of them athletic, were holding hands and talking to each other very tenderly, like people who are a little drunk: Yves and Jean [a childhood friend] – and I ran to them' (XVIII). Loti's seemingly jealous reaction to what he perceives as a 'very tender' moment makes clear the extent of his emotional involvement with Yves.

Shortly thereafter comes the scene that explains the novel's title. Yves's mother, aware of the power of drink on the male members of her family, asks Loti, whom she recognizes as someone of more importance than his disguise as a simple sailor would suggest, to watch over her alcoholic son. Loti replies through Yves's sister (their mother only speaks Breton): 'Tell her that I swear I will watch over him *for the rest of my life, as if he were my brother*' (XXII). Loti chooses the determining simile, 'brother,' and the connotations that it had acquired in previous works make this scene highly charged for him and alerted readers of Viaud. Loti's use of the word 'brother' may also have been a signal for Yves, who had been the one who wanted to transform that infantryman into a 'brother' in 'Blossoms of Boredom.' When Loti at the end of the chapter uses the word for the first time in addressing Yves – 'And you, will you obey me, will you follow me ... *my brother?*' – he and some of Viaud's attentive readers must have been deeply moved.

Subsequently, as already mentioned, Loti sails off to and returns from the Middle East with no mention of Aziyadé, thus deleting that heterosexual episode from his life. (There is no mention of Rarahu in *My Brother Yves*, either.) On his return, Loti gives his first real indication of the depth of his feelings for his new 'brother.'[18] One day two sailors fall from the rigging into the sea and another to his death on the deck. Loti, looking up at the remaining seamen, 'recognized Yves, one of those who was climbing – and then I got my breath, which the anguish had taken away, back' (XXVII). When the commanding officer orders the other men to return to the deck, Loti relays the command happily: 'I gave that order quickly, with joy' (ibid.). There is more than just physical desire at play here – though desire is an important component. Loti has grown to care deeply about Yves and the thought of losing him fills the officer with anguish.[19]

This incident also causes Loti to experience a nightmare that evening, *My Brother Yves*'s version of 'Blossoms of Boredom''s initial falling dream. To begin with, Loti imagines that he is sleeping next to Yves:

'Yves's hammock was close to mine' (XXIX). (On ship, of course, Loti sleeps in his officer's quarters and Yves bunks with the other sailors further below.) 'Below us there was a muddled agitation of something black that must have been the deep water – and he was going to fall into it.' Readers of this novel and 'Blossoms of Boredom' will note the unifying use of the first-person plural pronoun ('below *us*'). Since this time only Yves is falling, Loti can attempt to save him, and in a wish-fulfullingly erotic way: 'Then I was trying to keep him from falling with my hands ... I was trying to get my arms around him, to lock my hands around his chest.' 'I understood with anguish [that word again] that I couldn't do it, that I wasn't capable of doing it; he was going to get away from me and disappear in all that moving blackness that murmured below.'

Though the form is different, the basic preoccupation of this dream is the same as that of the one at the beginning of 'Blossoms of Boredom': Loti fears losing Yves, here to some unspecified blackness that, given the event that triggered the dream, must represent death, but may also signify anything else that could take Yves away: alcoholism, marriage, etc.[20]

Once they are back at sea, Loti intercedes with the commanding officer after Yves has returned to the ship drunk: 'I beg: I think I have never begged in my life, it seems to me that it is no longer I who am speaking.' Loti puts himself on the line, does not hesitate to set aside his own dignity to obtain clemency for the man whom he by now appears to love. When Yves leaves his protector's cabin to serve his reduced sentence, Loti says: 'I threw some water on his forehead, I readjusted his shirt a little' (ibid.). The affectionate intimacy of these details is remarkable. Eight days later, when the two leave the ship, each assigned to another, Loti asks Yves to keep in touch, and to allay his subordinate's hesitation, tells him to address him when he writes as '*my brother*' (XXXV).

Six months later the officer receives a letter that is not what he had hoped for, despite the 'My good brother' salutation; indeed, he describes it as 'this surprising letter' (XXXVI). Yves writes: 'I am very sad to ship out this time without you' and ends 'With much love,'[21] 'Your brother who loves you,' and 'Yours,' but he begins by informing Loti: 'I got married yesterday.'

The letter's recipient immediately dismisses its news as momentary foolishness:

... After they return from their campaigns, sailors commit a thousand extravagances with their money; that's the rule. Maritime cities are familiar with their slightly wild eccentricities.

Sometimes, even, as a pastime, they marry women of whatever sort in order to have an occasion to put on a black frock coat.

And Yves, who had already, in times past, gone through all possible foolishness, had ended up getting married in order to have a change.

Yves married? ... And to whom, my God? ... Maybe some brazen woman from the town, picked up at random in a drunken moment!

I had reason to be very worried, recalling a certain creature in a feathered hat whom he had almost married for amusement – when he was twenty – in that same city, Brest. (XXXVI)

The tone of these remarks, to the almost hysterical 'And to whom, my God?' demonstrates the extent of Loti's emotional investment in Yves and a need to dismiss the possibility that Yves has fallen in love with a woman.

A perhaps not fortuitous coincidence underlines the gravity of this event for Loti. According to the title page of *Aziyadé*, Loti/Harry Grant died beneath the walls of Kars on 27 October 1877. Yves's letter to Loti, dated 15 October 1877, and sent from Brest, must have reached the officer, then stationed in Athens, about that time. While Samuel Viaud in his notes to his father's *Private Diary* pointed out years ago that Viaud altered the chronology of the real events used as a basis for *My Brother Yves*, shifting up the early scenes based on events that actually took place in 1878 to as early as 1875,[22] no one has suggested why the novelist did so. A reader might wonder if Viaud antedated these early scenes in order to allow the arrival of Yves's 'surprising letter' to coincide with Loti/Harry Grant's violent death in the Ottoman wars, in order to suggest that the former was as horrendous as the latter.[23]

Subsequently Yves's wife gives birth to the couple's first child, something which could have created a more exclusionary family unit, but that does not stop Loti. He kisses the child 'with all my heart, because he is Yves's baby,' and goes with the father to register the infant, leaving Marie, Yves's wife, behind. '*We* find it funny to see both of *us* going through the legal formalities like everyone else. At the mayor's, at the curate's, *we* feel very much like stand-ins, *we* even feel like laughing at times' (XLV, emphasis added). The child is named Yves-Pierre. Loti's narration manages to exclude Marie almost entirely at this point, and the child seems to be, even to his name, an embodiment of Loti's relationship with Yves, not Marie's. It is as if Loti is not going to give up Yves without a fight. While Marie Kermadec recovers from childbirth, he takes her place with her husband.

In fact, Loti seems to imply that, in some respects, he is more deserving of that place than she. One afternoon, while visiting his wife and newborn child, Yves gets drunk and decides to return to the ship. Still convalescing, Marie is unable to stop him and begs Loti to intervene. Deciding that he is not up to reasoning with the sailor this time, the officer blocks the door with his body instead, noting, 'I no longer felt anything of that affection that had lasted so many years, forgiven so many things. Before me I saw the drunken pirate, ungrateful, insubordinate, and that was all' (XLVIII). Yves calms down, saying to Loti: 'You have to forgive me again, *brother*! ...' and the sailor stays out of trouble thanks to Loti's intervention and despite Marie's failure to stop him on her own.

The tone of Loti's language suggests, however, that his feelings for the topman have changed. Even though, from Loti's perspective, 'little by little ... we had rediscovered our customary manner ... [w]e talked pretty much like before,' etc., he still feels a certain resentment: 'After all, it was his place to ask forgiveness of me.' The narrator does not specify why he wants Yves to ask him for forgiveness and one could assume that he has the sailor's conduct infractions in mind, but the tone, which sounds like that of a wounded lover, suggests that Loti also wants Yves to ask forgiveness for his marriage to Marie.[24]

The next day the relationship between the two is strained even further. Loti counsels Yves not to go ashore again, but Yves prepares to go anyway. The discussion between the two becomes heated and defiant, and the officer finally orders the topman to be put in irons below. No sooner has he done this, however, than Loti thinks to himself: 'Was it over between us? I thought so. This time, I had really lost him ... Yves would not come back; his heart, once closed, would not open again' (LXVI). 'This time, I had really lost him': it is hard to read these words as something other than a lover's cry of despair.

Loti does not give up on his charge, however. 'I still loved my poor Yves like a brother,' he asserts shortly afterward, and fearing that his severity may have lost him his 'brother''s love, sends him a message in the brig begging forgiveness: 'I forgive you and I ask you to forgive me as well' (ibid). Yves accepts Loti's proposal, the latter speaks of their 'reconciliation,' and when he sees the topman again, 'I took his hand ...

in mine; I had to squeeze it very hard for it to feel the pressure' (LXVII).

Even more romantically intimate is the scene several months later when Yves and Loti, having again visited the Kermadec family in Brittany, return to 'their' lodgings in Lorient.

> When we had returned to the chance lodgings that we had rented in town, Yves, before going to bed, arranged *our* flowers from the Toulven woods in vases.
>
> He did such work for the first time in his life; he was surprised at himself and at finding these poor little flowers that he had never noticed before pretty.
>
> 'Well,' he said ... 'see, it's you who gave me the idea of these things.' (LXVIII, emphasis added).

The domesticity of the scene is remarkable, not to mention the image of a large, muscular sailor taking an interest in flower arrangement.[25] Yves's new-found interest is in line, however, with the already noted breakdown of conventional gender constructions, in particular in the object of homosexual desire.

Loti's first description of Marie is not much more than civil.

> When it came time to leave, I saw Marie Keremenen, whom I was apprehensive about meeting ... Without being downright pretty, she was almost charming ... It seemed to me that I would have wanted her to be precisely like that if I had been charged with choosing her myself for my brother Yves. (XXXVIII)

Since she is not 'downright pretty' and only 'almost charming,' it is easy to understand why Loti would have been happy to choose so uncompetitive a rival.

The narrator treats her far from kindly for most of the text. After she gives birth to their first child, Loti reports that 'her youth had vanished, she was pale and thin.' He is even so cruel, if not indeed spiteful, as to declare that 'Yves looked at her with an air of disappointed surprise that she could see ... And I foresaw sad things from this glimpse of disenchantment' (XLVII).[26] Repeatedly he refers to her as 'Marie, his wife' (XLVIII, LXXVII, LXXXVIII), as if no one would bother to remember who 'Marie' is.

Just as he does not hesitate to point out her physical inadequacies,

Loti also censures what he presents as Marie's other failings. If she wanders the streets looking for her husband it is 'like a bad woman' (LI). He even suggests that her own tiny son questions her having brought him to live in the miserable city of Brest, far from the rural comfort of Toulven (ibid). When she takes the boy in her search for her husband, Loti breaks into moralistic grandstanding: 'How could she have let him walk like that, and even take him outside, like that, before daybreak? What was she thinking of? Where was her head?' (LII). If she had not made these efforts to remain in contact with her husband she would have made things easier for Loti, so his remark is also coloured by self-interest.

Loti's most scathing condemnation of Marie is more powerful for not being so direct, however, and is in fact a carefully constructed dramatic high point of the novel. One day Yves gets drunk yet again and his wife attempts to keep him from leaving to rejoin his corrupting drinking companions. When he refuses to cede to her repeated entreaties, she locks the door. His anger mounting ever higher, Yves rips the knob out of the door, falls back, and injures their child. Seeing blood run down little Yves-Pierre's forehead, Marie picks him up, clutches him to her chest, and orders Yves to leave the house. Overcome by alcohol, confusion, and shame he flees. Two days later, haggard and too ashamed to return home, he decides to desert the navy and enlist on an American merchant vessel.

There is not a judgmental word from the narrator anywhere in this powerful if melodramatic scene, but there does not need to be. Parallelism, which Viaud had employed so skilfully in *Aziyadé*, does the trick here most effectively. Any reader will recall the similar, already discussed scene where Loti himself had also blocked passage to a drunken Yves to keep him from returning to his ship. Yves had given in that time, however, asking his 'brother' to forgive him (XLVIII). Marie fails to achieve the same result, creating a situation far worse than the one that she had sought to remedy. The parallel highlights the poor woman's failure to achieve the effect that Loti had so successfully brought about. Once again, it is as if the officer were suggesting that he is better suited to take care of this difficult seaman, and therefore more worthy of his love.

Loti's negative depiction of Marie is not simply a result of his sense of rivalry, however; it is also in line with the growing misogyny noted in *The Story of a Spahi*. The narrator presents the waiting wives of other sailors as alcoholics not above cheating on their absent husbands (LXXXVIII), and when he describes the burial at sea of Barazère, he recalls that the sailor had contracted a fatal venereal disease in Algiers (LXXXIX), an episode from *Blossoms of Boredom*. In short, *My Brother Yves* continues the generally negative depiction of sexually active women that started with *The Story of a Spahi*.

The text does not present all women in a negative light, however. Following in the path established by *The Story of a Spahi*, the mother – perhaps still sexually active, but not a woman who would call on the male protagonist to function heterosexually – appears as the object of unmitigated adoration. One of the first things we learn about Yves is that he closed his Breton heart to the Catholic church because a curate made his mother cry (II). While a cabin boy, he had missed his mother (III). When he returns to Brest after three years at sea, his mother is the object of his thoughts (III; VI). Indeed, at one point the narrator describes Yves as hating everything but his mother (VI). Near the end of the novel, in another series of intimizing first-person plural pronouns, Loti assures us that even in his greatest happiness, Yves's thoughts will turn to the inevitable loss of his mother, the person he loves the most: 'And we, my brother, we will die, and everything that we have loved with us – our old mothers first – then everything and ourselves, the old mothers in the Breton huts like those in the cities ...' (CI). It is very telling that when Marie, shocked by the immoral conversation of the other wives in the *For the mother of the family* tavern, leaves and, 'so as to be in honest company,' joins instead 'a group of women in large coifs who had remained out of the way to let the crowd of brazen women pass,' these good women turn out to be 'good, elderly mothers' (LXXXVIII).

While the novel is rich in indications that Loti loves Yves and no woman, there is also evidence that the feeling might be reciprocal. Some of this is directly reported action, as we have seen, and some the more suspect narrator's interpretation of the sailor's thoughts and emotions. Early in the novel the officer describes how, in Pernambuco, the topman had sold his own watch for one hundred francs to help Loti when the latter had lost all his money and gone into debt. Alerted readers of Viaud will recall that, in Pierre Loti's previous novel, Fatou-gaye had *stolen* from Jean Peyral a hundred francs (Introduction:IX) and his father's watch (II:XXXIII). This reinforces the erotic and romantic connotations of Yves's act of *giving* them *to* Loti.

There are other examples of Yves's affection for Loti as well. After describing how he and Yves woke up 'together' in 'their' bed in Yves's mother's house, Loti continues:

This 'Hello, Pierre!' preceded by a small, knowing smile, is said to me hesitantly, with an intimidated voice; Yves is used to saying 'Hello, captain,' and he can't get over waking up so close to me, with the order to call me by my first name. In order to make it believable for the people of Plouherzel and maintain the believability of my borrowed uniform [Loti was traveling with Yves disguised as a simple sailor], we had concocted this togetherness [*intimité*]. (XXI)

Loti's description of Yves's joy at such intimacy – 'preceded by a small, knowing smile,' 'said to me hesitantly, with an intimidated voice,' 'he can't get over waking up so close to me' – evokes a timid but quite happy young bride. Yves is reportedly very happy to be with Loti in the 'togetherness' (*intimité*) that 'we' have concocted.

After Loti's already discussed falling dream, he awakens to see Yves in his cabin. The latter has come to tell him, 'with a calm and very gentle manner,' 'I wanted to see you ... because I dreamed about you a lot last night' (XXIX). He then explains that he had dreamed that Loti was being threatened by Burmese dancing women they had seen on shore; these women had wanted to eat the officer and Yves had broken out into a sweat, so frightened was he by the thought. This would seem to be an unabashed declaration of caring. It is also a classic projection of someone's fear of sex with women.

In his 'surprising' letter to his 'brother' announcing his marriage, Yves assures Loti: 'I am very sad to be shipping out this time without you,' and closes the epistle with several standard but nonetheless potentially affectionate formulas: 'I close by sending you much love. Your brother who loves you. Yours' (XXXVI). Some of his other letters end with similar, albeit tradition-sanctioned formulae, leaving the reader – and no doubt Loti – to wonder and dream about how much they are simply formula and how much an expression of real emotions (cf. LIX; LXXIV; LXXVI; XCVI). Yves also names his first son Yves-Pierre, which to some could suggest that he saw the child as a product of their relationship and not of that between himself and his wife. (Yves-Marie is a common man's name in France.) Elsewhere he writes Loti a letter begging him to be allowed to serve with his 'brother' on the latter's outbound ship (LIX). Yves is so eager to do so that he pays another sailor one hundred francs for the chance to serve under Loti. The latter assures us that his 'brother' did so 'joyously' (LXI).

When Loti, having had Yves put in chains because of drunken insubordination, writes the seaman for forgiveness, the latter replies with the by now heavily connotation-laden 'Yes, brother' (LXVI). Later, when the sailor begins to plan his house, he assures the officer that there will be a special room in it for him (LXVIII), just as Loti had set aside one of his rooms in Istanbul for Samuel (*Aziyadé* II:XVIII). Yves would not be aware of the similarity between his action and the younger Loti's, but the officer – and his alerted readers – would have been.

When Yves worries about his son's appearance he consults Loti, though his wife is also standing there (LXIX). Yves designs his house with Loti's help during idle evenings on board ship; at least according to the narrator, Marie plays no role in the planning. Yves even starts to write his thoughts down in a diary as the officer does: 'he is modeling himself on me, there's no doubt about it,' the narrator assures his readers, and no doubt himself.

It is when Loti prepares to leave the *Sèvre* that Yves becomes particularly demonstrative, at least according to the narrator. 'Poor Yves,' he tells us, 'now it's he who, at the moment of my departure, is surrounding me with a thousand little kindnesses ... not knowing how to go about showing me all of his affection. And this way of acting is more charming in his case, because it's not part of his customary nature' (LXXIII). Affection that Yves does not customarily show: what more could Loti want as an indication of the seaman's feelings for him? What, that is, other than a simple declaration of love, which he could not have reported in this novel even if it had been made. The sailor does seem to come close, though. When Loti tells him to think about his 'brother,' Yves writes back: 'I swear to you that an hour doesn't go by that I don't fail to think about you, and even several times an hour' (LXXIV; cf. also Yves's subsequent letter, LXXVI), words whose intent any man would be happy to hear from the object of his affections.[27]

As part of determining whether Yves might love him, Loti wonders if he is open to love with another man. Again the evidence is ambiguous. On the one hand, he describes Yves's past with women as largely unhappy and unfulfilling. We learn, albeit through Loti's words, that when Yves first entered the navy he experienced

> more troubled years when love was born, took form in the virgin and uncultivated soul – then was expressed in brutish intoxications or naively pure dreams depending on the locations to which the wind carried him, the women thrown into his arms [note the implication that Yves did not make any effort to meet them]; terrible awakenings of the heart and the senses, and then a return to the ascetic life at sea, to sequestration in the floating monastery.

When the narrator explains that Barrada, Yves's extremely handsome friend and shipmate, 'made money off of everything, for example, even off of his beauty on occasion,' which suggests that Barrada sold his body for sex, Loti notes that 'Yves limited himself to saying: "Oh! that's not pretty, Barrada, believe me ..." and didn't dislike him because of it either' (XXVI). Since it is hard to imagine a sailor being that moralistic about one of his fellows selling his body to women, this would suggest that Yves was not shocked by male same-sex activity. Elsewhere, we find Loti's ambiguous remark that Yves is 'morally and physically large, strong, and handsome, with a few irregularities in the details' (VIII). Remember also the scene in 'Blossoms of Boredom' where he dances with other men.

One of the officer's comments near the end of the novel is particularly striking. Having spoken again of Barrada, he turns his thoughts to 'my poor Yves, who, with as good a heart, surely had transgressed against the law of proper behaviour much less' (XCVII). Although the narrator fails to specify what he means by 'the law of proper behaviour,' he leaves open the possibility that Yves may have participated in the same immoral acts in which Barrada engaged, including selling his body for money.

Earlier in the novel, when Yves reveals to Loti that he suffers from occasional bouts of sadness (depression?), the officer, 'surprised,' exclaims: '"You're taking on some of my qualities there, my poor Yves." "Some of your qualities, you say?" And he looked at me with a long, melancholy smile that expressed to me on his part new things that could not be put into words. That night I understood that he had a lot more of my qualities than I would have thought, ideas and feelings similar to mine' (XXI). Loti does not specify what new, inexpressible feelings he suddenly envisions – and wants us to believe – Yves shares with him.[28]

Yves also feels a desire to escape the world of convention and restriction. Early in the novel he rejects the idea of deserting the navy for America, but admits to himself: 'At least, there, you are freed from everything' (VI). Much later, when he has contracted with the captain of an American ship and is about to desert, 'he felt free, freed from all his past ties ... This idea of deserting had obsessed him in a strange way for years ... Feeling outside the law made him feel bigger' (LXXX). Yves clearly wants to be free from unspecified restrictions that limit behaviour.[29] The alerted reader of Viaud will recall Loti's admiring description in *Aziyadé* of the freedom to be had in Salonika and Istanbul. With these passages as a background, Loti's descriptions of Yves's actions and thoughts make it look as if the seaman might also be open to homosexual feelings and acts, and therefore be at least open to, if not share the romantic feelings of, his superior officer.

At the end of the narrative, Yann assures Loti: 'At least you know, brother, that I have changed now and that there is something that is quite finished.' The narrator concludes the novel with a remarkable sentence: 'Real-life stories should be able to be stopped at will like those in books ...' (CII). To what are the two men referring? The casual reader would assume that Yves's 'something' is his excessive drinking, in which case Loti's pessimism would be understandable. The sailor's circumlocution allows other interpretations, however, and some readers, as well as Loti himself, might instead choose to view Yves's line as a declaration that he has set aside his homoerotic activity once and for all, in which case Loti's remark could be seen as both a doubt and a hope.

In short, the description of Yves's feelings for Loti is not as unambiguous as that of Loti's for Yves, but it is still suggestive, and not just to a biased and interested eye. It becomes even more suggestive when viewed in the context of the sailors' world in which Yves has chosen to live, at least as Loti presents it.

Perhaps the most significant single description of this world occurs late in the novel, as the *Primauguet* sails through southern climes one warm summer night. Speaking of the sleeping sailors, Loti remarks:

> This warm darkness brought ideas of love that men might not have wanted. Men saw themselves ready to vanish again into disturbing dreams; they felt a need to open their arms to a much desired human form, to hug it with a strong and rough, an infinite tenderness. (XCII)

This is a very ambiguous but nonetheless remarkable passage. Loti could have written that these sailors, their hormones awakened by the balmy breezes, felt a desire to embrace a woman. He did not. Instead, he speaks of a genderless 'human form.' *Forme* is feminine in French, so the modifying adjective, *désirée* (desired), has to be feminine as well. This might lead careless readers to assume that the sailors dream of embracing female forms, but the text is careful not to be so specific. Whom, one might ask, are these sailors dreaming of embracing?

The rest of the passage remains equally elusive, open to more than one reading. Why would these sailors not want these thoughts of love? Why are these dreams troublesome? Because there are no women present with whom to satisfy them? Because the love in question is not universally accepted? Readers of Viaud's previous novel will also note certain key terms: Loti speaks of these men's 'need' to embrace someone with 'tenderness,' just as in *The Story of a Spahi* he had explained

Jean's non-conventional romantic attachment by speaking of his 'need to cherish someone ... need for tenderness' (II:XXX).[30] In short, Loti suggests that on board ship sailors' thoughts, while they turn to love, do not necessarily do so in a rigorously heterosexual fashion.

These sailors, though always depicted as large and strong and quite masculine, also exhibit a remarkable range of what Western culture traditionally views as feminine characteristics, in line with the gender blurring we have noted in previous novels. Early in the work Loti describes how Yves and his shipmates, about to go ashore in Brest after three years at sea, arrange their outfits, 'adjusting each other with an air of *coquetterie*' (III; cf. also LXVI). (*Coquetterie* can mean several things, including an attention to sartorial elegance and flirtatiousness.) Throughout the text the narrator is fond of comparing sailors to Viaud's favourite animal, the cat. When Yves pays his regular visits to Loti's cabin – Loti speaks of 'the hour that Yves was fond of ... paying a visit to my room' – 'he arrived quite quietly, making no more noise than a cat with his bare feet' (XII). Later on the *Primauguet* 'he had taken up his custom from before of arriving in my room in the evening, with little cat steps' (XCIII). His friend Barrada shows his white teeth – a feature Loti often remarks in men, as already noted – 'with a feline expression' (VI) and the narrator later comments on his 'feline smile' (XXV). At the beginning of the novel, the narrator describes how a group of sailors, having docked in Brest, 'climbed those stairs that led to the town joyously, shaking themselves like cats that have just been sprinkled with water' (II). Elsewhere Loti says of Yves and his fellow topmen that 'their balancing back and forth, the supple and easy fashion with which they placed their bare feet was cat-like in a way' (XI). When ordered to their post, this group moves quickly, 'like a band of cats' (XI). When they undress at night in the often flooded hold, the topmen walk carefully to avoid the filthy water, 'perching with fears like a female cat's' (XXVIII). This time the cats in question are even specifically female.[31]

Yves, though endowed with strength and courage, has a fair number of what Western society might view as feminine – but not effeminate – traits. When he boarded the *Belle-Rose*, on which he had signed with plans of deserting his ship, Yves washed and 'adjusted his clothing better, with a certain *coquetterie*, in his new uniform' (LXXX). Even Loti comments, on seeing the seaman sewing his stripes back on his uniform, that he is 'always funny, looking so much like a pirate, when he is busy sewing' (LXXXIII), though the narrator finds nothing amusing about Yves's previously noted interest in flower arrangement (LXVIII).

Other sailors give signs of equal gender flexibility. In a scene reminiscent of the already discussed episode in the dive in 'Blossoms of Boredom,' Loti recounts how men on board an American whaler dance with each other. The description is worth quoting at length:

> While dancing, the whalers looked at us with side glances like those of a cat, half out of curious timidity, half out of fierce disdain. They had the facial expressions that those who ply the sea have kept from primitive man; funny gestures for everything, an excessive mimicry, like animals in the wild. Sometimes they leaned back, their backs arched; sometimes, out of natural suppleness and the habit of deception, they crumpled up, arching their backs, as big cats do when they walk in daylight. And they all turned, to the sound of the soft, piped music, the skipping and childish little flute; very serious, acting like fine dancers, with gracious movements of their arms and circular movement of their legs ...
>
> Suddenly two of these dancers who were holding each other by the waist were seen falling to the ground, still holding each other, and then fighting, making a rattling sound in their throats, overcome with a sudden anger; they were trying to bury their knives in each other's chests, and their blood was already leaving its red marks on the boards.
>
> The captain with a head like a river god's separated them by lashing both of them with a lash made of hippopotamus hide. (LXXXVII)

This passage is interesting for several reasons. In addition to comparing the men dancing with one other, some intimately, to cats, Loti remarks that they have facial expressions left over from 'primitive man.' Given the situation, this resonates with the previously cited passage in 'Blossoms of Boredom' in which Plumkett might be suggesting that male same-sex desire was an original, primitive male instinct covered over by thirty centuries of civilization.

Something similar is suggested shortly afterward when Loti describes the sailors aboard the *Primauguet* mending their uniforms: 'Seeing them so absorbed in these little girls' preoccupations, in the unpacking of dolls, it is impossible to imagine what these same men can become capable of once again once they are released on land' (XCII). Here it is as if Loti is saying that, when free of society's constraints and expectations, these men undertake both 'male' and 'female' activities quite naturally.[32]

Along these lines, Loti suggests that sailors, after having been out at sea and away from women for awhile, are no longer preoccupied with them. Shortly before the quoted passage about the troubling but unspecified dreams that seamen have during warm nights, Loti writes that earlier in the evenings

> some distant image of a woman passed before their eyes, surrounded by a languid charm, a delicious sweetness. Or, with a sudden disturbance of their senses, they dreamed of some senseless festivity of lewdness and alcohol ...
>
> But afterward, the real night came, warm, full of stars, and the momentary impression was forgotten ... (XCII)

If 'momentary impression' refers to these dreams of women and sex with women ('lewdness'), Loti would seem to be suggesting that sailors, once they are removed from women and a society that dictates heterosexual behaviour, do not spend a lot of time dreaming about them. Could he, like Dominique Fernandez and other gay writers to follow, believe that heterosexuality, or at least exclusive heterosexuality, is a social construct? This passage would then reinforce the idea that the already quoted passage several paragraphs later dealing with 'ideas of love that men might not have wanted' might refer to homosexual desire.

Such an interpretation is supported by two aspects of Viaud's description of the sailors' world. First, Loti's sailors do not seem to be particularly interested in having sex with women. When a group of them, including Yves and Barrada, hire some Burmese women to entertain them, 'the sailors were overcome with fear at the idea that these women, paid for their pleasure, were waiting for them. One after the next, they left along the beach, not daring to approach them' (XXVI). The alerted reader of Viaud will recall the scene with Yves, the other Bretons, the Basques, and the Algerian prostitutes in 'Blossoms of Boredom.' As already noted, Yves subsequently dreams that these dancing women tried to eat Loti (XXIX), a nightmare that could be indicative of a fear of having sex with women. The very handsome Barrada speaks of his planned marriage in an apologetic fashion: '"What do you want! It's a childhood friendship!" he said, as if it had been necessary to apologize for it' (XXVI). Why would he feel a need to apologize? Because his future wife is Spanish? Because he is marrying a woman? As always, Loti's text is not specific.[33]

Second, and as already noted in part, Loti's sailors seem to be remarkably tolerant of albeit unspecified departures from society's sexual norms. Having explained that Barrada 'made money off of everything, for example, even off of his beauty on occasion,' Loti remarks that 'the others, who knew it, forgave him as if he were more of a child than they were' (XXVI). To whom Barrada sold his body is not specified, in typical Viaud fashion, but it is hard to imagine that it would be worth mentioning if it had been to women.

In short, the sailors' world depicted in *My Brother Yves* seems to be populated by men who are not preoccupied with women, tolerant of and occasional participants in non-standard sexuality. As Loti at one point remarks, the sailors themselves 'had the vague notion that their life was strange and against nature' (XCII).[34] Given this and all the other aspects of that world just examined, it would not be unreasonable for Viaud's readers, or Loti, to speculate on whether one of its voluntary inhabitants, Yves Kermadec, might be predisposed to reciprocate Loti's love.

This is reinforced by the apparent subject of the novel, alcoholism. More than one critic has suggested that *My Brother Yves* was Viaud's attempt to deal with the sort of gritty facts-of-life material then in vogue with Zola and his fellow Realists, which Viaud would criticize in 1892 with the speech that he gave upon his entrance into the French Academy. Clive Wake proposed, instead, that in portraying Yves's struggle with alcoholism, 'Loti [Viaud] ... intended a symbolic projection of his personal struggle [with homosexuality]' (96).[35] When read in the context of the narratives that the author had given his public previously, the issue does take on added dimensions, though different from those these critics have proposed.

'Intoxication' (*ivresse* in French), the word Loti uses in *My Brother Yves* to talk about Yves's excessive drinking, had already figured prominently in *Aziyadé*, as we have seen, and therefore acquired certain connotations for readers of Viaud. Specifically, Loti had used it repeatedly in his first novel to describe the positive effects of heterosexual desire. As of *The Story of a Spahi*, however, intoxication seemed more like a blinding power that led men astray than a source of happiness, and that intoxication was clearly linked to heterosexual desire. In *My Brother Yves*, 'intoxication' and the associated terms are never used in relation to desire, but strictly with reference to alcoholic inebriation. And, as in *The Story of a Spahi*, the connotations of these words are now uniformly negative. Yves's older brother Gildas, who 'must have been very handsome,' is seen in a hospital, paralysed and dying, 'lost because of liquor' (XL).

The hostess of the inn in St Pol-de-Leon recalls that their father 'ruined himself at the tavern' (IX). Their mother, whom he left penniless with thirteen children to raise, speaks to Loti about 'this scourge without remedy that devours the families of Breton fishermen' (XXII). Yves himself, under the influence, not only repeatedly risks losing his career in the navy; in one already discussed scene, he even loses control of his actions to the point that he injures his own young son (LXXVIII). In scene after scene the novel depicts drunken sailors and their wives always negatively; it speaks, for example, of 'old men and women filthy with intoxication, who had fallen and had been picked back up, and who were moving along in front of them their backs covered with mud' (III). *My Brother Yves* depicts intoxication in a negative light, leaving the alerted reader of Viaud to wonder to what extent this text is also, like *The Story of a Spahi* but more directly, undermining the positive depiction of heterosexual desire described as intoxication in *Aziyadé*. With *My Brother Yves*, 'intoxication' has become a totally negative state, and this negative valuation in turn would seem to rewrite the positive depiction of erotic heterosexual intoxication in Viaud's first novel.[36]

If 'intoxication' has taken on a negative connotation as of Viaud's fourth novel, is it also, as Wake argued, acting as a metaphor for male same-sex attraction, and more particularly for Viaud's own sexuality? Since Wake raised the issue, it is worth examining what the novel has to say about alcoholism.

To begin with, the text repeatedly suggests that alcoholism is hereditary. Yves's mother assures Marie, when the latter says that Yves is drinking less, that there is no chance of his changing. 'He's got his father's head, it's the same thing,' she assures Marie, 'It's all the same, and you haven't seen the last of it with him, I'm telling you' (LXIV). When Yves exclaims despairingly after having injured his child during one drunken episode: 'That's how I am and it's not my fault,' Loti remarks: 'And maybe he was right: It wasn't his fault ... He gave in to distant and mysterious influences that came to him through his blood: he was subject to the law of heredity of an entire family, of an entire race' (LXXIX). In an earlier scene where Yves had become drunk, Loti had also remarked: 'He couldn't do anything about it' (VI). This was already a modern conception of alcoholism as a hereditary medical condition that could not be controlled by simple will power. Was Viaud also arguing that male same-sex desire was hereditary and not a matter of choice? That, too, would have been a modern position to take.

Alcoholism is also depicted as something terrible that destroys not only its victims but also those who associate with them. Yves's mother's description of it has already been quoted: 'This scourge without remedy that devours the families of Breton fishermen' (XXII). Yves's father, an alcoholic, had abandoned his family, and his older brother Gildas had also been destroyed by drink. There is nothing in the novel to suggest that male same-sex desire destroys anything or anyone, however. Loti's interest in Yves is a continual source of help for the latter.

Other remarks regarding Yves's drunkenness are also of interest in this context. He asks his wife, when sober, to forgive his previous drunken behaviour, assuring her that '*that wasn't me anymore!*' (LV). When the sailor recovers from one of his drunks, Loti assures the reader that 'that wasn't him, in fact: it was the wild animal that intoxication awakened, when his real soul was blocked and had disappeared' (LII; cf. also XLVIII). Baudelaire and other of Viaud's contemporaries saw alcohol and drugs as a way of releasing the primal core of man covered over by social convention; Loti seemed to feel that liquor released a being that is not the person's true self.

Since 'intoxication' was associated in Viaud's previous texts with extreme heterosexual desire, it is tempting to wonder if Viaud was arguing here metaphorically that Yves's occasional heterosexual acts, such as his marriage, were an eruption of this 'other' into his life, a 'savage beast' that did not represent his true, homosexual self. Recall Loti's reaction upon learning of that marriage: 'Yves married? ... And to whom, my God? ... Maybe some brazen woman from the town, picked up at random in a drunken moment!' (XXXVI). The reader might also recall the ambiguity of the novel's last lines and Loti's scepticism regarding Yves's remark that he has really changed for good.

In *My Brother Yves* there is a distinction between 'primitive' and 'wild' (*sauvage*, again) that is worth noting on this point. Following on *Blossoms of Boredom*, there is a fascination in this novel with the primitive, man and life before civilization. For Viaud the Bretons seem to be a primitive people. Describing some women whom they meet while out picking fruit in the woods near Toulven, Loti says that 'their calm faces had primitive expressions' (L). When he and Yves pay a last visit to Marie's mother's house, the narrator observes around him 'nothing but things from the past, poor and primitive' (CI). He finds that the thatch and granite of which humble Breton houses were built 'still cast a note of the primitive epoch in Breton villages' (XLVI), and comments that the church in Toulven has 'a porch of a very primitive architecture' (XLVII). Looking out over Toulven, he notes 'completely wooded horizons, as they must have been in the ancient times of Gaul' (LXXVII). In fact, the primitive seems to have become a real preoccupation for Loti. As he looks out over the ocean, the narrator reflects that 'all these waters enclosed latent life in the rudimentary state like, in the past, the sad waters of the primitive world' (XI). He finds that the whalers who dance with each other have 'the facial expressions that those who ply the sea have kept from primitive man' (LXXXVII). Again, as in 'Blossoms of Boredom,' 'primitive' seems to suggest pre-civilized man free from what Plumkett in the former work had called 'what thirty centuries have brought to humanity.'

'Wild' (sauvage) has very different meanings, however. In The Marriage of Loti, as we saw in chapter 3, the adjective had had several different connotations. This seems to be true in My Brother Yves as well, though some of the connotations have shifted. When Loti describes Yves and his companions as 'wild children' early in the novel (IV), the connotation is that these men do not worry about social convention, though it is true that he later describes this group as frequenting 'bad places' and behaving there with 'the exuberance of wild gaiety' (IV), which would seem to recall the element of unrestrained sexuality.

A new connotation seems to be in play later in the text, however, when the officer tries to stop a drunken Yves from returning to ship. 'Deep inside each man there is always a hidden wild man [sauvage] who remains awake,' he states. 'It was our two wild men that were present and that were looking at each other; they had just thrown themselves at each other' (XLVIII). There is a distinction here between 'man,' who can be 'primitive' but still a man, and 'wild man,' which is something that lurks inside him. This is why, when Yves gets drunk two years later, Loti assures the reader that 'that wasn't him, in fact: it was the wild animal that intoxication awakened, when his real soul was blocked and had disappeared' (LII; cf. also LXIII). So for Loti there is a distinction between the primitive and the savage: the primitive appears to be man free of most of society's conventions and therefore admirable and enviable; the savage is something that has thrown off even the primitive self that defines man and separates him from the beast, something that is no longer man and cannot be controlled, is not, in fact, man. As we noted in the Introduction, in June 1881 Viaud had written to Émile Pouvillon 'My own wild man [sauvage] ... was turned over to himself very young, in contact with other wild men, real ones, without control, in countries where the thousand restraints of our policed societies do not exist and where the sun beats down hard on the passions' (Private Diary 1878–

1881). Here 'real' wild men are defined as those 'without control.' If Loti was fascinated by sailors and Bretons who were closer to the early stages of man when sexuality had not been – he imagined – so rigidly prescribed, he at the same time was leery of anything, like alcohol, that unleashed in man the uncontrollable beast.[37]

In short, there does not seem to be enough material to support Wake's hypothesis that with *My Brother Yves* Viaud was using alcoholism as a metaphor to depict homosexuality in general, or his own in particular. At one point the text explains Yves's alcoholism by saying that he 'fell victim to the law of heredity for an entire family, an entire race' (LXXIX). Unless one were to argue that Viaud meant to portray all Bretons as homosexually inclined, it would seem clear that he was not presenting Yves's alcoholism as 'a symbolic projection of his personal struggle [with homosexuality].' Rather, given the connotations associated with 'intoxication' in his previous novels, Viaud would seem, if he was making any metaphorical arguments, to have been using Yves's alcoholism to condemn the erotic emotional excesses that he had romanticized in his first work. This interpretation is reinforced by the fact that, in *My Brother Yves*, Loti returns from the Middle East in 1877 alive and with no mention of Aziyadé (XXIV), in effect erasing that whole episode from his life. It would not seem too extreme to propose, therefore, that with *My Brother Yves* Julien Viaud not only offered his first novel centred around homosexual desire and love; he even used its fashionable theme to undercut the importance of heterosexual desire that had played such an important role in his first novel.

My Brother Yves marks the end of the first stage of Viaud's development of the gay novel. It goes as far as he seems to have felt that he could go in portraying directly not only one man's attraction to another, but also one man's love for another. Beginning with his next novel, *Iceland Fisherman*, Viaud would explore indirect ways of portraying these issues, ways that, because they were less obvious, would allow him to discuss the feelings involved less circumspectly. We therefore need to turn now to that work.

CHAPTER SIX

Different Contexts, Different Sexualities: *Iceland Fisherman*

Iceland Fisherman (1886) has always been the most successful of Viaud's novels. The French Academy awarded it the Vitet prize upon its appearance,[1] and it went through 265 editions in France alone during its first twenty years.[2] Today it remains the best known of the author's works, in 1996 undergoing its fifth film adaptation.[3] At least in part, its popularity has been the result of the fact that it recounts in a very appealing way the heterosexual relationship between Yann Gaos, a huge, very masculine Breton fisherman, and Gaud Mével, a young Breton woman who falls in love with him. This would seem to suggest that, after the directness of *My Brother Yves* three years before, Viaud gave up, at least temporarily, trying to depict one man's desire and love for another man.

It is true that, for much of the novel, told largely from Gaud's perspective, Yann seems indifferent to the young woman's pursuit of him. He does not avoid all women, however; the text recounts his brief liaison with a music hall singer in Nantes (I:I), shows him with his arms around Jeannie Caroff (I:V), reveals that, while in Saint-Martin-de-Ré, he had taken up with 'a certain brown-haired woman, his mistress from the previous autumn' (III:XIV), mentions other 'previous mistresses' (IV:IV), and reveals that, 'in a moment of error, after a long voyage,' Yann had had dealings with Chinese female prostitutes (IV:VII). It is also true that he is rather indifferent about these affairs: when he encounters the music hall singer later in Bordeaux, for example, the text says that 'he ... had allowed himself, in an indifferent fashion, to be adored for eight more days' (III:XIV), just as he had treated the watch that she had given him earlier 'like a contemptible toy' (I:I). The text states that 'he didn't worry much about beautiful women' (II:III), and in the first scene of the novel, when his friend Sylvestre asks him when he intends to marry, Yann is described as 'shrugging his awesome shoulders in a very disdainful manner with regard to women ...' (I:I).

Yann does, however, finally marry Gaud and seem to love her. The text describes how, on their wedding night, he carries her off in his muscular arms: 'he couldn't believe he loved her so much!' (IV:VII; cf. also IV:I, IV:II, IV:IV, IV:VII, IV:VIII). Granted that one sexual tendency does not necessarily exclude the other, all this would seem to suggest that Yann is heterosexual.

There are, it is true, some strange aspects to his relationship with Gaud. When courting her, he restricts himself to chaste and basically non-erotic kisses. The text speaks of his 'brotherly kiss' (IV:IV), and adds that 'he did not dare to kiss her.' He refuses to think about possessing her physically, 'out of respect, almost wondering if he would dare commit that delightful sacrilege.' Even on their wedding night he at first kneels before her 'as if before the Holy Virgin' (IV:VII), and in the days that follow, though he presumably has sex with her, 'during the day, he no longer remembered their caresses' (IV:VIII).

The novel also presents a male-male relationship, that between Yann and his friend, fellow fisherman Sylvestre Moan, with whom he works aboard the *Marie*. Clive Wake spoke of 'the latent sexuality of this relationship'[4] but did not elaborate. In fact, some of the passages that describe the two of them together could seem homoerotic.

When the work begins, for example, we see all the sailors but Yann down in the hold of the *Marie*. 'However, Sylvestre was anxious, because of another seaman called Jean (a name that the Bretons pronounce Yann), who had not arrived yet' (I:I). Sylvestre evidently wonders, in one of the novel's many uses of free indirect discourse: 'Indeed, so where was Yann; still working up above? Why didn't he come down to have a little of his share of the festivities?' Later, having finished their fishing and gulped down breakfast, the two together 'had become extremely gay once again at the idea of going down to sleep, to be nice and warm in their little bunks and, holding each other by the waist, they went as far as the hatchway, with a rolling gait, singing an old song' (I:I).[5] When they are ashore, Gaud sees 'Sylvestre and [Yann] walking arm in arm' (I:IV), and the two men engage in similar physical intimacy on board ship when reading letters from home: 'Sitting together over to one side, in a corner of the bridge, their arms together and holding each other by the shoulders, they read very slowly, as if better to be penetrated by the things about home that were addressed to them' (I:VI). When Sylvestre enters the navy to do his compulsory service, he sings the endless *Jean*

François from Nantes 'in order to remember his brother Yann' (II:IX).[6] When Sylvestre dies, Gaud wonders how Yann will react: 'Will he at least cry for him? ... Perhaps, since he loved him' (III:VII).

The text undercuts the romantic implications of this homosocial behaviour, however, particularly as regards Sylvestre. In the novel's first scene, once Yann, after the younger sailor's expression of concern, descends to join the other seamen in the cabin, 'Sylvestre, putting his arms around this Yann, drew him against himself with tenderness' (I:I). The narration completes the sentence in a fashion that seems to deny its homoerotic potential, however: '... drew him against himself with tenderness, as children do; he was engaged to his sister and treated him like a big brother.' ('Brother,' of course, undercuts 'children.') Elsewhere the text shows us Sylvestre whispering to his fiancée Marie (I:V); if he ignores the streetwalkers in Brest (II:V), he is so 'fascinated' by those he encounters in India that he begins to move toward their alluring signals (II:X). An interest in women does not rule out a similar interest in men, but it is impossible to ignore the fact that the younger sailor repeatedly dreams of and works toward a marriage between his older friend and Gaud (I:I, I:VI, II:XIII), unlike Loti and his attitude toward the marriage of Yves and Marie Karemenen in *My Brother Yves*. The previous novel had also conveyed some ambiguity regarding the past sexual activities of the title character and his friend Barrada (VIII, XXVI, XCVII). There is nothing in *Iceland Fisherman*, however, to suggest that either Sylvestre or Yann has ever been involved sexually with other men.

The general maritime environment in *Iceland Fisherman* also lacks the occasional hints at sexual ambiguity that we saw scattered through Viaud's previous novel. Though groups of seamen are shown more than once strolling around on shore arm in arm (I:IV, II:V), other topics treated ambiguously in *My Brother Yves* do not receive similar treatment here. This is particularly striking in the respective descriptions of the sailors' dreams. Aboard the *Marie* in *Iceland Fisherman*, the monotonous work of fishing reduces the men to a semi-conscious state. 'They no longer gave any thought to women, because it was already cold; but they dreamed about incoherent or marvellous things, as if asleep, and the thread of these dreams was as scattered as a mist ...' (III:X). 'Incoherent or marvellous things' is vague, but not in any homoerotically suggestive way, unlike the already cited passage describing sailors' dreams in *My Brother Yves* (XCII).

Finally, one might note that *Iceland Fisherman*, unlike Viaud's previous and some subsequent narratives, does not, by and large, have a narrator with gay tendencies. Except in part III, chapters III–IV, the narrator of this novel has no name or identity. (As already seen, most of Viaud's previous works are narrated by Loti. This will also be true of several of his subsequent fictional ones.) The narrative repeatedly notes Yann's and Sylvestre's size, strength, and good looks, but never depicts the two men, or any of the work's other male characters, in a state of undress, as Loti frequently had in previous works, most especially, as we have seen, in *My Brother Yves*.[7] In part II, chapter XII, the narrative makes a clear comparison between Yann's growing emotional involvement with Gaud and the *Marie*'s stranding on some object, but male fear of commitment to a woman is not proof of homosexual tendencies.

In short, it is easy to understand why for over a hundred years people have read and enjoyed *Iceland Fisherman* as a heterosexual narrative. Since it has been enjoyed as that it can be that ... though, as we shall see, it does not have to be just that. Some critics have gone so far as to suggest that it is a retelling of Viaud's pursuit of the daughter of a Breton fisherman, thereby making it an assertion of the author's heterosexuality as well. This would seem to be going too far, however.

The problem here is not that this would be a form of the biographical criticism that has been rejected by some for the last half-century. In fact, biographically informed approaches to texts play a role in contemporary gay readings of literature: Proust is the obvious French example, but there are others.[8] The consideration of certain elements of the author's biography allows for an understanding of how he may have experienced his own work, and in the case of *Iceland Fisherman* such an approach will allow me to suggest how the work might have had a gay subtext specifically for Viaud. After that, we will see how the general reading public might also perceive the narrative as gay without needing knowledge of the author's biography.

The entry for 21 December 1882 in Viaud's published diary describes his unsuccessful pursuit of the daughter of a Breton fisherman (*Private Diary 1882–1885*). This has lead some critics to read *Iceland Fisherman* as a reworking of this episode. Helen Poggenburg, for example, wrote: 'While visiting [Pierre Le Cor] in his home near Paimpol, Loti [Viaud] met the daughter of Iceland fishermen who refused his offer of marriage and who became the Gaud of *Pêcheur d'Islande*.'[9] Jacques Dupont, in the Preface to his edition of the novel, was more circumspect but still saw the biographical episode as a key to understanding the text: 'The biographical element ... does explain many particularities of the work, which goes beyond and exceeds it.'[10]

What these and other critics who have taken the same approach over-look is that *Iceland Fisherman* recounts the pursuit of a man (Yann) by a woman (Gaud), and not of a woman by a man. They also overlook that Gaud, the Parisian-educated daughter of a wealthy Paimpol business-man, bears little resemblance to the provincial daughter of a small-town Breton fisherman.[11] They also overlook the extent to which Gaud resembles not this unnamed fisherman's daughter, but Julien Viaud himself.

The similarities are too striking to be coincidental, starting with the names themselves: Gaud, Viaud. Gaud is twenty at the beginning of the novel (I:III); she loses her father, her sole source of financial support, a year or so later, and is reduced to complete poverty because of his mis-management of his affairs. Viaud's father, a clerk for the city of Roche-fort, died when the author was twenty, leaving his family in penury because he had been accused of embezzling municipal funds and had been ordered to repay them. Gaud, though born in Paimpol, had been educated in Paris; Viaud, though born in Rochefort, had also studied in Paris. Gaud, after her father's and her cousin Sylvestre's deaths, takes care of the elderly Yvonne Moan, who had raised her in her mother's absence (I:III); Viaud, after his father's and his brother's deaths, took care of his mother, Nadine Texier Viaud, who was sixty when she was widowed and in her early seventies when Viaud wrote *Iceland Fisherman*. (Viaud's brother Gustave died at sea as the result of a fever contracted in Indo-China while serving with the French navy; Sylvestre dies at sea of a bullet wound he received while fighting in Vietnam.) Gaud, before she loses her house at her father's death, spends much time sitting at her window, looking out over Paimpol (I:III, I:IV, I:V, II:XI, etc.); in his recently published diaries, Viaud repeatedly shows himself sitting at his window, looking out over Rochefort.

While Gaud resembles Viaud, Yann definitely does not resemble any woman in Viaud's life. He is one of the most masculine of the author's male characters. At his first appearance, his captain addresses him sim-ply as '*the man!*' (I:I).

Those few critics who have noted general similarities between Viaud and Gaud have not followed though on the homosexual implications. For Poggenburg, Gaud 'in a very important sense ... is Loti' only in that she, like Viaud, experiences Brittany as something of an outsider.[12] Dupont noted that 'it is not forbidden to find projected in Gaud certain aspects of Loti himself, perhaps speaking about himself more freely behind this mask,'[13] and pointed out that 'Gaud is socially, compared to

Yann, close to being in the same situation as Loti compared to the fisherman's daughter.' But Dupont did nothing with this and went on to suggest that 'Loti seems to have slipped into the character of Gaud, giving her certain of his own reactions'[14] when he was turned down for a rendezvous by the fisherman's daughter, thereby reinstating the frame of heterosexual desire.[15]

The novel itself is too complex to allow for any sort of one-to-one biographical correspondence. If Gaud resembles Viaud, so, to a lesser extent, does Yann. Though based on Guillaume Floury, a real individual whom Viaud knew in Brittany[16] and whom he even refers to in the published version of his diary as Yann (*Private Diary 1882–1885*, 10 December 1885), Yann in *Iceland Fisherman* resembles Viaud in that both of them were pressured by their families to marry (for Yann, II:IV; for Viaud, Blanch *Pierre Loti* 149). Viaud's family was busy hunting for a wife for him while he was writing this novel;[17] in his diary for 24 December 1884, he mentioned 'plans of marriage for me, from different sides – a formidable decision to make' (*Private Diary 1882–1885*). Yann is also connected to his author by his strength: Viaud had been a weak child and was very short and slight. Joining himself to the huge, muscular Yann by having the latter share his familial pressures may have provided Viaud with vicarious wish fulfilment.[18]

The above demonstrates that it is hard to read *Iceland Fisherman* as a retelling of Viaud's pursuit of an unnamed fisherman's daughter, and hard not to read it as a metaphorization of Viaud's desire for some man. It seems that Viaud used Gaud to create a space for himself in the story, perhaps so that he could express more openly the love for Pierre Le Cor that he had suggested more ambiguously in *My Brother Yves*.[19] Even though, unlike most of his previous works, *Iceland Fisherman* does not recount the adventures of the largely auto-biographical Loti, some of its readers have felt that it, too, has a strongly auto-biographical component. Louis Barthou, for example, who knew Viaud well, wrote: '*Iceland Fisherman* was one of the books in which [Viaud], illustrious and fêted, had put the most of himself, of his life and of his soul.'[20] Barthou described the novel, most tellingly, as 'a confession.'[21] The only critic who suggested that the work expresses homosexual tendencies on the part of its author, however, is Clive Wake. He declared that 'it is more than likely, therefore, that through these two female characters [Gaud and Fatou-gaye, from *The Story of a Spahi*], Loti is representing his own sexual attraction towards the handsome sailor.'[22] For Wake, *Iceland Fisherman* marks the climax of Viaud's 'inner struggle with himself.'[23] It is 'a parable of Loti's last real confrontation with himself.'[24]

As we have seen, for Wake, homosexuality, like alcoholism, is something reprehensible that should and can be controlled, not just for moral reasons but primarily because 'both of them cause a deep-seated inability to adapt to the responsibilities of adult life.'[25] Imputing this view to Viaud, he continued: 'Marriage, as seen by Loti, is the fundamental recognition of one's commitment to a settled and responsible life. It involves the acceptance of the everyday responsibilities of maturity and the rejection of escapism.'[26] Gaud 'represents man's need to accept the responsibility of facing life, as symbolized by marriage and the raising of a family.'[27] From the perspective of this morality, Yann's 'death by drowning is the symbolic portrayal of [Viaud's] moral failure.'[28] Though it would be easy to raise objections to the homophobia of Wake's interpretation, what is relevant here is not his understanding of male same-sex desire but whether that misunderstanding provides insight into *Iceland Fisherman* as a key to its author's psycho-biography, that is, whether Viaud himself held the views Wake ascribed to him.

The simple answer would seem to be 'no.' Nowhere does the novel depict marriage in general, or Yann's marriage to Gaud in particular, as a 'responsibility.' Nowhere does it suggest that Yann does not want to be tied down to one woman; given his trade, marriage would not tie him down physically. Since he is careful with his money, giving most of his salary to his parents for their support (I:V), does not drink to excess, and, as his father tells Gaud, generally qualifies as 'a well-behaved man' (II:III), he is a model of responsibility and maturity without being married. Nor, finally, is there any indication in the novel that Yann drowns as the result of any failure on his part. He did, after all, marry Gaud.

In fact, in this novel where the sea is more than once compared to a woman, even by Yann himself (I:I), one might better argue that Yann's death is a metaphor for the engulfing potential of marriage to a woman. Viaud, then being pressured to marry by his family, might have seen it that way. As we saw previously, in *My Brother Yves* Pierre Loti had dreamed of the title character falling into 'something black which must have been the deep water' (XXIX). Since Yves subsequently married, becoming lost to Loti, it was not difficult to read the deep, black water that threatened to engulf the sailor as a metaphor for heterosexual desire and/or marriage. In that context, Yann's drowning and Gaud's loss of him could also be read as a retelling of Loti's (and Viaud's) loss of Yves (Pierre Le Cor) to marriage. In *The Awakened*, Viaud's last novel, published twenty years after *Iceland Fisherman*, the main character, Djénane, who is about to be forced into a marriage that she does not want, exclaims at one point: 'I feel like a person who has been drowned' (IV).

In short, *Iceland Fisherman*, like Viaud's previous novels, constitutes a working out of issues central to him, but as an expression both of Viaud's homosexual desire for another man, perhaps Pierre Le Cor, and of his fear of heterosexual marriage for himself or for any man in whom he was interested. Now I would like to go back to the novel itself, however, to show that, read only with the information available to its original, intended audience, it can also be a gay text.

To begin with, in many ways Gaud's relationship to Yann resembles Pierre Loti's homoerotic relationship to Yves Kermadec in *My Brother Yves*. In each case, the object of desire is a large, handsome Breton sailor in his middle twenties. Though they allow the person who desires them to believe that they might share this desire, these sailors do not provide any clear indications of their feelings – in Yann's case, not until part III, chapter XVII, seven-tenths of the way through the novel. Yves repeatedly gets violent when drunk (XXXI, XLVIII, LXXVIII, etc); though generally sober, Yann also gives in to acts of violence (I:I, I:V). Yann is also described as having 'white teeth' (I:I) and 'gleaming teeth' (I:V), a trait that he shares with several previous male objects of desire, among them Samuel (*Aziyadé*, I:VII) and Jean Peyral (*The Story of a Spahi*, Introduction:IV).

More important, Gaud's feelings for Yann often recall Loti's for Yves. This is particularly noticeable with the repeated use of the noun 'anguish,' the importance of which in *My Brother Yves* we noted in the previous chapter. One day, when Yann is still avoiding her, Gaud sees him approach on her path. 'She ... had raised her eyes, directing toward him in spite of herself a plea and her anguish' (III:XIII). (He passes by with just a 'Bonjour, mademoiselle Gaud.') As she sits with the elderly Yvonne Moan, Sylvestre's grandmother, wondering if she will ever marry Yann, 'she dreamed about him with more anguish' (III:XIV). When she hears that Yann has joined the crew of a new ship, the *Léopoldine*, 'this change, this *Léopoldine*, increased her anguish' (III:XV).[29] When Yann's family, after his marriage to Gaud, prepares for his imminent departure on that vessel, 'Gaud underwent these inexorable preparations with anguish' (IV:VIII). Not surprisingly, that fall, as the other ships return and the *Léopoldine* does not, 'in the evening she had the first little shivers of anxiety, of anguish' (V:VI). When September passes without any word, 'recollections of anguish returned, more horrible than before' (V:IX). As we saw in the previous chapter, Pierre Loti had repeatedly used the same word to convey his worries concerning Yves Kermadec in *My Brother Yves.*

Gaud fears repeatedly that she will lose Yann to the sea. Before he finally asks her to marry him, she wonders to herself: 'How would she contend with the sea for him' (II:II). After their marriage, as Yann explains in glowing terms how much he enjoys fishing off Iceland, where he will soon return, 'she lowered her head, feeling sadder, more defeated by the sea' (IV:VIII). In the previous novel, Pierre Loti had had that terrible nightmare about Yves falling into 'something black which must have been the deep water' (XXIX) and being unable to save him: 'He was going to get away from me and disappear in all that moving blackness that murmured below us.' In both cases, and especially in the second one, the sea/water may symbolize something else, such as women and heterosexual desire. The narration in *Iceland Fisherman* does refer to the sea as 'this thing that always draws people, that fascinates and devours' (I:III), and that certainly has erotic possibilities.[30]

Gaud also forgives Yann constantly, as Loti did Yves. After meeting Yann the second time, at a wedding, when he says things that she interprets as indications of more than passing interest, Gaud asks around about him to learn what sort of man he is. Though he has had his excesses, she is quick to excuse them: 'All that she forgave him; everyone knows how sailors are, sometimes, when the spirit seizes them ...' (I:V). When Sylvestre tells her that Yann had boasted about marrying no one but the sea, 'she forgave him his way of being, and, always finding in her memory his handsome, forthright smile from the night of the dance, she went back to hoping' (II:II). (Here her interpretation of Yann's smile is enough to counter Sylvestre's report of Yann's declared intent not to marry.) Later, when she, displaying an amazing amount of boldness for a woman in nineteenth-century Brittany, confronts Yann and asks him why he has been avoiding her only to have him utter a few unconvincing words and depart, 'she forgave everything, and a feeling of tenderness without hope took the place of the bitter resentment that had first risen up in her heart ... But, really, she forgave him, and there was no hatred mixed in with her hopeless love for him ...' (II:XI). When Yann finally asks Gaud if she will forgive him for having avoided her for so long and marry him, the narrative, in another example of free indirect discourse, explodes: 'Oh! if she would forgive him! She felt tears coming, very gently; it was the remnant of her grief from before that was finally vanishing with this avowal from her Yann' (IV:V). As we saw in the previous chapter, Pierre Loti behaved in the same fashion with Yves Kermadec in *My Brother Yves*.

There are other similarities between these two relationships as well. Perhaps most notable is the importance of the mother figure. In *Iceland Fisherman*, Yann finally shows an interest in Gaud and asks her to marry him when he sees her devotion to Sylvestre's grandmother (III:XVI–XVII). In *My Brother Yves*, as we saw, Loti had suggested to Yves that their affection for their respective mothers formed a tie between them: 'We, my brother, we will fade away, and everything that we have loved with us – our elderly mothers first – then everything and ourselves, the elderly mothers in the Breton huts like those in the cities' (CI). Gaud's relationship to Yann recalls Loti's homoerotic one to Yves in various ways, then.

The Sylvestre-Yann relationship in *Iceland Fisherman* also has elements that recall the Yves-Loti relationship of the preceding work, elements that therefore bring with them some of the earlier male-male relationship's homoeroticism. To begin with, Sylvestre is repeatedly linked to Yves. His matriculation number in the French navy, 2091 (III:V), is the same as Yves's (I). Despite their very masculine physiques, both are repeatedly described as having childlike qualities (Sylvestre: I:I, II:V, III:II; Yves: III, VII, XXXI, XLVIII, LVI, LVIII, LXIII, XCIX). Both are very devoted to an elderly mother figure, Sylvestre to his grandmother Yvonne Moan, Yves to 'his elderly mother' (XVI). Both begin to keep apparently naive diaries while serving with Loti (Sylvestre III:II, Yves LXXI).[31] Both serve as topmen in the crowsnest, both are the last surviving sons in their respective families.

The relationships between the men also have similarities. Yann functions with Sylvestre in the role of a protective 'brother' (I:I, II:IX, III:VIII, III:IX, III:X); as we saw, Loti used the same term repeatedly to describe his relationship with Yves.[32] Yann learns of Sylvestre's loss by letter while he is away from home (III:VIII), just as Loti learns in Athens of Yves's loss to him, the seaman's marriage to Marie Keremenen (XXXVI). Yann does not seem to take an interest in Gaud until after Sylvestre's death, and then does so, at least in part, because he mistakenly imagines that his young friend had dreamed of such a union on his deathbed (III:X). Whereas *Iceland Fisherman* states clearly that Gaud loves and desires Yann, it is less clear about Yann's feelings for Sylvestre. These parallels with *My Brother Yves* are suggestive, but the later novel also has a new, interesting way of talking about Yann's feelings for the younger sailor.

The day after receiving news of Sylvestre's death, Yann stands on deck, looking at the sky and thinking about his lost friend. The narrative remarks: 'But words, as vague as they may be, still remain too precise to express these things; one would need that uncertain language that is sometimes spoken in dreams, and of which upon waking people retain only enigmatic fragments that no longer have any meaning' (III:IX). The idea that each subject requires a special language and that one language is insufficient to describe all things runs throughout Viaud's writings. Here the problem is that standard language is too precise to express the unspecified 'things' running through Yann's mind at the moment. In *Iceland Fisherman*, Viaud does more than just complain about standard language's precision, however; he sets about undermining it, to create 'that uncertain language that is sometimes spoken in dreams.'

To begin with, Viaud loads his text with phrases and modifiers that undo the precision of words: 'probably,' 'almost' (60 times in 240 pages), 'rather,' 'perhaps,' 'a kind of,' 'it seemed,' and similar expressions constantly undo language's specificity. Looking just at the first chapter, the text describes the fishermen as gathered together not in 'a somber dwelling,' but in 'a *kind of* somber dwelling.' Outside, 'it *must have been* the sea and the night,' not 'it was the sea and the night.' The ship itself, the *Marie*, 'was *somewhat* old,' not just 'old,' and the captain '*could have been* forty.' The fishermen '*seemed to* feel a real well-being,' while the clock on the wall 'indicated eleven o'clock, eleven o'clock at night *probably*.' When Yann arrives, the text describes him as '*almost* a giant,' with teeth that 'were *somewhat* spaced apart and *seemed* very small.' And so on throughout almost the entire novel. It is not surprising that Alain Buisine felt that Viaud's descriptions render objects *less* distinct.[33] Even the words that he uses these expressions to modify and hence undermine are themselves often not precise. As N. Serban noted, 'It is remarkable to see to what extent abstract nouns are more frequent than concrete nouns.'[34]

Viaud makes particularly striking use of imprecise words when talking about colour. (He had studied art in Paris as a young man and was aware of contemporary developments in French painting. Monet's *Impression: Rising Sun* [1873] would make a very appropriate cover for *Iceland Fisherman*.)[35] Though he mentions colour *very* frequently, it is most often grey, and otherwise pink (rather than red), green, black, blue, brown, or white.[36] He also makes repeated use of approximations of colours: 'grayish' (*grisâtre*), 'bluish' (*bleuâtre*), 'greenish' (*verdâtre*), 'whitish' (*blanchâtre*). As Yves Le Hir remarked: 'These adjectives ... dematerialize whatever is too clear cut in feeling.'[37] Sometimes Viaud even focuses on colours that are beyond language: at one point he describes the sky near Iceland as having 'all that paleness of things [that] were of no nameable hue' (I:I). Elsewhere he writes that 'the sea ... hid under the discreet tints that have no name' (III:IX).

Just as he renders the language that he uses to describe things indefinite, so many of Viaud's descriptions focus on things that no language could depict precisely. In the first chapter of the novel, again, when painting the sea around the *Marie*, Viaud writes: 'Everything seemed diaphanous, impalpable, chimeric ... it had neither a horizon nor outlines ... above, formless and colourless clouds seemed to contain that latent light that could not be explained' (I:I). (Not surprisingly, this setting causes the men to see 'strange sights that are vague and troublesome like visions.') Indeed, 'that earlier light had been vague and strange like that of dreams.' Later he chooses to single out 'vague designs that became entangled in each other and lost their shape; very quickly wiped out, very fugitive' on the sea under a sun 'almost without boundaries' (I:VI), 'formless spots' in the sky (II:I), 'diffuse clouds [that] had taken whatever form' (III:IX), 'formless gray clouds' (III:IX), 'veils ... vaguer than vapours' (III:IX), etc.[38]

Given all this (not to mention what we have observed in certain of his earlier narratives), it should not come as a surprise that, in *Iceland Fisherman*, Viaud also blurs traditional gender distinctions. Indeed, it would very much seem that he created the ambiguous and ambivalent language and setting of this novel so as to have a domain in which such blurring would seem natural. (He had, as we have seen, been hinting at the naturalness, if not indeed the primordiality, of fluid gender since *Blossoms of Boredom*.) On the one hand, Yann is presented as the essence of traditional masculinity. When the reader first encounters him, he appears as the literal embodiment of manhood: ' – Yann! Yann! ... Eh! *man!*' the captain calls up to the still unseen protagonist. '*The Man* answered roughly from outside' (I:I). When Yann descends into the tiny cabin of the *Marie* moments later, Viaud substantiates the impression made by the previous text with his physical description of the fisherman: 'He entered, obliged to bend over double like a big bear, because he was almost a giant ... He exceeded the ordinary proportions of men a little too much, especially by the breadth of his shoulders, which were straight as a helm; when he faced you, the muscles on his shoulders, out-lined under his blue sweater, formed what looked like two balls on the tops of his arms. He had large, very quick brown eyes, with a wild and proud expression' (I:I).[39]

In his behaviour as well, Yann exemplifies traditional masculinity, in its negative as well as positive qualities. He sometimes demonstrates his impressive physical strength with acts of violence: 'One night, being drunk, in a Paimpol café where the fishermen celebrate, he had thrown a huge marble table against a door that someone didn't want to open for him' (I:V). Early in the novel, in a moment of anger, he hurls the ship's dog, Turc, against the wall for having bitten down suddenly on his hand (I:I).

As we noted earlier, Yann also has had sexual relationships with women, who find him attractive: after first meeting him, Gaud discovers that Yann 'went back and forth, to Lézardrieux as well as Paimpol, to be with beautiful women who desired him.' We learn elsewhere of his affairs with a dance hall singer in Bordeaux and a brunette in St. Martin-de-Ré. At their wedding banquet, Gaud learns that Yann had consorted with Chinese prostitutes while stationed there with the French navy (IV:VII). And, of course, Yann does eventually fall in love with and marry Gaud.

Sometimes Yann's relationships with women also involve violence. The text early on notes that 'when his physical being alone was involved, a soft caress was often, with him, very close to a brutal violence' (I:I). Earlier in the first chapter the narrative recounts the story of how, when ashore in Nantes, Yann had bought a bouquet of flowers for the singer, only to throw it in her face when he arrived at the nightclub where she performed.

Like some of the hyper-masculine fantasies of today, such as Arnold Schwarzenegger's 'Conan the Barbarian' films, *Iceland Fisherman* empha-sizes Yann's extreme maleness with references to the primitive.[40] The text at one point speaks specifically of Yann's 'primitive beliefs' (III:IX). More often, it depicts his fellow Bretons as a primitive people, referring to them as 'these primitive men' (I:I) and comparing the thatched roofs of their cottages and the interior of Yvonne Moan's cottage in particular to those of 'Celtic huts' (II:III; III:XII).

These references to the primitive make the text's use of the French adjective *sauvage* with respect to Yann understandable. At one point, in this respect differing from *My Brother Yves*, the novel even establishes a specific link between *sauvagerie* and the primitive. Describing Yann and his friend Sylvestre's actions during a storm at sea, the text speaks of their 'primitive *sauvagerie*' (II:I). Elsewhere the novel often describes Yann as *sauvage*.[41] Perhaps as a reflection of Darwin's three-decade-old theory of the origin of man, Yann is even sometimes specifically linked to animals, again all traditionally 'masculine.' In addition to the bear seen in the first description, quoted above, he is elsewhere likened to a lion (I:I) and a bull (II:XI, V:XI), and more generally to a wild animal (IV:VII) and a 'vigorous beast' (II:I). In short, *Iceland Fisherman* presents Yann Gaos as a model of conventional masculinity.

It also, however, presents him as endowed with characteristics that Western culture has traditionally categorized as exemplary of femininity. Even in the initial description of him, the opening of which we have already cited for its declaration of masculinity, the text mentions 'his lips which had fine, exquisite contours' (I:I). That same paragraph also explains that 'his cheeks had retained a fresh downiness, like that of fruits that no one has touched.' In the course of the novel, the text notes that his voice, 'which with others was brusk and decided, became, when he spoke to [Gaud], ever softer and more caressing' (I:V). When he dances with her, he moves 'with a grace that is both light and noble' (ibid). He can be 'very sweet ... when he was needed' (I:VI); once they are married, Gaud is surprised to find him 'so sweet, so childlike' (IV:VIII). When he learns of Sylvestre's death, he cries (III:IX), though the text admits that he had never cried before. When he finally offers to marry Gaud, he surprises her and evidently the shopkeepers of Paimpol by insisting upon buying her wedding dress: 'He took charge of everything, even the form that this dress would have' (IV:II). Though there is no indication of who chose them, the already surprising fact that Yann's bed curtains are pink is emphasized by the fact that it is repeated twice in close proximity (II:III).[42]

Viaud is not the first writer to have created male characters with female traits. Some of Balzac's creations, such as Charles Grandet in *Eugénie Grandet*, spring immediately to mind, and literature is full of others. In those cases, however, the authors in question usually employed gender ambiguity or mixing to suggest weakness, corruption of the traditional qualities of masculinity, etc. What makes Viaud's novel remarkable for its time and appealing today is that Yann's feminine qualities are not presented as existing in place of, as indicating an absence of, traditional male qualities, but rather as coinciding with and not contradicting them. In short, Yann is no less a man for having them. In this respect, Viaud is reconfiguring modern Western culture's construction of masculinity in a broader, more inclusive, and modern fashion that is in line with the work being done by contemporary feminist and gay studies theoreticians of gender.[43]

This is even more remarkable, and no doubt intentionally so, given the era during which Viaud wrote the novel. As Annelise Maugere has shown, French intellectuals, including some important French novelists, interpreted the humiliating loss of the Franco-Prussian War not simply as a series of upper-level military blunders, but as a glaring indication of the decline in their fellow Frenchmen's masculinity.[44] Not surprisingly, Maugere reports that women were castigated as one of the major culprits of this decline: their growing insistence on holding an equal place in society was condemned as leading to the weakening of men, who had previously held all power.[45] This irrational need to assign general social blame for something that resulted from the failure of a few individuals even led such otherwise intelligent writers as Emile Zola and Maurice Barrès to denounce clerical work as demasculinizing.[46] However they apportioned the blame, these thinkers became obsessed with what they saw as the French male's need to regain his lost power, to become as traditionally masculine as possible.

Given this intellectual climate, in which women and anything associated with them were seen as emasculating and undiluted masculinity was being promoted as France's great need, Viaud's nuanced depiction of the very masculine Yann appears remarkable indeed. When Gaud at one point removes her corset, a quintessentially modern imposition, and the narrator remarks that 'her body, once free, became more perfect; no longer compressed or excessively narrowed at the bottom, it regained its natural lines, which were full and soft like those of marble statues; her movements changed its forms, and each of her poses was exquisite to see' (I:V), it is difficult not to read this as yet another indication that, for Viaud, modern society was imposing limitations on men (and women) that restricted and thereby disfigured their nature and natural beauty, a nature that was fuller, more complex and complete, than the narrow, compressed image resulting from modern society's efforts to mould women – and men – into what it wanted and no more.

All of this creates a world of ambiguity and imprecision where both language and the things that language describes lose their boundaries and specificities. While it does not clarify what Yann is thinking as he stands on deck recalling Sylvestre, it evokes a state of mind that does not support the clear mutually exclusive divisions and distinctions of standard language, or of the nineteenth century's dominant depiction of male and female.

The dichotomous, negative, and often hostile nature of the writing on male same-sex desire that dominated France when Viaud created this world may also have had a lot to do with the author's attempt to create a new space in which to present Yann's thoughts about Sylvestre. As noted in the Introduction, beginning in 1857 with Ambroise Tardieu's *Medical-Legal Study of Assaults on Morality*, French psychiatrists and physicians had undertaken a detailed and often widely read study of the newly named male homosexual.[47] Their descriptions, at least until the publication of Marc-André Raffalovich's *Uranism and Unisexuality* in 1895, were generally negative and hostile, linking homosexuality with criminality, physical degeneracy, the dissolution of social order, and other horrors. They also maintained that all homosexuals were exclusively so.[48] With his years of experience at sea and in foreign cultures to contradict this, Viaud may have felt that he could not describe in contemporary language Yann's feelings for Sylvestre because they did not coincide with the clear-cut denotations and connotations that his contemporaries were giving to the words that Viaud would have had to use. It is no wonder that Yann himself cannot understand his feelings for his lost 'brother': 'He saw once again Sylvestre's gentle face, his good childlike eyes; at the idea of kissing him, something like a veil fell suddenly in front of his eyes, in spite of him – and at first he couldn't really explain to himself what it was, never having cried since he became a man' (III:IX). Yann would not be the first or last gay man to have been unable to understand his feelings for another man because he could not reconcile society's depiction of those who experience same-sex desire with what he knew to be true of himself.

In a famous passage from the first volume of *The History of Sexuality*, Foucault wrote that the appearance in late nineteenth-century medical and legal discourse of a largely negative presentation of the newly created male homosexual, while making possible the control of all men's sexual activity and even emotions, also 'made possible the formation of a "reverse" discourse; homosexuality began to speak in its own behalf ... often in the same vocabulary, using the same categories by which it was medically disqualified.'[49] One of the fascinating things about *Iceland Fisherman* is that in it, Viaud demonstrates the importance of not using 'the same vocabulary, using the same categories by which it was medically disqualified,' as, in many respects, Proust would do.

As I explained at the outset, *Iceland Fisherman* is not as direct as *Aziyadé* or *My Brother Yves* in dealing with male homosexual desire. Nor, unlike with Pierre Loti in *My Brother Yves*, does it present a male character who has no involvement with women. Nor, unlike *The Story of a Spahi*, does it attempt to justify unconventional relationships. What it does do, however, like *The Story of a Spahi*, is to universalize its issues – attraction to a man, frustration with not knowing whether he shares this desire and why he behaves as he does, grief at the feeling that he is being lost to something else, and even confusion about one's feelings for him – to the point that these issues can be appreciated equally by anyone, man or woman, gay or straight, who might experience them. With its parallels to *My Brother Yves*, the novel suggests the validity of a gay reading, but it does not restrict its audience to that. (My straight students, especially the women, have delighted in this novel as a heterosexual love story for years.) Gay men may find a certain satisfaction in the notion that, with this novel, Viaud managed to involve a considerable general public in what began, at least, as one man's love for another. Whereas Proust, perhaps in an effort to universalize it, perhaps simply to hide it, would, several decades later in *In Search of Lost Time*, transform his love for other men into Marcel's love for women, Viaud retained the sex of the original object of desire and provided clues that the person who desired him could also be read as a man.

For some the homosexual nature of this desire remains quite strong. As already noted, Michael Moon, the distinguished gay studies scholar, described *Iceland Fisherman* as 'perhaps the most pungently male homoerotic novel about a sailor before Jean Genet's *Querelle de Brest*.'[50] Others, those for whom homosexuality is not an issue, often see the work as comfortably heterosexual. I hope to have shown the extent to which it can be read as a gay novel, the commentary that it makes on the sometimes ambiguous and non-dichotomous nature of human desire, and the way in which it critiques and works to undermine conventional language's collaboration with and support of dominant society's dualistic ways of constructing sex, gender, and love.

CHAPTER SEVEN

The Origin of Sexual Ambiguity in the Madame Butterfly Legend: *Madame Chrysanthemum*

After the less direct but more intense approach to recounting one man's love for another in *Iceland Fisherman*, the year after, with *Madame Chrysanthemum* (1887), Viaud returned to using two male characters and the restrictions that imposed. As with *My Brother Yves*, this does not seem to have had an adverse affect on sales: *Madame Chrysanthemum* went through 222 editions in the thirty-four years before Viaud's death,[1] making it one of the most popular of his novels and a significant commercial success. Most of the tension that underlies the principal relationships in the two preceding novels is absent from this Japanese tale, however; this time there is no real concern with whether Yves Kermadec reciprocates Pierre Loti's love. This may account for why the work has struck some readers as rather flat, and why it has received little coverage in more recent books devoted to the author's novels.[2] Still, it should not be ignored in a gay reading of Viaud's works. If nothing else, it provided the basis for sexual ambiguity in what has become the legend of Madame Butterfly, romanticized by composer Giacomo Puccini and his librettists in the opera of that name first produced in 1904, and recently transformed by David Henry Hwang in his popular play, *M. Butterfly*.[3]

Madame Chrysanthemum is a fictionalized reworking of Viaud's one-month stay in Japan in 1885, during which time he 'married' an eighteen-year-old Japanese woman by the name of Okané San, apparently out of boredom. At the end of the month he set sail, but neither in real life nor in the novel did the woman commit suicide out of despair. (David Belasco added that and the child in his play *Madam Butterfly*.) In Viaud's novel, Chrysanthemum is last seen counting the money that Loti had left her, making sure that it is real (LII). Neither she nor he experiences anything like the emotional trauma that has reduced opera-goers to tears for almost a century.

Lest there be any misunderstanding, in the preface Loti informs his readers immediately that love, or even desire, had nothing to do with his decision to marry. 'Out of boredom, my God, out of loneliness, I lit-tle by little ended up imagining and desiring this marriage.' To make sure that there is no misunderstanding on this point, he repeats this declaration twice more in the body of the novel itself (VII, LII). Nor do things change once the marriage takes place and Loti begins to live with the woman. He weds her on 7 July 1885 (V), and by 27 August, he reports that 'Chrysanthemum ... bores me even more' (XXXVI). Noth-ing about her appeals to him. One evening, down in Nagasaki, faced with the prospect of climbing the hill to the house that he shares with her, he muses: 'And for what reason, my God, should I climb up to that district every evening, when nothing draws me to that lodging up there?' (XXIX). At times he even says that he hates her. One night, while in bed beside his wife, Loti recalls Aziyadé. 'I looked with a sort of hatred at that doll stretched out near me, asking myself what I was doing there on that bed, and I got up, seized with disgust and remorse, and left that little tent of blue mosquito netting' (X).

Loti seems to make an effort to exaggerate his lack of interest in his Japanese consort. He cannot carry on much of a conversation with her, as he does not speak her language to any extent and makes no effort to learn it: 'But, it's strange, since I have been living with her, rather than going further with my study of the Japanese language, I have neglected it, because I've felt to such a great extent the impossibility of even being interested in it' (XX).[4] Readers of Viaud's next work, *Autumn Japaneries* (1889), a collection of essays published under the name Pierre Loti, would see the narrator speaking Japanese, however ('Kyoto, the Holy City,' XI). In *Madame Prune* (1905), furthermore, a romanticized account of Viaud's second trip to Japan in 1900–1, the narrator will remark, shortly after arriving in the country: 'Words of that language ... are coming back to me more and more; I really think that once I have landed, I will know how to speak Japanese again' (II). These two pas-sages suggest that Loti had learned Japanese well enough to speak it during his first sojourn there, and that he had lied in *Madam Chrysanthe-mum* in order to exaggerate his lack of interest in his 'wife.'

When he leaves Chrysanthemum, Loti mocks Madame Prune's prayer, ending the novel with the line: 'Oh Ama-Terace-Omi-Kami, wash this little marriage off me until I'm completely white, in the waters of the river Kamo' (LVI).[5]

Critics not blinded by their notion of Viaud as an author of great heterosexual romances have seen that there is no feeling for Chrysanthemum on Loti's part. Michael Lerner stated: 'Loti never establishes real contact with Madame Chrysanthemum or Japan';[6] Blanch: 'There was never the slightest emotion in this arrangement';[7] Quella-Villéger: 'There is no love in these pages';[8] etc. In *Madame Prune*, eighteen years later, Loti himself would write: 'I had passed through this country without suffering and without love' (III). One can see *Madame Chrysanthemum* marking the latest ring in the downward spiral of romantic interest in women that began with *The Story of a Spahi*.

Quella-Villéger's 'There is no love in these pages' is not accurate, however. Yves Kermadec is in Japan with Loti, and though the officer's feelings for him are not the central focus of this novel as they had been in *My Brother Yves*, they are not absent from this narrative.[9] To some extent, Yves is paralleled with Samuel in *Aziyadé*, a work that Viaud evokes in this novel's pages several times (X, XXVII, LI). In the preface, telling the sailor that he intends to take a wife while in Japan, Loti assures him: 'You will have your room in our home,' just as Samuel, and then Achmet, had lived with Aziyadé and Loti in Istanbul. Furthermore, Yves is the one who points out Chrysanthemum to Loti (IV). In a sense, Loti marries a woman whom Yves has approved for him, somewhat as Yann had imagined Sylvestre giving him Gaud as his dying wish in *Iceland Fisherman* (III:X). Unlike in *My Brother Yves*, however, Loti pays almost no attention to Yves's body.

Typical of Viaud's style, as we noted in *Aziyadé* and *The Story of a Spahi*, responsibility for some of the intimacy between the two men is shifted away from Loti. When mosquitos make it hard for Yves to sleep in his own room, where he has no netting, Chrysanthemum is the one who brings him into hers and Loti's, which has only one bed (XXXIV). Loti puts her in between them, 'to observe, to see' – he suspects some sort of dalliance between the two – but reports that his wife rearranges this, putting her husband next to Yves. 'Oh, this is decidedly very good,' he exclaims.

When he suspects something between his friend and his wife, Loti always phrases it in terms of her causing trouble between himself and Yves, and never in terms of losing Chrysanthemum. 'I can't imagine that that little spouse, chosen by chance, could ever bring even vaguely serious trouble between this "brother" and myself' (XVIII). 'I thought I noticed very long looks, from Chrysanthemum to him, from him to Chrysanthemum ... I'm not at all concerned about that Japanese woman. But Yves ... that would be bad on his part, and it would strike a serious blow to my confidence in him ... I would begin to hate my little girl, if she led my poor Yves to a bad action that I would never, perhaps, forgive him for' (XXIX). Proust would argue that jealousy is the true mark of love. Still, other than his worry about Yves's possible involvement with Chrysanthemum, *Madame Chrysanthemum* contains no expression of any real affection on Loti's part for his fellow sailor, nothing like what we saw in *My Brother Yves*.

In 'A Forgotten Page From *Madame Chrysanthemum*,' which Viaud published six years later as part of *Carmen Sylva and Sketches from the Orient* (1893), and which, by its date of 16 September 1885, would be a missing part of *Madame Chrysanthemum*'s chapter L, there is a suggestive line that perhaps supplies a missing element for the 1887 novel. When Yves recalls a religious celebration that he and Loti had attended back in Brittany, the latter closes the scene with the exclamation: 'How many things have changed and passed, since that *pardon* last year ...' Not much to go on, certainly, but its tone suggests a feeling of loss. Perhaps, as in Proust, there is only jealousy in Loti's expression of his feelings for Yves in *Madame Chrysanthemum* because something has happened and there is nothing else left of them. Whatever the case may be, after *My Brother Yves* and *Iceland Fisherman*, which, directly and indirectly, are two powerful tales of the protagonist's love for a man, *Madame Chrysanthemum* seems very pale as a gay love story. As a heterosexual love story, it is altogether lifeless.

There are some other expressions of Loti's interest in men here. He repeatedly notes the naked, muscular legs of the various rickshaw drivers he employs (III, XI, XIX, XXIX), and near the end of the novel he says that the farewell he bid to his favourite driver, 415, whose muscular legs he had called 'the best in Nagasaki' (XIX), is 'the only handshake that I really give from the heart' (LIII).[10]

There is also a certain amount of gender ambiguity in the description of some of the men in *Madame Chrysanthemum*. When Loti arrives in Japan he notices that the junks plying the harbour are manoeuvred by 'little yellow men, completely naked, with their long hair combed in bands such as women wear' (II). Later, while talking to some bonzes, he notes that 'they played with their fans like women' (XL). Such gender confusion is not limited to Japanese men, moreover. Earlier, Loti describes a group of 'our sailors from the *Triomphante* who play with fans' going by in rickshaws (XI).

As we saw in previous chapters, the gender ambiguity of Viaud's objects of desire is not made by direct comparison with women, but rather with elements that Western society has traditionally linked to women. It is surprising to note, therefore, that all of the characters compared to cats or birds in this novel, unlike in the works that we have already examined and the ones that we have yet to treat, are women. Japanese women in general (Forward, II, XXXIV) and Chrysanthemum in particular (XXVI, XXIX, XXXVI, XLVII) are repeatedly compared to cats and, somewhat less often, to birds (XII, XLVI, XLVIII, XLIV, LII)

In the last analysis, however, there is not much to say about *Madame Chrysanthemum* from the point of view of a gay reading. It offers nothing new, confirming what we already know from previous volumes about Loti and his interests. As already remarked, the novel's racism makes it difficult reading today, especially for anyone who has dealt with prejudice of any sort. One thing that does make it of at least historical interest for those intrigued by gay literature, however, is the introduction of a considerable element of sexual ambiguity in the male protagonist of what has become the Madame Butterfly legend. David Henry Hwang's *M. Butterfly*, which won the Tony Award for Best Play in 1988, draws heavily on Puccini's completely heterosexual contribution to that legend, but reintroduces this element as well. Song Liling, the Chinese spy disguised as a singer, whom Rene Gallimard for twenty years takes to be a woman and with whom he has an affair, is homosexual; Comrade Chin roundly condemns him for that (II, x). Though Gallimard spends the entire play contending that he never knew that his 'mistress' was actually a man, his sexuality is open to question, not simply for the obvious reason – how could he not have known that Song Liling was a man? – but also because, in a scene with his friend Marc early in the play (I, iv), Hwang shows him to be uninterested in meeting women.

French film director Frédéric Mitterand is likely to have been familiar with *Madame Chrysanthemum*. His 1996 screen adaptation of the opera suggests that he may have been trying to reintroduce the novel's homosexual element in the legend as well. Most of his movie is a faithful adaptation of Puccini's work, but in the first act Mitterand added something that has no equivalent in either the Illica-Giacosa libretto or its American predecessors. For much of that act, Pierre Loti's operatic equivalent, Capt. B.F. Pinkerton, is accompanied by a black sailor who seems to act as his orderly, but who is remarkably intimate physically with his superior officer, constantly touching him and patting him on the back. In one scene that will recall 'Blossoms of Boredom' to readers of Viaud, this sailor exchanges articles of clothing with Butterfly's two male servants. Later, when he helps Pinkerton off with his jacket, he seems to look quite purposefully at the captain's torso. This is not much to go on, but the scenes with the black seaman leave the viewer wondering if Mitterand intended to suggest that the captain's sexuality was not as unquestionably hetero as Puccini's opera makes it out to be.

CHAPTER EIGHT

A Proustian Probing into Childhood and the Beginnings of Sexuality: *The Story of a Child*

Viaud's seventh novel, *The Story of a Child* (1890), has received little attention from literary critics, probably because it has been regarded as autobiography rather than a novel. Clive Wake, in *The Novels of Pierre Loti*, which devotes a chapter to each of Viaud's novels, wrote no chapter on it. Claude Martin, a major contemporary Viaud scholar, did not include it in his list of the author's novels.[1] Yet Viaud did entitle the work *Le roman d'un enfant,* which can mean *The Story of a Child, A Novel About a Child,* or both, since *roman* is used in French to mean someone's interesting life story as well as 'novel,' a fictional narrative. As we will see, *The Story of a Child* is not just a chronological report of autobiographical events, but rather a structured and cohesive reworking of the author's biography very much in line with most of his previous novels.[2] Furthermore, Viaud makes it clear that he is not simply recounting his own childhood here: on more than one occasion he gives the name of the character whose early life the narrative depicts as 'Pierre' (III, XX, etc.).[3] One can argue, therefore, that *The Story of a Child* is as much a novel as any number of other autobiographically based works that are regularly regarded as novels, like Proust's *In Search of Lost Time.*[4] Again, however, Viaud is clearly calling attention to the links between his protagonist and himself.

The comparison between these two works is not arbitrary. As we noted in the Introduction, Proust was an avid reader of Viaud's works and seems to have been particularly fond of *The Story of a Child*. He recommended it to his mother when it first appeared, and she quoted it at length in their correspondence.[5] Like the first volume of the *Search,* Viaud's novel is an attempt to recapture a young boy's reactions to the events of his childhood.[6] In fact, the similarities between the two works are too numerous to be fortuitous. The following reading of Viaud's narrative will evoke them because Proust's novel provides a singularly appropriate guide to and commentary on *The Story of a Child*, making more readily accessible what Bruno Vercier has called 'this book so simple in appearance but consisting of an infinitely complex tissue.'[7]

Viaud presents his seventh novel as having been suggested by Queen Elisabeth of Romania, to whom he dedicates it: 'The queen from whom I got the idea to write it.' His immediately previous writings show that he himself had been becoming progressively more preoccupied with his childhood for some time, however.[8] If the Romanian sovereign, a good friend of Viaud's, suggested a novel based on his childhood recollections, it is not difficult to imagine that the author must have been demonstrating this preoccupation in his conversation as well. Furthermore, Viaud had come to something of an impasse. Having married Blanche de Ferrière in 1886, he could no longer write about his latest romantic adventure. (*Madame Chrysanthemum*, though published in 1887, had been based on his sojourn in Japan in 1885.) Since, as he himself admitted, he had no imagination to come up with material that he had not experienced himself,[9] and since he had already mined all the major romantic episodes of his adult life in his previous works, his last untouched reserve of material was his childhood. It may also be worth noting that in *The Awakened*, Viaud's last novel, published sixteen years later, the female protagonist, Djénane, who, as we shall see, has much in common with both the Pierre of *The Story of a Child* and Viaud, writes at one point: 'When my soul ... suffers too much, the memories of my childhood return to haunt me' (III).

And yet, though Viaud talked a great deal about his childhood in *The Story of a Child*, he was evidently conflicted about how much of it to share. Throughout the novel, the narrator repeatedly assures his readers of its self-revelatory nature. 'This book [is], furthermore, the most intimate one that I have ever written' (V), he proclaims early on. Later, having recounted the story of the sunbeam he used to see when returning from church, he concludes: 'This whole chapter, which is almost unintelligible, has no other excuse than that it was written with a great effort at sincerity, at being absolutely true' (VI). Still later, having described the effort he made to keep his childhood diary secret, he comments: 'My God, I've changed a great deal since that era ... I've come to the point of singing about my sorrow and shouting it to whoever might be passing by' (LVIII). Yet, while he may be 'absolutely true' – since 'he' is Pierre and not Julien Viaud, he can be true about his own life without being true about the author's – the narrator also admits repeatedly that he is not being absolutely complete. Recalling his early formal education, for example, he hints at what he might say 'if I dared to be completely sincere' (XXI). He continues the just quoted passage, 'My God, I've changed ...' with the remark: 'And, who knows? As I get older, I may come to write even more intimate things that, at present, no one could drag out of me' (LVIII).[10]

Thus, the narrator makes it clear that he is not presenting a complete retelling of his early years. Just as Marcel, the narrator of Proust's *In Search of Lost Time*, repeatedly stresses that he is trying to recapture not the 'little things' that constituted his daily life but rather 'that reality [that] has its hidden existence ... *beneath* the surface of the little things,' a reality that he defines as 'what we have really experienced' (*Time Regained* 297–8), so the narrator of *The Story of a Child* repeatedly stresses that he is attempting to provide not a log of his youth, but rather a recollection of what he felt about certain events. Early in the narrative, recollecting the days he spent at Limoise, he speaks of 'the *impression* ... that I am going to attempt to convey: the impression of summer, of bright sunlight, of nature, and of a delicious terror upon finding myself alone in the middle of tall June grass that rose above my forehead' (III; emphasis added); he begins the next chapter by explaining that 'I would like to try to express now the *impression* that the sea made on me, at the time of our first meeting' (IV; emphasis added); etc.[11] When Marcel concluded the *Search* by asking if 'the re-creation by the memory of *impressions* ... was not ... one of the conditions, almost the very essence of the work of art as I had just now in the library conceived it' (*Time Regained* 525; emphasis added), one might wonder which narrator is speaking.

To make the distinction clear between what he is creating and the standard chronologically structured, event-focused autobiography, the narrator of *The Story of a Child* announces on the first page: 'Therefore I would rather not write a history [of my life], which would be fastidious; but only *note*, without connection or transitions, moments that *struck* me in a strange manner – that *struck* me in such a way that I still remember them with complete sharpness' (I; emphasis added).[12] This 'strange manner' is clarified later by means of the linking word 'struck' when Pierre, remembering an episode in which his mother came to get him after school, remarks: 'Mingled with my regret is a sort of undefinable anxiety, which, for that matter, occurs every time that I find myself in the presence of things that *struck* and charmed me with their *mysterious underside*, with an intensity that I cannot explain to myself' (LXI; emphasis added).[13] As this passage makes clear, it is these moments' link to a 'mysterious underside' – what Freud, just a few years later, would name the subconscious – that fixed them in Pierre's memory.[14] If it is these moments that he is going to recall, it is not surprising that Pierre will be intent on exploring the 'mysterious underside' that is attached to them and that gives them their intensity and permanence in his memory.[15]

As Viaud suggests elsewhere, writing down notes 'without connection or transitions' will, itself, facilitate his access to this 'mysterious underside.' Early in the novel Pierre recounts how, at the age of five or six, he made two drawings, the Happy Duck and the Unhappy Duck. Like most children's art they were basically sketches, but it is this very incompleteness that gives them, for Loti, great value:

> I have often noticed, for that matter, that rudimentary scribblings drawn by a child ... can make much more of an *impression* than skilful or inspired paintings, precisely because they are incomplete and we are led, in looking at them, to add thousands of things of our own, thousands of things arising from our *unfathomed inner depths*. (IX; emphasis added)

Since Pierre had just linked painting and writing at the beginning of the previous chapter, speaking in one phrase of those 'gifted in painting [with colours or with words]' (VIII), the applicability of this aesthetics to the novel seems clear. If *The Story of a Child* is presented as being casual 'notes' 'without connection or transitions,' it is because Viaud felt that such a lack of completeness would cause him, upon rereading it, to be forced to call up things from his 'unfathomed inner depths,' and thereby enter into contact with his 'mysterious underside.'[16] In this respect, Viaud was suggesting that the creation of this novel would constitute a means to self-analysis. One should also note that this aesthetic metaphorizes the coming out process, during which a gay individual delves into him or herself in order to understand the parts of his or her life that do not seem to connect and, in doing so, confronts his or her entire self for the first time. At the same time, of course, Viaud's literary technique would cause his readers to experience similar self-discovery.

Proust's narrator saw the same function for his magnum opus and said so more directly:

> The writer's work is merely a kind of optical instrument which he offers to the reader to enable him to discern what, without this book, he would perhaps never have perceived in himself. (*Time Regained* 322)

'My' readers ... would not be 'my' readers but the readers of their own selves, my book being merely a sort of magnifying glass like those which the optician at Combray used to offer his customers – it would be my book, but with its help I would furnish them with the means of reading what lay inside themselves. (Ibid., 508)

Though Pierre's description of the effects of his work evokes the surrealists who would follow Proust with their attempts to cause things to rise up from their audience's subconscious by jolting the mind, he shares with the author of the *Search* the conviction that the function of literature is to enable the reader to come to know him or herself.

One difference from Proust is important to note, however. Whereas Marcel complained that his attempts to 'rediscover days that were long past, the Time that was Lost ... had always defeated the efforts of my [voluntary] memory and my intellect,' producing only 'untrue recollections' (*Time Regained* 263), Pierre has no problems using voluntary memory to recapture past impressions. Recalling his first recollection of his beloved mother, for example, he exclaims: 'I rediscover *everything* ... Her face on that morning ... is still *absolutely present* to my eyes' (V; emphasis added). Of his drawing of the Unhappy Duck, he writes shortly afterward: 'Today, after so many years, I still see it as it looked to me then' (IX). For Marcel, who had no such faith in his own voluntary memory,

the chain of all those inaccurate expressions [preserved by voluntary memory] in which there survives nothing of what we have really experienced comes to constitute for us our thought, our life, our 'reality,' and this lie is all that can be reproduced by the art that styles itself 'true to life,' an art that is as simple as life, without beauty, a mere vain and tedious duplication of what our eyes see and our intellect records, so vain and so tedious that one wonders where the writer who devotes himself to it can have found the joyous and impulsive spark that was capable of setting him in motion and making him advance in his task. (*Time Regained* 298)[17]

This is why Marcel becomes so ecstatic when he discovers and understands the nature of involuntary memory: it allows him to recapture his past impressions in all their original power (*Time Regained* 506).[18]

Pierre does not undertake this exploration of the inner depths of the self lightly, by any means. Twelve years later, another sailor-turned-novelist, Joseph Conrad, had Kurtz speak of 'the horror!' that he experienced during his own self-discovery in *Heart of Darkness*. Pierre begins

The Story of a Child by confessing that 'it is with a sort of fear that I approach the mystery of my impressions of the beginning of life ... I feel something like a religious hesitation about fathoming this abyss' (I). The religious/moral language seems to suggest that Pierre suspects he will find something of which neither religion nor morality will approve. It also evokes and suggests acceptance of the values of the general reading public, making Pierre one of them and thereby drawing them into this effort at self-discovery, much as Plumkett had done at the opening of *Aziyadé* when speaking of Loti.

Pierre's hesitation may indicate that Viaud, if not Pierre, had a good idea by 1890 of what he would find in 'this abyss.' Again, the episode of the Unhappy Duck early in the narrative is significant here. Describing the 'impression' that it made on him, Pierre remarks: 'Then that little drawing ... suddenly took on a terrifying depth for me ... I was frightened by my work, finding in it things that I certainly had not put in it and that, furthermore, must have been barely familiar to me' (IX). Though a five-year-old could already have an awareness of being different, of lacking expected qualities, without being aware of what was involved, it is tempting to read this episode as a metaphor for the adult Pierre's, and Viaud's, discovery in his previous writings of 'terrifying' truths about himself of which Pierre, at any rate, claims to have been unaware before. Since they had already come to the surface in his/their previous works, it was perhaps time to confront this 'depth' directly, especially now, when an excuse for doing so was being provided by a queen.[19]

But what could there be in his subconscious, this 'mysterious underside' about which he speaks so often throughout *The Story of a Child*, that fills at least Pierre with such fear? Since 'subconscious' had yet to be defined by Freud, rather than risk imposing an anachronistic understanding on what Pierre is so intent upon discussing, we need first to see what the text itself has to say about this variously-named 'depth.'

For him, as it will soon be for Freud, the 'mysterious underside' of which Pierre speaks is that part of the psyche outside conscious thought. In the book's second chapter, recounting how, at age two, he learned to jump, the narrator recalls:

> While I was jumping, I *thought*, in an intense fashion that certainly was not customary for me. At the same time as my little legs, my mind had woken up; a somewhat brighter light had just flashed in my head, where the dawn of ideas was still so pale. And this fleeting moment of my life probably owes

its *unfathomable underside* to this interior awakening, and especially the persistence with which it has remained in my memory, ineffaceably etched. (II; emphasis added)

The text states that the 'unfathomable underside' results from the awakening of conscious thought: once part of Pierre's psyche experiences this awakening, what is left becomes distinct, different, beyond, and inaccessible to the thought that constitutes and enlightens the first part. At the same time, however, this 'unfathomable underside' remains linked to Pierre's 'impression' of the event and is what engraves it in the author's memory.

Since this 'unfathomable underside' is beyond thought, it is not surprising that it is also beyond the bounds of language. Throughout the novel, Pierre laments that he cannot put this something into words. For example, the extended passage quoted in the previous paragraph continues: 'But I will exhaust myself in vain looking for words to tell all that, the *blurred depth* of which escapes me' (II; emphasis added). He continues the passage about his first memories of Limoise cited earlier with the declaration: 'But here the *underside* is still more complicated ... I feel that I am going to become lost in it, without managing to express anything' (III; emphasis added). Shortly thereafter, having recounted his first recollection of his mother, he explains that, while writing this novel, he always keeps in mind Queen Elisabeth, 'with the assurance of being understood [by her] all the way, and even beyond that, in this *deep underside* that words do not express' (V; emphasis added). Speaking of his drawings of the two ducks, Pierre remarks, at least partly metaphorically, that

> rudimentary scribblings drawn by a child ... can make much more of an impression than skilful or inspired paintings, precisely because they are incomplete and we are led, in looking at them, to add thousands of things of our own, a thousand things arising from our *unfathomed inner depths* that no paintbrush could capture. (IX; emphasis added; remember the previous linking of those who paint with colours and those who paint with words [VIII])

Much later, in a passage to which we will devote attention later, Pierre, recalling a summer spent in the Midi, notes that 'other inexpressible feelings also came to me, also arising from the same *unfathomable underside*' (LVI; emphasis added). Remember also the narrator's remark in

Iceland Fisherman about the inadequacy of standard language to describe Yann's feelings for Sylvestre (III:IX).

Proust also recognized the difficulty of recovering the object of such a search. It was not sufficient, he had Marcel explain, simply to react to things. One must then undertake 'a laborious and inward-directed study' to discover what feelings are behind one's reaction (*Time Regained* 293). He did not seem to suggest, however, that once this 'inward-directed study' was carried out, there would be any difficulty in finding language to write up the results. At the end of 'Combray,' for example, the narrator is able to put his feelings upon looking at the Martinville church steeples into words. Here Pierre differs greatly from his successor.

Because this 'unfathomable underside' was beyond thought and language, it is not surprising that Pierre finds it very difficult to understand. At one point he admits that 'this book could just as well have borne the (dangerous, I realize) title: "Diary of My Great *Unexplained* Sadnesses"' (XXXVII; emphasis added).[20] The novel is full of examples of his failure to understand the 'depth' within him. Near the end of his first memory of his mother he remarks: 'I do not fully understand why this appearance of my mother at my little sick bed, that morning, struck me so [again, the verb 'struck'], since she was with me constantly. There is, again, a very *mysterious underside* there' (V; emphasis added). When recalling his previous summer in the Midi, which, as already noted, had meant that 'other inexpressible feelings also came to me, also arising from the same *unfathomable underside*,' 'this linking of the butterfly, the song and Bories [items to which we shall return, all connected to his sojourn in the Midi] continued for a long time to cause me sadness that everything I have tried to say does not sufficiently explain' (LVI; emphasis added). Similarly, in the already noted episode of his mother coming to meet him after school, he mentions that 'mingled with my regret is a sort of undefinable anxiety, which, for that matter, happens every time that I find myself in the presence of things that struck and charmed me with their *mysterious underside*, with an intensity that I cannot explain to myself' (LXI; emphasis added).[21]

This 'mysterious underside' is not always beyond understanding, however. When he viewed his paternal grandmother's body at the time of her death, Pierre's first experience with mortality, 'there then passed through me one of these sad little glimmers of lightening, which sometimes cross children's minds, as if to allow them to examine, with a quick glance, *abysses* they have glimpsed' (XVII; emphasis added). More significant, especially for those who know their Proust, is the passage near the end of the novel where Pierre explains that

> my awakenings ... have, today, become the moment of *terrifying* lucidity when I see, so to speak, *the underside of life* freed from all these still entertaining mirages that, during the day, return to hide them from me. (LXVIII; emphasis added)

Readers of Proust will recall the initial scene of the *Search*, in which Marcel explains how, when he first awakens, especially in a strange bed, he has a momentary struggle to impose upon his unfamiliar surroundings a familiarity that will comfort him – but, as he spends the next several thousand pages learning, one that also hides from him the reality of things, especially past events (*Swann's Way* 8–12). For Pierre, however, these moments of wakening are more like Proust's madeleine and other epiphanies: they are the moments when 'all these mirages' are caught off guard and he is finally able to see and presumably understand 'the underside of life.'[22]

The obvious question by now is what is in this 'underside' that so frightens Pierre? Since he makes a mystery of it, constructing the novel to withhold the answer until the last page, we may be forgiven if we build up to an explanation as well.

To begin with, the narrator suggests several times that some of the contents of his 'underside' may be inherited. Speaking of his strange reactions to a sunbeam, first in his home in Rochefort and later while in Istanbul, Pierre writes: 'Evidently, in the *underside* of all that there must be, if not recollections of personal pre-existences, at least incoherent reflections of the thoughts of ancestors, all things that I am incapable of freeing any further from their darkness and their dust' (VI; emphasis added). Commenting on his 'impression' of Limoise somewhat earlier, he had noted: 'Here the *underside* is still more complicated, more mixed with things that date from before my present existence' (III; emphasis added). Hereditary transmission of certain traits is something that had been on Viaud's mind for several years, it would appear. As we saw, he had used heredity to explain Yves's alcoholism in *My Brother Yves* (LXIV, LXXIX), and in *Iceland Fisherman* he had remarked that the little parrots the sailors bought in Singapore 'had inherited that colour unconsciously' (III:IV).

Whatever this 'underside' contains it is also something sufficiently out of the ordinary to frighten Pierre. In his already cited description of his reaction to his drawing of the Unhappy Duck, he explains:

> The thin paper, a page ripped from some book, had printing on the back, and the letters, the lines showed through in grayish stains that quickly produced in my eyes the impression of the clouds in the sky; then that little drawing, more shapeless than a school boy's scrawl on a class wall, was completed in a strange fashion by those stains from the underside, and suddenly took on a *terrifying* depth for me ... I was frightened by my work ... (IX; emphasis added)

Given his already quoted description of the effects of incomplete artworks on an audience and their subconscious, it is hard not to see the description of the drawing, 'more *shapeless* than a school boy's scrawl on a class wall,' as a hint that the 'stains from the underside' that complete the sketch should be read as a metaphor for the 'thousand things arising from our unfathomed inner depths' that a reader 'is led ... to ... add' to 'incomplete ... rudimentary scribblings,' especially since the 'stains' have their origin on the underside of a piece of paper, the usual material for writing. If one reads the passage in this way, the text says that Pierre found the elements of his subconscious with which he was completing the incomplete drawing – or, metaphorically, his more directly autobiographical adult works, which, since *Aziyadé*, he had described as being only very loosely constructed (*Aziyadé*, Preface) – to give his creations 'a terrifying depth,' such that 'I was frightened by my work.'[23] This 'depth' is frightening because it involves something in which Pierre fears that he might lose himself. Later in the novel he explains that he suffered an 'anxiety at not understanding, at always feeling himself lose his footing in the same *unfathomable underside*' (XXXVII; emphasis added).

This last fear suggests that the 'underside' in question has something to do with sexuality. In the dedication he assures the queen that 'I will stop my story early on, so that love appears in it only in the state of a vague dream,' but he is presenting 'the unfathomable underside' in the imprecise and metaphoric language of dreams.[24] As we saw in examining *Iceland Fisherman*, Viaud had already spoken four years before about 'that uncertain language that is sometimes spoken in dreams, and of which, on waking, you retain only enigmatic fragments no longer having any meaning' (III:IX), a language that would have been needed to describe Yann's thoughts of Sylvestre.

There are also a few passages in the novel that follows that can be read as hints, albeit ambiguous ones, at Pierre's sexual interests.

As a teenager, he explains, he once coloured in the drawings of Tahitians in a book that his older brother Gustave had given him. (Note that Pierre's brother is now Gustave, like Viaud's, and not George, as he had been in *The Marriage of Loti*.) This leads him to remark: 'My feeling about beauty has changed a lot since that time, and I would have been very surprised then if I had learned what sorts of faces I would come to find charming in the unforeseen continuation of my life ... [Adults'] ways of valuing things vary according to the formation of their mind and above all according to their senses' (XXVI). How different would the faces be that his senses would one day cause him to find attractive? Different just in colour, or also in sex?

At the age of twelve, he recalls, on the way to Limoise, he dutifully wound a white scarf around his neck to protect himself from dampness because he had promised his mother to do so, even though, since he had to pass a group of masculine 'boatmen tanned by the sea,' this made him feel an unspeakable shame (XLI).[25] Similarly, and again to keep his word to his mother, one sunny day while walking though les Chaumes he used a parasol, though it subjected him to ridicule from four schoolboys. These two recollections lead him to remark that 'in the years to follow, I had to go about my business many times without reacting to insults hurled by poor people ignorant of the causes' (XLI). What later in his life would cause others, particularly men, to hurl insults at him? Would those episodes also involve doing things that were not traditionally seen as masculine?

At nine, when he has no male playmates Pierre addresses his little female friend Lucette as Luçon, 'a *masculine singular proper noun* [name] that I had given her' (XXVIII). Does this indicate that even at that age Pierre felt a desire to be with other males? Several things in the novel would seem to suggest so.

First, there is his way of talking about the sea. Viaud had already made a connection between water and sex in at least two of his previous works. In chapter XXIX of *My Brother Yves*, as already mentioned, Pierre Loti had dreamed about Yves, the sailor with whom he was falling in love and whom he would subsequently lose to a woman, falling into 'something black that must have been deep water' (XXIX). *Iceland Fisherman* had ended with the actual drowning of Yann, who had shortly before married Gaud Mével. In *The Story of a Child*, Pierre's way of talking about the sea repeatedly suggests a link not only with sex, but also with his 'mysterious underside.' In recollecting his first encounter with the sea, Pierre speaks of its 'great expanses, green and *deep*' (IV; emphasis added).[26] 'It seemed unstable, treacherous, engulfing,' he also remarks, three adjectives that could suggest sexual desire or a sexual relationship. In the next chapter he links 'unstable' with romantic love, saying that 'my love for my mother ... was the only *stable* one among the loves in my life' (V; emphasis added). When, on the same page from which the first two quotations are taken, he remarks that 'I had the unflagging foreboding that [the sea] would end up one day taking me, despite all my hesitations, despite all the will power that tried to hold me back' (IV), it is difficult not to interpret the sea as a metaphor for some sort of dangerous sexual desire. This also ties the sea to the 'mysterious underside,' since, as noted, Pierre remarks elsewhere on his 'anxiety ... at feeling himself constantly lose his footing in the same unfathomable underside' (XXXVII). By association, these passages suggest that some dangerous sexual desire figures in his 'mysterious underside.'

Another remark on that same page is striking in this context: 'Had I already seen the sea, that I was able to *recognize* it in this way? ... Had it been looked at by my sea-going ancestors so often, that I was born with a confused reflection of its immensity already in my mind?' (IV). Given the narrator's previously cited preoccupation with the hereditary nature of certain character traits and his conviction that he may have inherited at least part of his 'mysterious underside,' it is tempting to suggest that here Pierre is hinting that his recognition of the sort of desire represented by the sea, itself linked to that subconscious 'depth,' is something that he may have inherited, in particular from male ancestors who had chosen to live apart from women in close quarters with other men.

More striking still is his remark on that same page: 'What I felt in [the sea's] presence was not only fear, but above all a sadness without name, an impression of *sorrowful loneliness, abandonment, exile*' (IV; emphasis added). Whatever the desire symbolized by the sea, he had the impression that it would leave him alone, abandoned (by whom?), exiled (from what?). The sea represents a desire whose fulfilment would require him to go outside the bounds of convention.

The only clear instance of gender inversion in the novel is related to these three emotions. At one point, Pierre recalls how his father, during an evening Bible session typical of Protestant families of the era, read the story of the foolish virgins (Matthew 25.1–13), in which several virgins arrive late to a wedding at which Jesus is present and are left outside in the darkness. Pierre, identifying with the virgins, is horrified at the thought of being shut out of paradise by God for unspecified sins (XIII). (As we shall see shortly, from the opening of the novel darkness is presented as something that both fascinates and terrifies Pierre, and is linked to homosexual desire.) This feeling of guilt leads the young Pierre to consider becoming a minister when he grows up, but that idea goes by the boards when he realizes that it would keep him from visiting unknown distant lands (XIV). For a while he considers a compromise: he could become a Protestant missionary and so get to visit 'unknown shores' while still working for God (XXXIII), but this idea disappears as well.

What little mystery may remain about the 'mysterious underside' is further diminished by the fascination that Pierre reports having had from his adolescence with sailors. At carnival, 'closed' in his room, he is intrigued by the sounds coming from outside of 'the sailors [who] were running, jumping, singing at the top of their lungs, with two-penny masks on their faces' (XXXII). 'They *troubled* me in a very strange manner, these people in the street!' The verb 'troubled' suggests that there was something more, something darker than just curiosity at issue here.[27]

In a chapter several pages before, the narrator recalls an ambulatory cake-seller who, after having left Pierre's house, would always move off toward 'the same low streets bordering on the port and the ramparts' of Rochefort (XXIII). 'The path of this merchant was invariable,' he explains, 'and I followed her in my thoughts with a *singular interest*,' because 'I had a sort of *uneasy* curiosity about these low neighbourhoods, toward which the merchant went so bravely' (emphasis added). 'What could be going on down there? What was that *brutal* gaiety that was expressed with *shouts*? What did they do to have fun, those people who had returned from the sea and the distant lands where the sun burns? What *harsher*, simpler, and *freer* life did they have?' (emphasis added).[28] Why did these sailors so fascinate and yet trouble the adolescent Pierre? What did their 'freer life' allow them to do that so concerned him?

Whatever the reason, whatever the quality they possessed, it was sufficiently attractive to Pierre that he wanted to join them. His way of expressing this is particularly striking, however: 'Already the seed of a *trouble*, an aspiration toward something *other* and *unknown* was planted in my little head' (emphasis added). Whatever they had to offer, it caused the adolescent Pierre to be troubled; whatever it was, it was something different, something *other* than what he knew already, something that remained to him, at that point at least, *unknown*.

The last line of the chapter only increases the suggestiveness of what has come before:

> A sort of *unspecific* and dull *desire* took hold of me, even – a *latent* one, if I dare to use that word – to run outside, myself, to the entertaining escapade, in the brisk air of the winter nights, or in the bright sun of exotic ports, and, like them, to sing the simple joy of living at the top of my voice. (emphasis added)

The sound of the sailors awakens 'desire' in him, though one that he did not yet, at least, fully understand ('unspecific'), like the contents of the 'mysterious underside.' As with his attraction to whatever desire the sea represents, as with that 'mysterious underside' inside him, this desire already seems to have been part of him ('latent'), as if inherited, before he became conscious of it.

Despite all this mystery, Pierre is clear about liking one quality with which he credits sailors. Talking about the groups of friends that he has formed in his life, he remarks: 'I preferred to constitute them in this fashion, with simpler beings, who did not examine my fantasies and never smiled at my childlike actions' (XLIII). Sailors, he explains subsequently, are just such people: 'Sailors, easy to get along with acquaintances ... generally turn out to be indulgent with regard to childlike actions – and for good reason' (LXIII). Read in the context of Viaud's earlier works, these lines become very suggestive. In *My Brother Yves*, as we saw, Viaud, and Loti, had presented sailors as non-judgmental and tolerant of sexual irregularities (XXVI). In *Iceland Fisherman*, Yann has feelings for Sylvestre that cannot be put into standard language (III:IX) and, when together, they are repeatedly depicted as behaving like children (I:I, I:VI). This could be read as an indication that 'childlike behaviour' may have been code for involvement between men. Reading *The Story of a Child* in the context of those two preceding works, we see that Pierre may have been drawn to sailors because he saw their world as one in which such involvement, 'childlike actions,' was tolerated, not subject to the 'insults' that others hurled at him during the course of his adult life. The maturation process for non-heterosexual individuals has often been delayed compared to societally accepted standards of progress because of their initial lack of self-awareness, role models, social identity, etc. Thus childlike behaviour would have been a particularly apt term to code homosexuality.[29]

As must be obvious by now, one element of the 'mysterious underside' that Pierre recognizes within himself and that frightens him, that had been surfacing in his earlier works, that may have been inherited, that calls to him like a great, engulfing, unstable sea that he fears will pull him under one day despite all his efforts to resist it, an element that could subject him to solitude, to being abandoned by others, that is different and unknown, at least at some point, at least to some extent, an element that troubles him and yet fills him with an indefinable desire, an element that sailors, accustomed to the ways of men living without women, excused, could be homosexual desire.

If homosexual desire is the aspect of his 'mysterious underside' that bothers him, it is interesting to see how young Pierre deals with it. Often he flees from it, seeking shelter with his mother. What has come before makes his description of her significant in this capacity. For him, she is 'the natural refuge, the shelter against all the terrors of the *unknown,* against all the *dark* sorrows that had no defined cause' (V; emphasis added).[30] So, when he is frightened by the sea (and what it symbolizes), he runs to her 'to console me for a thousand *anticipated, inexpressible anguishes,* that had wrung my heart at the sight of these great, green and *deep* expanses' (IV; emphasis added).[31] When he hears people, including the above-mentioned sailors, carousing in the streets and causing him, again, 'anguish' (XXXII) – 'they *troubled* me in a very strange manner, these people in the street!' – he runs to his mother: '*Feeling myself in distress,* I went downstairs to look for my mother' (emphasis added). In short, the adult Pierre seems to present his young self as seeking refuge from the urgings of gay desire in his mother.[32]

One might wonder to what extent this is emblematic of the whole enterprise of *The Story of a Child.* If his relationship to his mother can be read as a more general representation of his relationship to the protected state of childhood, one might wonder if Viaud's and Pierre's fascination with his youth and his desire to recreate it is, at least in part, an effort to return to an era before the complications of sexual desire.[33] Yet, as we have seen, writing about his childhood was not a way of putting sexual desire on hold for Viaud, since he encounters elements of it even in his recollections of his youth. Rather, *The Story of a Child* seems to have been Viaud's attempt to come to an understanding of the beginnings of his sexuality, perhaps so as to be able to realign or put into congruence the distinct gay identity that would still have been a very new idea in 1890, and that many non-heterosexuals are so long in confronting and constructing even today.

Pierre's – and Viaud's – fascination with his childhood has several facets, however. The narrator repeatedly remarks on the power and intensity of his feelings during his youth – what Marcel, in an already quoted passage, referred to as 'the joyous and impulsive spark' (*Time Regained* 298). When he was young, Pierre notes more than once, 'everything ... throbbed with a more *intense* life' (XXXIV; emphasis added). As a result, Pierre feels that his childhood writing had more power than what he creates as an adult:

> In terms of art and dreams, despite the lack of method, the lack of acquired knowledge, I went much further, and much higher than at present, it's incontestable; and, if that book of scribbles wrapped around a reed [his childhood diary], of which I was speaking just a moment ago, still existed, it would be worth twenty of these pale notes, on which, it seems to me, they have already scattered ashes. (LXII)[34]

Part of his fascination with his childhood, therefore, is an attempt to recapture that lost intensity, which he feels is necessary for literary creation and which he can access with his childhood recollections. In recalling a moment when his mother came to meet him after school, he says, for example: 'Mingled with my regret is a sort of indefinable anxiety, which, for that matter, happens every time that I find myself in the presence of things that struck and charmed me with their *mysterious underside*, with an *intensity* that I cannot explain to myself' (LXI; emphasis added).[35]

Why the adult Pierre has lost this intensity he never clarifies. Is it simply because youth has a power that is lost with age? (As early as *Aziyadé*, Viaud's writings demonstrate a preoccupation with being young.) Is it because acting on sexuality somehow diminishes one's powers, as many artists, including Viaud's much-admired Flaubert, have claimed? Or, on the contrary, is it because, now that one aspect of his self is confined to this 'mysterious underside,' he has lost contact with the creative force that it provided? As we have already seen, Viaud describes this 'mysterious underside' as having the ability to 'etch' (II), to produce writing that makes a long-lasting impression. Whatever the answer, the passages quoted make it clear that, for artistic reasons as well, he was intent upon reconnecting with his childhood.

It bears noting that attraction to other men is not the only thing that the narrator fears. The adolescent Pierre is also afraid of the future (XXIX, XXXIII, LXVIII, LXXIV, etc.) and of getting older.[36] In part, this fear stems from his not believing that his adult life will be any better than his childhood. At one point he speaks of 'the improbable better days of the future' (LVII). He does not look forward to change, either. If he cherishes certain physical things from his youth, it is because 'the persistence of certain things that have always been familiar manages to entice us concerning our own stability, concerning our own duration; seeing them remain the same, it seems to us that we cannot change or cease being' (XIX).[37]

Death in particular seems to terrify Pierre. Early on he speaks of 'the dark mystery of the final disintegration' (IX), and later he explains how, upon waking, he is confronted with 'the speed of the years, the crumbling of everything that I try to clutch with my hands, and the final nothingness, the large gaping hole of death, which is so close, and which nothing hides anymore' (LXVIII). In a continuation of a passage already cited he explains that one of his main reasons for writing is to make himself known to others before he dies: 'I've come to the point of singing about my sorrow and shouting it to whoever might be passing by ... and calling out with more anguish the more I have a foreboding of the *final dust*' (LVIII).

In this as well, Pierre resembles Proust's Marcel. The latter had been freed from 'all anxiety about the future' (*Time Regained* 255) once he discovered the power of involuntary memory to recapture the past: at the beginning of the famous madeleine revelation, Marcel exclaims: 'I had ceased now to feel mediocre, contingent, *mortal*' (*Swann's Way* 60; emphasis added). But Marcel, too, was horrified at the idea that, with the passing of time, he had come to be treated by young men as 'an old gentleman' (*Time Regained* 347).

All this explains, at least in part, the autobiographical nature of much of Viaud's writing. If Pierre talks about himself, and particularly about his past, it is a way of seeming to stop time, to create a stability that is contrary to the change and instability that has characterized his and Viaud's adult life. This has been, or so at least he claims, a preoccupation of his since his youth. If he has kept a diary since adolescence, for example, it is because 'I already had this need to note down, to *fix fleeing images*, to fight against the fragility of things and of myself, which made me pursue this diary in that fashion until the last few years' (LVIII; emphasis added).[38]

Some of Pierre's other remarks about his childhood are of interest from a gay perspective as well. Repeatedly he describes how his family kept him isolated from other boys to protect him from any rough contact (XXXI, XLIX, LXIX). He refers to his teenage self as a 'little creature too attached to home, too entwined by a thousand sweet ties' (LXXV), and in the penultimate chapter, looking forward to the life that would come, he announces: 'I had ... to pay cruelly for having been raised as a little sensitive, isolated creature' (LXXXI).[39] It is not surprising, therefore, that he often refers to his childhood as a form of captivity. Sitting in his enclosed garden reading at the age of nine, he notes that the birds he hears are 'free' (XXXI). In the passage just quoted he speaks about being 'too entwined by a thousand sweet ties' (LXXV), after having just recounted how his mother, upon his older brother's return to the sea, had taken him in her arms and exclaimed: 'Thanks be to God, at least we will keep *you*!' (ibid).

Such images of captivity also recur when he feels the lure of sailors and their life. Having bought some little cakes from the ambulatory merchant who would subsequently go down to the port and who caused Pierre to think of who and what was to be found there, Pierre states: 'I ended up, for a moment of barely appreciable length, feeling weak and captive' (XXIII). When, at Mardi Gras, he hears sailors outside singing in the streets, 'I suffered at being closed up' (XXXII), a feeling he links to the previously cited scene: 'It was, to a much more painful extent, an impression like the one that the song of the old cake merchant made on me, when she moved off in the direction of the low streets and the ramparts, on winter nights' (XXXII). His family's overprotective treatment of him not only deprives him of the strength, both of character and of body, that would enable him to function as he wishes in the adult world, in particular among men; it also cuts him off from any chance to experience actualization of the desire that he feels but did not, he says later, understand.[40]

His conservative Protestant family creates for him a world from which any expression or development of carnal desire seems likely to have been excluded. He terms the home education that they gave him 'austerely religious' (VIII), and characterizes the relatives whom he visited on the nearby Isle of Oléron as behaving with a 'Huguenot austerity' (X). Readers of Proust will recall that Marcel's mother skipped all the love scenes in *François le champi* when she read Sand's novel to her son (*Swann's Way* 56).

So far this chapter has shown how, when examined carefully, *The Story of a Child* constitutes Viaud's examination of the awakening of homosexual desire in his alter ego during childhood. It also suggests how Pierre learned, from an early age, to deal with his homosexual desires in a fashion so vague and ambiguous as to require such a careful reading. When his family finally sends him to school in his early teens and he comes into contact with the world, 'a certain superficial me, to meet the need of social relationships, was already forming like a thin envelop, and was beginning to know how to maintain itself largely on good terms with everyone, while the true, deep me continued to escape them entirely' (LXXV). The example he gives to demonstrate this is telling. When his two schoolmates, André and Paul, start to talk about their love for two female classmates, Pierre confides to them that he has similar feelings for a girl named Jeanne. 'To do as they did ... I tried to persuade myself of my love, but I have to admit that it was a little forced because, on the contrary, between Jeanne and myself the sort of comic little coquetry at the beginning of our relationship simply turned into a good, and true friendship' (LXXV). From early on Pierre had learned to present himself as experiencing a heterosexual desire that was acceptable to and expected by his peers, even though he did not really feel it.

He presents the desire that he did actually experience in a far more ambiguous and enigmatic fashion. 'My first true love,' he continues immediately, '... was for a dream vision' (LXXV). As he explains two short chapters later, on a warm spring night in his fourteenth year, as he listened to the singing of sailors in the distance, he fell asleep and dreamed of meeting a young girl in his family's enclosed garden: 'She was there as if in her own home ... She seemed to find it natural to be there, just as I found it natural for her to be there' (LXXVII). When he approaches, he finds that her eyes

> were the eyes of *someone*; more and more I recalled that already loved look and I *rediscovered* it, with bursts of infinite tenderness. Awakened suddenly with a start, I tried to hold on to her ghost, which fled, which fled, which became more elusive and more unreal ... Was it possible, however, that she was not and had never been anything but a nothing without life? (emphasis added)

Who is this person whom he has already loved and who leaves him with a final impression of fleeing, of becoming ever more unreal? Pierre does not believe it could have been someone who did not actually exist. Who, then, had actually been in Pierre's life, had been at home in his family's garden, had been the object of his love, and had fled?

One candidate would be Pierre's brother, who had left for the sea just shortly before, never to return (LXXIV), whose arrival Pierre had so eagerly awaited, whom he had so desperately wanted to please (LXVIII), and whose room he visits repeatedly after Gustave's departure. Since Pierre had linked this dream at its first mention (LXXV) to his admission that he lied to his schoolmates about the nature of his love, we might see this ghost, 'which fled, which fled, which became more elusive and more unreal,' like Gustave on the ship that had taken him away never to bring him back, as another tale of love altered to be acceptable to the general, heterosexual public. As noted in previous chapters, Viaud, and Loti, had used the word 'brother' in a sexually ambiguous manner in several works when describing relationships between men, and *The Marriage of Loti* had already presented the ambiguous nature of Pierre's love for his brother. One might also recall Pierre's earlier citation of Gustave's regret that Tahiti 'did not have a door that opened somewhere on the courtyard of our house' (XLVI) where Pierre dreams that the ghost appears.[41]

If Pierre and Viaud were so circumspect about discussing homosexual desire, it may not have been simply out of the obvious social and professional need for self-protection. As mentioned in chapter 6 in the discussion of *Iceland Fisherman*, Viaud may have found that, even had he wanted to discuss homosexuality openly in a positive fashion, he did not have the language to do so. Contemporary science had created the terms used to describe gay men, defining them in ways that would not have been acceptable to Viaud.[42] This might also suggest another reason for Viaud's turning to his youth for subject matter. Childhood provided a 'socially pure' context in which to explore the love that dared not speak its name.

Though Viaud is not forthright here in his discussion of homosexuality, he does discuss it, albeit in a manner that does not confront the casual reader. He stimulates thought concerning unfathomable unknowns, such as same-sex attraction, and lays a framework for the acceptance and open exploration of them. One can only wonder who the 'unknown friends' were whom he imagined reading this novel with 'a fine, distant sympathy' (V).[43] In a passage already cited, he says: 'I've come to the point of *singing about my sorrow* and shouting it to whoever might be passing by, in order to draw to me the sympathy of the most distant unknown people' (LVIII). Did he expect 'whoever might be passing by' to understand the nature of his 'sorrow' and feel 'sympathy' for him only in a more general sense, or did he imagine that they, too, might grasp his intent in its entirety?

Perhaps. If *The Story of a Child* deals with any issue, it certainly promotes the idea that art can have a powerful effect on any audience. Very much as in Proust, for Pierre (and, presumably, Viaud) many things are evocative. Shells leave the young boy 'dreaming about the countries from which they had come, imagining foreign shores' (XXVII).[44] Language is particularly evocative. The word 'colonies' has a very strong effect on him:

> Oh! what troubling and magic qualities that simple word, 'the colonies,' had in my childhood, a word which, at that time, designated for me all of the hot countries, with their palm trees, their large flowers, their blacks, their animals, their adventures ... Oh! 'the colonies'! How can I tell everything that tried to awaken in my mind, at the very call of that word! (XIV)

The strange word 'Bianoris,' found in Virgil's ninth eclogue, which recounts the love of two male shepherds for each other, has a particular effect on his imagination:

> The sonority of that word *Bianoris* finishing the sentence, evoked for me, suddenly, with an extraordinary magic, the impression of the music that the insects must have made around the two travellers, in the silence of a very hot noon under a very yellow sun, in the serene tranquillity of an Antique June month. I was no longer in class; I was in that countryside, in the society of those shepherds, walking on slightly burnt little flowers, on slightly browned grass, on a very luminous summer day – but yet one attenuated and seen through a certain vagueness, as if looked at through field-glasses in the depths of past ages ... (LXV)

Proust's Marcel, especially when young, has many similar reactions to exotic names (cf. for example *Swann's Way* 10).

More than objects and just words, however, for Pierre (and Viaud) it is art that has the power of evocation. When, as a child, he is read to about a boy who returns home after having been away several years, he reacts: 'Oh! then I got up, asking that they stop reading, feeling sobs that were coming up inside me ... I had seen, absolutely seen, that lonely garden, that old emptied cradle, and, half hidden under those reddish leaves, that blue pearl' (XII).[45] Two pages before, he had recounted how the playing of a violinist whom his parents had invited to dinner

> was for me like an evocation of dark paths in the woods, of a vast night where you felt abandoned and lost [those same fears]; then I saw very distinctly Gaspard [Pierre's recently lost dog] wandering in the rain, to a sinis-

ter crossing, and, no longer knowing his way, leaving in an unknown direction never to return ... [again, the image of being abandoned by a loved one]. Then my tears came, and since no one noticed them, the violin continued to cast into the silence its sad calls, to which, from the depth of the *abysses from beneath* visions that no longer had any form, any name, any sense replied. (XI; emphasis added; readers of Proust will recall the effect in *In Search* of Vinteuil's music, first on Swann and then on Marcel, but this passage also resembles the description of the effect of the duck drawing.)

Art not only invokes a scene, sometimes even one unknown to or previously unexperienced by the audience; it also calls forth sympathy, and even, in the first example, empathy. Could *The Story of a Child* and Viaud's/Loti's other works do the same with a general audience for gay men, or at least for this one gay man? And if they could do so in an emotional manner, like the examples just cited, rather than through rational, intellectual argument, would they not stand a better chance of not being countered, of succeeding?

The most significant example of the power of evocation, both by objects and by art, involves a butterfly, a song, and an estate. At the age of twelve, while in the south of France during a summer vacation, some young friends give Pierre a rare, dawn-yellow butterfly that, they explain, they found on their estate, Bories.

And when I received it from their hands, we heard, off to one side, my big cousin who was singing, with a voice tapered to the plaintive falsetto of a mountaineer. He sometimes took on that voice, which now caused me to feel *a strange melancholy* in the silence of the last September mid-days ... Beginning with that moment, then, the Bories property, the dawn-coloured butterfly, and the little melancholy refrain of the 'good story' were inseparably linked in my memory ... (XLVIII; emphasis added)

Immediately afterward, Pierre exclaims: 'Really, I'm afraid of speaking too often about these incoherent associations of images that then were so customary for me' and promises: 'This is the last time. I won't come back to it anymore. But you will see how important it was, for what will follow, to make note of that association.' He is right, as we shall see.

After having returned to Rochefort, Pierre one day looks at the butterfly. In the best Proustian manner he promptly hears in his mind

the dragging, drowsy song in a mountaineer falsetto: 'Ah! ah! the good story! ...' Then I saw once again the whitened porch of the Bories property, in the midst of a silence of sun and summer. [Note the order: butterfly, song, Bories.] Then I was seized with an immense nostalgia for the past vacation; sadly I noted the distance it had already retreated into the time gone by and the distance at which the vacation yet to come still remained. (LVI)

The rest of the paragraph is particularly significant:

Then other *inexpressible feelings* came to me as well, also arisen from the same *unfathomable underside,* and completing a very *strange* whole. This linking of the butterfly, the song, and Bories, continued for a long time to make me feel *sadness that everything I have tried to say does not explain sufficiently.* (emphasis added)

What are these 'inexpressible feelings' connected to the butterfly, the song, and Bories? They are 'also arisen from the same *unfathomable underside* ... completing a very strange whole.' Shades of Pierre's reaction to the Unhappy Duck drawing. Why 'very strange'? Why do they cause 'sadness' that Pierre cannot explain? What is the 'very strange whole' that they complete when added to the three elements?

Several years later, having returned to his uncle's home in the Midi, Pierre stands in the garden and, looking over the wall, sees Bories. 'As soon as I looked at it, the plaintive song: "Ah! ah! the good story! ..." came back to me, strangely sung, at the same time that that "yellow-dawn" butterfly, which had been pinned for two years beneath a display window in my little museum, reappeared to me' (LXXX). This time the order is: Bories, song, butterfly.

On the last page of the novel, having returned one final time to his uncle's house, Pierre sees Bories in the distance, then recalls the butterfly, and finally 'I heard inside me a little voice that took up, very sweetly: "Ah! ah! the good story! ..." And the little voice was flute-like and bizarre; above all it was sad, sad enough to make you cry, sad as if to sing, over a tomb, the song of the years that have vanished, the summers that have died' (LXXXII). This final time the order is: Bories, butterfly, song. Since the novel ends on the evocation of the song, it is worth taking a close look at it.[46]

Or its singer. Pierre begins chapter XLVII by telling his readers: 'I had very quickly become attached to my big cousin,' the singer of that song. The nature of this attachment is only made clear later, however, by those things that are associated with him. He is twice described as singing his song with a voice typical of a mountaineer (XLVIII, LVI). Pierre describes the butterfly that is linked to the sound of his voice as 'a sort of gris-gris' (LVI). The little friends who gave it to Pierre are named Peyral (XLIII).[47] These three elements, especially when taken together, will remind the alert reader of Viaud's previous works of *The Story of a Spahi*, in which the main character, the very handsome spahi Jean Peyral, originally from the mountains of the Cévennes region in France (I:I), had gone to Africa, where he became involved with an African mistress who surrounded herself with 'gris-gris' (amulets). Suddenly the 'big cousin,' who does not have a name in *The Story of a Child*, is connected to the attractive Jean Peyral. Suddenly the novel closes on the evocation of an attractive male. Proust's madeleine, tasted in association with tea, began the process of recalling to active memory Marcel's entire youth. The estate at Bories recalls, to close Viaud's novel, memories of a large, attractive man.[48]

There is no commentary here, no 'interpretation,' to use Marcel's words. Does Pierre understand why he is giving his cousin such an important place? Does Viaud? The earlier passage about how the feelings from the unfathomable underside *completed* his association of the three elements (LVI) would seem to suggest that they do.[49] Do they expect their readers to make these connections as well? If so, which readers? Just those 'unknown friends,' or others as well? The fact that, immediately after declaring his intention to enlist in the navy the fourteen-year-old Pierre gazes at Bories in the distance and thinks about the special butterfly and his cousin singing that song (LXXX), now reinforces the possibility of homoerotic motivation for Viaud's desire to enter the navy that we broached in chapter 1.[50]

If art in general, and literature in particular, can be so evocative, it is, as already noted, because of the power of language. In addition to the already-cited examples of the evocative effect that words have on Pierre, one could note that, when he catches scarlet fever at the age of eight, 'that word itself seemed to me to have a diabolical physiognomy' (XVIII); when his uncle speaks to him about the countries in Africa that he had visited, 'I became drunk on the music of those words' (XXVII). Near the end of the novel, it is the evocative power of the words he reads in an old ship's log that causes Pierre to overcome his fear of going to sea (LXXIV).

In order to convey the full power of a subject, however, one must, according to Pierre, use an appropriate, specific language. This is no simple matter. On the first page of the novel, before getting into the narration, Viaud – or is it already Pierre? – wonders aloud: 'Where will I find at present words that are fresh enough, words that are young enough?' – 'fresh' and 'young' because he is about to recount his youth and wants the language he uses to match the subject of his narrative. Shortly thereafter, when he is introducing his mother for the first time, he exclaims: 'And, for the first appearance of that blessed figure in this book of memories, I would like to greet her with different words, if that is possible, with words made for her and such as do not presently exist; words that, all by themselves, would make charitable tears flow, would have a certain consoling and forgiving sweetness' (V).[51] As this last quotation makes clear, he is looking for a language that has the power not only to describe his subject, but to move the reader and to awaken in him or her a 'consoling and forgiving sweetness.'[52]

Given his intended subject matter – the difficult content of his 'mysterious underside' – it is understandable that Pierre might have felt it necessary to create a special language, ambiguous and yet suggestive, simple and yet not simplistic, for this novel.[53] Its ambiguity would offer protection from those who might hurl 'insults,' limiting full comprehension to those mysterious 'unknown friends, who follow me with a fine, distant sympathy' (V), who, working in the context of Viaud's previous writings, would have been prepared to understand his 'mysterious underside.' Its simplicity might be able to awaken such 'sympathy,' and indeed a 'consoling and forgiving sweetness,' not only in those select and predisposed readers, but in a more general public. If the incompleteness of this simplicity called up hitherto unperceived elements of the reader's subconscious, moreover, more than one reader might be moved to such 'sympathy' and 'sweetness' by a discovery of similar traits within himself.[54] Viaud makes no suggestion that his work would 'transform' heterosexuals; one might argue, however, that by causing readers to delve into themselves in order to complete the apparent lacunae in this book, Viaud might have hoped that suppressed gays, often, as Proust would argue, the most vehement homophobes, would develop self-awareness and then empathy for men similar to themselves. If, as I proposed in chapter 5, Plumkett intended to suggest that homosexual desire was natural to all men and only covered over by 'thirty centuries of civilization,' Viaud might even have imagined that *The Story of a Child* could speak to all men on this issue.

And then, finally, as already pointed out, the ambiguous if highly suggestive discourse might also have been the appropriate language for

Viaud, or at least Pierre, who repeatedly claims that, at least in childhood, he usually did not understand his 'mysterious underside.' He
remarks at one point: 'Words, as uncertain and floating as they may be,
still give a *too precise* form to these dream conceptions' (V; emphasis
added).[55] In that sense, it could be said that, because he wanted to convey not the facts of his childhood, but the 'impressions' that they made
on him at the time, impressions that were themselves not precise or
even clear, he had no choice but to be ambiguous. In that sense, the
style of *The Story of a Child*, however frustrating it may be for those who
want to learn facts or those who do not understand why others in other
times were not as open as we can be now, may be the appropriate language to describe the events and feelings depicted, if not their ultimate
meaning.

According to Viaud's aesthetics, the novel is not insufficient, but
rather intentionally incomplete, leaving readers, and especially gay
readers, the opportunity to fill in the gaps with their own thoughts and
experiences, thereby enabling them not only to understand and, presumably, sympathize with the author, but also to do the same for themselves. The gay man who does not find himself augmenting this novel
with experiences from his own past, which he will then have to consider,
will be rare indeed. Viaud has constructed the novel in such a manner,
however, that gay men are not the only readers who will be able to identify with Pierre's feelings of isolation, confusion, and difference.

Still, readers, and especially gay readers, will be troubled by the
'terror' Pierre experiences at glimpsing the content of his 'mysterious
underside.' Did Viaud really share these feelings? Was he only coming
now to an understanding of his feelings? Did their nature not confront
him until he discovered it reading over his own works? Viaud seemed to
have come to a moment of crisis, one that would shape his next works.

CHAPTER NINE

Works of Self-Doubt: *A Phantom from the East* and *Sailor*

On 21 May 1891, at the age of only forty-one, Julien Viaud was elected to the French Academy, a body created in 1635 by Richelieu to oversee the French language and one to which election has ever since been regarded as a signal honour. For the rest of his life, Viaud had the privilege of joining the gatherings in the Mazarin Palace where some of France's most distinguished writers discussed their native tongue and considered ways to keep it pure. Not the least of its appeal to this man who loved exotic outfits was the uniform, the famous Green Suit, which he got to wear at formal Academy functions.

The first two narratives that Viaud published the year after his election are the least obviously homoerotic of his output. It is not clear whether this is chance, or whether the added attention and distinction brought about by Academy membership made him decide to try to change his literary ways. As we saw in chapter 8, Viaud had recently had his alter ego, Pierre, express surprise and terror at what he had found in his own artistic creations. The first of the two works, a novella entitled *A Phantom from the East*, is a pleasant enough piece that seems to have been designed to reshape readers' understanding of *Aziyadé* and that offers some interest to a gay reading. *Sailor,* the weakest of his novels from any perspective, gay or otherwise, contains a few things of note.

A Phantom from the East had its origin in Viaud's second trip to Istanbul, in October 1887. This was a three-day sojourn during which he attempted to learn what had happened to those whom he had encountered there a decade before, the individuals whom he had immortalized and romanticized in *Aziyadé*. As the published version of his diary shows, he had a fairly definite notion of their fates before making the trip. In 1878 he wrote that he was sure that Achmet (Mehmed, in real life) must be dead (*Notes of My Youth* 2 March 1878, 8 March 1878, April 1878) and that Samuel (Daniel) had returned to Greece (2 March 1878), and he gave up on further communication with Aziyadé (Hakidjé) as of that year (8 March 1878). By 1879 one of his diary entries suggests that he wanted to forget about the odalisque (*Private Diary 1878–1881*, 28 May 1879). Thereafter, with the exception of a mention of having his orderly dress as Achmet while he smoked a hookah in the Oriental room of his house in Rochefort (1 June 1881), these individuals fade from his personal journal, and in May 1880 he wrote that he could not recall Turkey anymore. In *A Phantom from the East*, Loti's initial ignorance and the intensity of his desire to learn what had happened to these individuals is therefore a part of the fiction. This demonstrates again that Loti was not Julien Viaud, though often he seems to have been the person who Viaud wanted to be. *Phantom*'s interest, especially for a gay reading, is that it offered Viaud a chance to rewrite or skew *Aziyadé*, a novel he had supposedly published before having any thought of becoming a regular novelist, and which had come to be one of his most popular works. At the beginning of *Phantom* the narrator, who, unlike the Loti of previous narratives, is now a writer and specifically the author of *Aziyadé*, explains that he had published his first novel 'not thinking, for that matter, that I would continue to write, and that people would know later who the anonymous author of *Aziyadé* was' (I). As we have seen, Viaud had already done some rewriting of the *Aziyadé* story in certain of his subsequent works, like *Blossoms of Boredom*, but *Phantom* gave him a chance to reconfigure his first novel in a major way.

In the opening pages of *A Phantom from the East*, as Loti talks about his return to Istanbul, Viaud phrases his anxiety in an ambiguous and open fashion. On the first page, rather than referring specifically to his affair with Aziyadé, the narrator remarks: 'An unforgettable act in the black fairy tale that has been my life must have been played out there as I am so worried by the thought of returning there' (I). 'A charm that I will never free myself from was cast on me by Islam, during the time when I lived on the shore of the Bosphorus, and I was influenced by that charm in a thousand ways.' What suppressed 'unforgettable act' occurred that now subconsciously worried him? What were the 'thousand ways' in which he was influenced by the charm of that culture? We know that Aziyadé is not the only person whose fate he wishes to pursue on his return: he speaks of 'beings who are still living and real' and begins to imagine 'my house as I had left it, with its dear guests from times gone by' (III). The other inhabitants of that house, as readers of *Aziyadé* will recall, were Samuel and later Achmet. What aspects of his first stay in Istanbul are drawing him back?

The ambiguity continues as he talks about his feelings concerning his previous sojourn there. 'To reread it, during this evening while I am waiting, I go to look, with fear, for a book that I published once upon a time, out of a need even then to sing out my sickness, to cry it very loudly to whoever was passing by along the road, and that, since the day that it appeared, I have never dared open again' (I). The last part of this passage repeats almost verbatim a passage in *The Story of a Child* (LVIII) that we saw in chapter 8, suggesting that the 'fear' he experiences in rereading *Aziyadé* is related to the desires that he experienced during his youth and later confronted during his first Middle East trip and recorded in that first novel, desires that he now views as 'sickness.' Not surprisingly, and in a style familiar to readers of *The Story of a Child*, he shortly afterward remarks:

> All of the unexpressed material that was sleeping between the lines, between the powerless and dull words, wakes little by little, comes out of the long night where I had let it vanish. They reappear to me, those unfathomable undersides of my life, of my love from that time, without which, for that matter, there would have been neither profound charm nor intimate anguish in it. From time to time, because of a memory, because of a suffering that this book evokes, I feel that sort of frozen jolt or shiver of the soul that comes from glimpsing the great abysses, from brushing against the great mysteries. Mysteries of pre-existences, or of I don't know what else that cannot be vaguely formulated ... What are these little things, that are barely graspable, barely existing, what are they linked to in the unknown inner depths of the human soul, what inside us do they attach themselves to? (I)

The key terms and phrases from *The Story of a Child* reappear here – unfathomable undersides, pre-existences, inexpressibility – linking Loti's 'anguish' at the thought of returning to Istanbul to Pierre's anguish over his homosexual feelings in the previous novel. To which 'love from that time' was he referring? What 'great glimpsed abysses' that cause him to shake and shiver does *Aziyadé* open up to him? What 'unexpressed material' was 'sleeping between the lines,' like in the drawing of the Unhappy Duck? Is this a reference to his relationship with Samuel (or Achmet), developed, as we saw in chapter 2, largely by implication in that first work? It is interesting that he refers to that first

sojourn as 'the era of transition in my life' (III); in doing so, Loti effaces
the implications of the passage in *Aziyadé* that had spoken of how he had
'tasted a little of all pleasures' (I:XV) at the age of sixteen before ever
leaving Europe, and recalls Jean Peyral's discovery of new sexual experience in the Africa of *The Story of a Spahi*.[1]

With all of this ambiguity regarding what happened ten years before
and how Loti feels about it set forth in the opening pages, the protagonist begins the tale of his second, three-day sojourn in Istanbul. One of
his principal reasons for the excursion was to determine what happened
to Aziyadé, with whom he had lost touch some time after returning to
France. From the start, though he has no proof of it, Loti expresses the
'conviction, both sweet and infinitely sad, that I have of her death' (I; cf.
III). At one point he even writes: 'It's almost sacrilege to say it: at this
moment, I think that I would prefer to be sure of finding only a tomb
there. For her and for me, I would prefer that she had preceded me in
the final dust that neither thinks nor suffers' (I). Why would he prefer
that she have died? So that he does not have to re-engage in the heterosexual affair that she represented? Because, after the subsequent, unsat-
isfying heterosexual relationships that he has had, most notably with
Madame Chrysanthemum, he is convinced that the one woman who
seemed to accept him under any terms could not still be alive? He had
just remarked that 'it does not matter; even if she has become old and is
dying, I still love her' (I), which would suggest that physical attraction
no longer plays a role in his feelings for Aziyadé. Once he learns that
she did die after his departure, he pays a visit to her tomb and can tell
her spirit 'I love you' (IV) with no risk of involvement. Shortly after visiting her final resting place, Loti sets off for the grave of Achmet, who, he
has learned, also passed away during the intervening years. Even while
at Aziyadé's grave, however, he admits that he cannot keep his mind on
her: 'I allow myself to be distracted even here by I don't know what,
maybe by the immensity of the funereal setting, by all this charm of
desolation with which, to my irresponsible eyes, the scene of my visit to
this tomb is surrounded and enlarged' (V).[2]

Before returning to Istanbul, Loti had been haunted by a dream that
he would not have enough time to see Aziyadé.

> But, since I left her, I am constantly pursued in my sleep by this vision,
> always the same: my ship makes an unexpected, quick, furtive stop in Istan-
> bul ... in haste, I disembark, with a fever to reach her, and a thousand
> things prevent me, and my anxiety grows as time passes; then suddenly the

moment of departure arrives, and then, I feel so much anguish at having to leave without seeing her again and without even having rediscovered anything of her lost trail, that I wake up ... (I)

The mentions of 'anguish' and the unpleasant awakening tie this passage to Loti's conflict over gay desire that we have observed in previous works, most particularly *The Story of a Child*, leading the alert reader to wonder if this dream could be understood as the expression of a desire to recapture a comfortable sexual identity (Aziyadé, the woman who was willing to accept Loti on his terms) that has been perpetually thwarted by a thousand obstacles that prevent him from doing so. Is that a heterosexual identity, one that a thousand gay desires since his first sojourn have prevented him from recapturing, or an accepted open sexuality such as he seemed to enjoy in Istanbul and that a thousand things have kept him from realizing since? Since Loti writes later that 'something of myself is buried in the Turkish earth, with Aziyadé' (III), and since, in *My Brother Yves* and *Madame Chrysanthemum*, we have the narration of Loti's subsequent involvement with Yves Kermadec and a failed affair with a woman, it is tempting to suggest that the part of himself that Loti feels he buried with Aziyadé might be the person – and the setting – who could be comfortable with his being involved with both Aziyadé and Samuel. Once the trip to Istanbul is over, Loti closes *A Phantom from the East* by saying that 'this anguish-filled dream that had pursued me for so many years, this dream of a return to Constantinople always held up and never arriving at its goal – this dream has not come back to me since I completed that pilgrimage' (VII). By the end of the work, Loti seems to feel that he has finally dealt with the desire or need to reunite with whatever Aziyadé had come to represent for him.

This is not to suggest that the narrator's second stay in Istanbul is devoted solely to remembrance of heterosexual affairs past, however. As mentioned earlier, Loti announces from the beginning his intention to revisit 'the dear guests' who had once shared his house in Istanbul with him (I). Once he arrives in that city he spends as much time learning about Achmet as about Aziyadé, explaining: 'I am looking for Achmet because I loved him tenderly' (III). When Anaktar-Chiraz leads him to the Armenian's final resting place – he had died in military combat almost a decade before – the narrator exclaims: 'Oh! the poor little one! How painful it is to see the place of his grave' (IV). Unlike in the parallel scene at Aziyadé's grave, there is no mention of Loti being distracted. When Anaktar-Chiraz, an old woman who had known Achmet, asks if she may kiss him, Loti writes: 'Oh! most willingly ... And with all my heart, for Achmet, I return her kiss, on her poor old woman's wrinkled cheek,' just as, during his second, solitary visit to Aziyadé's grave, 'I stretch out softly and kiss this earth, above the place where the dead face must be' (V). Lerner wrote that 'Achmet['s] death seems to cause Loti more grief than that of Aziyadé in the novel,'[3] but that is excessive. Viaud was using parallels again to suggest some sort of equivalence, but the fact that Loti conveys his kiss for Achmet not directly, but through kissing a woman, seems to lessen the homoerotic potential.

Later, finding himself in front of the Mehmed-Fatih mosque 'by chance,' words that, we have seen, are often associated with erotic encounters in Viaud's work, he recalls a passage in his diary describing 'Achmet and myself, in front of its great grey stone portals, stretched out in the sun, without a care in the world, pursuing some dream that cannot be translated into any human language' (IV). It is interesting that Loti should recall this as being a passage in his diary, since the scene is an important one in *Aziyadé* (III:XIX), one that we examined in chapter 2 to show how it paralleled, in a non-homoerotic way, an earlier scene with Samuel and Loti in the countryside (I:XIV). Some of the intervening works make the final phrase more suggestive, however, especially *The Story of a Child* and the passage in *Iceland Fisherman* that recounts Yann's dreams upon learning of Sylvestre's death, again dreams that could not be expressed in language (*Iceland Fisherman* [III:IX]). If Loti remembers Achmet with that scene in particular, eroticized by what Viaud had published since *Aziyadé* and already paralleled with an erotic scene with Samuel in the first novel, are we to see Loti's current memories of Achmet as homoerotic? For that matter, are we to re-examine the way we read *Aziyadé*, at least with regard to the Loti-Achmet relationship?

Or is Viaud skewing this relationship in light of what Loti has learned since his return about Achmet's affection for him? Earlier, at his first meeting with Anaktar-Chiraz, the old woman had told him: 'His last night, [Achmet] called for you all the time: Loti! Loti! Loti!' (III). Shortly after that, the narrator exclaims: 'Oh! but, if these two poor little ones [Aziyadé and Achmet], who loved me so much and whom I am almost confusing with each other now in the same tenderness that no longer has anything earthly about it, were returned to me for an instant, with what unspeakable joy, with what profound, nameless emotion I would take them in my arms.' If he is confusing the two, is it because he has come to see their love for him as similar, or his love for them, or both? Then again, he describes his own feelings for both of them as no longer having 'anything earthly about it.'[4]

Missing, of course, is Samuel. When Loti speaks, in the passage just cited, about 'these two poor little ones, who loved me so much' and more strikingly, later, about 'my two poor little companions in Eyoub' (IV), any reader of *Aziyadé* will be struck by the absence of Samuel. Has Loti no interest in finding out about the 'faithful friend' (*Aziyadé* II:II) with whom he had spent so many intimate moments a decade before, who introduced him to those underworld dens in which 'a strange prostitution' took place (I:XIII)? It would seem not. With *A Phantom from the East*, Viaud wrote Samuel out of his, or at least Loti's past.

Or perhaps he did so only for his general public. While initiating his inquiries into the whereabouts of Aziyadé and Achmet, Loti meets Salomon.

> I employed this Salomon often [during my first sojourn]; he went to make purchases for me with Achmet, and even knew about the clandestine comings and goings of a Muslim woman in my house. At the moment of my departure, I had chased him off, it is true, for I no longer remember what dishonesty; but what difference does that make, as long as he guides me. I was even almost joyous to see him again, like everything that was mixed with my life from before ... I had left him a large, superb man; I found him now all bent over and his hair white. (III)

In the notes for his edition of the French text of *A Phantom from the East*, Claude Martin asserted that this Salomon was the Saketo of *Aziyadé*, in real life a man named Isaac (391 n. 21). All we know about Saketo from *Aziyadé* is that he was a childhood friend of Samuel's who went back and forth between Istanbul and Salonika (II:IX).

More seems to be at stake here, however. To begin with, how many people would Loti have confided in, other than Samuel and Achmet, regarding his affair with Aziyadé? Far more significantly, the mention of chasing Salomon, a Jew (III), at the moment of his departure from Istanbul, will evoke in the mind of any attentive reader of Viaud's works the scene in 'Blossoms of Boredom' where Loti had described his 'real' parting from Samuel. Declaring that the moving scene near the end of *Aziyadé* was a fiction, he had explained, as we saw in chapter 5: 'One day, when I was feeling nasty – I don't know why anymore – I had sent him away' (122). Since Samuel had also been large and strikingly handsome with a beard like a Greek statue (*Aziyadé* I:VII), one begins to wonder if this Salomon is not Saketo but rather Samuel. If he is, why does Loti not say so? Was Viaud now trying to write the honest portrayal of homoerotic desire in *Aziyadé* out of his work, or just the overly emotional Samuel? Note the typically Viaudian modifying phrase immediately after what could be taken as an expression of desire: 'I was even *almost* joyous to see him again, *like everything that was mixed with my life from before*' (III; emphasis added). Did he expect any of his readers to make this connection by association?[5]

Similarly, when recounting his passing 'by chance' in front of the Mehmed-Fatih mosque, Loti notes at the end of the scene:

> Then, I stop in the middle of [the Turks gathered there], in the same square where, ten years ago, we had one evening seen appear on the steps of the mosque a visionary who was raising his eyes and his arms to the heavens, crying: 'I see God, I see the Eternal One!' ... In truth, I don't know why this stop in this square made such an impression, among so many other memories of my pilgrimage; nor why I feel the need to set it here, to keep it from going away too quickly, in the flight of everything. (IV)

When describing this scene in *Aziyadé* (IV:XX), he had remarked on the young mystic's 'admirable mystic head' with a 'handsome, wide forehead.' Now he makes no mention of the elements that may have made the incident stick in his memory. He also mentions here that 'we' saw the visionary, whereas in *Aziyadé* he makes no mention of being with Achmet during the episode.

Several critics have expressed a real fondness for *A Phantom from the East*, generally based on aesthetic criteria,[6] and the work does have beautiful passages. Nevertheless, and especially after *The Story of a Child*, it cannot help but be a disappointment, since it seems like an attempt to refocus *Aziyadé* in a way that denies much of that work's homoerotic interest and daring. The confusion and paralleling of Aziyadé and Achmet are suggestive, but the erasure of Samuel from Loti's recollection of his previous sojourn in the Middle East remains a salient and negative feature of the novella. What aspect of himself has Loti put to rest when he ceases to dream of trying to revisit Aziyadé? Does this imply that he has come to accept his homosexual tendencies and stopped longing to recapture a wholly heterosexual self? Or, as we will see suggested with a similar case in *Sailor*, the other narrative that Viaud published in 1892, has Aziyadé come to represent Loti's entire first Middle East experience with its variety of sexual involvements, and is it his fascination with that variety that ceases to haunt Loti at the novella's end? *A Phantom from the East* remains one of Viaud's most ambiguous, open-ended works, but also one of his most frustrating.

Readers may also experience frustration with *Sailor*, the other narrative that Viaud published in the year after his election to the French Academy. In this case they are unlikely to encounter defence of the work from literary critics, however. Of all the author's novels, *Sailor* is the least admired, both by the general reading public and by Viaud scholars. Claude Gagnière left it out of his recent one-volume collection of the author's novels, and there is almost no criticism devoted to it. While it is not a major work of literature and is the weakest, least developed of Viaud's fictional narratives, it is not totally devoid of interest. Because that interest is not immediately apparent, however, the novel requires some attention.

The traditional view is that Viaud based *Sailor* on events in the life of his new friend, Léo Thémèze, and it is true that some of the episodes in the life of the protagonist parallel Thémèze's biography. Clive Wake declared that the novel is not Thémèze's story, however, but that of the author himself,[7] and it is also true that Jean Berny's life sometimes resembles Viaud's. Viaud evidently identified with the protagonist to some extent. As the published version of his diary shows, the author had repeatedly used the pseudonym Louis Berny when disguising himself as a simple seaman for some of his incognito excursions in Paris (*Private Diary 1878–1881*, 27 August 1878, 22 May 1879). In the novel, as in Viaud's life, the central male character is raised by his mother and an elderly relative. Adverse circumstances force them to sell their beloved house, as the Viauds had done, and the protagonist feels anguish and guilt because of this. There are also differences between Berny and Viaud, however. Viaud repurchased the family home once he became a successful novelist; Berny never does. Viaud passed his exams and entered officer's training for the French navy; Berny fails his and becomes a simple sailor, like Yves Kermadec. *Sailor* turns out to be Viaud's story, like his other novels, but, like them, in a more complex fashion than Wake and other critics have suggested.

It is worth noting that there are also connections between Jean Berny and previous members of the Pierre Loti lineage, in particular the Pierre of *The Story of a Child*. As a young man living at home with his mother and grandfather, Berny dreams of escaping family life and going far away, like young Pierre. During an Easter dinner, his mother 'grew more hopelessly sad when she saw him with his head ceaselessly turned toward that open window, through which the port appeared, with the ships, the tartans, and the blue space of the sea ...' (II; cf. also III, V, XVIII, etc.; Jean thinks back on that dinner throughout the rest of his life). Berny gazing out the window recalls not only young Pierre, but also Gaud in *Iceland Fisherman*. Like Pierre, Jean fantasizes about such foreign lands from his readings in books, and the words describing those countries ignite his imagination (V; cf. also XX), as 'colonies' had for Pierre (XIV). Like Pierre (and Djénane in *The Awakened*, yet to be written), Jean becomes attached to objects from his past as a way of holding on to it (IX, XV, XVIII, XX, etc.). Quite surprisingly, however, the narrator several times ridicules such 'useless baggage' (XVI), the 'poor objects to which we are so childish as to cling' (LIII), and dismisses an attachment to them as 'the most puerile form of human cults' (XXI).

Like the young Pierre, the young Jean also has a garden where he goes to read, and which he recalls in his adulthood (XXV). He also has an affection for the humble and simple (IV, XX, etc.) but, contrary to Pierre, often feels superior to them. Unlike Viaud's other narratives, this novel is often marred by a strong sense of class distinctions and snobbishness on the part of both Berny and his mother. This leads the reader to wonder how much ironic distance one should imagine between the characters and their creator, who just two years before had written of Pierre: 'It took me many years to correct this pride [a feeling of superiority with regard to his fellow students at school], to become once again simply someone like anyone else; especially, to understand that one is not above one's fellows because – to one's own misfortune – one is a prince and magician in the domain of dreams' (*The Story of a Child* L; Jean Berny is repeatedly described as a dreamer).[8] Like young Pierre, when Jean enters the world he develops an exterior persona that allows him to hide his deepest thoughts from others (XXII), but this time there is nothing sexual, much less homosexual, about the ideas that he keeps to himself.

Like the Pierre of *The Story of a Child*, Jean Berny also has feelings that come from a 'mysterious underside' of his being. During his voyage to Asia, the text states that 'Jean had already felt troubled, in the most mysterious undersides of his soul, by a thousand things that his friends had perceived in a much more confused fashion or with much less profundity' (XXXVIII). It is somewhat of a letdown when the text subsequently specifies these things as 'the sands, the mirages on the Red Sea, and, every evening, the terrible apocalyptic splendour of its blood sun,' which is very different from the things that had bothered Pierre's 'undersides' in *The Story of a Child*. Similarly, speaking of Berny's relationship with Madeleine (of which more momentarily), the text remarks: 'His love for her had been more complex, more amalgamated to that great mystery of the human inner depths that we call the soul' (XLVIII). Here, again, 'that great mystery of the human inner depths' is specified with a definition ('the soul'); this had not happened in *The Story of a Child*, where the mystery of Pierre's 'inner depths' had been preserved in all its ambiguity. Interestingly – and this is a point to which we will return shortly – the text later speaks of the 'unknown inner depths' of Jean's mother's soul as well (LIII).

For all of these similarities between Jean and previous members of the Pierre Loti lineage, none of his childhood memories, rarely mentioned inner feelings, or adult life suggests any erotic interest in men. When he makes friends with Morel, the son of a Protestant minister, the only thing that the text says about Jean's attitude toward him is that 'they had immediately charmed each other' (XXVIII), feeble wording even for as ambiguous a writer as Viaud.

On the other hand, Jean is constantly described as chasing women or thinking about doing so (IX, XII, XX, XXVIII, XXX, XXXI, XXXII, XXXIV, etc.). Furthermore, his first romantic adventure reads like an intentionally heterosexual rewriting of *Aziyadé*. Again the location is Greece – Rhodes, this time, rather than Salonika – and again there is an encounter with a young woman, though this one never has a name. From the beginning of the brief episode, the text states repeatedly that she was all that he saw in the East: in her 'the East suddenly was personi-fied for him' (X); 'she incarnated for him the charm and the delicious troubling feelings of this country' (XI); 'this girl personified [the East] in his imagination' (XIII), and so on, as if to make it clear that, unlike the Loti of *Aziyadé*, Berny is attracted only to women while in the Ori-ent.[9] It is *she* who speaks *sabir* here (XI), whereas in Viaud's first novel it had been Samuel. This suggests that there may have been an attempt to conflate Aziyadé and Samuel into one female figure, thus ruling out the possibility of the clandestine existence of another Samuel. When his fel-low sailors take Jean to a local dive one night, the text specifies that the only people he meets there are 'Greek women' (XII), which contrasts with the ambiguous 'strange prostitution' that Loti had encountered in similar dives while wandering the streets of Salonika at night with Samuel (*Aziyadé* I:XIII).

Granted, Berny's other, more extended involvements with women are not very convincing. First, during a voyage around the world, he becomes engaged to a Canadian girl. The text says: 'He allowed himself to be led into this family' (XXV), which does not suggest any real passion on his part. Shortly afterward he loses interest, leaving Canada suddenly without even bothering to notify his never named fiancée. Then, back in Brest, he meets Madeleine, a pale woman whom Viaud never develops to any extent, and begins a quiet courtship, though not without chasing easier conquests late at night (XXVIII). When volunteers are requested for an expedition to the Far East, which could mean a promotion, Jean hesitates only a moment. Besides deciding to go, he also leaves Madeleine without even writing to explain (XXXVII). When, as the result of an illness contracted in the Far East, his health begins to decline,

> the images of women and of love had stopped appearing: for I do not know what reason, probably something very darkly physical, those images were the first to die, in his memory which was also ready to die ... He still thought back only about Madeleine, on occasion, because his love for her had been more complex, more amalgamated with that great mystery of the human inner depths that we call the soul; it sometimes happened that he saw again her pale face and her young, shadowed eyes, or heard again her timid sunset conversations, in the sad little alley, under the blossoming linden trees, under the new leaves where the warm rain of the April evenings made a drumming sound. But he quickly returned to his mother ... (XLVIII)

Viaud does note that, if his relationships with women were the first things to disappear from Jean's fevered mind, it was probably because of some 'physical cause,' that is, not because he was not attracted to them sexually. Still, these pale and undeveloped heterosexual relationships suggest that Viaud tried to create an unambiguously heterosexual character but could not bring him off in a convincing fashion.

And yet, *Sailor* is not the unambiguously heterosexual tale that it has been read, and certainly seems, to be. There is gay content. For that we need to look elsewhere, however. 'Pierre Loti' and his homoerotic desires are present in this novel, but, like Samuel in *A Phantom from the East*, hidden from ready view.

As noted earlier, the text at one point speaks of the 'unknown inner depths' of Jean's mother's soul (LIII), noting that she experiences

'awakenings [that] with each new occurrence had a more rending clair-
voyance' (LIII). As slight as they are, and they are very slight, these reminiscences of Pierre in *The Story of a Child* indicate that Viaud has found
yet another way to talk indirectly about Pierre Loti's love for another
man. Rather than transforming him into a young woman, as he had
done with Gaud in *Iceland Fisherman*, he has now metamorphosed him
into a somewhat older woman, Jean's never named mother. Whereas
Gaud, being an eligible young woman, had given Viaud greater freedom
to depict physical and romantic desire for a man than he had dared in
previous works, Jean's mother's relationship to Berny, presented as very
traditional and non-incestuous, undermines the erotic potential of any
feelings attributed to her, however.[10] Once Jean's mother's position in
the Pierre Loti lineage has been grasped, much of the novel takes on an
interesting second dimension.

   Jean's mother has several of the crucial Pierre Loti elements. Several
times, like Gaud and the Pierre of *The Story of a Child*, she appears looking out her window (XIX, XXI, XXVII, XXIX), though, given Jean's
own similarities to Pierre Loti, it is not surprising that on most of these
occasions she is joined by her son.[11] Just as *Sailor* undercuts the worship
of mementos of the past, however, so in this novel the significance of
the window is distorted when, having learned of the death of her son,
Jean's mother repeatedly envisions jumping out that opening to her
death (LIII). Like Gaud in *Iceland Fisherman* and Pierre Loti in *My
Brother Yves*, Jean's mother also experiences the 'joy of ... forgiving' the
male object of her affection (VI). Just as Gaud experienced 'anguish'
when Yann, after their marriage, prepared to set sail for a season of
fishing on the *Léopoldine* (IV:VII), so Jean's mother 'anguishes' the day
before he sets off on his first voyage (XXI). It is the anguish that she
experiences later upon her son's death that causes new feelings to rush
up from the already noted 'unknown inner depths of her soul' (LIII),
joining those two elements of the Pierre Loti lineage together in one
sentence.[12]

   Jean's mother also has certain qualities that we have seen in Viaud
himself, though not necessarily in representatives of the Pierre Loti lineage. Like Viaud in his description of his idyll with Joseph Bernard in
Africa, quoted in chapter 1, Jean's mother is repeatedly described as
having decorated the apartment in Brest to please the male object of
her affection (XIX, LII). (Gaud would like to do the same for Yann after
they move into Yvonne Moan's thatch-roofed cottage on their wedding
night but does not have the money [*Iceland Fisherman* IV:VII]). Also like

Viaud, Jean's mother, at the end of the novel, is horrified at the thought of being left alone in her old age with no son to take care of her (LIII). She, like Viaud, also has difficulty praying to God (XLII, LIII), though she does find faith at the very end, which the narrator notes that he – like Viaud – has been unable to do (LIV).

It is not surprising, then, that Jean's mother is involved in several of the relatively few descriptions of Berny's physical beauty, the 'gay gaze,' limited though it is, in this novel. While the two of them are together at the window of their Brest apartment, the text, perhaps conveying her thoughts, notes that Jean, 'his neck tanned [had] changed somewhat in his face, for example; more handsome, perhaps, because of his beginning black beard' (XIX). Later and more directly, when Jean returns from his voyage to Canada the text describes how his mother 'looked at her son with admiration, in the splendour of his twenty-one years, tall, his waist narrow and his shoulders broad; his profile so pure, his complexion so warm in the sharp frame of his black beard' (XXVI). At the end of the novel, the text notes that while he was at sea she had got in the habit of waiting for a Jean who was 'altogether a man and completely handsome' (LIII). None of this suggests any sort of erotic desire. On the contrary, the fact that these tame appreciations of Jean's physique are presented as those of a largely conventional mother rob them of the homoerotic connotations that similar, more voyeuristic ones had had in *My Brother Yves*, or even of the erotic connotations that Gaud's descriptions of Yann had in *Iceland Fisherman*. Unlike in works such as *The Story of a Spahi* or *My Brother Yves*, there are few physical descriptions of Jean Berny or other men in *Sailor* and those few are circumspect.

Pierre Loti also seems to be present, albeit briefly, in Morel, Jean's Protestant friend, but again in a way that appears intentionally to undercut the homosexual potential of the relationship. Being the son of a Protestant minister, he recalls the young Pierre of *The Story of a Child*, who for a time had considered becoming a minister himself (XIII). Like the young Pierre as well, Morel was 'drawn [to the navy] by dreams of voyages and by the unknown sea' (XXVIII). But *Sailor* repeatedly describes Morel as being 'frail and timid' (XXVIII), a 'pale boy,' and 'the frail son of the pastor' (XXIX), all of which would seem to be a self-hating attack on the physical weakness of young Pierre (and, in his early years, Viaud himself). Similarly, the text's remark that 'Jean became attached to him ... after first having simply taken him under his protection out of pity' (XXVIII) suggests no physical attraction, and the possibility of authorial self-contempt. (Recall the repeated contempt for devotion to mementoes of one's past in this novel, a distinguishing characteristic of the Pierre of *The Story of a Child*, and of Viaud.) As already noted, the description of the two young men's feelings for each other is bland: 'They had immediately charmed each other' (XXVIII).

It is interesting that Jean is presented as sneaking out on both his mother (XX) and Morel (XXVIII) to chase after women, in each case lying about his absence when he returns. He feels some guilt at doing this, but in neither case do we have access to the grieved party's feelings. In this respect, Berny resembles Yves Kermadec, who 'left' Pierre Loti to marry a woman in *My Brother Yves* and, sometimes, to chase after women in port, including, perhaps, Madame Chrysanthemum.[13] Jean's 'cheating' on both Morel and his mother with women could be read as a de-eroticized metaphor for Pierre Loti's – and perhaps Viaud's – feelings of having repeatedly lost a male object of affection – Yves Kermadec, Pierre Le Cor, Léo Thémèze – not to other men, but to women.

Given all this, other elements of Jean Berny's character situate him more clearly in the Viaud corpus. Like the male objects of desire in previous narratives, Berny is repeatedly, if not so often as his counterparts in *The Story of a Spahi* and *My Brother Yves*, described as being large, strong, and handsome (IX, XIV, XXVI, XXX, XLVII; Loti, in the first two novels, fancies himself to be handsome, but never large or strong). Though he is from Antibes in the Provençal region of France, he is also repeatedly noted as having an Arab or Oriental quality in his face and his soul (I, V, XXV, XXVI). The text remarks early on, though not in reference to this, that the Berny family had a blood line that 'had not been crossed with foreign blood at least since the Saracen era' (I). It now makes sense that this should be significant since, as we have seen, previous objects of Pierre Loti's desire, starting with Samuel and including such unlikely subjects as Jean Peyral and Yves Kermadec, had also been described as having Arab features. If Jean's mother is the latest in the Pierre Loti lineage, Jean himself, while sharing certain biographical elements with Loti (and Viaud), definitely also belongs to the lineage of Samuel, John, Jean Peyral, Yves Kermadec, and Yann Gaos. Again, and as in Viaud's last (largely) non-Pierre Loti narrative, *Iceland Fisherman*, the author has distributed elements of himself and those around him in real life among various of his characters, so there are no simple one-to-one biographical correspondences. Like *Iceland Fisherman, Sailor* is far from being a *roman à clef.*

Still, Jean remains resolutely heterosexual, without any of the ambiguities of John, Yves, or Yann. At one point, while on deck during an early voyage, Jean 'finished stretching out on those very clean boards that were his most customary bed, resting his head on some neighbour, as custom permits, in order to sleep more softly' (XXIV). The phrase 'as custom permits' suggests that Viaud felt a need to assure his readers that such physical intimacy in no way indicated homosexual tendencies on Jean's part. Nowhere in *My Brother Yves* or *Iceland Fisherman,* both of which, as we have seen, are filled with such instances of sailors in close physical contact, had those texts ever bothered with such a disclaimer. Though only a few words, this passage, along with the repeated insistence on Berny's womanizing and the almost total absence of male-male relationships in this work, suggests that, with *Sailor,* for whatever reason, Viaud was trying to write a non-gay novel, having tried to erase the homoeroticism from his first with *A Phantom from the East.*

Sailor reads as an unhappy work, however, one in which Viaud repeatedly seems to have ridiculed himself, both with the character of Morel and with the dismissal of affection for mementoes of one's past. On the one hand, it is as if he had lost respect for himself, not because he experienced homosexual desire, as we see Proust do with the often virulent homophobia of *In Search of Lost Time,* but because he was unable to inspire such desire in another man. On the other hand, when, near the end of the novel, Jean's mother, in her despair over her son's death, breaks many of the objects that they had saved from their life in Provence (LIII), there would seem to be a metaphor for Viaud's own disillusionment with his attempts to derive happiness, or at least escape from the sorrows of the present, from recollections of his past. (Again, recall the repeated disparagement of mementoes noted earlier.) [14]

Could one even read this last episode as a disillusionment with literature, or at least Viaud's literature, which is so involved in a resurrection and preservation of the past? Jean's mother subsequently regrets her destructive actions, which may speak for the author as well, but in a very vague way the novel could suggest that its author had passed through some crisis involving his most central beliefs, including perhaps his belief in the power of literature. In the famous madeleine episode of *Swann's Way,* Proust's Marcel experiences an 'exquisite pleasure' at having recovered the past in a way such that 'the vicissitudes of life had become indifferent to me, its disasters innocuous, its brevity illusory' (60). For Viaud, for at least a moment, the keys to his past seem to have lost their power to protect him from the sufferings of the present.

Still, despite its Proustian premonitions, in the last analysis *Sailor* is a disappointment. Viaud seems to have remained in this crisis stage for several years, but with his next novel, *Ramuntcho*, he found a more artistically satisfying vehicle with which to express it.

CHAPTER TEN

Creating the Allegorical Gay Novel: *Ramuntcho*

Viaud's ninth novel, *Ramuntcho* (1897), like *The Story of a Spahi, Iceland Fisherman,* and *Sailor,* does not appear autobiographical. It deals with a group of poor Basques, one of whom, Ramuntcho, runs contraband by night and plays pelota during the day. It does not seem to have potential for a gay reading, either: the main plot focuses on Ramuntcho's love for a poor young Basque woman, Gracieuse Detcharry, and his efforts to marry her despite her mother's opposition. The title character does have male friends, but his relationships with them are not erotic or romantic, unlike Loti's with Yves in *My Brother Yves* and *Madame Chrysanthemum* or Samuel in *Aziyadé,* or even Yann's with Sylvestre in *Iceland Fisherman.* After the apparent attempts to write gay desire out of his narratives in *A Phantom from the East* and *Sailor, Ramuntcho* might give the impression of being another effort of the same sort.

Yet, like *Iceland Fisherman,* which it resembles in many ways, *Ramuntcho* is actually less different and more gay than it first appears. If read in the context of some of Viaud's previous fiction, and especially *The Story of a Child,* this apparently heterosexual tale turns out to have significant gay content. Unlike the story of Gaud and Yann, however, *Ramuntcho* is constructed allegorically: once the symbols are understood, the novel tells its story directly and does not rely on the use of ambiguity or parallels that was central to the earlier work. As we shall see, anyone with a knowledge of Viaud's previous novels, such as those 'unknown friends' whom he mentions in several earlier volumes, is equipped to view his latest narrative with its hidden dimension. To show how it operates, we shall approach Viaud's ninth novel as we did *Iceland Fisherman,* examining it first in isolation and then in the context of its predecessors. The parallels with those predecessors will show both how heterosexual *Ramuntcho* appears by itself and, therefore, how striking the effect of a gay decoding can be.

As we mentioned at the outset of this chapter, the major relationship in *Ramuntcho*, that between the title character and Gracieuse, is not gay. Ramuntcho is a man, and Gracieuse, unlike Gaud, proves to be a woman from any perspective. What is more, unlike Yann in *Iceland Fisherman*, Ramuntcho is unambiguously interested in this unambiguously female character from the beginning of the novel. Whereas Yann avoided Gaud and her attempts to get him to marry her for most of that narrative, Ramuntcho asks Gracieuse early on to wed him, and when she indicates her consent the text states: 'They staggered, almost ... like two children drunk with youth, joy, and hope' (I:5). In a later scene, when he hears the approach of a religious procession in which Gracieuse is taking part, the protagonist is described as being 'thrilled above all at the thought that they would go to the Detcharry's and that he would see Gracieuse again for a moment' (I:9). More examples could be added, but these suffice to show that from early in this novel, Ramuntcho experiences a physical, sexual attraction to Gracieuse. This is very different from Jean Berny's pale relationships with the unnamed Canadian woman and Melanie.

The one element that might give some alerted readers pause is that Gracieuse is described as resembling her handsome brother, Arrochkoa (I:14).[1] Even here, however, as if aware of what readers might surmise, the text explains that Gracieuse 'continued to resemble her brother, the same regular traits, the same perfect oval; but the difference in their eyes became continually more accentuated' (I:14). How much can one read into this one passage? Could the progressive differentiation suggest that Ramuntcho is moving ever further away from the possibility of a gay or at least bisexual orientation and toward a uniquely heterosexual one? The protagonist's relationship to Arrochkoa also needs to be examined.

Though Ramuntcho plays pelota with his friend during the day, even then he thinks constantly about spending the evening with Gracieuse. As the text at one point is careful to explain:

During [summer], Ramuntcho, during the day, lived his active life as a *pelotari*, constantly going, with Arrochkoa, from village to village, to organize handball games and to play them.

But, in his eyes, only the evenings existed.

The evenings! ... In the fragrant and warm darkness of the garden, seated very close to Gracieuse; wrapping his arms around her, little by little drawing her and holding her against his chest so as to press her tight, and remaining that way a long time without saying anything, his chin resting on her hair, breathing in the young and healthy smell of her body. (I:23)

Think back to Yann or the other sailors on the *Marie* and how they forgot about women while at sea.

Arrochkoa's interest in Ramuntcho seems equally devoid of the erotic. Early on, in an extended description of him, the text notes that the contraband runner 'loved Ramuntcho for his triumphs at handball' (I:4). For what it is worth, he subsequently gets married and has a child. More significantly, Arrochkoa seems to enjoy his girlfriend's company. At one point, he and Ramuntcho journey to another village, Erribiague, for a festival. The two arrive late at night and stay at an inn where, at the end of chapter I:15, the text is careful to note that they go up to their respective and separate 'room*s*.' This seems to be a conscious effort on Viaud's part to make clear that there is no sexual relationship between the two men. Two such poor individuals, in such a rural setting, would, especially at that time, most likely have taken one room and not two; moreover, in the episode in Viaud's diary on which this scene is based, one that describes a trip taken by Viaud and his orderly Joseph Brahy, the two men not only shared the same room, but the same bed.[2] The next morning Ramuntcho and Arrochkoa awaken full of joy, not, as in *My Brother Yves*, because they are together, but because 'this morning they plan to go to the home of cousins of Madame Dargaignaratz down in the countryside, to pay a visit to the two little ones who must have arrived the evening before, by carriage, Gracieuse and Pantchika [Arrochkoa's girlfriend]' (I:16). Again, there is no mention of women in the diary entry that served as the model for this excursion, but Viaud was careful to insert such mention when transforming it into part of the novel.[3]

There is virtually no physical contact between Ramuntcho and Arrochkoa. If, in the episode just mentioned, the text is careful to make clear that the two did not sleep in the same room, so earlier, after having journeyed to Zitzarry for a pelota match, the two also spend the night at an inn, but the text describes the protagonist waking up in his room the next morning without ever mentioning where Arrochkoa slept (I:7). Contrast this with the scene in *My Brother Yves* (XXI), where Viaud wrote of a similar awakening of two male friends, Pierre Loti and the title character, in such a way as to suggest that they had been sleeping side by side, when in fact they had been sleeping in bunk beds. Given the unrealistic mention of the two rooms in the first of these examples, it is hard not to think back to the instance of 'homosexual panic' that we noted in chapter 9 with Viaud's description of life aboard ship in *Sailor* (XXIV).

Yet another indication of the non-gay nature of the relationship between Ramuntcho and Arrochkoa, this one similar to its parallel in *Iceland Fisherman*, is that Arrochkoa is intent on helping his friend marry his sister Gracieuse. Whereas Sylvestre had simply offered an occasional suggestion regarding Yann and Gaud, Arrochkoa is a major catalyst here, doing much of the planning and carrying out of the attempted abduction of the young woman from the convent. Interestingly, given the context of some of Viaud's previous narratives, Ramuntcho thinks of Arrochkoa as his 'brother' only when he contemplates this abduction of a potential wife (II:3). The unidentified narrator does the same, referring to the two men as 'brothers' when they plot her abduction (II:13).[4] Both passages seem to undercut the homoerotic connotations of that word from previous narratives. During the abduction scene near the end of the novel, the mother superior of Gracieuse's convent asks Arrochkoa if the man whom he has brought with him is his brother. "'Oh! no" said Arrochkoa, in a singular tone of voice, "he's only my friend"' (II:13), seeming to deny any closer relationship.[5] At the end of the novel the text reports that Ramuntcho, having failed to bring off the abduction and deciding to leave the Basque region altogether, wants with all his heart to take Arrochkoa in his arms for a final 'embrace with the brother of his beloved' (II:13). Here Arrochkoa is no longer Ramuntcho's brother, but Gracieuse's. Even so, Arrochkoa will have nothing to do with this.

> No, Arrochkoa had once again become the Arrochkoa of the bad days, the handsome player without a soul, who was interested only in things having to do with daring. In a distracted manner, he touches Ramuntcho's hand:
> 'Well, then, farewell! ... Good luck over there! ...'
> And, with his silent step, he left to rejoin the contraband runners, toward the border, in the propitious darkness. (II:13)

In short, there seems to be no grounds for a gay reading of the Ramuntcho-Arrochkoa relationship.

Nor is the depiction of the other members of Ramuntcho's male group, the contraband runners, particularly suggestive along these lines, especially if we think back to the open-minded crews in *My Brother*

Yves and 'Blossoms of Boredom.' All the members of Ramuntcho's group are either already married or get married and have children during the course of the narrative. Florentino is almost embarrassed to talk to Ramuntcho about his 'happiness' (II:2) in marriage; Marcos is associated 'joyously' with his new wife (II:3); Arrochkoa, as already mentioned, gets married and has a child (II:3). The ambiguously suggestive lines that we saw in *My Brother Yves* regarding the sexual open-mindedness of sailors have no equivalent in the descriptions of Ramuntcho's fellow contraband runners.

Finally, unlike several of the narratives that we have already examined, *Ramuntcho*'s narrator does not exhibit a 'gay gaze.' In this novel the narrator does not have a name and an identity. Though he does on occasion notice and describe the men in the narrative, there is almost none of the erotic focus that we found in *The Story of a Spahi, My Brother Yves*, or even *Madame Chrysanthemum*. The text speaks once of the title character as 'ce beau joueur' (II:3), but that can mean 'this fine player [of pelota]' as well as 'this handsome player.' More often, the narration comments on the male characters' size and strength along with their looks. Early in the novel, as the first pelota match is about to get under-way, the narrator portrays the participants as 'the handsome players of the country, the fine flower of the nimble and the strong' (I:4). Toward the end, Ramuntcho and Arrochkoa are described as 'handsome beings of instinct and force' (II:13).

When describing the male characters in the novel, however, the text generally focuses strictly on their size and strength. In depicting one of the open-air festivities during which the young Basques dance, the nar-rator notes that the men's 'great strength is revealed by the thickness of their tanned necks, the breadth of their shoulders' (I:5). At the end of that first pelota match it mentions 'the muscles of this entire youth of alert and vigorous men, who, shortly, are going to exercise their iron hamstrings and arms at handball' (I:4). Elsewhere the text notes the pelota players' 'athletes' arms' (I:4). Florentino, Ramuntcho's friend and fellow contraband runner, is presented as 'an athletic boy' (I:4). When Ramuntcho returns from military service three years later, some-one – whether it is the protagonist or the narrator is not clear – notes that Florentino is 'very changed, having even broader shoulders than before, altogether a man now' (II:2). The text singles out the 'powerful neck muscles' (I:4) of two other contraband runners, Marcos and Joachim, as they perform a song, stating that 'they recall, in their serious immobility, the figures that one sees on Roman medals.' In the final scene of the novel, the text twice notices Ramuntcho and Arrochkoa's size and strength, mentioning their 'broad shoulders' and their 'wide shoulders' (II:13), as well as Arrochkoa's 'powerful shoulder.'

As in *Iceland Fisherman*, however, the description of the men in *Ramuntcho* seldom seems erotic. There are scenes such as the depictions of the pelota matches where one would expect to find mention of naked male torsos, but they are noticeably absent. The players either compete completely clothed (I:4), or there is an indication that they might be shirtless but no actual mention of it. During one match, for example, the text speaks of 'players with chests and foreheads streaming [with sweat]' (I:17), but there is no indication of whether those chests are visible or not. Again, in the description in Viaud's diary of the pelota game that served as the model for the first of these scenes, there is mention (unlike in the novel) that the players 'took their vests off.'[6]

There is one striking exception to the general lack of erotic description of men's bodies to which we will have reason to return later. Near the end of the first part of the novel, while describing a warm summer night, the narrator notes carts being driven by 'half-naked men' (I:23). Having returned from his military service, one day Ramuntcho encounters similar cart drivers, 'their shirts of pink cotton exposing their chests' (II:2); 'the width of their jaws and the muscles of their necks give an expression of massive solidity.' It is only subsequently that we discover that one of these cart drivers is Ramuntcho's friend and former fellow contraband runner, Florentino, whose increased shoulder breadth is also noted in this scene. We also are told that this impressive figure of a man has 'a naked chest covered with bushes of red fur,' and that he is 'altogether a man at present.' This is the only time that the narrator gives a possibly erotic description of a man, however; as readers of earlier chapters will recall, this is far more circumspect than the narratorial discourse in some previous Viaud novels.

As with *Iceland Fisherman*, this lack of obvious gay content has facilitated several critics' attempts to interpret the novel as the retelling of a heterosexual event in Viaud's private life, thereby making the work heterosexual as well. Again, however, as with *Iceland Fisherman*, that is going too far. If we go outside the work itself for context, we will discover that this novel also takes on a significant gay autobiographical dimension, thus defying any attempt to make it uncomplicatedly heterosexual.

For now, however, unlike in our chapter on *Iceland Fisherman*, let us hold off on the biographical context and start by examining how the novel can be read against the background of Viaud's previous works, and in particular *The Story of a Child*. Since Viaud had mentioned 'unknown friends' in that novel and *Carmen Sylva and Sketches from the Orient*, one might suspect that he was hoping his understanding and sympathetic readers would do exactly this, and that he had such thoughts in mind when constructing his latest work.

To begin with, Ramuntcho recalls Pierre in *The Story of a Child*, with whom he has much in common. At the beginning of *Ramuntcho*, the title character is sixteen or seventeen (I:1), almost as if he were meant to be seen as a continuation of Pierre, who at the end of his novel was almost fifteen (LXXXI). More importantly, Ramuntcho experiences many of the same emotions as Pierre, and they are described in the same way, often with the same vocabulary. Like Pierre, the young Basque often has strange, sad feelings coming from his inner depths that he cannot explain – though this time, Viaud will be more intent on interpreting them. At the opening of the novel, for example, as Ramuntcho climbs toward the house that he shares with his mother, he sees below him a cart driver singing a song while he leads his team. The young Basque stops to watch, 'pensive,' and when the cart and driver disappear into 'a ravine bathed in an already nocturnal shadow,' 'Ramuntcho felt the embrace of a sudden melancholy, unexplained like most of his complex impressions' (I:1).

> In his mind had passed an intuitive uneasiness about *other places*, about a thousand *other* things that one can see or do in this world and that one can enjoy; a chaos of troubling half-thoughts, of atavistic recollections and of ghosts had just made a furtive appearance in the inner depths of his wild child's soul ... In him, the chaos of *other* things, of luminous *other places*, of splendours or of fears foreign to his own life was moving around in a confused fashion, trying to become clear ... But no, all that, which was not graspable or comprehensible, remained without a connection, without a continuation and without form, in the shadows.

This passage is like an encapsulated summary of Pierre's feelings in *The Story of a Child*. Ramuntcho suffers from an unexplained melancholy that is described as an 'impression.' Striking is the fact that this particular instance of melancholy is triggered by hearing a distant song, like the effect of Pierre's recollection of his cousin's song linked to Bories and the butterfly, and that this song is sung by a cart driver, who, as we have seen, is among the few erotically described men in the novel. (Remember that Pierre's singing cousin's size had been noted, too.)

Ramuntcho also experiences a desire to be elsewhere, where he could 'enjoy' a thousand things unavailable to him in his small Basque town (*jouir*, in French, can have a sexual connotation), just as Pierre had fantasized about enjoying the unknown while listening to the distant singing of virile sailors (XXIII). This fills Ramuntcho with '*troubling* half-thoughts, atavistic recollections,' somehow passed down to him from his ancestors, which is how Pierre had explained some of his feelings (III, VI, XXXII), such as his first impression of the ocean. These thoughts and recollections, which arise from his 'inner depths,' remain 'not ... comprehensible.'

Also like Pierre, Ramuntcho has a sense that there are things that he wants to know that can only be discovered elsewhere. He has a 'desire to become familiar with what there is outside, and outside that ... Oh! to go elsewhere! ... To escape, at least for awhile, from the oppression of this land ... to escape from this existence, always the same and without exit. To try something else, to leave here, to travel, *to know!*' (I:13; emphasis added). Ramuntcho experiences 'chaos' inside his head (ibid), a fascinating line that projects the homoerotic connotations of the original chaos presented in earlier works such as 'Blossoms of Boredom' into Ramuntcho himself, but that also shows why he feels a need to go elsewhere and learn things, so as to be able to make sense of this confusion inside him, '*to know!*' This chaos also shows why, again recalling *The Story of a Child,* in the Basque region, far from the knowledge that he experiences a need to discover, Ramuntcho 'feels like a prisoner here, with always his same aspiration toward something unknown, that disturbs him at the approach of night' (I:6). In short, Viaud creates a clear link between his protagonist and Pierre in *The Story of a Child.* Since by now we are sufficiently attuned to his work to number among his 'unknown friends,' this leads us to start wondering how a knowledge of the previous novel might enhance our reading of this one.[7]

Given what we have seen in the opening pages of this work, it is not surprising that Florentino – who, we recall, is later described as a large and virile cart driver – triggers 'unexplained anguish' (I:4) in the title character when he sings a song. The connection with the singing cousin in *The Story of a Child* is clear here, since Florentino is described as someone 'who knows only old mountain refrains' and who sings this one in an 'Arab falsetto,' just as the cousin in the earlier novel had sung in the 'plaintive falsetto of a mountaineer' (XLVIII). Here Ramuntcho's feelings are further analysed by the narrator, however. He is experiencing 'worry about living ... forever in these same villages, under the oppression of these same mountains; the notion and the confused *desire* for other places; the trouble caused by the thoughts of unknowable distant places.' There is a definite sense that his 'desire' is presently unfulfilled, and that it leads him to wish that he were some-place else where there would be other possibilities. Furthermore, 'he felt exiled, without understanding from what country, disinherited, without knowing by whom, sad to the depths of his soul; between him and the men who surround him arose, suddenly, unyielding hereditary dissimilarities.' Ramuntcho feels exiled – a key term in several earlier Viaud novels, but only really explained here – separated from those around him, as a result of something that he has inherited, and yet at the same time he feels disinherited, as if cut off from the source of whatever it is that has made him feel different from those around him.[8] As any therapist who works with troubled gays could point out, Ramuntcho here exhibits all the classic traits of a gay man who feels dif-ferent from the straight world around him because of his sexuality and cut off from a sympathetic culture because he is not part of a gay com-munity that can help him put his feelings into some sort of meaningful context. Our modern idea of a distinct gay identity emerges from the pages of this text.

All this makes particularly telling the scene in the second part of the novel, after Ramuntcho's return, when he encounters Florentino again.

> The two friends embrace. Then, they look at each other in silence, sud-denly bothered by the wave of memories that is coming back up from the depth of their souls and that neither of them knows how to express, Ray-mond no better than Florentino, because the depth and the mystery of his thoughts are also much more unfathomable.
>
> And this oppresses them, conceiving of things that they are unable to say; then their embarrassed looks turn in a distracted way to the large, handsome cattle standing still. (II:2)

The fact that they are disturbed by a rush of memories that come up from the *depth* of their souls makes it easy for anyone who has read *The Story of a Child* to understand their discomfort as the result of feelings of attraction and eroticized love for each other. The fact that they cannot express these feelings may be a reflection of their shame or, as we have seen in several earlier Viaud texts, of the problem of not having a lan-guage that would allow them to put what they feel into words. The fact that they feel 'oppressed' by their inability to talk about these feelings is new with *Ramuntcho,* however. Yann had not felt oppressed when he could not understand his feelings for Sylvestre (III:9); it had been the narrator who could not find the necessary language. One might go so far as to suggest that this is the beginning of a desire for gay community that will play an important and remarkable role in *The Awakened.*

Ramuntcho is further linked to previous manifestations of the Pierre Loti 'lineage' by the fact that he, too, has bad moments upon awakening, but there is a major difference with this novel. Once Gracieuse has agreed to marry him, the title character wakes up one morning 'with a persistent impression of his joy from the day before, instead of that confused anguish that, so often, used to accompany the progressive return of thoughts for him' (I:7). He has changed, and this change seems to be for the better. A similar passage a few chapters later makes the reason for this change clear:

Ramuntcho's awakenings were permeated, now, with peace and humble serenity. For that matter, his awakenings as a fiancé were full of joy, since he had the assurance of finding Gracieuse again in the evening at the promised rendezvous. The vague worries, the indefinite sadness, that used to accompany the daily return of thoughts in him had fled for a while, chased away by the memory and the expectation of those rendezvous; his life was altogether changed because of them; as soon as his eyes opened, he had the impression of a mystery and an immense enchantment, enveloping him in the middle of this greenery and these April flowers. And this spring peace, seen again every morning like this, always seemed a new thing to him, very different from what it had been the other years, infinitely sweet to his heart and full of sensuousness to his flesh, having unfathomable and entrancing undersides ... (I:12)

Many will see here the notion that marriage to a woman will 'cure' a man of his homosexual desires. There seems to be something more at play, however. First of all, rather than saying that the knowledge that Gracieuse will marry him has ended Ramuntcho's uneasiness at wakening, the text states only that this uneasiness has left 'for a while.' Second, Ramuntcho's new peace seems, to him at least, to have 'unfathomable and *entrancing* undersides.' The positive adjective 'entrancing,' along with earlier parts of the sentence, suggests that Viaud meant to indicate that Ramuntcho was discovering aspects in himself that corresponded to a heterosexual affection for Gracieuse. This does not mean that he was changing, being 'cured,' but rather that, thanks to his association with Gracieuse, he was tapping into another part of what we would call his sexuality. Many gay readers will not be happy about the suggestion that Ramuntcho's unhappiness was caused by a feeling of being gay and that he begins to feel happier as he begins to see himself as at least bisexual, but we will deal with that issue later.

First, to continue with the similarities between *Ramuntcho* and previous Viaud novels, especially *The Story of a Child*, it is worth cataloguing the themes and images that the author's latest work repeats from previous ones. As we have already seen, there is talk in *Ramuntcho* of a person's inner depths, though the phrase is used less often here than in *The Story of a Child*. The sea also plays an important part in Viaud's Basque novel, as it did in the earlier work, but this time it is linked more clearly to negative connotations of sexual desire. From the Basque perspective the sea, here the Bay of Biscay, is 'the noisy and bad sea, down below, at the bottom of the Biscay Golf' (I:9). It is always associated with a lower, negative world. Similarly, darkness – night, shade, shadows – also has a more clearly negative connotation. This image, like several others reprised from *The Story of a Child*, takes on a more complex set of connotations in Viaud's latest work, however. Night is now also linked with positive notions of rebirth and growth: as Ramuntcho and Gracieuse sit talking on a warm spring evening, the text remarks in a Bahktinian way on 'the great, caressing mystery of this April night, which incubated around them so much mounting sap, so many germinations and so much love' (I:11).

As we have already seen, heredity is also an important concern in *Ramuntcho*. The title character's desire to be 'elsewhere,' which Pierre had also experienced in *The Story of a Child*, is seen again as being inherited, now specifically from his father. Ramuntcho's 'fear of coming back to close himself in [the Basque region], when he knows that there exist throughout the world such vast and free *other places*' (II:2), is depicted as 'an inheritance from his unknown father.'[9] It is not surprising, therefore, that Ramuntcho wants to know who his father was. When he sees the only person who could tell him, his mother, begin to fail, he leans over her and dares to ask: 'Mother! ... Mother, tell me now who my father is!' (II:6). Since the emotions that make him feel like an exile come from his father, and since being cut off from his father prevents him from understanding those emotions, it makes sense that he would want to learn about his father. In this sense, he is like the adult Pierre and narrator of *The Story of a Child* who, as we saw, went back into his childhood so as to understand his adult self better; Ramuntcho has the added dimension of wanting to know about the world from which his feelings come, and in which they had a meaning.

Another carry-over from previous Viaud works, but this time largely from *My Brother Yves* and 'Blossoms of Boredom,' is the importance of primitivism. Like the location of that novel and *Iceland Fisherman*, the 'set' for *Ramuntcho* is repeatedly presented as primitive. At the beginning of the narrative, the text describes the house that the title character shares with his mother as a 'primitive lodging' (I:1), and the word is used repeatedly to depict the dwellings of the Basques thereafter.

An important part of the primitive in this novel is the 'Spirit of Ancient Eras.' For René Doumic, 'in this spirit of ancient eras ... Loti personifies the force of tradition,'[10] but more is involved. We first encounter this spirit as Ramuntcho and Florentino are preparing for a contraband expedition one night. In a Proustian passage, the protagonist, half lost in thought, is surprised to find himself

> thinking confusedly about older times, of an imprecise and obscure antiquity ... The Spirit of Ancient Eras, which sometimes comes out of the earth during calm nights, in the hours when the perturbing beings of our days sleep, the Spirit of Ancient Eras is probably beginning to float in the air around him; he doesn't see it clearly, because the sense of an artist and a seer, which no education has sharpened, remains rudimentary in him; but he has a notion of it, and of the uneasiness that comes with it ... In his head, there is still a chaos, which perpetually tries to become clear, but without ever succeeding ... However, when the two enlarged and reddened horns of the moon plunge slowly behind the altogether black mountain, the aspects of things take on, for an imperceptible moment, something ferocious and primitive; then, a dying impression of the first eras, which had remained somewhere in space, becomes clear to him in a sudden fashion, and he is troubled by it to the point of shivering. Indeed, now he dreams without wanting to about the men of the forest who used to live here *in the past*, in the incalculable and dark past, because suddenly, from a distant point on the shore, a long Basque cry rises out of the darkness in a lugubrious falsetto, an *irrintzina*, the only thing in his country that he has never been able to get to know entirely. (I:13)

This is a crucial passage. Whatever this Spirit of Ancient Eras represents, it troubles Ramuntcho. It is linked in his head with 'chaos,' a word that has important connotations in this text, and which in 'Blossoms of Boredom,' as we saw in chapter 5, was linked to the origins of the world and humankind, when the rigid and mutually exclusive distinctions that 'thirty centuries' of civilization have imposed upon 'natural' man did not yet exist. This chaos is perpetually trying to come to the surface of Ramuntcho's consciousness, to make itself clear, but the Basque, for lack of education, is not able to help it do so. Nonetheless, he is troubled to the point of shivering when confronted with an impression of 'the primitive,' 'the first epochs.' In this mind frame, the strange Basque cry, the *irrintzina* – sung, again, in a falsetto – sets him thinking about the primitive *men* who had once lived in his region. In 'Blossoms of Boredom' there had been the suggestion, from Plumkett, that primitive men had lived in a world that did not condemn the homosexual; as we saw, there had even been a suggestion that male-male attraction had been man's first, natural impulse, one repressed later by 'thirty centuries' of civilization. The text here does not go as far, but the reader is left wondering what aspect of primitive man represented by the *irrintzina* Ramuntcho has not yet been able to know entirely, and why it troubles him so.

Late in the novel this mysterious, primitive Spirit, or one similar to it, returns. This time it is in association with the establishments where the contraband runners meet.

> In these cider-houses ... a little of the Spirit of the Past still comes to life, during the winter evenings ... Sometimes someone sings a lament handed down from the night of centuries past; the beating of a drum makes old forgotten rhythms come alive; the scraping of a guitar awakens a sadness from the era of the Moors ... Or, one in front of the other, two men, castanets in their hands, suddenly dance the fandango, swaying with an antique grace.
>
> And, from these innocent little cabarets, they withdraw early – especially on these bad, rainy nights whose dark shadows are so particularly propitious for contraband, each person here having something clandestine to do out there, in the direction of Spain. (II:10)

Here again this mysterious Spirit is linked with a melody from the distant past, and this time, recalling the scene in 'Blossoms of Boredom,' with men involved in what is potentially a homoerotic activity: dancing. Since the Moors were linked to the Arabs who, as we have seen, have homosexual connotations in Viaud's work, mention of them further heightens the homoerotic atmosphere here. The adjective 'antique' also links this to a primitive past, and the last line connects all this to 'something clandestine.'[11]

The strange cry that triggers Ramuntcho's vision of primitive men is explained further elsewhere. During a smuggling expedition, one of the contraband runners gives forth with an *irrintzina* (I:8). The text describes it this time as being made of 'those very high notes that ordinarily belong only to women, but with something harsh and powerful that indicates, rather, the savage male; it has the biting quality of the voice of jackals, and it keeps, nevertheless, something human that makes one tremble even more.' Here there is gender blending associated with it, as well as the primitive, again. In addition, the mention of jackals recalls the association of night scavengers with a potential homosexual attack in *The Story of a Spahi*; in fact, in his diary Viaud had compared the Basque cry to the call of a hyena, a carnivore, and not a jackal.[12] While the other contraband runners let out this cry for fun, 'Ramuntcho remains silent and without a smile. This sudden savagery chills him, although he has been familiar with it for a long time; it plunges him into dreams that trouble and do not become clear.' If this cry is being used as a metaphor for some sort of primitive, male-male sexuality, there is something about it that troubles Ramuntcho.[13] Or at least something that troubles him about it now, as he finds himself being more involved with Gracieuse even as she is becoming more distinct from her handsome brother. Michael Lerner saw *Ramuntcho* as an expression of Viaud's 'despair' at being alienated from the simple Basque lifestyle.[14] The truth is much more complex. As this passage shows, Ramuntcho himself is uncomfortable with what Viaud was presenting as part of Basque life.

The contraband runners themselves are also presented as primitive, more so than their fellow Basques. During one of the nocturnal smuggling scenes, the narrator explains that the tension of their undertakings

> causes them a sort of almost animal joy, it redoubles their life of muscles, they who are beings of the past; it is a recollection of the most primitive human impressions in the forests or the jungles of the first eras ... It will take centuries of policed civilization yet to crush that taste for dangerous surprises that pushes certain children to the game of hide and seek, certain men to the ambushes and skirmishes of war, or to the unforeseen things involved in contraband ... (II:9)

Much is significant here. The contraband runners are linked to the primitive men in the forest that Ramuntcho had imagined when he heard the *irrintzina*. They represent man as he was before centuries of civilization, seen as policing, have smothered his taste for exploits that involve hiding, danger, and the unexpected. Viaud's 'unknown friends' will remember not only Plumkett's passage from 'Blossoms of Boredom' about the effects of thirty centuries of civilization, but also Loti's remark in *Aziyadé* that he loved Turkey in part because the Turks had not yet imported the European police who track you down in three hours for things that bother no one in the Middle East (IV:XI, IV:XXV).

It should not come as a surprise, therefore, that in *Ramuntcho* the contraband runners serve as a metaphor for talking about gay men. They are not necessarily gay themselves, though that is left open to interpretation, but Viaud describes them in such a way that they become a metaphor for gays. In order to ply their 'trade,' they move back and forth over the Bidassoa River, which serves as the border between France and Spain. (Generally, they take merchandise from France to Spain.) This establishes that their activity involves crossing borders or boundaries. The description of this border is significant, furthermore. One night when Ramuntcho waits for Florentino during a contraband expedition, the text notes that the Bidassoa acts as a 'mirror the colour of a night sky in which the stars are reflected inverted' (I:13), thus suggesting an inversion of the standard order.[15] In addition, the contraband expeditions are carried out at night, in the darkness, and these images were associated with the tempting but frightening in *The Story of a Child*.[16] The men always sneak back to their homes at dawn – 'returning at the break of dawn ... is the habitual follow up to contraband runs' (I:2) – just like (closeted) gay men who have to seek their pleasure under cover of night.[17] The text describes these runners as Ramuntcho's 'companions in *adventure*,' a term used regularly in French to refer to sexual escapades. They share 'the reciprocal devotion of brothers, especially during the nocturnal outings' (I:4), a phrase that the ambiguous use of 'brother' in previous works loads with homosexual connotations. After one of these outings, the text describes the runners as 'dull with the comfort of sitting after the exertions of the night' (I:4), which suggests men who are exhausted from a night of sexual activity, and adds, tellingly, that they 'barely lift their heads to look at ... the young women who are passing by.' Moreover, the literal explanation for their activity is thrown into question, since the text states that contraband 'barely provides a living' for some of them (I:4).

Other elements reinforce the metaphorical dimension of the runners. As part of the scene just mentioned, the narrator notes that the returning men 'speak and joke in their mysterious language, of such an unknown origin, which seems more distant than Mongolian or Sanskrit to the men of the other countries of Europe' (I:4). Since this is a strange place to put another disquisition on Basque, which everyone in the novel has been speaking for several chapters by this point, here Viaud seems to be using the uniqueness of the Basque language to suggest metaphorically the existence of some sort of slang or coded language among gay men.[18] Some characters in the novel even have separate names, as gay men living a double life often do. Arrochkoa, for example, is really named Jean Detcharry. The contraband runners delight in telling stories about how they outwitted the police, and when they finally arrive in Spain, the place where they carry out their clandestine and forbidden activities, they experience a 'noisy joy' (II:9). The text remarks that 'with the return of this beautiful weather, night contraband was exquisite to engage in ... It was also favourable and tempting for lovers' (I:10), thereby linking contraband and sexual activity.

If the contraband runners in general serve as a metaphor for gay men, the principal ones serve as interesting but different types. Itchoua, the leader of the group, is immoral and powerful, a dangerous combination.[19] To Ramuntcho, Itchoua seems 'closed to anything having to do with [heterosexual] love ... the calm husband of an ugly and old woman' (II:11). He is also cynical about women, assuring Ramuntcho in an insulting way that once Gracieuse has 'tasted' sex, all her scruples will vanish, like any woman's (II:11). He also claims that he would have no problems killing a man if he felt that he had to in order to escape capture, and tries to convince the others to share his view (I:4). Just as he is immoral, so he is materialistic. He offers to help Ramuntcho and Arrochkoa with the abduction of Gracieuse, but only for a substantial sum of money (II:9). Interestingly, Itchoua at one point announces his intention to leave France altogether and settle in Spain (II:11), the land where the contraband runners carry out their clandestine activity. Ramuntcho wonders what secrets may lie hidden in his past (II:11). He is the dominating force among the outlaws, and more than once puts a heavy hand on Ramuntcho's shoulder as if 'to take possession' (II:3; cf. also II:9). At the end of the first chapter, the text refers to Ramuntcho as Itchoua's 'new recruit,' recalling the passage in 'Blossoms of Boredom' where Yves and the other Breton sailors had exchanged clothing with a young zouave and set off with their 'new recruit' to find adventure in Algiers. Itchoua is not blamed for leading anyone into the clandestine activity, but once they become involved, he certainly plays a role in trying to keep them there.

If Itchoua evokes unfavourable memories of Balzac's Vautrin, the portraits of the other contraband runners are not negative. Florentino, like Ramuntcho, takes pleasure in singing the song of the spinning woman (I:4), thereby introducing again the breakdown of traditional gender distinctions that we have noted in previous male objects of desire. He gets married while the title character is away fulfilling his military service, but the narrative has a strange way of presenting his marital happiness. Having announced to his friend that he wed two years before, he speaks not about his wife but about the fact that he has been able to buy another pair of bulls like the ones that he is leading (II:2). Now that he is married, he has given up contraband (II:12).

Arrochkoa, Ramuntcho's closest friend, does contraband not out of need but only as a lark: 'contraband runner out of caprice ... without any necessity whatsoever' (I:4). He is the son of a customs officer, the enemy of contraband runners, but that is so far in his past that he remembers nothing of it (I:15). He is proud of his father and his father's profession, however (I:15), which would seem to suggest that he is ambivalent about his participation in the running of contraband. He is repeatedly compared to a cat (I:4, I:8, II:3, II:13), which, especially after *My Brother Yves*, reinforces the suggestion of his sexual ambiguity.[20] As we have already seen, after the failed kidnapping attempt Arrochkoa goes off to join the other contraband runners for another escapade (II:13). Allegorically, Florentino is the man who has given up homosexual activity for marriage, Arrochkoa the one who still plays with it, but only as it moves him and not out of any necessity.

In short, Viaud's presentation of the contraband runners as an allegorical representation of gay men is ambiguous. In this text they are 'respected' by the Basque population in general 'for their daring and their strength' (I:1). Franchita does not look down on them because her father had been one (ibid.), which introduces again the notion of heredity. Even the nuns in Gracieuse's convent raise no objection to their trade: many of them have known runners in their own families. On the other hand, there is the description of them wading across the sometimes very shallow Bidassoa to reach their destination: they move through 'the muck into which their feet plunge' (I:8). The 'unknown friends' might recall that in Plumkett's preface to *Aziyadé* the English officer, describing his late friend Loti, had cited Victor Hugo's lines about how the human soul can contain both heaven and muck. It is important to note, however, that this is the first time that homosexual men as a group have been portrayed, even if only metaphorically, in Viaud's work. That is an issue to which we shall return in chapter 11.

The contraband runners as symbols for gay men comprise the most striking new image that Viaud introduces with *Ramuntcho*, but there are more. The other major new image in this novel is the mountains, and specifically the Gizune, which towers over Ramuntcho's world. It is linked with darkness: at the end of the day, after a pelota match, the narrator remarks that 'above everything else, filling the sky, the gigantesque Gizune, indistinct and somber, is like the centre and the source of the darkness, little by little stretched out over things' (I:4).[21] Later in the novel, 'twilight descends from the peaks, invades the earth, seems to emanate and fall from the brown Pyrenees' (II:2; cf. II:13). Because of their size, these peaks seem to tower constantly over Ramuntcho's life below. Early in the novel the narrator describes how the 'mountains ... seem to have advanced today to the point of jutting out over the church' (I:3), how Etchézar, Ramuntcho's village, is 'under the great shadow of the Gizune, the overhanging mountain' (I:4). These mountains often work with night to increase darkness: when Arrochkoa and Ramuntcho go to Erribiague for a pelota match, the town is described as 'dwarfed, and lost in its ravine hollow, and one has the feeling that the night here is a blacker and more mysterious night than elsewhere' because it is dominated by 'the terrible overhanging peaks' (I:15). While focusing on Etchézar itself, at the end of the day, the text speaks of 'the vast night, that the mountains, rising up everywhere like giants of darkness, made more veiled and black' (I:5). Over and over, the Pyrenees in general, and the Gizune in particular, appear to loom over Ramuntcho's life and to be linked with darkness and all that it represents. (Not surprisingly, the contraband runners are repeatedly associated with the mountains as they are with night.)

Given the foregoing, it will come as no surprise that there is also, again more developed with *Ramuntcho*, an opposing image cluster centred around light and white, linked not to the contraband runners and their activities, but to Gracieuse and, therefore, heterosexual desire. Viaud sets forth the opposition clearly and repeatedly. He describes a June religious festival:

> The mountains seemed close and somber, a little ferocious with their brown tones and their tawny tones, above this white procession of little girls walking on a carpet of leaves and cut grass.

> All the old banners of the church were there, lit by this sun ...
> The large one, that of the Virgin, in white silk embroidered with dull gold, moved forward, carried by Gracieuse, who walked dressed all in white ... (I:21)

Here, as often in the novel, the white, light world of heterosexuality has the dark world of homosexuality constantly hovering over it. Not surprisingly, Gracieuse has blond hair (I:16).

Just as cold and winter are part of the opposing image cluster, so summer here becomes part of the cluster of light: the text describes the first summer as 'the season of light' (I:23). It is the season of outdoor festivities, and so of heterosexual dances and courting. Spring and everything associated with it also play a part in this cluster, with repeated mention of sap, greenery, etc. When Ramuntcho begins to plan the abduction of Gracieuse from the convent, which will allow him to marry her and confirm a heterosexual identity, the text remarks in the next sentence that 'sap was rising everywhere around him, on the slope of the brown Pyrenees; there were longer and warmer nights; the paths were lined with violets and periwinkle' (II:11).

Viaud does not set up these two image clusters as mutually exclusive, however, and this is one of the things that makes the novel interesting. He explains, for example, that all of this life and greenery owes its existence to vapour that comes from the sea and is turned into precipitation by contact with the mountains:

> May! The grass grows, grows everywhere like a sumptuous carpet, like velvet streaked with silk, that had emanated spontaneously from the earth.
> To water this region of the Basques, which throughout the summer remains humid and green like a sort of warmer Brittany [an interesting link to the two Breton novels], the vapours scattered over the Sea of Biscay all come together at the bottom of the gulf, stop at the Pyrenean peaks, and dissolve into rain. (I:18)

What, one has to ask, does this mean in the allegorical context of this opposition? Is Viaud suggesting that homosexual desire is a necessary beginning, or component, of a man's development, something without which he cannot go on to function successfully as a heterosexual? Or should one see this in broader terms as an explanation of the sexual development of man?

Other elements in this second image cluster include the south wind, which is repeatedly described as 'chasing in front of it the cold, the clouds, and the mist' (I:2; cf. also I:4, II:2). This wind comes from Spain, however, the destination and centre of activity of the contraband runners. It is 'the country that is the perpetual goal of their dangerous expeditions' (I:2), a land that 'is constantly occupying their thoughts.'

Ramuntcho himself makes the connection between Spain and contraband, and the opposition to Gracieuse and therefore heterosexuality, clear when, one evening, as he is taking his leave from her he answers her question, 'Will you come back tomorrow?' with the line: 'But yes, of course! ... Tomorrow and every night! ... Every night that we do not have work for Spain' (I:11). It is interesting but by now not surprising that when, at the end of Part I, Ramuntcho leaves his homeland to fulfil his military obligation, the last sentence reads: 'And down there on his left, at the bottom of a sort of black pit, Spain still stood out in profile, Spain which, for a very long time, no doubt, would no longer trouble his nights' (I:27). Spain is linked to the desires that trouble Ramuntcho – remember, that is where Itchoua would like to retire, despite the dangers (II:11) – but it is also the source of the beneficial south wind that clears the Basque sky.[22]

One major but also ambiguous constituent of this second image cluster is the Catholic church. Just as each town in the Basque region has a handball court, so it has a church. Viaud establishes the opposition between the church and the images of darkness early on in the already quoted passage describing the mountains that seem to jut out over the church in Etchézar. In general, the church appears to serve a protective function: at one point the narrator refers to the sound of its bells as a 'dear, protecting voice' (I:20). It is not surprising, therefore, that somewhat earlier, in a significant passage, the text had explained how, once the church bells fell silent, Ramuntcho had heard the sound of the sea, which is linked to the mountains. 'And, now that they have just stopped, he hears, with an undefined sadness, coming from down there that powerful and dull sound, almost incessant since the beginnings [of time], that the breakers of the Biscay sea make, and that, in peaceful evenings, is heard in the distance even behind the mountains' (I:13). This passage makes clear, metaphorically, that the church protects, at least in part, by blocking out the dark desires represented by the sea and the mountains.

In general, the church is repeatedly shown as being in opposition to, and indeed dulling, desire. When Ramuntcho and Arrochkoa enter the convent to abduct Gracieuse, the text notes that 'in the depths of their chests, their hearts beat with great, dull beats, but the words of love or violence, those words die before passing their lips ... And this peace becomes more and more established; it seems that a white shroud little by little covers over everything here, calming and extinguishing' (II:13). Similarly, when Gracieuse, who outside had been as passionate as Ramuntcho, enters the church, she experiences 'an appeasement of all her desires, a renouncement of all her earthly joys' (I:18). When she sits in front of the church, talking to the nuns, she experiences 'a serenity detached from things and as if freed from all links with the senses' (I:19).

This peace has its negative aspects. When at the beginning of Part II the text explains that Gracieuse has entered a convent, it wonders 'how she had allowed herself to be walled up in that tomb' (II:1). When Ramuntcho finally confronts her there at the end of the novel, the text suggests that 'she has already left for the regions of the great forgetfulness of death' (II:13). One passage in this scene is particularly interesting, moreover. It states that 'it is as if she were looking at him from infinitely far away, as if from behind impassable white mists, as if from the other side of the abyss, from the other side of death; her look, though very sweet, indicates that she is as if absent, departed for tranquil and inaccessible other places' (I:13). Some of the images associated with the opposite cluster – mists, abyss, and other places – appear here as well, a fact to which we shall return later.

The church is also an impediment to the realization of the heterosexual identity that Ramuntcho seems intent upon constituting for himself: the text at one point speaks of 'his hatred against this church that had stolen his fiancée from him' (II:3). In fact it was Dolorès, Gracieuse's mother, who forced her to enter the convent. Nevertheless, the text seems to share Ramuntcho's view that the church is at fault here. When, after speaking with Itchoua, Ramuntcho becomes firmer in his resolve to kidnap her, the narrator remarks: 'Now religious scruples were the only thing that was still holding him back' (II:11). Even once he has entered the convent to carry out the abduction, it is the remnants of his religious faith that defeat his resolution: 'Inside him, the mysterious white powers that are here in the air are probably acting; religious heredity, which had been sleeping in his inner depths, fills him at present with an unexpected submission and respect; the antique symbols dominate him: those crosses encountered that evening along the paths, and that plaster Virgin, with the colour of immaculate snow, against the spotless white of the wall' (II:13). (Again, there is an interesting crossover of images from the opposite cluster: heredity, inner depths.) Finally, the text announces that 'the rebel Ramuntcho is defeated, oh! quite defeated by the tranquil white powers' (II:13).[23]

One of the most intriguing parts of the allegory in *Ramuntcho* is one of its major components, the game of pelota, a kind of handball. The title character is proud of being a great *pelotari*. As we have already noted, this skill wins him the friendship of Arrochkoa (I:4) and the respect and admiration of his fellow Basque men. After a match, 'men in berets [the standard Basque headgear], of another essence than his, surrounded him to congratulate him' (II:4; cf. also I:4).[24] In fact, for Ramuntcho pelota plays a role somewhat analogous to that of Gracieuse. Having returned from his military service to discover that she is in a convent, the thought of resuming his career as a *pelotari* for a moment makes him forget about her loss (II:2). It is also interesting to note that more than once, the mountains end a game of pelota, throwing the court into darkness (I:14). During one match, Ramuntcho's resentment at this is made clear. In a passage that may be reporting his thoughts through indirect discourse, the text describes

higher than everything, dominating everything, dwarfing everything, the abrupt mass of the Gizune, from which comes so much darkness, from which there descends on this lost village a very hasty impression of evening ... Truly, this mountain encloses too much, it imprisons, it oppresses ... And Ramuntcho, in his youthful triumph, is troubled by the feeling of that, by that furtive and vague attraction of the *other places* so often mixed with his sorrows and his joys ... (I:4).

Not surprisingly, just as Ramuntcho had made an opposition between Gracieuse and Spain/contraband, so the text makes a similar opposition between pelota and his nocturnal escapades. It describes his life as 'the wandering life that the game of handball made for him during his days, and contraband during his nights' (I:17). It would seem that, allegorically as well as literally, pelota here represents the title character's integration into general heterosexual society, especially the society of heterosexual men. Just as homosexual desire is in opposition to his marriage to Gracieuse and the heterosexual identity that marriage to her would provide him, it also threatens his integration into and acceptance by the world of heterosexual men.

At the opening of the novel, however, in describing Ramuntcho's life, the text states that 'contraband runner and pelota player [are] two things, furthermore, that go well together and that are essentially

Basque' (I:1). This suggests that the physical force and endurance involved in the world of contraband, which is repeatedly described as 'the life of the muscles,' is also a component for success in the activities that earn the respect and acceptance of heterosexual men. It also raises the question of the allegorical meaning of the Basque region itself, situated up in the Pyrenees and isolated from the rest of the world, between France and Spain and, except politically, part of neither of them.

In fact, it is tempting to suggest that, in *Ramuntcho*, the Basque land serves as a sort of ideal, or at least unreal, primitive territory between rigidly distinct heterosexuality and homosexuality, a place where the border is vague and fluid and a man can go back and forth at will, albeit under cover of night and at some real risk, yet still be accepted by general society.[25] (Recall, again, the descriptions of primitive man in 'Blossoms of Boredom' as well as nineteenth-century French science's insistence on the mutual exclusivity of homosexual and heterosexual desire.) In the Preface to his French edition of the novel, Besnier asserted that the Basque lands as Viaud depicts them are a place of 'perpetual adolescence.'[26] One could argue that adolescence, for some men unsure of their sexual identity, is a sort of borderland where they experiment with either facet: the contraband runners in *Ramuntcho* are mostly young men who, like Florentino, leave the band when they marry. In the first chapter, the text notes that Ramuntcho himself 'began [his involvement in contraband running] for the fun of it, out of bravado, like most of them' (I:1). One might also wonder, however, given that the text later describes the Basques as 'a very mysteriously unique people, without analogue among mankind' (I:4), if the country does not, more generally, represent any sort of unique, isolated culture, such as those aboard ships, that allow men to experiment and move back and forth with relative ease.[27] Though Ramuntcho is uncomfortable with the other contraband runners, the text at one point asserts that 'in the later days of his existence, during the exiles [of which more later], the memory of these delicious returns at dawn, after the nights of contraband, would cause him indefinable and very anguish-filled regrets' (I:2). Whatever else it represents, the Basque region and the possibilities that it offers make it for some a unique and beguiling place, not unlike, perhaps, the sexual openness that Aziyadé and Istanbul seem to have come to represent for Viaud.

Given all these images and metaphors and how they play out with and against each other in the novel, it is not difficult to see the struggle in this work as an attempt to construct a heterosexual identity, an alternative to the gay activity symbolized by involvement with the contraband runners that encroaches on a desire to bask in the admiration and acceptance of men in general, symbolized by success at pelota. (Whether this is also Ramuntcho's struggle or only the allegorical implication of it remains unclear.) In this sense, *Ramuntcho* follows in the path started by *A Phantom from the East* and *Sailor*, but it is a more complex work. Rather than simply an effort to write gay desire out, it shows a struggle with the issue and the emotions involved. Rather than simply presenting Ramuntcho as a womanizer, as he had Jean Berny in *Sailor*, Viaud from the very beginning presents the title character as 'a mixture of two very different races' (I:1), someone 'composed of two very diverse essences.' On the plot level, Viaud is talking about the fact that Ramuntcho is the illegitimate son of a Frenchman and a Basque woman, but in a text that operates so consistently on an allegorical level as well, it is not hard to see that there must be other conflicting natures in the young man. In the Preface to his French edition, Besnier pointed out that 'even his name reflects this refusal to fit into one identity,'[28] since the protagonist is referred to variously throughout the novel by either his Basque name, Ramuntcho, or by his French one, Raymond.

Given these repeated indications of Ramuntcho's dual nature, it is interesting that there is some suggestion of gender ambiguity as well. When we first see him, he sings the song of a female flax spinner bemoaning the fact that her lover, off at a distant war, is slow to return (I:1). (As we saw, Florentino sings this same song later.) Elsewhere the text speaks of the 'sweet and refined side of his nature' (I:4).[29] He is also twice compared to a cat (I:16, I:23).

The narrator envies those who do not experience such internal conflict, symbolized in this text by the general run of Basque manhood. At one point early in the novel, describing the Basques during a church service, he exclaims: 'Doing the same things that their ancestors did for centuries without number, and repeating blindly the same words of faith, is a supreme wisdom, a supreme force' (I:3). Elsewhere, describing how Ramuntcho threw over his religious education, the narrator exclaims: 'It is wise to submit, with confidence, to the venerable and consecrated formulas, behind which is hidden, perhaps, everything that we can glimpse of the unknowable truths' (I:13).

In part, this is because such faith provides peace in the face of death, something that, as we will see in the next chapter, was of more concern to Viaud himself than to most of his characters. As the passage in question goes on to state: 'For all these believers who were singing there, a sort of peace, a confused but sweet resignation regarding subsequent annihilation emerged from this unchangeable ceremonial of the mass.'

In part, however, these men are admired because they do not question, and ignore anything different from their traditions. At one point, the narrator describes a group of peasant men that Arrochkoa and Ramuntcho see in the distance as 'Basques from the past, almost intermixed, when you look at them from here, with that red earth from which they came – and where they will return, after having lived like their ancestors without having any suspicion of the things of our time, of the things *of other places*' (I:16). The term 'other places' (*ailleurs*), repeatedly associated here, as in *The Story of a Child*, with the protagonist's desires for something still unknown, also suggests that these simple Basques are at peace because they are unaware of the full range of sexuality, whose alternatives, or at least their metaphors, trouble Ramuntcho, that is, the 'unknowable truths' that are hidden behind tradition's 'venerable and consecrated formulas.'

Viaud conveys the uniformity of these men most clearly with the single item that, to his late nineteenth-century readers, typified a Basque man: the beret. (Today we think of it as typically French, but at the time of *Ramuntcho* it had not yet been imported into French culture.) After a Mass early in the novel, the narrator describes the men exiting from the church as 'all dressed in the uniform national beret' (I:4), and elsewhere, describing a crowd at a pelota match, he speaks of 'hundreds of Basque berets, all the same' (I:4). Besides wearing the same berets, these men all wear them identically. Portraying the crowd at that pelota game, the narrator remarks on 'all the wool berets lowered in the same fashion on the shaved faces of the men' (I:4). These men, who never question anything – including, one must assume, their sexuality – are different from Ramuntcho, as the text makes clear when it describes how, after another pelota game, 'men in berets, of a different essence than his, surrounded him to congratulate him' (II:4).

As much as the narrator admires the peace that these unquestioning men enjoy, however, he also realizes that Ramuntcho cannot be one of them. Recounting how Ramuntcho abandoned his religious education, he remarks: 'His soul is no longer simple enough to admit blindly dogmas and observances' (I:13).[30] He resents this. Having returned from three years of military service in France, he surveys his homeland, and the narrator wonders: 'What is there that is so particular that resides in his soul that keeps him from feeling comfortable here, like the others? Why, my God, is it forbidden for him, for him alone, to finish out here the tranquil destiny of his dream, when all his friends have achieved theirs?' (II:2). His travels have only distanced him further from his fellow Basques, however: 'His removal from his native surroundings, his travels, his new conceptions have shrunk and ruined his mountain home for him' (II:2).[31] Looking at some cart drivers after his return, 'he felt the primary differences between himself and the working men more accentuated than ever' (II:2).

Ramuntcho also feels more disconnected from the contraband runners, however. Once he has exposed his plans to abduct Gracieuse to Itchoua, the text remarks, understandably given the metaphors at work, that 'among these men, who are less than ever his equals, he becomes isolated in an immense hope of love' (II:9).[32] In the next chapter, the narrator says that 'during his three years of travel, of reading, of conversations with various men, too many new ideas had penetrated into his already open mind; he felt more out of place than before with his companions of the past, more detached from the thousand little things of which their life was composed' (II:10). He cannot be one with those who have never questioned their sexuality, but neither is he at ease with those who, like Florentino, can join the contraband group for awhile and then leave it for married life. After having met the now married, settled, and apparently happy Florentino upon his return, Ramuntcho wonders to himself: 'What is there that is so particular that resides in his soul that keeps him from feeling comfortable here, like the others? Why, my God, is it forbidden for him, for him alone, to finish out here the tranquil destiny of his dream, when all his friends have achieved theirs?' (II:2; remember the homoerotic connotations given to dreams in *Iceland Fisherman*).

The answer to Ramuntcho's anguished question would seem to be found earlier in the novel, when the text notes that 'between [Ramuntcho] and the men who surround him [the other contraband runners] arose suddenly irreducible hereditary differences' (I:4). The text at one point had remarked that, long before he became involved with Itchoua and his band, Ramuntcho 'just out of childhood ... began to follow contraband runners in the mountains' (I:9; note again the link of the runners with the mountains). If Ramuntcho has come to feel a real, basic difference even from the contraband runners, one that the narrator attributes to heredity, it would seem to be because, for him, contraband is not just a temporary pastime, as homoerotic activity can be for young men who will grow up to be comfortably heterosexual adults. If 'he had begun [contraband] for fun, as a dare, like most of

them ... little by little [Ramuntcho] had developed a need for this continued adventure of black nights' (I:1), a passage that is readable as a
description of a young man's introduction to and involvement in homosexual feelings. Ramuntcho's case recalls the first two of the four 'axes
around which,' according to David Bergman, 'one can distinguish
the homosexual from other sexual discourses': (1) Ramuntcho has an
indefinite feeling of 'otherness'; 'he is distanced without definition';
and (2) his attachment to contraband is 'a lifelong condition. It is not a
"phase" that one goes through,' as it is for Florentino and Arrochkoa;
he has a sense of contraband's 'genuineness of experience'; it is not, for
him, a substitute for something else.[33] In other words, Ramuntcho is
developing a distinct and, even if only metaphorically, gay identity, one
that, in line with *The Story of a Child*, is linked to heredity. (Even in the
first pages of the novel, the narrator had had remarked that Ramuntcho
'did not feel altogether the same as his companions in sport or healthy
exercise' [I:1].)

This provides an added dimension to the scene between Florentino
and Ramuntcho after the latter's return from military service. The narrator notes that 'between the two, an abyss of different conceptions
opened wider during these three years' (II:2). Why is the abyss between
the two wider now? Because Florentino is happily married? Because
Ramuntcho cannot understand how Florentino could have given up
contraband for marriage? As the cart driver moves off, Ramuntcho
thinks to himself: 'He has made a success out of his life!' Does
Ramuntcho envy him his married status, his financial stability, or something else?

Besides finding himself distanced from both the general run of men
and the other contraband runners, the protagonist also feels disconnected from the very different world of his father. Just as his fellow
Basques are too simple for him to share their unquestioning view of life,
the world of his father is too refined for him. Early in the novel, when
the young man still knows nothing about his French parent, the text
speaks of 'the elegant men whom Ramuntcho's father chose as his companions' (I:1). Because Franchita has intentionally kept him from all
contact with his father, Ramuntcho 'would no longer be able to attain
the dangerous regions of dizziness to which the intelligence of his father
had risen.'

After Franchita's death, her son finds the letters that his father had
written to her twenty years before and feels 'a sudden execration against
the man who had given him life out of caprice' (II:8). Part of this hatred

must be attributed to a sense of having been abandoned. Though Ramuntcho's mother was still alive at that point and loved him very much, the narrator had had no problem early in the novel describing the protagonist as 'alone and without support in the world' (I:6). Later, after Franchita dies and her son wonders whether he should go through her papers to find some trace of his father, the text reports his thoughts through indirect discourse: 'So then, what should he do? ... And for that matter, whom should he take counsel from, when he has no one in the world?' (II:8). It is not surprising that, when his uncle Ignacio offered to help him and his wife, Ramuntcho told Gracieuse: 'It's no longer like in the past, you understand; I am no longer abandoned like I used to be' (I:20), or that, when this offer later fell through, he saw himself once again as an 'exile' (II:13). Ramuntcho feels the need for a guide in life, and perhaps more specifically someone who can explain to him where he came from, the source and context for his different desires.[34] Viewed from our modern perspective, the young Basque, though he does not realize it, is suffering from a lack of community, an inability to communicate with others like himself who could help him give his feelings context and create an identity that incorporates them.[35] As Bergman has remarked, since 'no homosexual is raised *as* a homosexual ... gay men grow up without support, recognition, or modelling of others, all of which are needed for consonance of signification.'[36] Remember Ramuntcho's feelings of oppression at not being able to express his emotions to Florentino (II:2).

Part of Ramuntcho's hatred for his father also seems to result from a strong dislike of certain qualities that the young man resents having had passed down to him. When he comes across the Frenchman's photograph among the letters, he discovers that '*That man resembled him!* ... He found, with a deep terror, something of himself in that unknown man. And instinctively he turned around, worrying that the ghosts in the dark corners had approached from behind to look as well.' Since Ramuntcho is troubled by the thought that someone might notice the similarity that he has just detected between himself and this elegant man, there must be something in his father that he would be ashamed to have others see in him. Having already tossed the letters into the fire, he does the same with the picture. 'He threw it, with a gesture of anger and terror, into the ashes of the last letters.' Why would he be terrified that someone might notice a similarity between himself and the Frenchman? What qualities could that elegant Frenchman, the source of his difference from other men and his desires for something else, have? What elegant man associated with France would someone in the last decade of the nineteenth century who saw himself as gay-tendancied and who desired the acceptance of straight men not have wanted others to see him resembling?

Dare one suggest Oscar Wilde? Always interested in things French, Wilde had sent a copy of his French play, *Salomé*, to Viaud in 1893,[37] and moved to France after his release from Reading Gaol in 1897. Gide, recalling his 1895 meeting with the Irish author in Africa after the trial had started, remarked in his memoirs that by that point 'frequenting Wilde had become compromising, and I wasn't happy about it when I met him again.'[38] As many studies have shown, Wilde's 1895 trial brought homosexuality to the attention of the western world and went far to establish the image of the elegant dandy as the type of the gay man for the general culture. As Joseph Bristow has written, 'So familiar is this queer stereotype that it is easy to forget that the connection between effeminate behaviour and same-sex desire was firmly established in the public imagination only after Wilde was sent to Reading Gaol for two years in solitary confinement with hard labour.'[39] Robert A. Nye confirms that, at this time, 'in France the concept of the effeminate invert invariably subverted all other varieties.'[40] We will come back to this idea later when we consider the autobiographical context for the novel, but it is clear that Wilde, or at least the elegant dandy in general, is yet another identity from which Ramuntcho wants to distance himself.[41]

If *Ramuntcho* is the allegorical depiction of a man's effort to establish a heterosexual identity for himself, and since that identity is bound up in marriage to Gracieuse, it would be difficult not to notice that the problems that get in his way all seem to come from outside Ramuntcho. (This is definitely typical of Viaud, as we saw in earlier chapters: responsibility for sexual involvements is often shifted to others.) The most obvious guilty party is his mother. Besnier, in fact, went so far as to assert that in Viaud's Basque world mothers, 'having visibly devoured and digested their husbands long ago, can now devote themselves entirely to their task: causing the unhappiness of their children.'[42] This is excessive – Franchita never sets out intentionally to make life miserable for her son, and has been hoping that he would be able to marry Gracieuse for the last ten years (I:1) – but she has a deleterious, if unintentional, effect on her son's efforts to realize this goal.

The text is categorical about this. For reasons that no one can remember, Franchita and Dolorès, the young woman's mother, had a falling out many years before, and this, along with Ramuntcho's illegitimacy, disposes Dolorès against any union between her daughter and Ramuntcho. Franchita closes the door on the possibility of a reconciliation altogether when she gets into an argument with her old enemy after her son's departure for military service (I:27). The text subsequently states flatly: 'After this sort of challenge hurled at Dolorès out in public, it was cruelly true that, this time, she had broken her son's life forever!' (II:1). Interestingly enough for whatever it may signify, Franchita does not try to prevent him from running contraband (I:1).

While this is the worst of her (unintentional) impediments to her son's happiness, Franchita makes other mistakes as well. 'In addition, with a thoughtless investment, she had lost a part of the money given by the foreigner for her son. Truly, she was an excessively blundering mother, compromising the happiness of her beloved Ramuntcho in every way' (II:1). One might argue that this is being extremely harsh on the poor woman, an uneducated peasant who could not have been expected to be a skilled investor. (None of the mothers in Viaud's previous works had received anything like this condemnation.) Later, for what it is worth, the text blames these losses on 'unfaithful notaries' (II:8) instead.

In general, the text presents Franchita as being very controlling. As we have already seen, she chose to separate her son from his urban heritage, and the narrator expresses this in an unfavourable tone: 'Ramuntcho, the son of the foreigner, could have aspired to the less harsh existence of men in the cities if, with an unthinking and rather wild decision, she had not separated him from his father to bring him back to the Basque mountain' (I:1). As a result, we recall, she left her son feeling 'disinherited' (I:4), cut off from the source of his different feelings. Out of a fear of losing him, rather than out of a concern for his well-being and development, she decided to keep him in ignorance of his father and this heritage. Although she wished Ramuntcho to marry Gracieuse, her desire to spite Dolorès enables the text to state that 'she decided her son's future on her own' (I:1). It is interesting that, when he leaves to fulfil his military service and she insists on accompanying him to the station, the young Basque does not allow her to stay with him all the way (I:26). His words to her, 'I don't want my mother to go any farther,' do not give us any indication of why he does not want her to accompany him to the train station, but it is hard not to compare this scene to Sylvestre's departure for military service in *Iceland Fisherman*. That young sailor did not mind his grandmother coming to spend three days with him in Brest before he shipped out, bidding her an emotional good-bye in front of everyone at the train station (II:VII–VIII). It seems that the young Basque is intentionally trying to break Franchita's overwhelming efforts to control him. Twice the narration (I:27, II:1) and once Ramuntcho himself (II:8) refer to her illicit relationship with his father as a 'fault,' suggesting a certain amount of blame and resentment, something not found in the depiction of protagonists' mothers in earlier narratives.[43]

Although Ramuntcho's mother is presented as the major obstacle in his pursuit of marriage and whatever it represents, she is not the only one. Dolorès is also a guilty party. In addition to what we have already seen, she whisks her daughter off to the convent when, after the young man's departure for the military and Franchita's disastrous argument with her, Gracieuse refuses the hand of a wealthy suitor whom her mother tries to impose upon her (II:1). Elsewhere the text states that 'that woman is the only person in the world who has the power to chill him, and, nowhere else than in her presence does he feel the blemish of being the child of an unknown father weigh down upon him' (I:4).

The novel also presents Gracieuse as partially responsible for Ramuntcho's failure to achieve his goal. Though her mother takes her to the convent, the text does not allow readers to assume that Dolorès is solely responsible for her daughter's entrance into religious orders. 'No one knew what pressures were exercised on the little one with the golden hair, or how the luminous doors of life had been closed before her, how she had allowed herself to be walled into that tomb' (II:1).[44] Late in the novel, during their final meeting in the convent, the text suggests more clearly that Gracieuse played a role in taking orders, stating that she has within her 'that flame that pushed ... [her] toward mystical dreams, toward the mortification and the annihilation of the flesh' (II:13).

While her single greatest impediment to Ramuntcho's attainment of his goal is clearly her withdrawal from their planned marriage, Gracieuse does other things to hinder him as well. As a Basque, he is not obligated to perform military service, but she asks him to do so (I:5). As a result, she inadvertently prevents him from accepting his uncle Ignacio's subsequent offer to come to South America and manage his estate, which would have provided the two with enough income to overcome Dolorès's objections and get married immediately. The text makes the young woman's responsibility here clear. Ramuntcho reminds her: 'It is, for that matter, you who ordered me to undertake those proceedings'

(I:20), and the narrator chimes in: 'She was tortured at present at being the cause of this, of having herself pushed him to that act, which made so black a threat hang over the barely glimpsed joy!' Like Franchita, Gracieuse is presented as at least somewhat controlling, and one might wonder what to make of the sentence that mentions 'the same ardour that, later, no doubt, she would put into entwining Raymond, when caresses would no longer be forbidden between them' (I:5).

Another significant obstacle in Ramuntcho's attainment of his goal, as we have seen, is the church and religion. In several passages that we have already quoted, the narrator makes it clear that the young man's religious training causes him to hesitate in his resolve to kidnap Gracieuse.[45] It is also true that in this novel religion is almost uniformly associated with women. In one of the first scenes in the narrative, the reader sees Ramuntcho accompanying his mother to church (I:3). Later Gracieuse leads him to church to do penance for blaspheming (I:10), buys a statue of the Virgin for 'our [future] house' (I:17), and is portrayed as going to church 'at all hours of the day' (I:18). When she is there, at times she dreams 'of forgetting everything, and feeling pure, sanctified, and immaculate,' and only the warm spring air reawakens her desire to be with Ramuntcho. As this and other passages show, the church instills in the young woman a feeling that her desire for her beloved is somehow impure. Later, during the religious procession, 'when, from time to time, the memory of Raymond's lips crossed her dream, she had the impression, in the midst of all this white, of a burning, though delicious, stain' (I:21).

The preceding analysis could easily be adduced to argue that in this novel Viaud was blaming women for Ramuntcho's failure to develop a heterosexual identity. There is truth in this, but one should note that Ramuntcho's uncle Ignacio, by getting married, cuts his nephew off from the means to support himself and Gracieuse if he managed to kidnap her (II:13). Perhaps it would be more accurate to say that, while in this novel Viaud casts a great deal of blame for Ramuntcho's problems on women, in the end, true to his earlier novels, he is less concerned with accusing women than with shifting any responsibility away from the protagonist.

One interesting idea comes out of Viaud's description of Gracieuse's motivation for abandoning Ramuntcho and entering the convent. In a passage already quoted in part, the narrator states that 'the same flame ... pushed [Arrochkoa] toward adventures and the great life of the muscles, [and Gracieuse] toward mystical dreams, toward the mortification

and the annihilation of the flesh' (II:13). Gracieuse is as subject to the
desires of the flesh as any man in the novel (cf. I:18, I:19). Could Viaud
have been suggesting that homosexual activity (Arrochkoa's participation in contraband) was another way of dealing with extreme desire, no
different, and therefore no more reprehensible, than taking religious
orders?

Once all of the metaphors in *Ramuntcho* have been elucidated, the
novel reads simultaneously at two levels, almost like a medieval text. A
few instances should suffice to illustrate what readers will discover
throughout the volume. In the opening scene, for example, the title
character arrives 'on foot from very far away,' like a pilgrim at the start
of a medieval allegory, climbing 'from the regions that border the sea of
Biscay' [gay desire] to his house 'in a great deal of shadow, near the
Spanish border' [the zone between gay and straight desire]. He is surrounded by 'distant areas, ever deeper, [that] fall away on all sides,
greatly dimmed by twilight and fog': even though he is trying to move
away from it, he is still surrounded on all sides by gay desire. Because of
his dual nature, 'he did not feel altogether like his companions in the
games or healthy labour': he is comfortable in neither the straight nor
the gay world.

At the end of the first chapter, Itchoua comes to get Ramuntcho for a
contraband expedition, leading him off 'into the thick night, into the
rain, into the chaos of the mountains, toward the dark border': into the
realm of gay desire. (Again, note that Ramuntcho is lead by someone
else this first time and does not take off on his own: more shifting of
responsibility.) When the men come back the next morning, 'they
returned like people never having had anything to hide,' suggesting
that they did have something that they needed to keep secret from others. (This makes more sense allegorically than literally, as the contraband runners had no need to conceal their activities from their fellow
Basques.)

The next contraband scene is surrounded from the beginning with
images associated with gay desire: 'Midnight, a winter night black like
hell, with much wind and lashing rain. On the bank of the Bidassoa, in
the middle of an unclear stretch on the traitorous ground that awakens
ideas of chaos, in muck where their feet plunge, men carry crates on
their shoulders' (I:8). Ramuntcho's boat gets loose and starts to carry
him toward the sea; he has to row back against the current at the risk of
being discovered: his efforts not to be carried altogether into gay desire.

Other scenes can be read in the same fashion, but one of the most remarkable is the final one in the convent. When Ramuntcho and Arroch-koa first set off, it is as if the forces of gay desire are threatening to stop this attempt at creating a heterosexual identity. Ramuntcho has decided to reject Itchoua's offer of help, feeling assured that this way he will not 'stain himself with some crime' (II:13). Is he here rejecting gay help entirely? (Remember, Arrochkoa does contraband not out of necessity, but as a lark.) The two young men move through terrible mountain ter-rain, but now 'a powerful, tranquil greenery has been thrown over all this tormented geology': the powers of heterosexuality are beginning to dominate those of homosexuality. Even once the two enter the white convent, however, the sisters remind them that the night outside is still very black, and rain threatens.

Recalling Viaud's own description of the Breton fisherman's daugh-ter who refused his offer of marriage as his last possibility for salvation, Ramuntcho now decides that Gracieuse 'was his hope ... without her, there is nothing more.' This makes less sense on the literal level than it does on the allegorical, where the young woman represents the protago-nist's hope for constructing a heterosexual identity. When she fails him (as the text presents the story; it is actually Ramuntcho who fails him-self, in that he does not go through with the abduction), he leaves the Basque land, this frontier between the two sexualities, and sets off for the New World, which is described as 'exile,' obeying 'an ancient impulse,' a man 'whom a gust of adventure carries elsewhere.'

What is one to make of this final scene? For Quella-Villéger, it was an indication that 'Ramuntcho ... has been defeated.'[46] Wake argued largely the same thing, but saw it as autobiography as well, claiming that '*Ramuntcho* records the measure of [Viaud's] failure as a man.'[47] Read in the allegorical context that has been developed in this chapter, the scene is less clearly defeatist. True, the protagonist has failed in his attempt to construct a heterosexual identity for himself. (In thinking that Gracieuse is his only hope, he would seem to suggest that, after this attempt, there will not be others.) At the same time, in leaving the Basque land, he is also giving up both the homosexual possibilities rep-resented by the contraband runners, men who can engage in the illicit for awhile as a lark and not out of necessity but then abandon it for con-ventional married life, and the glory and acceptance from the general populace associated with pelota.[48] Nevertheless, he is going 'elsewhere,' and in doing so obeys 'an ancient impulse,' leaving the reader to won-der if he is abandoning the realm of desire altogether, or moving to a new kingdom where he will be able to construct an identity more in congruence with his different feelings and nature. The text suggests that in America 'his strength [will have to] spend itself and use itself up who knows where, in unknown labours and battles.' Readers might recall that the title character of *My Brother Yves*, when overcome by a desire to be 'freed from everything' that seemed to be constraining him, had fantasized about deserting from the navy and fleeing to America (VI). The conclusion of *Ramuntcho* does not have a positive tone, but it nevertheless suggests that the title character, however unhappily, has abandoned efforts to compromise himself and has resolved to try to construct an identity in congruence with his nature as he has come to see it. Even today many homosexual men do not go as far.

All of the above can be seen when *Ramuntcho* is read in the context of Viaud's previous fictions. To read the novel in the context of his life is also informative. Validating such an approach to *Ramuntcho* is not new, furthermore. Quella-Villéger maintained that 'it is good form, especially in the work of Pierre Loti, to look for the author in his fictional characters,'[49] and Besnier called 'the real scope of the book ... its most correct perspective.'[50] The latter even suggested that 'the novel is useful for expressing the truth on points where the diary only puts forth fictions.'[51] As we have seen, Viaud often used his novels not to record his life, but to work out ideas that were important to him.

Unfortunately, those who have attempted biographical interpretations of *Ramuntcho* have generally tried to make it a retelling of Viaud's bizarre relationship with Crucita Gainza, the Basque woman whom he brought to France while working on the novel so that he could father children, and specifically male children, with her hardy Basque blood.[52] The first of these sons, Raymond, or Ramontcho, was born on 29 June 1895, a year and a half after the author first began to develop the idea for the novel,[53] and, according to Viaud's legitimate son, Samuel, about as long before he completed the work on 8 November 1896.[54] Since Viaud's diary entries from this period make it clear that he had no romantic interest in the young Basque woman, biographical critics have not gone to any great effort to see Ramuntcho's feelings for Gracieuse as a transposition of Viaud's for Crucita.

Instead, they focus on the fact that Ramuntcho is an illegitimate child and see in the scene where he burns his father's picture an expression of guilt on Viaud's part for his relationship with his own illegitimate son Ramontcho.[55] According to Besnier, for example, '*Ramuntcho* is nourished by this bad conscience, sometimes taking the character of self-punishment.'[56] Moulis, having presented Viaud's diary entries for the period, concludes: 'The protagonists Franchita and her son Ramuntcho are only a considerably transposed pre-figuration of Crucita and Raymond G.'[57] Quella-Villéger, arguing for the same interpretation, claims that Viaud 'appears ... completely present in the [French] officer.'[58]

As with the attempts to read Viaud's courtship of the Breton fisherman's daughter into *Iceland Fisherman*, this effort can only be achieved by ignoring the reality of the text itself. To begin with, unlike the Frenchman, Viaud never abandoned Raymond or his other two illegitimate sons. On the contrary, as already mentioned, he brought Crucita to Rochefort and raised his second family there, even introducing the children to his mother.[59] There is a famous photograph, reproduced in many books on the author, of Viaud standing together with his legitimate and two illegitimate sons. He had no reason to feel guilty about his treatment of them.

Second, and as we have already seen, the novel describes Ramuntcho's father as elegant, a man of the world, one of a group of 'refined men ... exchanging between themselves, with light banter, thoughts about the abyss' (I:1). As every biography and recollection of Viaud makes clear, nothing could be farther from a description of the author, a timid little man, stiff and always off in a corner, who hated society and was not given to clever banter. Again, given the dates of composition of the novel, it is difficult not to see the Frenchman as a portrait of Oscar Wilde, or at least his French equivalents in the Parisian literary salons of the day. When Ramuntcho burns his father's photograph, it is hard to see this as Viaud expressing hatred for himself, but easy to see it as an expression of his 'terror' at the recognition of some of the flamboyant Wilde in himself, and his desire to eradicate any noticeable connection. Indeed if, as it seems, Viaud intended to end his novelistic production and hence his literary depictions of gay desire with *Ramuntcho*, one might ask to what extent this renunciation was born of a fear that, after the Wilde trial, at least some of his readers might begin to see something of the outlandish Irishman in him. As Rivers wrote, 'the Wilde affair cast a pall of paranoia over the subject of homosexuality'[60] and, as Bristow noted in a passage cited earlier in this chapter, the Wilde trial did a great deal to convince Westerners that all gay men are effete and effeminate, not the sort of image that Viaud, a career naval officer so proud of his physical strength, would have wanted imposed upon himself.

If *Ramuntcho* cannot be read in good faith as a commentary on his relationship with his illegitimate son, it can be seen as containing reflections on other aspects of Viaud's life. The most obvious one has to do with the relationship between Ramuntcho and Franchita, which in many ways seems to parallel that between Viaud and his own mother, Nadine. As noted in chapter 1, Nadine Viaud was also in her own way a controlling and dominating parent. Since she died on 12 November 1897,[61] four days after he completed the novel, it is not difficult to see in Ramuntcho's pain and sense of isolation at Franchita's passing a reflection of Viaud's own sorrow in a similar situation.[62]

More intriguingly, one might wonder what other aspects of Franchita may reflect Viaud's feelings toward his mother. Could one read into Franchita's decision to separate her son from the world of his father Viaud's feeling that his mother had separated him from participation in the homosexual culture of the time? Remember the passages in his diary, cited in chapter 1, where Viaud spoke of playing one role for his mother and another when he was away from her (*Private Diary 1878–1881*, April 1881). For that matter, in ascribing Ramuntcho's feelings of difference specifically to his father, whereas Pierre's, in *The Story of a Child*, had only been ascribed to unspecified ancestors, did Viaud mean to suggest something specific about his own father, or perhaps his father's family? Again, as with *Iceland Fisherman*, *Ramuntcho* may have been a way for Viaud to work out his feelings for his mother, and perhaps this time his father, as well as to express his problems with the conflicts of sexuality that may have informed his life and had informed most of his fiction.[63]

As we have seen, Viaud's Basque novel is more concerned with gay issues than it would appear on first reading or when read in isolation. Furthermore, it creates a system of metaphors to talk about these issues. Although the system was borrowed from *The Story of a Child*, it is greatly developed here. One might also ask if the story deals with these issues at its literal level. Does Ramuntcho feel actual desire for Florentino? Do the contraband expeditions involve anything sexual? By constructing his narrative in this sort of allegorical fashion, Viaud universalized the questions that he examines – feelings of difference aggravated by a claustrophobic society that stresses uniformity, etc. – to the point that, as in *Iceland Fisherman* or *The Story of a Child*, more than just gay men can identify with them. And they have, for *Ramuntcho* became one of Viaud's most popular novels. Puccini considered turning it into an opera, and one of his lesser contemporaries, Stefano Donaudy, did. That is all to the good.

Many will not be happy with what, for the first time in Viaud's novelistic output, might be seen as negative portrayals of homosexuality, however: Itchoua, the muddy crossing of the Bidassoa, the way the shadows cast by the mountains threaten Ramuntcho's pelota games, his means to acceptance by men in general, and the fact that Ramuntcho wants to marry a woman. Though he decides in the end to abandon the marriage and sets out to create a new life, it is not with optimism or exhilaration, but rather 'without courage' (II:13). Still, he had inherited from his father 'a fear of being closed up [in the Basque region], when he knew that vast and free elsewheres existed throughout the world' (II:2). If this were Viaud's last novel, as he seemed to have planned, and this the last chapter in my presentation of his works, it might leave a bad impression in the minds of some of the readers I hope to interest in him.

Fortunately, that is not the case. Whatever Viaud may have intended in 1897, nine years later, for remarkable reasons, one of which involved a remarkable feminist, he published one more novel, one that cannot help but delight anyone with an interest in gay issues, not to mention feminist ones. It is to that work, *The Awakened,* that we now need to turn.

A Defense of Homosexuals and a Consciousness Raising: *The Awakened*

With the conclusion of *Ramuntcho* and the title character's departure for an unknown that he would confront 'without courage,' Viaud seemed to abandon the issue of homosexual desire that had informed most of his previous fiction. Thereafter he published two collections of short pieces originally written for various venues, *Impressions* (1897) and *On Life's Byways* (1899), and three travel narratives, *The Last Days of Peking* (1902), *India* (1903), and *To Ispahan* (1904). He also wrote three works for the theatre: a play about one of his ancestors, *Judith Renaudin* (1898), the book for an operetta based on *The Marriage of Loti, The Isle of Dreams* (1898), and, in collaboration with Judith Gautier, *The Daughter of Heaven* (1903; not published until 1911).[1] He even collaborated with his friend Émile Vedel on a French translation of *King Lear* (1904). Viaud seemed to give up on telling stories about characters and relationships that involved desire. In 1904 he told Marc Hélys, of whom more shortly, that he no longer wanted to put himself on stage,[2] a line that emphasizes once again the extent to which he saw himself working out his issues in his novels. Since he did not seem to be able to write a novel without doing that, he apparently gave up on them.

The effect of this resolution on his work can be seen in *Madame Prune* (1905), a retelling of his return to Japan in 1900–1. Claude Martin lists it as one of Viaud's novels,[3] but many readers are likely to disagree. The opening description of a storm upon Pierre Loti's arrival in Japan (I) repeats much of the dark imagery from *Ramuntcho* and would seem to announce a novel, but thereafter there is neither tension nor plot. Loti meets several women, but makes it clear that he has no erotic or romantic interest in any of them. He finds April Rain, the thirteen-year-old geisha whom he encounters, 'asexual' (V; cf. also XVI), and describes

Inamoto, whom he meets in a cemetery over Nagasaki and for whom he has far more respect, as a 'friend' (XXXVII), repeatedly declaring that their tête-à-têtes were innocent (XXXVII; XLII). He goes through the brothel district one night, since it is on his way home, but makes it clear that sex did not interest him (XXIX). Although he flirts with several older Japanese women, he always explains that nothing else was intended or expected. Novels can exist without love stories, but once he had set aside desire, Viaud did not seem interested in constructing a narrative.

Men attract a little attention in *Madame Prune*, but again, it is brief and subdued, and is sometimes recollection rather than observation. When he arrives in Nagasaki harbour, for example, Loti notices that the junks that used to fill it, manoeuvered by 'little yellow athletes, naked like the men of antiquity' (II), are gone. Similarly, he remarks that Japanese peasants, 'so broad in the shoulder, of short, well-shaped stature, with athletic limbs' (XXIV), are dying because, unlike their ancestors, they can no longer live naked. Early in his stay Loti comments on the 'muscular and thick-set legs' (V) of a rick-shaw driver, as he had so often in *Madame Chrysanthemum* during his previous sojourn in Japan, but later he travels behind drivers without such remarks (XIII, XVIII). Otherwise there are brief mentions of water sellers who are 'athletic and half-naked' (XXI), acrobats who are 'astonishingly thick-set, with bull necks, their white muslin outfits letting the bulging of their thick muscles show through' (XL.2) and, on the sacred island of Miyajima, fishermen gathered in front of their shacks 'half naked, with magnificent musculature ... you would say that it was a scene from the golden age' (XLIX). Stopping for a few days in some port towns, Loti finds the inhabitants to be different from their city-dwelling compatriots.

> An alert and vigorous population, singularly different from the one in the cities, tanned by the sea air, built with strength, thickness, with red blood in their cheeks. Men naked like men of antiquity [again], often admirable, with their thick-set torsos, their excessive musculature, resembling smaller versions of the Farnese Hercules. (LI)

As often as not, however, where readers of Viaud's earlier works might expect to find attention paid to men's physiques, it does not figure in this book. Loti mentions the sailors on his ship exercising above him (XVII), a giant Breton seaman (XXII, XLIII), and a drunken Russian sailor (XXIX), without devoting erotic notice to their appearance. In short, there is no sexual tension in this book and no story: Pierre Loti goes from place to place as an observer but never gets involved with anyone he sees. *Madame Prune* is not a novel, but a personalized travelogue ... which seems to be what, and all, Viaud wanted to write.[4]

And that is probably all that he would have written had something remarkable not occurred to trigger the creation of his last novel, *The Awakened*.[5] Thereby hangs a tale, one that has often been told by previous writers on Viaud, but that merits further examination.

During Viaud's lifetime, *The Awakened* (1906) was the second most popular of his novels, after only *Iceland Fisherman*.[6] It went through 419 editions in French alone by 1923.[7] Much of that success was the result of its feminist stance. Even feminists who lambast Viaud's works today for not having their late twentieth-century ideas a hundred years before their time make an exception for *The Awakened*. Szyliowicz, for example, who faulted Viaud for not respecting women in his books while she slandered gay men in her own, found the novel to be 'one of Loti's positive contributions to French literature,'[8] and even declared that the work 'represents a milestone in feminist thought for the early twentieth century because it pleads for equal rights for women at a time when they were mostly regarded as second-class citizens.'[9] Since the author's death, however, the book has lost its standing among his works, largely, I suspect, because of a revelation made the year after about its creation.

Briefly, the novel recounts the story of three Turkish women trapped in harem life in Istanbul who, because they know the works and popularity of a French novelist and naval officer named André Lhéry, ask him to plead their case and that of Turkish women in general through a novel that would tell their story to the world. They offer to provide him with information about harem life, and the leader of the three, Djénane, writes Lhéry a series of letters recounting her experiences and her feelings about a marriage that she is about to be forced to accept. Though the first line of *The Awakened* is 'This is an entirely imagined story' (Preface), Viaud made no pretence of denying his source, preceding the Preface with a dedication to the memory of Leyla Hanum, one of the three women whom he had met in Turkey and on whose lives the novel was based. It is hard to say how much help the original audience who bought those hundreds of thousands of copies of *The Awakened* believed that Viaud had received from the three Turkish women. In the novel, Lhéry speaks of collaborating with Djénane (XXIII), but that is part of the novel.

In 1924, however, shortly after Viaud's death, a French feminist, Marie-Amélie Léra (or Lerat, 1869–1964), who wrote under the pen name Marc Hélys, published *The Secret of 'The Awakened,'* in which she announced that she and two friends, descendants of a Frenchman who had moved to Istanbul and wed a Circassian woman, had played a hoax on the novel's author. They had presented themselves as Turkish women suffering under harem law – one, Zeyneb, widowed after a terrible marriage; one, Mélek, divorced after much suffering; and one, Leyla Hanum (Hélys), facing a loveless and degrading match – and had asked Viaud to tell the world about their plight and that of all Turkish women. Though Hélys did not take credit for the entire novel and praised Viaud for the beauty that he had brought to it,[10] she claimed to have played a major role in its creation. According to her, Viaud had agreed to send the women the work chapter by chapter for their suggestions and corrections and did so.[11] Furthermore, she showed, providing the originals, that in *The Awakened* Viaud had used, sometimes almost verbatim, many of the letters that she had written to him. In short, she not only made Viaud look like a middle-aged dupe who had let his ego and three flattering women make a fool of him, she also made it appear that he had, at best, been only a partial creator of the novel.[12]

Since Hélys published her version of the creation of *The Awakened* after Viaud's death – to avoid causing him pain, she said[13] – he never had a chance to respond. Writers on the novel have all repeated her story with total acceptance, and it may, in fact, be completely accurate. Then again, it may not. In *The Awakened*, André Lhéry makes fun of Djénane's 'little literary ideas' (XXIII; cf. also XXX), finding them clichéd and predictable. Hélys, an author in her own right, albeit mostly of journalistic works, may have spent the intervening eighteen years rankling under that widely diffused public ridicule and wanted, when telling her part of the story, to lessen Viaud's standing in turn. There is also a brief scene depicting a female journalist whom Djénane describes as someone who 'still wore her dirty gloves from the ship: indiscreet, prying, avid for copy for a recently created newspaper, she asked me the most astonishing questions, with a complete lack of tact' (IV). Whether Hélys might have seen herself as the object of this unflattering passage is impossible to determine. The most suspicious thing about her book is what she presents as the originals of her letters to the author, letters that, as already mentioned, figure in *The Awakened*, sometimes almost without change. Their style is remarkably, sometimes astonishingly like Viaud's, often using words, images, and ideas that are central to his way of writing.

There are several possible explanations for this. On the one hand, as she told Viaud, Hélys had been a devoted reader of his books and had them all.[14] It is possible that she had read them thoroughly and couched her letters to him in their terms to have a better chance of winning him over. It is also possible, however, especially after the mild ridicule to which he had subjected her in the novel, that she altered or even created some of her alleged originals using Viaud's text in order to depict herself as a better writer than he had made her out to be.

Just as Hélys's participation in the writing of the novel is not as clear as she and subsequent critics have claimed it to be, so the extent of Viaud's gullibility has, perhaps, been exaggerated. When Djénane first contacts André Lhéry by letter he dismisses her as a fraud: 'Ah! no, this woman was having fun at his expense! Her language was too modern, her French too pure and too flowing ... she must have been some traveller passing through Constantinople, or the wife of an embassy attaché, who knows? or, at the outside, a Levantine educated in Paris?' (I) Later, when he arrives in Turkey and receives her first invitation to meet, he assures his friend Jean Renaud: 'It's a trap ... This lady is no more a Turk than you or I' (V). Whether Viaud, who included this doubt in the novel and so raised it in his readers' minds, later changed his own mind like Lhéry (VI) remains a question. As Quella-Villéger has shown, the author quickly pierced the disguise of Zennour (Zeyneb in the novel) and Nouriyé (Mélek), 'Leyla Hanum''s two supposed cousins.[15] This would certainly have given him reason to suspect Leyla Hanum as well. We know from *Supreme Visions of the East*, as well as from his correspondance, that Viaud had doubts about Leyla Hanum's authenticity in the years after the novel's publication.[16]

But why, if he suspected fraud, would he have gone on with the charade and written the work? For that matter, why did he devote so much effort to defending a feminist cause, he whom feminists like Szyliowicz have found to be so lacking in respect for women, he whom, furthermore, critics and even Viaud himself have described as incapable of writing about anything but himself?[17]

The answer to either question can be found in *The Awakened*. As an attentive examination of the book shows, while it is about the sufferings of three Turkish women trapped in the harem system, it is also about something closer to Viaud's heart: the sufferings of individuals whose culture forces them to accept partners not of their choice and live double lives hidden behind a veil and on the margin of society. As we will see, Viaud managed to put together the material that Hélys had given him in such a way that, while he satisfied her and others who wanted a plea for Turkish women's freedom, he was also able, behind the veil of that plea, to write a defence of gay men and a call for them to come to a realization of their worth, dignity, and rights.[18] As with *Ramuntcho*, however, he turned to allegory to discuss these difficult issues.

Clive Wake, in his study of Viaud's novels, saw *The Awakened* as less personal than its predecessors: 'All of Loti's previous novels were the product of his own most intimate preoccupations.'[19] As we will see, however, it is as personal as those that came before. Though Alain Buisine claimed that there was little evolution from one novel to the next,[20] *The Awakened* treats some of these intimate preoccupations differently. In its own careful fashion it is bolder than its predecessors, in a way that should make it interesting even to activist contemporary gay men and others. It is time, now, to examine the second, previously unrevealed, 'secret' of *The Awakened*.

In the past, as we have seen with *Iceland Fisherman* and, to a limited extent, *Sailor*, Viaud had already used a woman to portray a gay man's feelings. This time he did not go quite so far. In one of her first letters, Hélys told him to think of her and her two cousins not as women, but as souls – 'these formless, graceless packets were not women, but souls, one soul'[21] – and, with some stylistic improvement, Viaud carried the idea over into his book: 'And then, above all, you have sensed, we are sure of it, that these formless, graceless packets were not women at all, as we had been telling you ourselves, but *souls, one soul*' (VII). Later in the novel the text states that Lhéry 'treated them like equals, like intelligences, like *souls*' (XIV). Since they generally appear wearing veils and shapeless clothing, it is easy for the reader to treat them in a similarly genderless fashion. As a result, it is also easier for a reader to see the description of their suffering as that not just of Turkish women, but of anyone of either sex who might have to wear a veil, however metaphoric, in public. Nevertheless, in using women to speak allegorically about the plight of gay men, Viaud was once again breaking down traditional exclusive gender constructions.[22]

It would be easy to say that the similarities between the sufferings of (closeted) gay men in an intolerant society and those of haremed women in Turkey are sufficient to establish a link between them, so that there would be no particular value in reading *The Awakened* in this allegorical way. More than just general similarities are present in *The Awakened*, however, making it clear that Viaud constructed the work with an allegorical reading in mind. He did this primarily through the character of Djénane whom, as much if not more than André Lhéry, he created in the mould of *The Story of a Child*'s Pierre and *Ramuntcho*'s title character, thereby establishing a link between *The Awakened* and some of its predecessors.[23] Like both of those earlier characters, and particularly the second one, Djénane dreams of living her life 'elsewhere.' In her diary (of which more in a moment), she writes to a then only imagined Lhéry: 'I will live my life elsewhere, I don't know where' (IV). So intent is she on this that she even dreams of a river whose waters 'hastened in their course toward the unknown distant lands' (III).[24] Like the Pierre Loti of *My Brother Yves*, Gaud in *Iceland Fisherman*, Pierre in *The Story of a Child*, and Jean Berny's mother in *Sailor*, Djénane also repeatedly experiences anguish (III, X, LIII), though now at the thought not of losing a man, but rather of having one whom she does not want forced upon her.[25] Like Jean Peyral in *The Story of a Spahi* and others who followed him, Djénane, too, confesses to a 'thirst for affection' (XXVIII). Like Pierre in *The Story of a Child*, she spent much of her childhood in a walled garden (II), sitting dreaming on a bank at the back (III). Viaud assures this connection by repeating even a small detail: just as Pierre's garden had a little grotto with a pool built by his brother (XIX), so Djénane's had 'a water spout in a marble basin' (II). These elements go past the general similarities between closeted gay men and haremed women, establishing a clear connection between Djénane and Viaud's previous protagonists.

The connections do not stop there. Djénane is repeatedly described, or describes herself and her fellow harem residents, as 'cloistered' (XIX [the word is absent from the same passage in Hélys's original, *Secret* 126], XXXI, XXXV, etc.), and also as a 'prisoner' (II, III, IV) and a 'captive' (III). All this, including some of the vocabulary, comes out of Pierre's description of his feelings in *The Story of a Child* and the narrator's description of Ramuntcho's emotions, as we saw in the chapters devoted to those works. Like both of them, Djénane is also 'eager for independence' (II). Like them as well, and to a lesser extent Gaud before them, she relies on a real window as her opening onto the world from which she is being kept (III, LIII, etc.). This time, however, the view is blocked because her window is covered with iron grills (II). On the other hand, she does have a freedom that Pierre did not have: whereas the young boy's family had carefully supervised his reading, forbidding him Musset, for example, because of its possible effect on his emotions (LXXVI), she, lacking a mother, has the freedom to read what she wants (II) and takes advantage of it to devour authors like Baudelaire and Verlaine, who would no doubt have horrified Pierre's family. As we shall see later, reading is very important for Djénane.

Other connections cement the link between the odalisque and central characters in Viaud's previous fiction. Just as Pierre had been fascinated by the songs of sailors, suggesting a rugged masculine world that he did not know but that entranced and called to him (XXXII), so the young Djénane, still living in the countryside, had delighted in the 'wild songs' of equally exotic and masculine Circassian soldiers (III).[26] Just as Pierre saved objects associated with his youth as a way of holding on to it, in Djénane's room the text notes 'humble knickknacks ... they didn't have any value at all, but they recalled vanished moments of that life, whose rapid disappearance without return constituted a great subject of anguish for them' (III).[27] Djénane explains this preoccupation with her childhood to Lhéry in a letter that explains the creation of works like *The Story of a Child* as well: 'When this soul suffers too much, it is the memories of my childhood that come back to haunt me' (III).[28]

What follows is equally interesting, however: '[These memories] reappear, imperious, coloured and brilliant; they show me a luminous land, a lost paradise, to which I neither can nor would want to return.'[29] Already in *The Story of a Child*, as we saw, Viaud had realized the futility of returning to childhood to escape the difficulties caused by gay desire. In leaving the Basque region, Ramuntcho also had stopped living in the location of his childhood. If anything, Djénane is even clearer about her resolve not to try to escape to her past.

After all this, it is not surprising that Lhéry at one point remarks to himself concerning Djénane: 'You would think, sometimes, that between us we have common memories of some unknown past' (XXV).

The most striking and important connection between Djénane and preceding Viaud characters, in particular the Pierre Loti of *My Brother Yves* and Pierre in *The Story of a Child*, is the fact that she, too, keeps a diary. She began it at the age of thirteen (III), exactly the age when Pierre began his (LVIII). Given this coincidence, the explanation of why Djénane began to write down her thoughts cannot help but reflect back on Pierre's decision (and perhaps Viaud's own) in the mind of any reader who has been following Viaud's works in chronological order. The text explains that the odalisque began a diary on her thirteenth birthday because it was then that 'she had *taken the tscharchaf* (to use an expression from there), in other words the day when it became necessary, for ever, to hide her face from the world, to cloister herself' (III).

In Djénane's case this is real, but since the connection with Pierre has already been established, the reader has a right to wonder if an allegorical interpretation of those same words should be applied back to him and Pierre Loti as well. Did Pierre start keeping his diary because he realized that there was something about himself that he could not share with the world, that he had to hide his face, or at least part of it, from the world?[30] In *The Story of a Child* he explains that in it he put 'less the events of my little, tranquil existence, than my incoherent impressions, my sadness at evening, my regrets over summers past and my dreams of distant lands' (LVIII), which could be a description of a thirteen-year-old child's feelings about initial (homo)sexual desires.

It is with this passage in *The Awakened* that another 'secret'· of the novel begins to unfold. The links between Djénane and previous Viaud characters serve to tie her to what one might call the Loti lineage, giving her a gay male dimension that Hélys did not envision for her and that she does not appear to have if the novel is read in isolation. In turn, however, because Viaud in his last novel makes comments about her state that can be applied to that of gay men in the author's time, she allows him both to elucidate aspects of her lineal predecessors, thereby reshaping our reading of his earlier works, and to make comments on the state of gay men in general.

This is true, for example, of some of the comments on Djénane's diary. The text notes that she wrote it in a foreign language, French, 'in order to be certain that neither her grandmother, nor anyone in the house, would read it for fun' (II). In *The Story of a Child*, Pierre had explained that in the first year he wrote his diary in code but thereafter switched to French to make composing it easier, though he was still careful to keep the volume hidden, 'like a criminal work' (LVIII). Is Viaud's remark about the odalisque's linguistic practice meant to refer just to Pierre's one-year coding, or is it meant to suggest more generally that all of Viaud's diary, and therefore at least some of the works drawn from it, have been similarly disguised? (Djénane continues to write her diary in French.) The second suggestion could mean that we were being told to read some of the events in Viaud's works as coded representations of Viaud's biography.[31] There is no one answer here, but it is clear that *The Awakened* is designed to cause Viaud's readers to rethink some of their previous understandings of his works.

Similarly, Djénane is described as writing her diary as if it would be read by Lhéry, because she envisioned him as 'a true friend, a big brother' (III). Elsewhere, using a noun that will have great importance in this novel, the text describes her diary as 'the letter to the unreal confidant,' and Djénane herself describes Lhéry, once she has met him and got to know him, as 'my confidant' (XXIV).[32] One could wonder what this might say about Viaud's reasons for keeping his diary, but more interestingly, it suggests an explanation for his intent in writing novels. As we have seen with his comments in certain previous works where he spoke of being read by 'unknown friends,' here the author suggests that he wrote not only to entertain the general public with artistic refashionings of his adventures (real or imagined), but also to confide his secret thoughts and feelings to those among them whom he could take as confidants, because they were real, trustworthy, understanding friends. The fact that Djénane views Lhéry as a 'big brother' is particularly suggestive, given the connotations that word had taken in earlier narratives. (Cf. also 'his role as big fraternal older brother' [XXXVI].) To what extent did Viaud imagine his 'unknown friends' to be gay men?

There are also links between Djénane and Viaud. Just as the music she writes is described as being 'inspirations that came from no one' (III), so Viaud's work had often been described, perhaps to his liking, as being *sui generis*. For example, one of his publishers, Juliette Adam, in a letter that he saved in his diary, wrote him: 'No one in French literature resembles you. You have no peer. To compare you to someone is to falsify you or to falsify the other person' (*Private Diary 1878–1881*, 28 January 1881).[33] Djénane loves to play the piano because its music allows her to fantasize a better life (III); Viaud's diaries are filled with references to his love of playing music on the piano.[34]

In addition, there are links between Djénane and Aziyadé/Hatidjé. Hélys was open about trying to associate herself in Viaud's mind with Aziyadé/Hatidjé in order to win his sympathies. In her first letter to him, Hélys closed by referring to herself as 'the present-day Aziyadé,'[35] and Viaud carried her claim over into his novel, having Djénane refer to herself as 'the Medjé of today' (V).[36] Lhéry eventually comes to accept this idea. At first 'he almost had the sacrilegious feeling that [Djénane] was a continuation of [Hakidjé]' (XI), but later he begins to equate them: 'He associated them in his memory, Nedjibé [Hakidjé], Djénane' (XVII), until finally, sensing an 'emanation of feminine souls' floating over the city, 'feminine souls that he had loved and that were becoming mixed together,' he wonders: 'Did it come from Nedjibé, or from Djénane, or from both of them, he didn't really know.' Indeed, he gave Djénane green eyes (XXII, not in the corresponding passage in Hélys's original letter, *Secret* 139; XXX), like Aziyadé/Hakidjé, and, in common with Hakidjé, a Circassian heritage (XXXI), though in reality it was Zeyneb and not Hélys who had spoken to Viaud of her Circassian background.[37] In the novel, Lhéry is clearly reliving something though Djénane. (Whether Viaud did the same it would be more difficult to guess.) Hélys did everything in her power to foster this confusion. She wrote Viaud: 'Let them become mixed together, let everything be mixed together ... all these shadows: the beloved from the past ... and these other shades who wanted to be your friends. Mix them all together ... mix them together well, and keep them together in your heart – because in your memory is not enough!'[38]

And yet, Djénane is not Aziyadé or Hakidjé. More independent than her predecessor, who was never portrayed as complaining about the system in which she functioned, Djénane is 'like the banner carrier of the feminine insurrection against the severities of the harem' (III), and when her forced marriage to Hamdi falls apart she approaches the Sultan himself for a divorce (X).

Nevertheless, something remarkable happens in the course of all these connections. Since Viaud created Djénane as another in the Loti lineage, it is easy to imagine that he would have felt a strong sense of identification with her. But, by association, if he linked her to Aziyadé/Hakidjé as well, he might also come to understand his early flame. In fact, that is what happens, at least to Lhéry: half way through the novel the text states that 'he understood better than ever before ... the mortal ennui of sequestrations' (XXXIII). He, and perhaps Viaud, have undergone a radical change. In the process of creating similarities between Djénane and himself so that he could use her to express his feelings, Viaud, himself sequestered by a society that would not allow him to express certain desires openly, ended up understanding the feelings of his fellow sequestered, or at least saying that Lhéry, his literary counterpart, did. The readers of *Aziyadé*, who will recall no such understanding on Loti's part for the title character in that novel, can only marvel at the change. In the course of trying to talk about himself, Viaud had finally learned to understand others as well, regardless of sex or gender.

This explains how Viaud could have used odalisques as a metaphor for (closeted) gay men. He describes them as living 'on the margin of the other [world], that they brush against in every street' (III), and says that they constitute 'that world that you feel everywhere around you, troubling, drawing you, but impenetrable, and that observes, conjectures, critiques, sees many things through its eternal mask of black gauze,' all of which is phrased such as to make it equally applicable to closeted gay men living in a homophobic culture. (It is probably not by chance that at one point the text observes that, when the three women bend over, 'their face veils hung like long Capuchin beards' [XIII], a strange image if the author were not trying to point out these characters' 'real' sex.) Viaud uses such careful phrasing throughout his descriptions of this cloistered society, so that his 'unknown friends' can move from one level to the other with ease. If Djénane, speaking of the Turkish woman, writes that foreigners have not previously been able to 'penetrate the mystery of her soul' (VII), Viaud meant the same to be understood of gay men, particularly in an era when science was proclaiming so many pejorative falsehoods about them. If one of the three women, at their first meeting with Lhéry, tells the author that they are 'three poor souls in pain, who need your friendship' (VI; cf. also XI), in large part because of their lack of freedom and forced, miserable marriages, the allegorical meaning, again, would not have been difficult to see. (Viaud's own marriage, though not forced, was the result of pressure from his family, and was not happy for either him or his wife.) When Mélek, forced into another marriage that she does not want, dies of a cerebral fever caused by 'so much nervous over-excitement, revolt, terror, which this new marriage caused her' (XLV), the text's comment that her father 'by his implacable observance of old customs ... had led her to die' (XLVII) is a stinging condemnation of such 'old customs.' The worst of it, moreover, as Viaud points out with Mélek's death and as he has Djénane reinforce in her final letter, is that it is the very people who love these individuals who cause them such misery: near the end of her missive Djénane writes: 'May their tears, all of them, may my anguish at this hour finally touch the poor blind ones, who love us, indeed, but who oppress us!' (LVI).[39] Earlier, in a less forgiving tone, the text had spoken of 'the tyranny of men' (XIII).

Though the condemnation of this oppression and tyranny is an important part of the novel, the central focus of *The Awakened* is Djénane's fear and hatred of entering into a marriage not of her choosing. This is a theme not explored in Viaud's previous novels, with the possible exceptions of *Madame Chrysanthemum* as we saw in chapter 7 and the end of *Iceland Fisherman* as we saw in the analysis of Yann's drowning.[40] This time, however, with the irony that marks much of Viaud's last novel, his protagonist is distraught not about being forced to marry a woman, but rather about being confronted with marrying a very handsome man, Hamdi-Bey.[41] Unlike in either of the two previous novels just mentioned, however, here Viaud presents the pressured individual's feelings at great length. Djénane is 'thrown off balance ... by the terror of this marriage' (II), in part because, as she tells her cousins, 'none of my days and none of my nights will belong to me anymore' (III).

In part, as well, Djénane hates the thought of the marriage because she knows that she will have to begin leading a double life, playing a role for her spouse who will not want her as she really is. She writes to Lhéry: 'So that was marriage ... those other hours where I had to play a part' (XIX).[42] As we saw in the chapter devoted to *The Story of a Child*, Pierre had spoken of developing an outer social self to disguise his true one when he first entered the outside world (LXXV).[43] With *The Awakening*, however, Viaud shows an awareness of others in this same situation: the text speaks of 'that sort of doubling customary to many young Turkish women' (IV) and Djénane, writing of Turkish women in general, bemoans 'this doubling of our being' (VII).[44] Taking Hélys's letters as a basis, for the first time the author presents the suffering not just of one individual but of a whole segment of society.

The text concedes that life with an unwanted partner can become bearable with time and habit, but it also argues that such a life is never true fulfilment. As Djénane writes to Lhéry, 'Often, it is true ... we become attached to him, with time, but that affection is not love' (VII; cf. *Secret* 34). Most interestingly for some modern readers, such a life is presented as a denial of an individual's fundamental dignity and being. Early in her marriage, Djénane starts to feel an attachment to her imposed husband (IV) and is lulled into forgetting her resentment (VIII), but then he is unfaithful to her with another woman, whom he even decides to take as his second wife. This reawakens Djénane's spirit and she writes Lhéry: 'I regained my dignity, I found my soul again and resumed my ascent' (XXII).[45] No doubt influenced by the ideas of the feminist Hélys but still rethinking and expressing things in his own way, Viaud, with *The Awakened*, asserted his subjects' fundamental right to be true to themselves and their desires, and found dignity and value in that state. This is well past even his justification of a 'need for tenderness' in *The Story of a Spahi*.[46]

According to the text, prisoners such as these say to themselves: 'My soul, which was not consulted, still belongs to me, and I'm keeping it closed up, jealously, in reserve for some ideal lover ... whom I will, per-haps, never meet, and who, in any case, will probably never know any-thing about it' (IV). But for the modifying 'probably,' this sounds close to Marcel's repeated assertion in *In Search of Lost Time* that gay men were doomed to lead unfulfilled lives. What makes *The Awakened* radically different from Proust's work, however, is that it proceeds to call for a world in which this will no longer have to be true. The three women's repeated complaint is that they are unable to turn their dreams into action. In a letter to Lhéry, for example, Djénane speaks of 'hearts in which a young sap boils, and to which action is forbidden, who can do nothing ... who are consumed or worn out by unrealizable dreams' (XXVI),[47] a line full of potent eroticism. Later she suggests that the heroine of his book should die 'from the inflexible exigencies of the harem that do not allow her the means to *console herself for her love and her dream with action*' (XXX).[48]

Not content to accept this situation, what the women, and particularly Djénane, call for is the right to have a partner of one's choice, to be able to realize their dreams with actions. Rephrasing Hélys's letter to give it more power, Viaud has Djénane write, using a comparison to *Aziyadé* that should drive home the point to readers of his previous works: 'Your Medjé is in the cemetery ... the little Circassian, whom overpowering feelings cast into your arms, is no longer, and the time has come when ... instinctual love and love born out of obeying have given way to love born out of *choice*' (VII).[49] Other things may be requested later, in half a century, the odalisque tells him, but now all they want is freedom to make their own choice of a partner (XLI). If they request this freedom, moreover, it is because they have the right to do so. In her last letter, written as she is dying after she has taken that poison, Djénane proclaims to Lhéry: 'I had the right to live and to be happy' (LVI). Viaud may have taken the line verbatim from Hélys's last letter to him,[50] but the fact that he used it in the novel casts all its meaning for his cause as well. It is made clear that part of this right concerns sex. Djénane's letter continues: 'And where are the arms that I would have loved?' altered from Hélys's less assertive, 'And the arms that I loved ...' This is particularly suggestive in the context of some of Viaud's previous work, which had focused on the virile arms of admired men. Hélys and her friends had asked Viaud for 'a book that shows ... that we have the right to have freedom in deciding our fate.'[51] Viaud provided that, and for the first time dared, albeit covertly, to claim that right for gay men as well.

This is not all that is new with *The Awakened*. While it repeats preoccupations found in some of Viaud's earlier works, his last novel also offers a number of striking new elements, several of which suggest a remarkably modern viewpoint. As already mentioned, Djénane, unlike the unquestioning Aziyadé, 'was like the banner carrier of the feminine insurrection against the severities of the harem' (III). When he wrote this, the novelist was certainly thinking of the outspoken and cogent Leyla, but in describing the latest embodiment of the Pierre Loti lineage in that fashion, did he see himself as being in a similar position among those who would, after his death, come to be called gay liberationists? He repeatedly remarks on the revolutionary zeal of his protagonist: 'She had preached so many times to others the feminist crusade' (III). Rather than accepting her fate, she tells her diary: 'I am ready for a fight' (IV), and dares to approach the sultan himself for a divorce (IX). Whether he saw himself as a potential gay activist like Djénane or not, Viaud was holding her proactive character up for admiration, something he had done in no previous work. It is perhaps worth recalling the chapter in *The Story of a Child* where Pierre, remembering how his Protestant ancestors had been excluded from French society because of their faith, explains that he had become so indignant that he was ready to undergo martyrdom for such a cause himself (XXIX).

Equally new with *The Awakened* is the protagonist's sense of working for someone other than herself, born of an awareness that she is not the only one to suffer in her situation. As already noted several times, Djénane speaks to Lhéry not just about herself and her cousins, but about the plight of Turkish women in general. If she wants him to call the world's attention to it through a novel, it is because she believes that, by making such efforts, she and her contemporaries will be able to initiate change. Granted, she writes: 'We are the rung in the ladder, we and probably those who will follow immediately, the rung by which the female Muslims of Turkey are called to climb and to free themselves' (XIX), but she definitely envisions both the possibility of change and the need to work together for the general good. None of Viaud's previous protagonists had worked for anyone but themselves.[52]

This is tied to one of the most striking features in the novel, the notion of community. In all of Viaud's previous novels, the Pierre Loti representative had always been conscious of being isolated and alone. From the beginning of this novel Djénane functions with her cousins, relying on them for support through her trials. She refers to them repeatedly as her 'sisters' (III, VI, VIII) because she shares with them 'their intimacy of sisters' (III, VIII).[53] Equally striking is the repeated talk of confidants. Djénane thinks of Zeyneb and Mélek as 'her confidants, her soul sisters' (III), and trusts them with her every thought.

Viaud drives the newness and difference of this development home by showing that, when Jean Renaud, Lhéry's friend, whom the text at one point describes as his 'confidant' (V), 'confided in him with burning expressions of sorrow his pain at being in love with a beautiful woman from the embassies [who was] indifferent to his desire in a very amiable fashion' (XL), Lhéry 'wanted to cry out to him, in a sort of triumph: "Well, imagine, I am more loved than you!"' but did not.[54] A community is based, at least in part, on the ability to confide in others, but for some, that ability was still hard to come by.[55]

Finding a person worthy of confidence is not easy, either. When she first moves into her husband's home, Djénane meets Durdané, an attractive woman about her age. 'To her, who had been married and who was young, I could, I thought, tell my sorrows' (XIX), but when she tries to confide her pain to the woman, Durdané just laughs at her and subsequently starts sleeping with Djénane's husband.[56] Furthermore, marriage makes having confidants more difficult. Hamdi's house is high above the city, 'in that high area that was accessible only with difficulty' (IV). Once there, Djénane feels, she will be 'exiled,' a word that Viaud had used repeatedly throughout his earlier narratives to describe his protagonists' isolation from others.

As often, a comparison with Proust is revealing. In *In Search of Lost Time*, Marcel repeatedly assures his readers that community is impossible for 'inverts.' He warns about the

> lamentable error of proposing (just as people have encouraged a Zionist movement) to create a Sodomist movement and to rebuild Sodom. For, no sooner had they arrived there than the Sodomites would leave the town so as not to have the appearance of belonging to it, would take wives, keep mistresses in other cities where they would find, incidentally, every diversion that appealed to them. They would repair to Sodom only on days of supreme necessity, when their own town was empty, at those seasons when hunger drives the wolf from the woods. (*Sodom and Gomorrah* 44)

This is because, according to Marcel, 'the invert brought face to face with an invert sees ... an unpleasing image of himself which ... could at the worst only injure his self-esteem' (*Sodom and Gomorrah* 432).[57] Was Viaud more optimistic because he was less homophobic? He would seem to have been envious of the three odalisques' ease in establishing and maintaining community and, with the above-cited scene between Lhéry and Renaud as well as the one between Ramuntcho and Florentino, to have regretted some men's (his own?) difficulty in doing the same.

The Awakened begins with a description of Lhéry 'believing himself suddenly isolated in life' (I). In the past there had been Viaud's readers, those 'unknown friends' of whom he had spoken more than once in his books.[58] But now they seemed too distant to suffice: on that same first page Lhéry views them as 'scattered and forever distant creatures.' No wonder Viaud found the story of these three Turks, functioning in 'their intimacy of sisters,' to be so appealing. Was he calling for a similar 'sisterhood' among gay men? Once Djénane is forced to return to her husband and Mélek has died of cerebral fever, Zeyneb writes Lhéry that she finds herself 'in a terrifying isolation' (LIV). Viaud's previous characters had known such isolation, as had he. Community looked like a wonderful, and perhaps possible, alternative.

One way to establish that community, especially at the turn of the century, was through books, and books play an important role in *The Awakened*. This, too, is basically a new development with Viaud's last novel, though Pierre in *The Story of a Child* had mentioned a few books that awakened his imagination, and there was some mention in *Ramuntcho* of the effects of the title character's reading on his feelings of being different (II:10). *The Awakened*, however, contains a veritable paean to the value of books for those forced to live 'on the margin' of society. When Djénane discovers the misery of Turkish marriage and decides that things must be otherwise elsewhere, she 'set about studying it with passion in literature' (XXVI). As the text explains later speaking of all three women, 'everything that they knew about life in general, things about Europe, about the evolution of the intellects there, they had learned in solitude, with books' (XIV), and this novel, unlike some of its distinguished nineteenth-century French predecessors, makes no suggestion that there was anything wrong with such a tutelage. If the cousins' mother cannot understand the three young women's suffering under the harem system, if 'she ... would not have understood' (II), it is because 'she was of another generation,' a generation that is described in terms of its lack of reading of modern literature, 'having read only Alexander Dumas senior.'

Granted, that older generation is at peace: 'She didn't resemble them, her beautiful eyes reflected a somewhat naive peace that was not found in the look of the admirers of André Lhéry (II),' a description that links the mother with the unreflective Basques in *Ramuntcho*. A similar link is established with the unquestioning faithful when Lhéry observes a group of believers 'cast their foreheads to the earth, all at the same time, with a regular group movement' (XVII), just as the Basque men had worn their uniform berets all in the same fashion (I:4). 'These simple and ... wise people here ... later, with reassured souls, will die like you set off on a nice trip!' the text observes with a tone of envy, again recalling the Basques's calm in the face of death (I:13). But those who have read cannot go back to that peaceful ignorance. When Lhéry suggests such a return, hypothetically, Djénane promptly replies: 'That return is impossible: you can't go back up stream on the flow of time' (XIII), just as Ramuntcho was no longer simple enough to accept the dogma and observances that provided his fellow Basques with their calm (I:13).

Literature in *The Awakened* provides several different types of learning. For those who are kept from discovering things through their own experience, books can teach what they are unable to encounter directly. Djénane tells Lhéry in one of her letters: 'For us, the eternally cloistered, you hold out the mirror that reflects the world forever unknown; it is through you that we see it' (XIX).[59] As a result, they are able to live experiences that are denied them in the real world. Mélek tells Lhéry: 'You can't imagine what we have already lived with you' (XI). Elsewhere, the text says: 'It was true that for a long time now they had been living in his company, through his books' (XIV).

More important, perhaps, literature teaches cloistered individuals about themselves. (As we saw in the chapter devoted to *The Story of a Child*, Viaud had already put forth this idea there.) In one of her letters Djénane exclaims to Lhéry: 'How good it would make me feel to tell you, you who must understand them, so many heavy things that no one has ever heard; things in my destiny that baffle me; you who are a man and who *know*, you would explain them to me, perhaps' (XXIV).[60] This passage, original with Viaud, shows quite strikingly his refocusing of Hélys's story to express his own, different ends. Since the odalisques had the advantage of community and confidants, it is hard to imagine that they would have needed to turn to an outside figure, and a man at that, to explain their feelings to them. On the contrary, Djénane's letters and conversation suggest that she already had a remarkable sense of herself before ever meeting Lhéry. For closeted gay men at the turn of the century, however, cut off from almost any sort of community and thus communal sharing, the desire to look to other gay men as a way of understanding things about themselves that they were not able to encounter in their general culture must have been a very strong one.

(Remember Ramuntcho's desire to learn about his father and more generally 'to know!') Many gay men, especially those new to an awareness of their sexuality, continue to feel such a desire today, often still turning to books for answers to their questions about who they are finding themselves to be, in particular if they live outside areas with readily accessible gay communities. David Bergman devotes a considerable portion of the Introduction to his study of gay American literature to explaining 'the importance of literature for developing gay identity,' part of 'the disproportionate importance given to writing in gay communities.'[61] As Dominique Fernandez has pointed out, however, until recently most books on homosexual men, including most literature, gave such men only 'the portrait ... of an inferior being condemned·to suffer.'[62]

This was not always an easy experience. Their tutor laments: 'I regret having been one of the instruments that put the microbe of suffering in these women of tomorrow' (XXXII), but the awakened themselves do not seem to regret the pain. Addressing Lhéry in her diary before she ever imagined meeting him, Djénane remarks: 'The carefree and gay child has become a young woman who has already cried a lot. Would she have been happier continuing her primitive life? ... But *it was written* that she would leave it, because she *had* to be changed into a thinking being, her orbit and yours *had* to cross one day' (III).[63]

Books not only explain questions about the self for which the cloistered often have no other place to find answers; they can also cause readers who have not yet done so to begin to ask such questions, to come to an awareness of who they are and what they have a right to expect. This awareness might be unknown to readers if their reality is one that their culture has not already shown them to be a possibility, or if it has done so only in a negative fashion. Improving on a line from one of Hélys's letters,[64] Viaud had Djénane write to Lhéry: 'In us, Muslim women, almost everything was still asleep. Our consciousness of ourselves, of our value, was barely awakening' (XXVI), and elsewhere: before reading Lhéry 'we had never thought that we might deserve to be felt sorry for' (XXIV). Their reading is what awakens the three young Turks, giving them the 'awareness of ourselves, of our value.'

If Djénane and her fellows ask Lhéry to novelize the story of their lives and suffering, it is, in part, because they are intent on bringing about a similar consciousness raising for others in their situation. In her last letter to the author, the odalisque cries: 'May my death at least serve my Muslim sisters! ... I had caressed this dream of trying to awaken them all in the past' (LVI). Subsequently she retreats somewhat, wondering if she should disturb those who have not already begun to question on their own:

> Oh! no, sleep, sleep, poor souls. Never become aware that you have wings! ... But those who have already begun to soar, who have glimpsed other horizons than that of the harem, oh! André, I entrust them to you; speak about them and speak for them. Be their defender in the world where people think. And may all of their tears, may my anguish at this hour finally touch the poor blind ones, who love us, indeed, but who oppress us![65]

This is more ambitious than anything Viaud had undertaken before, even *The Story of a Child*. Here, for moments at least, he presents the function of literature not simply as responding to the questions of those who have come to a realization that they are not at one with those around them or with themselves, but even as a way of awakening others who are still in the oblivion that their culture has inculcated in them, still 'asleep/enchanted.' In calling for them to come to a 'consciousness of their value,' furthermore, he was offering all such oppressed individuals a valorization that society in general and even other gay men would be a long time in conceding.[66]

André Lhéry is sceptical about his ability to live up to the three women's request. Well before the end of Djénane's last letter, they had called upon him to defend them to the world: 'Monsieur Lhéry, take our defence; write a book in favour of the poor Muslim woman of the twentieth century!' (XIII). Lhéry listens to them 'without in any way giving himself an illusion about the extent of what he could do for them' (XLI). Nonetheless, Viaud proceeded to make the changes in Hélys's letters and suggestions that, as we have noted, enabled him to produce a defence of gay men and a call for their own consciousness raising.

How he went about this proceeds to the heart of Viaud's literary aesthetic and is reminiscent of *The Story of a Child*. As we have already seen, near the end of her last letter Djénane exhorts Lhéry: 'Be their defender in the world where people think.' Implicitly at least, Djénane – and Hélys, whose text Viaud repeated verbatim here[67] – envisions the author making a reasoned plea, appealing to his readers through their intellect, which, as Djénane makes clear, works only with those who function rationally. Lhéry, however, had already explained earlier that rational argumentation was not his gift. At one of their meetings he had said: 'A book that tries to prove something? Do you, who seem to have read me carefully and to know me, think that that is the sort of thing that I can do?' (XIII). What he decides to do instead, and what we have already seen Viaud talk about in *The Story of a Child*, is to win his readers over by appealing to their emotions. Using indirect discourse to report what may be Lhéry's thoughts, which certainly also echo the author's, the text shortly afterward mentions 'these ardent affections that one awakens here and there, at the far ends of the earth, in unknown souls – and that are, perhaps, the only reason that one has for writing!' (XIV). Rational discourse, the traditional way of addressing 'the world in which people think,' can always be rejected by blindness and bigotry. Emotion circumvents such responses and goes directly to the generally unprotected depths of the audience. (One is not always sentimental simply to' sell books.)

These and other things already mentioned show, not surprisingly, that André Lhéry is also a representative for Viaud in this novel. The author models him so clearly on himself as to make the previously mentioned prefatory remark: 'This is an entirely imagined story,' altogether risible. Not only does Viaud present Lhéry, a French naval officer and celebrated novelist, as the author of a work describing his romance with an odalisque in the Middle East, he at one point also has Lhéry explain that 'once upon a time, I took pleasure in having people call me Arif Effendi' (XXXI), one of the pseudonyms that Loti had used in *Aziyadé* (II:XVIII, etc.). Since he makes such obvious efforts to equate Lhéry with himself and Loti, it is hard not to see Lhéry's portrait as an intentional public presentation of the author's self.

As in *Madame Prune*, this Viaud figure does not make any pretence of seeking a romantic adventure here: 'This time he didn't even dream of starting the adventure [of Aziyadé] back up' (V). 'With this Djénane, young enough to be my daughter, how could there be on either side anything more than a gentle and strange friendship?' (XVII). Zeyneb at one point writes him that 'this innocent adventure ... will be, in your life, a page without a reverse side' (XII), recalling the episode of the drawing of the Unhappy Duck in *The Story of a Child* (IX) in which, as we saw, the lines on the reverse side of the paper became a metaphor for hidden sexual desires.[68] He seems to have given up on involvement in any sort of desire.

Lhéry wants to see the faces, and especially the eyes, of the three women who appear to him under heavy veils, however; he repeats this desire several times (XIV, XXV, XXIX, and elsewhere). In part this is a question of ego: he asks his friends, the Saint-Enogats, who know

Djénane, if she is attractive (XV), no doubt because he would like to think of himself as appealing to attractive persons.[69] More important, however, since Lhéry elsewhere expresses his belief that 'souls are revealed to another soul above all else through the expression of the eyes' (XIII), one can assume that he wants to see what the three Turkish women, and especially Djénane, really think of him. When one lives behind disguises, one grows to suspect that others do as well.[70]

One of the more unsympathetic sides to Lhéry is his constant preoccupation with his age. He is convinced that other people's interest in him is based on his looking young. When he thinks the three Turkish women have stood him up, for example, he says to himself sadly: 'They were expecting me to be young, and they must have been too disappointed' (IX). The text distances itself from this preoccupation, however, and inserts a critical stance. At one point it speaks of how beings like Lhéry indulge in 'puerile and lamentable despair, because their hair is turning white and their eyes are growing dull' (XXXIX). 'Puerile' suggests a lack of sympathy; here Viaud is distancing himself either from himself, or at least from incarnations of this aspect of Pierre Loti. Earlier, a member of the English embassy had made fun of Lhéry's 'excessive efforts' to appear young (VIII).

There is another possible insight into Viaud and closeted gay men of the time in the character of Lhéry as well. Mélek at one point writes him: 'You never enjoy anything fully, because you tell yourself: "It will end"' (XXXV), and it is true that he does not believe that the affection of others for him will last. When Djénane is faced with having to return to her husband, Lhéry muses: 'Now that she has been taken back by Hamdi, who was young and whom she probably had not stopped desiring, she was going to be altogether lost to him' (XLI; cf. also LIII). Viaud's diary, at least in its published form, is full of examples of a fear that friends and potential lovers will leave him (*Private Diary 1878–1881*, 1 November 1879; 7 April 1880; April 1881; etc.). One could argue, nonetheless, that such would logically be the state of mind of any gay man who lived in a culture that, he felt, would reject him the moment that it discovered his true sexuality.

Particularly interesting, however, is that the character of André Lhéry allows Viaud to talk about himself in relation to his books and his readers. He indulges in no little ego gratification here as well. Djénane has a veritable 'cult for him' (II) as a result of reading his works. In a passage that he added to Hélys's corresponding letter,[71] Viaud went so far as to have the odalisque write him that, having read widely in modern fiction,

'I understood yet better why all of us ... owe you thanks, and why we love you more than so many others. It is because we found ourselves to be in a close kinship of the soul with you' (XIX). Was Viaud arguing that, more than any other modern writer, he was someone whose works struck a chord in gay men? In the same sense, when he wrote that the 'peace' experienced by the sister's mother 'was not found in any way in the faces of the admirers of André Lhéry' (II), was he describing just the three Turkish women, or his own suffering gay readers as well?

Certainly meant to be read metaphorically is the passage early in the novel where, having received a letter from Lhéry, the three women 'undertook to plumb the mystery of the writing' (II). All knowing readers of Viaud's work, those 'unknown friends' to whom he referred in previous volumes, would have been in the habit of plumbing his work to see what lay hidden in it. Here in *The Awakened* Viaud changed the term for these understanding readers to 'unknown souls' (V), which resonates with the fact that, as we saw earlier, he refers to the protagonists of this work repeatedly as genderless 'souls.'[72] There is also no little irony in the fact that Djénane describes Lhéry as living in 'the feverish and free West' (XX), when in fact he must discuss homosexuals through metaphor there.

Finally, it is interesting to note the probingly personal nature of Lhéry's readers in *The Awakened*. One of the first questions that the trio ask him at their initial meeting is whether *Medjé* (*Aziyadé*) depicts the author's own life: '"Will you tell us if the story of 'Medjé' is true," the third one asked' (VI). As we noted in the Introduction, this seems to have been a question on the minds of many of Viaud's readers. Furthermore, Djénane informs André: 'I like this book [*The Land of Kaboul*, Viaud's *To Ispahan*, one of the non-fiction books that he had published after *Ramuntcho*] less than its older brothers: there isn't enough of *you* inside it' (XVI). Already in *The Story of a Child*, as we saw, Pierre had expressed horror at the way that his artistic creations revealed aspects of his innermost self (IX), and as we also saw, Viaud had made one of the conditions of writing this new book not putting himself on stage again.[73] Still, in addition to a plea for the cause of Turkish women, one of the things that Djénane hopes to get out of the book that the three women are commissioning from Lhéry is another glimpse into the author's most private self:

Will I find in it what I have been looking in vain to discover since we have known each other: the depths of your soul, the intimate truth of your feelings, everything that neither your brief letters nor your infrequent words reveal? I have, indeed, sometimes felt emotion in you, but it was repressed so quickly, so furtive! There were moments when I would have liked to open your head and your heart, in order to learn, finally, what was there behind your cold and clear eyes! (LII)[74]

What she says elsewhere on this topic is striking, because it may suggest, in an important way, how Marc Hélys convinced Viaud to return to the composition of the personal novel. In one of the feminist's letters, she wrote him, having complained that she no longer found him in his last several books: 'Oh! Don't keep writing with just your mind! You told us that you don't want to put yourself on stage? What does it matter what the envious might say about it? So write with your mind what your heart will tell you.'[75] Perhaps it was such support from Hélys that gave Viaud the strength to write the most courageous of his works in terms of its stand on gay issues. One might propose that it was Hélys who gave Viaud the courage that Ramuntcho had lacked when he set off to find a new world at the end of the author's previous novel.

Some may find 'courageous' to describe *The Awakened* excessive. In regard to gay issues, it is the most hermetic of Viaud's novels. There is nothing in it that overtly suggests the possibility of a gay reading, less even than *Ramuntcho*. For a reader not already familiar with at least certain of Viaud's previous narratives, *The Awakened* is not likely to appear as anything other than what it has always been read as being. In this respect, it would seem safe to say that the author did not, in any realistic sense, imagine the allegorical meaning of his text to be perceivable by any but his most sympathetic and understanding readers.

In his defence, however, it needs once again to be remembered that he was writing in the first decade of the twentieth century and not the twenty-first. Though Gide wrote *Corydon*, his defence of pederasty, in 1911, he was not convinced to publish it until 1924. In 1889 Zola, who risked much in the defence of noble causes, turned down an offer to use the diary of a young Italian homosexual as the basis for a novel.[76] Though he talked about 'inverts' extensively in his masterpiece (1913–27), Proust was careful to assert a heterosexual identity for his apparently autobiographically based protagonist and to fill his work with much of the homophobic scientific thought of his day. Forster did not publish *Maurice* (1911–12).

In fact, the gay value of *The Awakened* lies in its application of feminist consciousness raising to gay men, or at least to those 'unknown friends' who read his books. Marc Hélys ended her book with the exclamation: 'What a joy and what an honour it was for those who were his volunteers and modest inspirers to see their thoughts and their feelings understood and interpreted in this way!'[77] Our reading of the novel has shown that, through working with Hélys, Viaud also came to a better understanding of the issues that were facing gay men. In universalizing them, moreover, as he had already done to an extent in *Iceland Fisherman*, *The Story of a Child*, and *Ramuntcho*, he facilitated contemporary acceptance of his work, with the possibility that some 'outsiders' would see and profit from his hidden meanings, just as André Lhéry, by a series of associations, came to understand Medjé/Aziyadé better.

In one of her last letters to Lhéry, Djénane expresses her fear that he will forget her (LIV). We have already seen Lhéry's similar fear of being forgotten. Perhaps this gay reading of *The Awakened* will find the work a new audience that will guarantee both these characters and their author the immortality that they all sought, and deserve.

Conclusion

After publishing *The Awakened,* Julien Viaud lived seventeen years and published ten more volumes. He wrote no more novels, however. Instead, he went back to what he had been doing after *Ramuntcho,* producing a dramatization of that novel (1908), another collection of previously published short pieces, *Sleeping Beauty's Chateau* (1910), and two more travelogues, *Egypt* (1909) and *A Pilgrimage to Angkor* (1912).[1] The travelogues still evince the 'gay gaze' noted in some of the novels, but there is no further creation of plot or characters. Thereafter, from 1913 to 1920, Viaud became involved in politics, devoting his literary efforts to defending Turkey and condemning Germany in a series of pieces for various newspapers that he subsequently collected, revised, and published in five volumes.

During that time he also worked on *Supreme Visions of the East,* the first part of which was published in installments in 1915. This is a collection of reworked diary entries and newspaper articles concerning Viaud's trips to Turkey in 1910 and 1913 that contains reflections on both 'Aziyadé' and 'Djénane' and therefore sometimes resembles *A Phantom from the East* or *Madame Prune* more than the other travelogues. Viaud's son Samuel completed it after his father's health failed.

In 1919 Viaud also published *First Youth,* a recollection of adolescence that was presented as a sequel to *The Story of a Child.* Unlike *The Story of a Child,* however, *First Youth* is not moulded into a novel. Furthermore, it recounts the adolescence not of the literary creation Pierre, but of J., presumably Julien Viaud. This suggests that it is a non-fictional autobiographical work and not another addition to the presentation of the persona first introduced as Loti. (Autobiographical works are seldom altogether non-fictional, but that is another issue.) *First Youth* repeats several elements from *The Story of a Child*, such as the butterfly and the ambulant cake vender, but without their homoerotic associations. As mentioned in chapter 1, it also presents two heterosexual encounters. The gypsy, J.'s first heterosexual experience, speaks a French that includes some Spanish (XXIX), just as Samuel, Loti's first described homosexual encounter, had been presented as speaking a *sabir* that included some Spanish (*Aziyadé* I:IX). Still, *First Youth*, the most literary of the works that Viaud penned after *The Awakened*, is not really a novel and certainly not a gay one. Marc Hélys had charmed Viaud out of fiction retirement to put himself 'on stage' one final, affirmative time, but then Pierre Loti the character and evidently alter ego disappeared.[2] After *The Awakened*, it is hard to imagine what Viaud could have done next. It would be half a century before gay fiction began to produce anything as positive.

What Viaud had created in the twenty-seven years from *Aziyadé* to *The Awakened* was already a remarkable achievement. Though the ten novels and one novella that he produced during that time function as discrete works, I hope that I have shown the extent to which they in fact constitute a whole, one that traces the development of the persona often named Loti from his encounter with Samuel and same-sex desire in the Middle East through his realization of the extent to which that desire means that he is different to an affirmation that those who experience such desire have a right to dignity and fulfilment. Starting from a position that does not yet recognize a distinct gay identity, Viaud explores the various elements that may have disposed his protagonist to homosexual attraction, including heredity, and early on calls for toleration of differences in desire. Eventually, with *The Story of a Child*, he presents his protagonist as essentially different from most other men, and shows how he learns to play a role in order to hide that difference and function in society. For a while, there seems to be regret, especially of the extent to which this difference risks excluding the gay male from general social participation, but even at this point Viaud's protagonist does not deny his different nature in order to achieve such participation. Finally, with the help of a feminist, Viaud learns to reject this longing for participation in general society and instead calls for the development of gay community, which will help the gay individual come to an awareness of his dignity and self-worth.

Given the unity of Viaud's works, not simply their common protagonist but, as we have shown, the way that later ones play off earlier ones to constitute meaning, the description of an ideal literary critic that he offered in his 1891 speech accepting his election to the French Academy is striking: 'A critic worthy of the name who has to speak about a writer would be fortunate if he were ... to read him ... from beginning to end in the exact order in which his books had been written, and in that way to follow the development of his talent, the appearance of his personality, if he has one, and to see take shape in his work the unity without which there is neither greatness nor duration' (Loti, *Discours de réception de la Séance de l'Académie française* 61). Again, it would appear that Viaud was signalling at least some of his readers to look for the interplay between his texts, what he terms their 'unity,' which we have found so significant.

To the extent that he actually wrote one extended work that traces the development of a single protagonist, Viaud was a precursor of and surely an inspiration for Proust, who would begin to develop his own multivolume account of one man's intellectual and emotional development, though a far less gay-affirmative one, just two years after Viaud had completed his.[3] Moving beyond what Proust and many of his successors would attempt, Viaud also, in the course of his work, questioned and broadened the concept of masculinity while being one of the first to argue for the importance of gay community.

As I have argued throughout this volume, comparisons with Proust are particularly revealing, not just because the two were roughly contemporaries – though no two authors with such similar beginnings went on to have more radically different lives – but because they treated so many common themes. One point does separate them, however: whereas Proust, apart from his often objectionable presentation of homosexuality, captures our attention with a wealth of other elements, the most fascinating aspect of Viaud's work for modern readers may well be his treatment of male same-sex desire. This is why I felt that it was imperative to illustrate this treatment, which, as we have seen, can be understood only though an examination of all his novels. Viaud was a more limited writer than Proust, but once his treatment of this issue is revealed, he becomes an important and enjoyable one.

Some might argue that Viaud should have been more direct in his treatment of homosexual desire and love. Lawrence R. Schehr, for example, complained that 'Loti himself translates his personal erotics into heterosexual exotics for the sake of safe publication.'[4] Such discontent is unrealistic, however. As Robert A. Nye pointed out, Georges Eekhoud was put on trial as late as 1900, three years after the publication of all of Viaud's novels except *The Awakened*, for his largely positive depiction of gay desire in *Escal Vigor*.[5] Mark G. Guenette, in his perceptive study of Marcel's homosexuality in Proust's masterpiece, stated quite simply that 'the admission of the narrator's sexual orientation is the limit past which even *A la recherche du temps perdu* cannot go' because of 'what could and what could not be written during the first quarter of this century.'[6] On the other hand, Jeffrey Meyers, defending the homophobia of *In Search of Lost Time*, wrote that 'Proust had to devise a strategy that would allow him to portray inverts and include the drama of their lives in his fiction without sacrificing the interest and sympathy of his readers.'[7] To Viaud's credit, his strategies, if not particularly direct, at least never resort to gay bashing to win such 'interest and sympathy.' In the best examples, *Aziyadé, Iceland Fisherman, The Story of a Child, Ramuntcho, The Awakened*, they give his works a complexity that adds to their richness.

As I mentioned in the Introduction, this virtual absence of homophobia constitutes one of the real and permanent values of Viaud's fiction, one that does not have to rely on allowances for change over time. Some of his characters, such as Ramuntcho, and perhaps also the Pierre of *The Story of a Child*, seem to regret their difference, but nowhere in Viaud's novelistic output does one have to deal with the sort of homophobic self-hatred that makes so much early gay fiction, including much written well after *The Awakened*, so very unpleasant to read. Proust's masterpiece is a compendium of much of the worst that his contemporaries had written on the gay male. As Christopher Robinson has noted, 'Gide clearly entertained classically heterosexual views on all forms of homosexuality except his own [pederasty].'[8] Genet may glorify homosexuality in his novels, but there is still much self-hatred associated with it and an inability to conceive of gay relationships as a partnership of two equals. Bersani described him as 'the least "gay-affirmative" gay writer I know.'[9] Julien Green's novels dealing with homosexuality, such as *The Transgressor*, have even more self-hatred and no glorification. Paul Robinson noted 'Green's profound revulsion from his own desires ... his chronic inability to find peace with his sexuality.'[10] No man in Viaud's novels is punished for desiring another man, however; no Viaud male hates himself for doing so; no one else, nor the texts themselves, ridicules him for this desire. Even Ramuntcho, for all his vacillating, finally elects not to marry Gracieuse and sets off for America, which Yves had seen as an escape from the constraints that others sought to impose. Djénane proclaims every individual's right to take a partner of his or her own choosing. In an era filled with negative depictions of gay men, many by gays themselves, Viaud's novels stand out as truly remarkable.[11]

This is why I spent the last several years preparing a gay reading of Viaud's fiction. Once their gay content has been revealed, his better works become truly fascinating, highly enjoyable tales dealing with issues still very important today. I hope that this study will convince those fond of well-crafted literature to search out these better novels and discover the pleasures that they have afforded me and my students repeatedly over these last several years.

Some authors are appreciated immediately. Others have had to wait until long after their deaths. In the case of Viaud, once one of France's most popular writers, it is time to appreciate him again, in a new way, as he, at his best, can be.

Notes

Introduction

1 James, 'Pierre Loti,' 151. For a fine study of James's views on Viaud's works, see Melchiori, 'Feelings About Aspects.'

2 Woodress, *Willa Cather*, 189.

3 One indication of the extent to which Viaud's novels were viewed in the English-speaking world largely as travelogues is that their titles were often changed to focus on their location. Thus *Aziyadé* was published in English as *Constantinople*, *Madame Chrysanthemum* as *Japan*, *The Marriage of Loti* as *Tahiti*, *My Brother Yves* as *A Tale of Brittany*, *Ramuntcho* as *A Tale of the Pyrenees*, and *The Story of a Spahi* as *The Sahara*.

4 Fernandez, *Le rapte de Ganymede*, 75.

5 Ibid., 228.

6 Camus, 'Monsieur Ouin à Châteaudouble.'

7 Martel, *Le rose et le noir*, 155.

8 Rivers, *Proust and the Art of Love*, 2.

9 Jeffrey Meyers, for example, in *Homosexuality and Literature 1890–1930*, asserts that 'Wilde ... was the first novelist to defy literary convention and to write about homosexuality in a manner that was obvious to the sophisticated reader. He burst the restrictive barriers, and the others followed in his wake' (13).

10 Proust's depiction of homosexuality is, at best, ambiguous; Georges Eekhoud, a Belgian author, created a very positive depiction of homosexuality in his 1899 novel *Escal-Vigor* and was prosecuted for it.

11 I have found the following American school editions of Loti's novels, all apparently edited for high school use: *Mon frère Yves*, abridged and edited with introduction, notes, exercises and vocabulary, by Henry Ward Church

(New York: H. Holt and Co., 1924); *Pêcheur d'Islande,* edited with notes by R.J. Morich (Boston: D.C. Heath, 1896); *Pêcheur d'Islande,* edited with introduction and notes by O.B. Super with vocabulary (Boston: Heath, [c. 1902]); *Pêcheur d'Islande,* edited by Colman Dudley Frank, illustrated by Richard L. Marwede (Garden City, N.Y.: Doubleday, Doran & Co. [c. 1933]); *Pêcheur d'Islande,* edited with introduction, notes, exercises, and vocabulary, by Winfield S. Barney (Boston, New York [etc.]: Allyn and Bacon, [c. 1922]); *Pêcheur d'Islande,* with explanatory notes, by C. Fontaine (New York: William R. Jenkins, 1896); *Pêcheur d'Islande,* edited with introduction, notes, exercises, and vocabulary, by D.S. Blondheim (New York: The Macmillan Company, 1935); *Pêcheur d'Islande,* edited with notes and vocabulary by James F. Mason with exercises by Osmond T. Robert (New York: H. Holt [1932, c. 1930]); *Ramuntcho,* abridged and edited with notes and vocabulary by E.F. Hacker (Boston, New York: D.C. Heath and Company [c. 1926]); *Ramuntcho,* abridged and edited with notes by C. Fontaine (Boston: D.C. Heath & Co., 1903); *Ramuntcho,* abridged and edited by Victor W. Ritchie (Paris: Librairie Hachette; Garden City, N.Y.: Doubleday, Doran, [1923?]). Some of these went through several editions, and many are available at larger public and university libraries.

12 Martin, 'Edward Carpenter and the Double Structure of *Maurice,*' 45.
13 Anders, 'Willa Cather, France, and Pierre Loti,' 17.
14 Mayne, *The Intersexes,* 327–8.
15 Ibid., 187.
16 Moon, 'Disseminating Whitman,' 260. Genet's novel, which he published in 1953, sixty-seven years after *Iceland Fisherman,* contains striking parallels to Viaud's *My Brother Yves.*
17 I take as my definition of 'gay novel' the one put forth by Michael N. Stanton in his entry, 'The Novel: Gay Male,' in *The Gay and Lesbian Literary Heritage.* 'The gay male novel is a form of fiction in which male homosexuality is central – not always a central problem, but certainly a central concern' (518).
18 Summers, ed., *The Gay and Lesbian Literary Heritage.*
19 Robinson, *Scandal in the Ink,* 44.
20 Rivers, *Proust and the Art of Love,* 73.
21 A few critics have argued that Proust's presentation of homosexuals and homosexuality in his great novel is not as negative as Rivers – and most readers – would claim. For such arguments see, for example: Muller, 'Sodome I ou la naturalisation de Charlus,' who maintains that by linking Charlus's meeting with Jupien to nature Proust glorifies it; or Cairns, 'Homosexuality and Lesbianism in Proust's *Sodome et Gomorrhe,*' who, taking a deconstructive approach, asserts without proof that the novel is so full of contradictions and

ambiguities that the negative remarks concerning homosexuality are undercut. Along the same lines, Sedgwick, in her chapter on Proust in *Epistemology
of the Closet*, wrote: 'Every analytic or ethical category applied throughout *A la
recherche* to the homosexuality of M. de Charlus can easily be shown to be subverted or directly contradicted elsewhere' (230). Sedgwick points out some
fascinating and very important contradictions in the discussion and depiction of homosexual men in Proust's novel, but they do not necessarily sub-
vert the text's apparent and repeated negativity on this subject.
21 Rivers, *Proust and the Art of Love*, 32.
22 Nye, *Masculinity and Male Codes of Honor in Modern France*, 123. For further
details on these duels, see, for example, Carter, *Marcel Proust: A Life*.
23 Rivers wrote that 'to contradict [the medical theories of the day on homosex-
uality] in his novel might have reduced the chances of winning a wide audience for *In Search of Lost Time*' (*Proust and the Art of Love*, 157), but how
could Proust have reconciled this with his averred intention to tell 'the
truth' about mankind, including gay mankind, unless he believed that
these theories contained the truth? It seems that Proust did actually accept
most of what contemporary medicine said about homosexuals, as terrible
as it was. Rivers remarked: 'It is clear from Proust's correspondence and
notebooks that he actually believed, at least at certain junctures of his life,
that homosexually oriented people are sick, that they are a "third sex," and
so on' (204). Many passages in Carter's recent biography seem to support
this.
24 Gide, *Corydon*, 179, 311–12. As Martha Hanna notes in her fine study of *Corydon*, 'Gide defended pederasty – the only type of homosexuality he judged
"normal"' ('Natalism, Homosexuality, and the Controversy over *Corydon*,'
205). Leo Bersani remarked: 'It is one of the least attractive aspects of Gide's
presumed defense of homosexuality in *Corydon* that the argument excludes
what most of us would identify as homosexual desire' (*Homos*, 121).
    In 'How to Do the History of Male Homosexuality,' David M. Halperin
provides a clear delineation of effeminacy, inversion, pederasty, and male-
male love, which he presents as 'the four prehomosexual categories of male
sex and gender deviance' (91). Unlike Viaud, Proust and Gide both seem to
have conceived of male same-sex relationships at least partly in terms of
these older 'prehomosexual' categories, so their work might be said to be
less gay/homosexual than the novels examined in this study. We will get to
the specific meaning of 'homosexual' shortly.
25 Robinson, *Scandal in the Ink*, 74.
26 Michel Foucault, in his *History of Sexuality*, asserted that these pseudo-
scientific efforts were part of what he saw as the nineteenth century's

attempt to bring sexuality into the open so as to gain control over it. For a critique of Foucault on this issue, see Bristow, *Sexology*, 179.

27 On these early French studies of male homosexuality, see Rosario's fascinating 'Pointy Penises, Fashion Crimes, and Hysterical Mollies,' and Copley, *Sexual Moralities in France, 1790–1980*, 135–54.

28 Rivers, *Proust and the Art of Love*, 204.

29 Fernandez, *Le rapte de Ganymede*, 83.

30 Alex G. Hargreaves maintained that Viaud's 'conceptual framework, preoccupations and value system were intensely personal, but they owed virtually nothing to non-European cultures' (*The Colonial Experience in French Fiction*, 80). I believe he underestimated the influence of non-European attitudes toward homosexuality on Viaud and his work.

31 For these people, of course, 'lesbian' refers to women attracted to other women.

32 'Some in the media still insist on using the "H" word,' *Gay People's Chronicle*, 2 August 1996, 14.

33 Halperin, *One Hundred Years*, 24.

34 On the development of the idea of sexualities, see Bristow, *Sexology*.

35 For example, Dr Barry, to whom E.M. Forster's Maurice goes for help with his 'perversion' and who, Forster is careful to point out, 'had read no scientific works on Maurice's subject,' refers to same-sex desire as an 'evil hallucination,' a momentary 'temptation from the devil' that could befall any man, but not as a sign of an essential difference or sexuality (*Maurice*, chapters 31–2).

36 Foucault, *History of Sexuality*, 43.

37 Halperin, *One Hundred Years*, 27.

38 Ibid., 29.

39 See also Halperin's remark:

> Throughout the nineteenth century, sexual preference for a person of one's own sex was not clearly distinguished from other sorts of non-conformity to one's culturally defined sex-role: deviant object-choice was viewed as merely one of a number of pathological symptoms exhibited by those who reversed, or 'inverted,' their proper sex-roles by adopting a masculine or a feminine style at variance with what was deemed natural and appropriate to their anatomical sex. Political aspirations in women and (at least according to one expert writing as late as 1920) a fondness for cats in men were manifestations of a pathological condition, a kind of psychological hermaphroditism tellingly but not essentially expressed by the preference for a 'normal' member of one's own sex as a sexual partner. (*One Hundred Years*, 15–16)

The view that it was unnatural for a man to be fond of cats is something that will be recalled when we reach *My Brother Yves* in chapter 4.

40 Summers, 'Introduction,' *The Gay and Lesbian Literary Heritage*, xiii.

41 For Halperin, for example, 'sexual categories and identities are objectivated fictions' (*One Hundred Years*, 28).

42 Robinson, *Scandal in the Ink*, 7.

43 Fernandez, *Le rapte de Ganymede*, 228.

44 See, for example, Bray, *Homosexuality in Renaissance England*. The distinction between Foucault and his followers on one hand and those who argue for an earlier origin for a distinct homosexual identity on the other resides in part in Foucault's insistence that the idea of homosexuality was developed by individuals who did not themselves necessarily experience any significant same-sex desire, but rather constructed the concept as a way of controlling society (both those who experienced such desire and those who did not), i.e., by those who were hostile to male same-sex desire. Others such as Bray have argued that homosexual-tendancied men first created the idea of an independent, distinct, (homo)sexually based identity on their own.

45 This is why constructionists object to the use of the word 'homosexual' to describe pre-nineteenth-century men. As William B. Turner phrased it in his history of queer studies, 'the debate between social constructionists and essentialists took the form of disputes about whether men who had sex with other men, predominantly or exclusively, before the creation of the category "homosexual," still fit that category' (*A Genealogy of Queer Studies*, 63).

46 Summers, 'Introduction,' xii.

47 Creech, *Closet Writing/Gay Reading*, 60.

48 Ibid., 194

49 As Eve Kosofsky Sedgwick, among others, has very correctly pointed out, there really is today no one universally held conception of what this male homosexual is like (*Epistemology of the Closet*, 47). Halperin speaks of 'a man distinct from other men in absolutely no other respect besides that of his sexuality' (*One Hundred Years*, 9), an idea that much of modern psychology and many gay men share, but as Halperin himself remarks in a passage to be quoted shortly, the acceptance of this understanding of the homosexual/gay man is far from universal, even in Western society and even among gay men. In Turner's phrasing, 'the history of "homosexuality" does not move in a straight line. Competing conceptualizations overlap and interact, often in unpredictable ways' (*A Geneology of Queer Studies*, 80). In *Gay New York*, George Chauncey demonstrates the various ways that gay men have envisioned themselves, and been envisioned by others, in part of the United States.

50 Halperin, 'How to Do the History of Male Homosexuality,' 109.

51 Ibid., 108.
52 Ibid., 111.
53 Woods, *A History of Gay Literature*, 9.
54 Gide, *Corydon*, 216, 280; Fernandez, *Le rapte de Ganymede*, 18.
55 A good study of gay autobiography is Paul Robinson's *Gay Lives*. He deals with the autobiographies of three of Viaud's successors in French literature, Gide, Genet, and Green.
56 In addition to the various scholarly studies that, in treating gay literature, now constitute a canon of significant works, there have also been popular books such as Drake's *The Gay Canon*.
57 It is sadly ironic that Proust, who felt that he had to transpose his own gay experiences into heterosexual ones in his novel, did not share this view. In the last volume of *In Search of Lost Time, Time Regained*, he at one point had Marcel, with no little homophobia, say: 'A writer should not be offended when an invert puts male faces on his heroines. This rather aberrant peculiarity is the only way that an invert can give what he reads its full generality ... If Mr. Charlus had not given the unfaithful woman over whom Musset cries in "October night" or in "The Memory" Morel's face, he would have neither cried nor understood, because it was only by means of this narrow and wandering route that he had access to the truths of love' (217).

1. Was Julien Viaud Gay?

1 Millward, *L'Oeuvre de Pierre Loti et l'Esprit 'fin de siècle,'* 166 n. 57.
2 Blanch, *Pierre Loti*, 128. Blanch, like many critics who have written on Viaud, often refers to him as Loti, and often does not distinguish between the author and the character in his books of that name.
3 Szyliowicz, *Pierre Loti and the Oriental Woman*, 23. One might think that the author of a study decrying how Oriental women have been unjustly depicted would refrain from unjustly depicting homosexual men, but that is not the case here.
4 Vercier, Quella-Villéger, and Dugas, 'Du "Roman d'un enfant" au Journal d'un adulte,' 10.
5 Ibid., 15.
6 Blanch, *Pierre Loti*, 128.
7 Pseudonyms are never really empty of meaning. Even gender-neutral pen names like O. Henry, Voltaire, or Molière still suggest a nationality or at least a language-specific culture. Most pseudonyms also indicate a gender – Mark Twain, Anatole France, etc. – though sometimes, as in cases like George Eliot and George Sand, they are misleading in that respect. 'Loti' is not just a pseudonym, however. Since it is the name of the principle character in the

first two of Viaud's anonymously published novels, *Aziyadé* (1879) and *The Marriage of Loti* (1880), it already referred to a specific and known individual with his own personality and history when Viaud began to use it in 1881 as the name of the author of the books that he was publishing. He went on to use Pierre Loti as the name of a character in several subsequent narratives. As a result, 'Pierre Loti' is not an empty term that corresponds perfectly to Julien Viaud and like it refers only to that real world person. Instead, the name designates a literary character, one in many ways similar to Viaud but not the same individual, as well as the 'author' of any of the works signed 'Pierre Loti.' (As we will see, the unnamed narrator in some of Viaud's fictional works has a distinct and describable personality, one that coincides with that of Loti as we know him from the novels in which he does appear.) In other words – and this is an important issue which we will examine at length in the chapter devoted to *The Story of a Spahi* – Viaud, having created the character Loti in his first two novels, thereafter used this person in subsequent works not just as a character but also as a sort of alter-ego to whom to attribute his work, which he could then argue to be an intentionally crafted expression of Pierre Loti's, rather than his own, self.

Once I make this distinction between Julien Viaud and Pierre Loti, I have no problem asserting that the latter was gay – is, really; literary characters never die – because he, the character who bears this name, is, as we shall see, definitely attracted to other men and, after the first few narratives, not particularly attracted to women. In this sense, it is easy to argue that the 'author,' or at least the named author, of Viaud's novels was/is gay, regardless of Viaud's own sexuality. That is, however, a rhetorical game of questionable usefulness.

8 Cited in Lefèvre, *La Vie inquiète de Pierre Loti*, 45n. The quotation comes from de Robert, *De Loti à Proust*, 219.

9 On de Robert's relationship with Proust, see Carter, *Marcel Proust*.

10 Edmond de Goncourt and Jules de Goncourt, *Journal*, 4:861. 'Pédéraste,' as other of Goncourt's entries make clear, did not for him have its etymological meaning of someone who engages in sex with minors, but rather denoted simply a man who has sex with other men. On this word's usage in nineteenth-century France, see Peniston, 'Love and Death in Gay Paris,' 143.

11 Ibid., 3:758.

12 Desbruères, Préface, *Mon Frère Yves*, 14. The quotation comes from Odette Valence and Samuel Pierre-Loti-Viaud, *La Famille de Pierre Loti*, 218. Desbruères's preface is aggravating for a piece written so recently. He talks around the issue of Viaud's sexual orientation without ever using the words 'gay' or 'homosexual' and concludes by saying: 'Unless we find new docu-

ments, it is best to limit ourselves to the known texts [*Aziyadé* and *My Brother Yves*] and refrain from putting forth hypotheses that would appeal to some and irritate others without helping to arrive at the truth' (20). His conclusion is sound, but his reticence to specify what he is talking about is difficult to accept in so recent a text.

13 Edmond de Goncourt and Jules de Goncourt, *Journal*, 4:227.

14 This rumour that Aziyadé was a pre-Proustian Albertine, a female character based on a real-life man, recurs repeatedly. See Vercier and Quella-Villéger, *Aziyadé suivi de Fantôme d'Orient de Pierre Loti*, 178. One can find it even in the recent scholarly *Gay and Lesbian Literary Heritage*, where Gretchen Schultz, in her article 'French Literature: Nineteenth Century,' wrote that '*Aziyadé* (1879) tells the story of a sea captain who falls in love with a harem woman who, quite likely, is really a man in female dress' (298; Loti is an ensign in the British navy, not a sea captain). Schultz's subsequent remark, 'the character of Aziyadé returns in *Fantôme d'Orient* (1891), where her gender is again ambiguous,' makes it clear that she did not read that work, since Aziyadé never appears in it, having died before its story begins.

15 Edmond de Goncourt and Jules de Goncourt, *Journal*, 3:1230.

16 Brodin, *Loti*, 71.

17 Alain Buisine wrote that Viaud's homosexuality, or homosexual tendencies, can be seen, in part, as an effort to find his lost brother (*Tombeau de Loti*, 351). It would make more sense to assume the inverse of this. Clive Wake asserted that Viaud did not grow out of the homosexual hero-worship stage of his adolescence because of his fixation on his brother (*The Novels of Pierre Loti*, 20), which would raise the eyebrows of more than one developmental psychologist today. (To be fair, Wake wrote in 1971.) Wake also asserted that 'the affection that bound him to Gustave was also a sexual one' (32), but offered no proof of this.

18 One could speculate on the extent to which Viaud's lifelong devotion to his brother's memory was tied to a feeling that Gustave represented efforts to maintain the young Julien in a conventional heterosexual sexuality.

19 Szyliowicz goes into an extensive analysis of this scene, arguing that the opening of the grotto where it takes place is a 'vagina dentata' image, and proceeds from there to ascribe a castration complex to Viaud (*Pierre Loti and the Oriental Woman*, 61–3).

20 Ibid., 62.

21 Proust did this same sort of thing with Marcel in the first pages of *In Search of Lost Time*, having him mention that he dreamed of sleeping with a woman to establish immediately his heterosexuality.

Viaud's next volume of autobiography, *Notes of My Youth*, begins with a chapter that the author composed to serve as the opening for what he evidently intended to be another narrativization of his diary entries, similar to *First Youth*. (Since Viaud died before being able to complete that project, the rest of *Notes of My Youth* is simply excerpts from his diary, edited by his son Samuel.) In that chapter, there begins a story about a young girl who attracted Viaud's attention, but it does not continue in the diary entries for the same period.

22 Vedel seems very intent on asserting Viaud's heterosexuality in his preface. After summarizing *First Youth* with those two heterosexual encounters, he proceeds to list memorable characters in Viaud's novels – Rarahu, Aziyadé, Fatou-Gaye, and Madame Chrysanthemum – leaving out all the male friends.

23 This scene is considered further in the Conclusion.

24 Gustave was also evidently eager to leave home, and once he joined the navy stayed away as much as possible.

25 The extent to which Viaud created in Pierre Loti not the person he was but the person he wanted to be, suggested by this quotation, will be further explored later in this study.

26 In a diary entry for 9 April 1897, five months after his mother's death, Viaud wrote: 'Now that I no longer have a mother ... no longer have a brake on my life, a passion has little by little arisen in me that is irresistible, all-powerful, wiping out all those from before and all memories ... I love as I had never loved ... I thought that I was done with that mystery, which had tortured my entire past life' (*Cette éternelle nostalgie*, 400). Nothing in the entry allows us to determine the sex of the object of this love, however, much less his or her identity.

27 It is interesting to note that in *Time Regained*, Proust's Marcel singles out a seaman's life as having the most rigorous discipline of any profession (147).

28 Valence and Pierre-Loti-Viaud, *La famille de Pierre Loti*, 114.

29 Blanch asserted that 'Julien lavished the whole of his emotional craving for the long-mourned Gustave on Joseph' (*Pierre Loti*, 64), but there is no proof that Viaud's relationship to Bernard had its origin in the one that he had had with his brother.

30 During a later stay in Toulon, when he was sharing a room with Lucien Jousselin, Viaud noted that 'I really love the streets of Toulon at these uncustomary hours [2:00 a.m.] ... You witness scenes that proper middle-class people will never suspect' (*Private Diary 1878–1881*, 188). Exactly what Viaud witnessed there, and perhaps participated in, the published diary entry does not specify, but this wording very much recalls an important passage in *Aziyadé* (I:XIII) that will be discussed in chapter 2 and that talks about the

'strange prostitution' that Loti encountered while visiting the dives of Salon-ika at night. In a subsequent diary entry, Viaud, back again in Toulon a little more than a year later, recalled his nocturnal wanderings there in 1880 as 'the freest and happiest season of my adult life' (*Private Diary 1878–1881*, 277), suggesting that the port city had a great deal of openness and toler-ance. Again, nothing is specified, but one might note Jean Cocteau's descrip-tion of Toulon in *The White Book*, which he wrote in 1927:

> It is unnecessary to describe this charming Sodom where the fires of heaven fall in the form of playful sunlight without hitting anyone. In the evening, an even sweeter indulgence bathes the city and, as in Naples and Venice, a crowd of lower-class revelers moves through squares deco-rated with fountains, cheap boutiques, waffle sellers, and hucksters. From all the corners of the world men smitten with masculine beauty come to admire the sailors who roam alone or in groups, answer glances with a smile, and never refuse an offer of love. A nocturnal salt transforms the most brutal criminal, the roughest Breton, the most ferocious Corsican into revealingly dressed, swaying, flower-bedecked girls who love to dance and lead their dance partners, without the slightest embarrassment, to the dilapidated hotels of the port. (Cocteau, *Le livre blanc*, 45–6)

31 Pierre Loti, *Correspondence inédite 1865–1904*, 120.

32 Ibid., 141.

33 *Notes of My Youth*, January 1876; *Cette éternelle nostalgie*, 38, 43, 47, 61; *Private Diary 1878–1881*, 32, 267.

34 Blanch, *Pierre Loti*, 99.

35 For the original 1872 text, see Pierre Loti, *L'Ile de Pâques: Journal d'un aspirant de La Flore*, 23–59. For the revised 1898 text, see Viaud's *On Life's By-ways*, 'Easter Island.'

36 Blanch, *Pierre Loti*, 83.

37 Millward, *L'Oeuvre de Pierre Loti*, 52.

38 Wake, *Novels of Pierre Loti*, 81.

39 For another example of this, see his description of the end of his relation-ship with a woman in Brest (*Private Diary 1878–1881*, 21).

40 Valence and Pierre-Loti-Viaud, *La famille de Pierre Loti*, 201.

41 Quella-Villéger, *Pierre Loti l'incompris*, 104.

42 Elsewhere, in a letter to his friend Lucien Jousselin, Viaud exclaimed that 'when it came to affection and friendship, there is none surer than that of an uneducated man who loves you without control and without reserve' (*Notes of My Youth*, 20 June 1878).

43 Blanch, *Pierre Loti*, 128.

44 Desbruères included letters from Le Cor to Viaud in his edition of *Mon Frère*

Yves (273–310). As he himself remarked (17), they offer nothing conclusive regarding the nature of the relationship between the two men.

45 Valence and Pierre-Loti-Viaud, *La famille de Pierre Loti*, 216.

46 Lerner, *Pierre Loti*, 77.

47 Brodin, *Loti*, 180. He was quoting from Loti, *Correspondance inédite*, 221.

48 Blanch, *Pierre Loti*, 281.

49 Viaud's diary entries concerning the first years of his involvement with Crucita have been published by André Moulis, 'Amours basques de Pierre Loti,' 99–131. The author mentions her after that, but not often, and usually with no sign of affection. Cf. *Cette éternelle nostalgie*; *Soldats bleus: Journal intime 1914–1918*.

50 Millward, *L'Oeuvre de Pierre Loti*, 145.

51 See, for example, de Robert, *De Loti à Proust*, 61.

52 Brodin reported that, during Viaud's first sojourn in Africa, 'Julien allowed himself to be tempted by Corydonesque experiments. [Corydon is a figure from Greek mythology associated with male same-sex love. Note Brodin's effort to deny that Viaud sought out these experiences of his own volition: 'Julien allowed himself to be tempted by ...'] They were probably experiments, but nothing more. In any case, they would not leave any deep marks on Julien's moral makeup' (*Loti*, 68). What effect these alleged experiences may have had on Viaud's moral development is probably impossible to say. Brodin gave no documentation for his report. We will return to it in chapter 4 when we examine Viaud's novel set in Africa, *The Story of a Spahi*.

53 Students of French literature will be reminded of the last line of Proust's *Swann in Love*, where the protagonist, Charles Swann, exclaims over his foolishness at having loved 'a woman who did not please me, who was not my style.'

2. Contextualized Suggestion and Ambiguity

1 The origin of Grant's nickname will be explained in Viaud's second novel, *The Marriage of Loti*.

2 Barthes, 'Pierre Loti: *Aziyadé*,' 113.

3 Ibid., 112.

4 Ibid., 113.

5 Ibid.

6 Ibid., 121, 113.

7 For a criticism from one of contemporary France's leading gay authors of Barthes's refusal to be open about his homosexuality, see Fernandez, *Le rapte de Ganymede*, 132.

8 Buisine, *Tombeau de Loti*, 64.

9 Saint-Leger, *Pierre Loti l'insaisissable*, 10.

10 Blanch, *Pierre Loti*, 111.

11 Ibid., 128.

12 In a passage cut before publication, the manuscript continued: 'That is how things go in Turkey: women are for the rich, who have several of them, and the poor have young boys' (Claude Martin, ed., *Aziyadé* suivi de *Fantôme d'Orient*, 365 n. 19). Exactly who cut this sentence and why we do not know. In the preface to his edition of the work, Claude Martin explains how many hands were involved in cutting the novel so that it would not offend contemporary readers. See also Bruno Vercier's preface to his edition of *Aziyadé*, 33–7. While this sentence simply summarizes the implications of the scene with Kaïroullah that occurs elsewhere in the novel (II:XXVII), of which more later, it also reinforces that scene's implication that in Turkey pederasty was understood not as a form of what Western society terms homosexual behaviour, but rather as an alternative form of what we conceive of as heterosexual behaviour. (This reinforces the constructionist argument, summarized in the Introduction, that our ideas on sexuality are social constructs that have no necessary basis in nature.)

13 For a colonialist perspective on Viaud's first three novels, see Bongie, *Exotic Memories*, 79–106.

14 Said, *Orientalism*, 190.

15 Rather than appearing as the product of a classical unified voice, a tale told by one narrator, *Aziyadé* is presented as a series of disparate writings – diary entries and letters by and to Harry Grant – that have been gathered together by his friend William Brown and published with a preface by his friend and fellow naval officer, Plumkett. With Plumkett's opening comment, Viaud makes sure that his readers notice the unconventional form of the novel to follow, perhaps as a sign that it could convey unconventional ideas. A decade later, as we will see, in *The Story of a Child*, he would develop a pre-Surrealist aesthetic around the (apparently) loosely constructed narrative and the reader's reaction to it.

16 Robert de Troy compared Viaud to Gide, describing them as 'creatures of desire, hedonists whom every possible sensual delight inebriates ... curious about all the possibilities that are offered' (De Troy, *Pierre Loti*, 173). De Troy managed to spend an entire chapter comparing Viaud to Gide and Proust without ever touching on the issue of homosexuality, however. Henry James found Viaud's 'almost inveterate habit of representing the closest and most intimate personal relations as unaccompanied with any moral feelings ... singularly vulgar' (Melchiori, 'Feelings About Aspects,' 177).

17 Gundermann, 'Orientalism, Homophobia, Masochism,' 164. On homosexual panic, see Sedgwick, *Between Men*, chapter 5.

18 Martin (ed. *Aziyadé* suivi de *Fantôme d'Orient*, 365 n. 22) felt that letter III:XXIII, though placed far after it, is the missing epistle to which Loti's early I:XV is a response.

19 There is no indication that 'gai' had its current meaning of 'homosexual' in French in 1879 or for some time thereafter, though, as we shall see, Viaud sometimes used it in a suggestively ambiguous way.

20 One curious subsequent line from Plumkett comes halfway through the novel, when he informs Loti: 'I commit all possible extravagances; shut up in my room I abandon myself to the craziest acts, after which, relieved, or rather exhausted, I calm down and become reasonable' (III:XXIII). A reader of Proust, much less Sade, might give these words, especially 'relieved' (*soulagé*), an autoerotic connotation. Of course, heterosexual men masturbate, too. In his earlier letter, Plumkett had stated that he and Loti 'are in no way responsible for the profound imperfection of our natures' (I:XVIII), but what he meant by that he did not explain.

21 Gundermann, 'Orientalism, Homophobia, Masochism,' 163.

22 Rosario, 'Pointy Penises,' 157.

23 Proust, *Time Regained*, 116, 252.

24 Gundermann asserted that Loti 'dresses up in "ethnic drag"' ('Orientalism, Homophobia, Masochism,' 156). He doesn't.

25 This is the first of many comparisons in Viaud's writings of the object of male desire to Greek statuary. Dominique Fernandez pointed out that until recent times Greek statuary provided many gay men with their only opportunity to view naked male bodies (*Le rapte de Ganymede*, 103). Whether it had such connotations for Viaud is not clear.

26 This initial description of Samuel can be seen as an icon for the novel as a whole, which allows the alerted and interested reader to peer through various suggestive passages to catch a glimpse of male same-sex eroticism. In *The Pleasure of the Text*, Roland Barthes wrote about the erotic pleasure of peering through tears and gaps such as those in Samuel's 'shirt in tatters' (9–10).

27 Loti remarks again on Samuel's 'handsome head' (IV:IV) and speaks of 'his handsome and sweet face' (I:XIII). He also remarks that Samuel 'looks better than the others' (II:XV). Near the end of the novel, as he prepares to leave Istanbul, he notes 'a young man who had an admirable mystical head. The white turban of the oulemas surrounded his large, handsome forehead' (IV:XX). Millward wrote of Viaud: 'His passion for beauty included physical beauty, especially male beauty' (*L'Oeuvre de Pierre Loti*, 156; cf. also 166 n. 57).

Elsewhere Millward noted that Viaud describes female beauty less often than its male counterpart (159).

28 In a later scene, Aziyadé 'fixed her eyes on mine with so much penetration and persistence that I turned my head away from that gaze' (III:XXI). Near the end of the novel, as Aziyadé and Loti say good-bye, the latter remarks: 'It was as if my most hidden recesses had suddenly been penetrated by her ...' (IV:XIII). Elsewhere, however, Loti dreams of being able to 'penetrate finally Aziyadé's apartment' (III:XIV). He is not always the passive object of that verb. This is the sort of redistribution of traditionally masculine and feminine roles that Robinson singled out as an essential component of truly gay writing (*Scandal in the Ink*, 253).

29 Quella-Villéger, *Pierre Loti l'incompris*, 359 n. 5.

30 *Aziyadé* suivi de *Fantôme d'Orient*, ed. Martin, 365 n. 20; *Aziyadé*, ed. Vercier, 249, where the passage goes on further.

31 Barthes, 'Pierre Loti,' 113. Blanch assured her readers that in Viaud's description in his unpublished diary of the real-life incident that was the source for this scene one can see 'Loti's [Viaud's] uneasy reaction to Samuel's [Daniel's] advances' (*Pierre Loti*, 111); 'Loti's unpublished journals reveal his ambiguous attitude to such advances' (109). As already noted, however, in the novel at least it is Loti who makes the advances, not Samuel. In speaking of this scene between Loti and Samuel, Blanch wrote: 'In the final version of the book, hero Loti gently yet firmly disengages himself from such a tricky situation, telling Samuel that kind of love is criticized – forbidden, even, in his country. "Never think of it again, or I shall have to send you away from me," says Loti in the book (and probably on the advice of his publishers). "Samuel buried his face in his arms and remained silent. But from that night, he had been at my service body and soul ..."' (110). In fact, this passage figures not in 'the final version of the book,' but in Viaud's journal (see *Aziyadé*, ed. Vercier, 249). Someone – Viaud, one of his friends, or his editor – suppressed it as the journal passages were transformed into a novel.

32 In addition to the scene in the boat in I:XXI, already discussed, see III:XXXVIII.

33 See, for example, Jacob Press's fascinating essay, 'Same-Sex Unions in Modern Europe,' particularly 315–19, in which he demonstrates how Theodore Hertzl reacted against this rhetoric in developing the Zionist movement.

34 'Shadowy' is also used to suggest male same-sex activity when Loti says of the procurer Kaïroullah: 'He exercised all the shadowy professions typical of the *déclassé* old Jews of Constantinople, one especially as part of which he dealt with Yuzbachi Suleiman and several of my Muslim friends' (II:XXVII). In light of Viaud's earlier description of Turkey as being remarkably tolerant in

sexual matters, it is not surprising that he has Loti go on to explain that Kaïroullah 'was, however, admitted and tolerated everywhere ... When men met him on the street, they said: "Good day, Kaïroullah!" and even touched the tips of his big, hairy fingers.' Whether this is an accurate depiction of how a procurer was treated in Istanbul in Viaud's time is another issue.

35 The diary at this point read: 'Daniel ... is, out of everyone, the one to whom I am most attached' (*Aziyadé*, ed. Vercier 251). Note that here Viaud speaks of his attachment to the boatman, which in the novel becomes mention of the boatman's attachment for Loti.

36 Discretion does not appear to be an issue; there are no scenes of Achmet and Loti visiting disreputable establishments that feature 'a strange prostitution,' no linking of the young man in any way with same-sex desire.

37 At one point Viaud writes that Achmet has 'his apartment' in Loti's house (III:XXXII). Since an earlier description of the house mentions only three bedrooms, one for Loti, one for Aziyadé, and one for Samuel (II:XVIII), it appears that Achmet also takes Samuel's place in Loti's household.

38 The relationship with Achmet is developed further in *A Phantom From the East*, as we will see in chapter 9.

39 Cf. also: I:X.

40 Cf. also: III:XLIX; IV:XV; IV:XXVII; IV:XXX; V:IV.

41 Loti also spoke of 'the fevered love of the senses' when describing his 'imprudent adventure' with Greek and Armenian women (II:V).

42 Barthes, 'Pierre Loti,' 114.

43 Wake, *The Novels of Pierre Loti*, 65.

44 Szyliowicz, *Pierre Loti and the Oriental Woman*, 83.

45 Gundermann, 'Orientalism, Homophobia, Masochism,' 163.

46 The depiction of a bisexual Loti also contradicts contemporary French scientific writings. Beginning with Tardieu, French physicians maintained that all men attracted to other men were so exclusively. Cf. Victoria Thompson, 'Creating Boundaries,' 114; Rosario, 'Pointy Penises,' 151. Marcel repeats this idea several times in *In Search of Lost Time*. As we will see in subsequent chapters, the character Pierre Loti in Viaud's later novels, *My Brother Yves* and *Madame Chrysanthemum*, is presented as having no romantic involvement with women, but only with another man, Yves Kermadec.

47 In *In Search of Lost Time*, Proust argued that homosexual men could never have fulfilling relationships because they were 'inverts,' women trapped in men's bodies who, being women, would only be attracted to 'real' men, who, in turn, would never feel anything but repulsion for 'inverts.' Cf. Rivers, *Proust and the Art of Love*. This idea was prevalent in the pseudo-scientific writing of the era on homosexuality. See Rosario, 'Pointy Penises' 162; Copley,

Sexual Moralities in France, 139. Viaud's characters are never trapped in this sort of internalized homophobia.

48 Robinson, *Scandal in the Ink*, 11.

49 Thompson provides a survey of depictions of homosexuals in nineteenth-century French literature, 'Creating Boundaries.' Nye noted that during that time 'openly sympathetic homosexual novels were rare indeed' (*Masculinity and Male Codes of Honor*, 119).

50 Sedgwick, *Epistemology*, 165.

51 Lefèvre, *La vie inquiète de Pierre Loti*, 61.

52 Brodin, *Loti*, 356.

53 Wake, *The Novels of Pierre Loti*, 174.

54 Viaud advised his mother not to read *Aziyadé* (*Private Diary 1878–1881*, 73), but we do not know why.

55 As we will see in later chapters, the major narrative recounting Pierre Loti's love for another man is *My Brother Yves* (1883). The relationship between Loti and Yves Kermadec also plays a role in 'Blossoms of Boredom' (1882) and *Madame Chrysanthemum* (1887).

3. Discovering a Fuller Range of Sexuality

1 On the work's initial success, see Bruno Vercier, Préface, *Le Mariage de Loti*, 14, and Lefèvre, *Le Mariage de Loti*, Part III. *Aziyadé* had not captured the attention of the reading public at the time of its initial appearance, though it did so subsequently.

2 On the changes that Viaud made in his diary in order to create a novel, see Lefèvre, *Le Mariage de Loti*, 20–65.

3 Blanch wrote: 'A feminine streak in Loti's [Viaud's] nature always made him crave a confidant to whom he could pour out his problems, hopes and griefs' (*Pierre Loti*, 265). The desire for a confidant is certainly not a gender-specific trait.

4 Viaud had originally written 'a sorrowful shock,' but changed it to 'surprise' at his friend Lucien Jousselin's suggestion in order to avoid the repetition with 'shock' earlier in the passage (Lefèvre, *Le Mariage de Loti*, 88).

5 De Troy noted 'a nostalgia for purity' in Viaud's characters (*Pierre Loti*, 116).

6 I:IV, I:XV, I:XXIX, II:VIII, III:XIV, III:XLVII, IV:VIII. In *Aziyadé* Loti, writing in a later period, at one point recalls 'the land of the black men where I lived a year with the brother that I lost!' (IV:XIII). A knowledge of Viaud's biography makes it clear that the models for both John and the lost brother of the African period are Joseph Bernard, but the reader of the novels has no rea-

son to assume that they are the same. The word 'brother' is never applied to Samuel in *Aziyadé*.

7 Achmet once described himself as Loti's brother (IV:XVIII), but Loti never used that term in reference to him.

8 See, for example, Wake's uncertainty when he wrote of John and Loti that the term 'brother' 'purifies their intimacy and *apparently* obscures its sexual overtones' (*The Novels of Pierre Loti*, 32, emphasis added).

9 Szyliowicz came to a gay interpretation of this relationship: 'It appears as though the South Sea episode disguises a less conventional relationship between John and Harry Grant.' She continued: 'Loti's hints concerning alternative sexual attraction emerge almost in spite of himself. It appears that he cannot fully suppress the evidence or that, in his candour, he intimates the truth without explicitly revealing it' (*Pierre Loti and the Oriental Woman*, 86). There is no reason to think that these 'hints' emerged 'in spite of' Viaud, though he may have claimed the contrary to protect himself, his family, and his career. Szyliowicz's second explanation for these 'hints' seems more plausible.

10 Girard, *Deceit, Desire, and the Novel.*

11 The last part of this passage is very similar to Viaud's description, in his diary, of how he lost interest in Dakar after Joseph Bernard and the unnamed woman had left. See the summary of Viaud's sexual biography in chapter 1.

12 Lefèvre, *Le mariage de Loti*, 42.

13 Vercier, Préface, *Le mariage de Loti*, 25.

14 Wake was quite straightforward on this point with regard to the author: 'The affection that bound him to Gustave was also a sexual one' (*The Novels of Pierre Loti*, 32).

15 Vercier, Préface, *Le mariage de Loti*, 19.

16 Cf. I:V, I:IX, I:XXI, I:XXIII, I:XXIV, I:XXVIII, I:XXXVII, II:VIII, II:XXII, II:XXXIV, III:VII, III:XXVI. Loti also describes himself as being like a child while on the island (I:XXVIII, II:XXXIV) and finds that being there allows him to recall his own childhood (II:XXII, II:XXXVIII, III:XXIII). Wake noted that Rarahu and the Tahitians were the uncorrupted innocence of childhood to which Loti/Viaud sought to return (*The Novels of Pierre Loti*, 67).

17 Remember Loti's comment that the last thing that he could see as he sailed away from Constantinople was the spot where Samuel and Achmet used to wait for him (*Aziyadé*, IV:XXVIII).

18 Given their highly charged appearances in *The Marriage of Loti*, it is interesting to remember that John and Georges are each mentioned only once, and neither by name, in *Aziyadé* (IV:XIII and V:IV, respectively), a work that, chronologically, follows *The Marriage of Loti*.

19 Remember Loti's description of Turkey as a land free of European moral policing (*Aziyadé*, IV:XI).

4. A Plea for Sexual Understanding

1 Given the sometimes racist tone of the text, this passage is particularly striking, especially since the protagonist also has a close white friend in Africa, Fritz Muller.

2 Jean also dreams of bruising Cora with his spurs and crop after she betrays him (I:XVI) and he experiences 'a mad desire to use his riding-crop' on his superiors when they deny him a promotion (II:I).

3 In a fascinating chapter, 'Cannibals and Queers: Man-Eating,' David Bergman shows that several gay American writers have used cannibalism as a metaphor for homosexuality, among them Viaud's sailor-author predecessor, Herman Melville, in whose *Typee*, set in Tahiti, the protagonist Tom's 'cannibalistic phobia is a screen for anxiety about the desire for egalitarian sexual relations with Mahevi [a Polynesian man]' because 'the prospect of an egalitarian homosexual relationship fills Melville with terror – a terror he converts to the more understandable and acceptable fear of being eaten – for such equality represents for him a new, untried loss of power and privilege' (*Gaiety Transfigured*, 148–9). Granted, there is no direct mention of cannibalism in *The Story of a Spahi*, but by linking the homoerotically charged dancers with the carnivores that finally devour Jean and his comrades, there is certainly the suggestion of cannibalism at one remove. Whether Melville, or Viaud at this point, saw homosexuality as 'egalitarian' I would hesitate to assert; as 'a ... loss of power and privilege,' certainly.

4 Brodin, *Loti*, 68.

5 When the novel first appeared, serialized in Juliette Adam's *La Nouvelle Revue* in five bi-monthly installments from 15 March to 15 May 1881, it was presented as being 'By the author of the *Marriage of Loti*.' See *La Nouvelle Revue* 9 (1881): 337–69, 599–633, 836–69; 10 (1881): 102–25, 411–37. When Calmann-Lévy brought out the novel in volume form on 13 September of that year, however, it was signed 'Pierre Loti.' See Quella-Villéger, 'Sources et contextes,' 130–1. On 26 September 1881, shortly after the novel's publication in book form, the Parisian daily *Le Figaro* revealed to the general public that Pierre Loti was naval officer Julien Viaud (Quella-Villéger, *Pierre Loti l'incompris*, 52).

6 If one wanted to go to unnecessary contortions to maintain the illusion, one could argue that since Tahiti was a French colony, an English captain might have had to work through a French-Tahitian interpreter to speak to Queen

Pomaré IV, and that the passage in question does not therefore flatly undercut the pretence that Loti and his fellow sailors were British.

7 Prior to this one might have wondered if Harry Grant/Loti had written his journal, the source of the two previous novels, in English, such that the excerpts from it in the first two novels were translations by Plumket(t), or if he had, for whatever reason, written them in French himself.

8 Various critics have speculated on possible personal reasons for the choice of 'Pierre.' Blanch saw the name as a reference to Viaud's grandfather (*Pierre Loti*, 155), whom the writer never knew. Jean Balcou opened his article by asserting that 'when Loti changed his first name, "Julien," to "Pierre," that signified that he was drawing a new birth from Pierre Le Cor [the sailor on whom Viaud would base the Yves Kermadec of subsequent narratives], an inhabitant of the hamlet of Kergrist en Plounez near Paimpol' ('La Vision bretonne de Loti,' 153). In the already-cited Preface to his edition of *Mon Frère Yves*, Desbruères noted that 'we know that Sarah Bernhardt called her friend Julien Viaud *Pierre* as early as 1878' (10).

9 One could also mention that Forster, though he wrote *Maurice* in 1913–14, never published it, though it needs to be remembered that in England, unlike in France, homosexual activity was a crime until 1967.

10 On Jean's handsomeness, see Introduction:IV, Introduction:VI, I:I, I:III, I:VII, I:XII, I:XXI, II:I, II:III, III:I, III:III, III:XIX, III:XXXI; on his strength, Introduction:IV, I:I, I:IX, I:XX, I:XXI, II:I, III:I, III:VII; on his size, I:I, I:IX, II:XXVIII, III:I.

11 I chose 'gaze' rather than a synonym for the alliterative effect. Since gaze is now a term in vogue in film criticism, its presence here may evoke for some the work of Laura Mulvey and others in that field (see, for example, Mulvey's pioneering essay, 'Visual Pleasure and Narrative Cinema'). There is little similarity in our uses of the word, however. Mulvey, a feminist intent on showing other women 'the patriarchal order in which we are caught,' discussed the way male directors and cameramen have shot movies for (heterosexual male) viewers. For her, there are 'two contradictory aspects of the pleasure structures of looking in the conventional cinematic situation.' On the one hand, the (heterosexual male) viewer sees the woman as 'an object of sexual stimulation through sight' and separates 'the erotic identity of the subject from the object on the screen,' objectifying and demeaning her in the process in order to control his fear of women arising from a castration complex. On the other hand, the viewer identifies with the men on the screen who, like himself, are also pursuing women.

Loti's case is different. He can both desire and identify with the men at whom he gazes and does not have any reason to objectify or demean them, as they are not different from or threatening to him. He can simply enjoy looking at them and let his so disposed readers do the same. His gaze is therefore very different from the one Mulvey quite understandably finds objectionable.

12 Lefèvre, *Le mariage de Loti*, 72–4.

13 *The Story of a Spahi* is in many respects racist, but the negative comments regarding blacks are generally restricted to black women, whereas Nyaor-fall is perhaps the most admired character in the novel. The racism of this book is therefore at least in part misogyny, though nonetheless misogyny reinforced with at least an element of racism.

14 For an African's reaction to *The Story of a Spahi*, see Osaji, 'The African Image By a Non-African Novelist,' which does not, unfortunately, take into account these non-racial reasons for the novel's largely negative depiction of black African women. Similarly, T. Denean Sharpley-Whiting devotes a chapter to pointing out the novel's obvious negatively racist depictions of black women (*Black Venus*, 91–104), but never puts them in the context of Viaud's surrounding work.

15 Szyliowicz's assertion that 'homosexuals ... frequently need to vilify women as a compensating mechanism to deal with their guilt for their own sexual persuasion' (*Pierre Loti and the Oriental Woman*, 58) is yet another example of her uninformed homophobia. It is also inaccurate: Viaud's novels portray some women more positively than others, but really 'vilify' none of them.

16 Rarahu had been described to readers, who had not yet seen Gauguin's depictions of Tahitian woman, as almost white (II:XIV).

17 In 'Les figures zoomorphes dans "Le Roman d'un spahi,"' Bernard Magne studied in detail Viaud's use of animal comparisons to demean black Africans.

18 Wake, *The Novels of Pierre Loti*, 86.

19 Pierre Loti sometimes uses 'love' in places where one would expect a less romantic term.

20 Alain Buisine wrote that the Jean Peyral-Fatou-gaye relationship is 'presexual,' as if between children (*Tombeau de Loti*, 139). This is very much at odds with the text.

21 Intoxication, either literal or metaphoric, had played no significant role in *The Marriage of Loti*, but, as we saw in chapter 2, it did appear quite often, usually metaphorically, when speaking of the power of (heterosexual) desire (as distinct from love) in *Aziyadé*. The few references to literal intoxication in Viaud's first novel show what a different, non-negative connotation the term had in that work. At Izeddin-Ali's party the guests partook of hashish and drink: 'And very gently there arrives intoxication, the desired forgetfulness of all human things!' (III:LIV). Similarly, at the party Aziyadé staged before

Loti's departure, 'the ear-splitting sound of this music, the aromatic smoke of the hookah gently brought intoxication, that light oriental intoxication that is the destruction of the past, and the forgetfulness of the dark hours of life' (IV:VIII). Extreme physical pleasure there had no negative connotation; it made one forget one's unhappy moments, but there was no depiction of it as a force that undermined one's morality – not a concern for the amoral Loti of *Aziyadé.*

22 Going back to the Renaissance, one could cite Michelangelo and other artists who defined 'monsters' in this fashion. Much closer to Viaud chronologically, Flaubert had already linked the time of primordial creation with monsters and a lack of differentiation in *Salammbô* (1862) and *The Temptation of Saint Anthony* (1875). According to Millward (*L'oeuvre de Pierre Loti*, 130), *Salammbô* was one of Viaud's favourite books. On Flaubert's depictions of monsters and primordial chaos, see Berrong, '*Salammbô*: A Myth of the Origin of Languages.'

23 Troy, *Pierre Loti*, 126.

24 Wake, conflating author and character, observed Viaud's 'inordinate and insatiable craving for affection and devotion' (*The Novels of Pierre Loti*, 21). Millward noted 'Loti's' 'great need for affection' (*L'oeuvre de Pierre Loti*, 48), and went on to declare that this desire to be loved was proof of 'Loti's [Viaud's] passivity' and even a 'masochistic trait' (226). Both critics' comments say more about their own constructions of sex roles than Viaud and his protagonists.

25 Twenty-nine years later, in a collection of occasional pieces entitled *Sleeping Beauty's Chateau*, Viaud would write, again in a non-sex-specific way, of 'this need that all souls have for another soul, and ... this desire that all bodies feel for another body, a body pleasant to caress and to hug, in order to overcome the anguish of feeling oneself alone before the mystery of those things that are impossible.' On the same page he explained that, for him, tenderness gives 'the brutality of love a certain infinitely good and superiorly fraternal something' (*Sleeping Beauty's Chateau*, 'An Old Necklace'). The choice of the adjective 'fraternal' is striking in this passage and recalls the eroticization of 'brother' in *The Marriage of Loti* discussed in the previous chapter.

26 Wake declared that 'initiation into sensuality is the cause of the Spahi's corruption' (*The Novels of Pierre Loti*, 84), ignoring the more complex explanation/justification that Viaud/Loti devotes so much of the novel to developing.

27 Wake asserted: 'It is more than likely, therefore, that through [Fatou-gaye], Loti [Viaud] is representing his own sexual attraction towards the handsome sailor' (*The Novels of Pierre Loti*, 86; 'gay' does not seem to have taken on the meaning 'homosexual' in French until long after the writing of *The Story of a*

Spahi, so Fatou-gaye's name, which might look to modern readers like a signal of such a metaphor, probably was not intended as such). If this is true, the negative tone of much of the description of the African woman's love for the spahi, cited above, would indicate a great deal of self-hatred. Since nothing in either *Aziyadé* or *My Brother Yves* reflects that, I would hesitate to read Fatou-gaye's obsession with Jean as a metaphor for Viaud's possible sexual attraction to men. As I argued above, their relationship seems to reflect the author's continuing movement away from heterosexual attraction. Other critics have been quick to identify Peyral with Viaud, especially in the depiction of Jean's affair with the married Cora in the first part of the novel. (Recall that Viaud evidently had a relationship with a married woman, from which a child seems to have resulted, while stationed in Africa.) This equation does not necessarily exclude a similar equation of the author with Fatou-gaye, but with this novel biographical criticism becomes particularly speculative for lack of documentation. One could as easily read the Peyral-Fatou-gaye affair as a metaphor for Viaud's alleged relationship with that married woman, as it too produced an illegitimate child.

5. Man (Men?) in Love

1 Yves Kermadec is based, at least in terms of his actions, on a sailor named Pierre Le Cor whom Viaud knew well from 1876 to 1891. We may never know what Viaud felt for Le Cor, though the author did describe the novel as 'this book in which I put and I continue to put a great deal of my life' (*Private Diary 1882–1885*, 16). Nevertheless, we have all the material necessary – *My Brother Yves* itself – to determine if Loti loves Yves. Given the frequency with which Viaud equated himself to and even presented himself as Pierre Loti, it would seem reasonable to assume that he was using this novel to work out his feelings for Le Cor.

2 There does not seem to have been any published English translation of this work. All quotations from *Fleurs d'ennui* are taken from the 1893 edition published in Paris by Calmann Lévy. The translations, as always, are my own.

3 When Viaud repeats this scene in *My Brother Yves* [X] there is no mention of Yves sitting on the head of a gargoyle nor any homoerotic image to take its place.

4 Millward, *L'Oeuvre de Pierre Loti*, 130.

5 In a letter from April 1881, Viaud had written his friend Émile Pouvillon that 'Plumkett [Lucien Jousselin] ... affirms ... that the me that is deep down inside me, the real one, is a primitive man.... Yves ... also being a primitive man, he is always sure of coming in touch with that within me that is least

artificial and most profound.' He continued: 'This theory is extravagant, like all the ones that Plumkett comes up with' (*Private Diary 1878–1881*). Note that Viaud refers to Pierre Le Cor as Yves even in a letter.

6 This recalls Jousselin's letter of 16 February 1879, in which he told Viaud that, with *The Marriage of Loti*, the author awakened a certain poetry 'by means of a perpetual re-evocation of ancestral feelings buried under the millennia of your civilization' (*Private Diary 1878–1881*).

7 As David Bergman has remarked, 'Gay writers are at pains to show that exclusive heterosexuality is an artificial barrier erected against the polymorphous perversity of nature' (*Gaiety Transfigured*, 35). Among contemporary gay writers, Dominique Fernandez has argued that 'nature is homosexual, culture organizes the survival of humanity' (*Le rapte de Ganymede*, 18). This is in opposition to nineteenth-century scientific thought, which held that homosexuality was the result of physical and mental degeneration (Rosario, 'Pointy Penises,' 158, 167). Interestingly, one of the sailors Steven Zeeland interviewed in his study of male-male sexual behaviour in the contemporary American navy, Joey, seems to have come to a similar conclusion:

> Modern society downs homosexuality, outlaws it, bans it, but way long ago I don't think it was that big of an issue. I think it was a hush-hush thing, but I think that people still did it. Especially sailors at sea, like in the 1500s and 1600s? Even though they'd hit ports and they'd go with women, it was probably new to them. Or they were attracted to women, too, but while they were at sea they always had their buddy. (*Sailors and Sexual Identity*, 283)

8 Flaubert's *Salammbô*, which, as already mentioned, Viaud cites several times in *My Brother Yves*, and which seethes with a lot of suggestive homoeroticism, has some remarkably tolerant – but not positive – depictions of male same-sex involvement among the 'Barbarians' in its penultimate chapter. Flaubert does not go so far as to propose that these relationships, born of the soldiers' 'need for tenderness' – a phrase that Loti used so tellingly in *The Story of a Spahi* – were in any sense natural; he speaks of them as 'strange loves – obscene unions' (285–6). He does seem to depict them as a 'natural' result of an unnatural situation, however: the Barbarians, trapped in a rock formation, live without women for an extended period of time and finally turn to each other for affection. None of this is offered as a 'primitive' justification of homosexuality, but Loti, who knew the novel well, may have seen the seeds for such an argument there.

9 As we will see, Loti repeats this scene in *A Phantom from the East* (III), though there he changes Samuel's name to Salomon.

10 Loti will have a similar dream about falling involving Yves in *My Brother Yves* (XXIX), of which more later.

11 Plumkett's explanation recalls the 1878 episode at Le Cor's mother's house, recounted in chapter 1, where Viaud's bed collapsed on top of Le Cor.

To the extent that the categories 'top' and 'bottom' are worth anything, it can be noted that Plumkett's interpretation, which puts Yves under Loti, corresponds with Loti's dream, which depicts Yves sitting on the head of a phallic gargoyle. Millward wrote: 'It is obvious that Loti [Viaud] has a need to be dominated; there is, in him, an almost feminine passivity' (*L'oeuvre de Pierre Loti*, 50 n. 44). Millward did not support his assertions with concrete examples, either from Viaud's texts or from his life, but passages such as these do not support a reading of the character Loti as sexually passive.

12 In Viaud's published diary, Jousselin, in a letter of 1 August 1878, wrote to Viaud:

There is a multiplicity of different beings in you, such that, if one of them, or even a group of them, inspires a deep and violent love to which a woman gives in as the result of an irresistible feeling of being carried away – other individualities, rising up from within you, will cause the woman who gave herself to you in that passionate, momentary feeling of being carried away to hesitate to turn her entire life over to unknown beings whom she fears, unknown beings of yourself, one might almost say. If you really want to be loved, you have to hide a whole part of your complete personality, the part that is so complex, so deeply disturbing, *that people distrust it* ... (*Private Diary 1878–1881*)

What part of Viaud did Jousselin feel he needed to keep concealed in order to keep women from leaving him?

13 This is part of what may strike some contemporary gay readers as an intriguing passage:

However the little handkerchiefs dried on the naked backs of the young men ... There were some of these little handkerchiefs that were completely white, others that had designs with several colours, and even some that had fine ships printed in the middle in red borders. (XI)

Modern sailors' handkerchiefs, like the rest of their clothing, are uniform by regulation. Could enlisted men at the time that Viaud was describing wear different-coloured handkerchiefs, or was he creating a scene here out of his imagination? If the latter is true, was he making reference to something like the modern hanky code, by which some American gay men now indicate their sexual preferences? There is not enough here to permit any assertions, but the speculation is interesting.

14 When Laura Mulvey talks about the 'gaze' that (male) directors and cameramen focus on women in movies, she argues that it operates in part to neutralize the threat that (Freud claims) men feel women pose to them because

of their lack of a penis and alleged castrating powers. Loti's gay gaze, while it concentrates on the various sailors' physical attributes, never works to dehumanize or demean them. He takes pride in Yves's ability to socialize on a par with his fellow officers (LXVIII), just as he had praised Samuel's intelligence (*Aziyadé*, I:VII).

15 'Topman' is the English term for a sailor who is stationed in the crow's nest; the French *gabier* does not have the same sexual connotations.

16 Whether Loti participates in the undressing and bathing of Yves early in the novel is not clear. Having insulted an officer while drunk, Yves is put in irons in the hold. Barrada comes to visit him and, when Yves says that he would like to get out of his wet clothes, the text continues:

> *They* undressed him, *the two of them*, he letting himself be coddled like a child. His chest, his shoulders, and his arms were carefully wiped, dry clothes were put on him, and he was laid back down, putting a sack under his head so that he could sleep better.
>
> When he thanked *them* ... (VII, emphasis added)

'The two of them' could refer to Barrada and Yves; there is no mention of anyone else coming down into the hold. The 'them' in the second paragraph, on the other hand, definitely indicates that there are at least two people down in the hold with Yves. All the impersonal constructions in the first paragraph carefully disguise the number of men involved in helping bathe and undress the prisoner. Since he is able to describe all this, was Loti down there with Barrada? Why would he have tried to hide this?

17 To those who might object that men on board ship are often partially naked – Loti remarks at one point that 'men wear very little on board' (LXXXIII) – and that the narrator, in describing them, does not therefore necessarily evince a gay gaze, I would point out the frequency of this focus here as compared to what one finds in other novels that depict men equally likely to be in a state of undress, such as *Salammbô*.

18 It would be tempting to attribute Loti's development of the capacity to have romantic feelings for another man to the experience of his relationship with Samuel, but no mention is made of the boatman, either. What is the reader supposed to retain of Loti/Harry Grant when reading about Pierre Loti?

19 'Anguish' was the term Loti had used in 'Blossoms of Boredom' to describe his feelings at the thought of Yves falling from the Creizker spire. He uses it repeatedly in *My Brother Yves* when he sees Yves in trouble (cf. XXXII, etc.). The word will have an important role in Viaud's subsequent novels as well, again linked with feelings for a man in trouble.

20 Wake read Loti's dream as an indication of 'the frightening power of the nat-

ural self hidden within the subconscious' (*The Novels of Pierre Loti*, 111), but provided no details to make clear what he meant.

Two decades later, in describing his tour of India, Viaud would pen a striking passage about worlds falling into an eternal blackness (*India*, I).

21 'En vous embrassant de tout mon coeur' means, literally, 'embracing/kissing you with all my heart,' but it is a standard epistolary closing in French and bears only the force of something like the translation that I have given. This is not to say, of course, that one could not read more into it, and mean more by it, than its standard usage suggests.

22 Loti, *Private Diary 1878–1881*, 70 n. 1.

23 Loti at one point asserts the artlessness of his narrative – 'I recount things that have remained in my memory at random' (XLIX) – but that is one of literature's great *topoi*.

24 The careful reader of Viaud may note the ironic similarity to a passage in *The Marriage of Loti* cited in chapter 3, in which John, Loti's 'brother,' 'experienced a sorrowful surprise' when he learned of Loti's nocturnal strolls with Faïmana but, less upset than Loti became when the shoe was on the other foot, 'was inclined to forgive his brother Henry everything, when it was a question of her' [*Marriage*, I:XV]. A late-night stroll with a Tahitian woman, however, was not as permanent as marriage to a French woman.

25 The line '*our* flowers from the Toulven woods' is intriguing. The flowers in question are those that little Yves-Pierre had picked that afternoon while wondering through the woods with Loti (LXVIII), yet here they become 'our' (Loti and Yves's) flowers. This would seem to suggest that for Loti, little Yves-Pierre was an extension of Yves.

26 This is only one of many examples in Viaud's texts of the narrator's lack of knowledge of future events. Whether it was by design or simply because Viaud took passages from his journals without changing them, this sort of narratorial ignorance regarding the outcome of events is rather unique in Viaud and often quite striking.

27 Yves's sentence is a strange one, and it is possible that Viaud was imitating such sailors' awkward and sometimes incorrect way of expressing themselves in writing. It would have made sense for Yves to have written: 'an hour doesn't go by that I don't think about you,' rather than 'that I don't fail to think about you.'

28 Loti will talk more about his own childhood bouts of depression in *The Story of a Child*, as we will see in chapter 8.

29 Wake read Yves's desire to desert as 'the urge to desert the community and to give up the struggle with oneself' (*The Novels of Pierre Loti*, 104). While this fits his overall reading of Viaud's works as expressing a struggle between a

feeling of responsibility to family and community and a desire to flee that responsibility, the just quoted texts in *My Brother Yves* do not support such an interpretation. As the first of the two quotations proves, Yves dreams of deserting well before he has a family. (He has no obligations to the community.) Nor, by deserting to a merchant vessel, would Yves escape the need to control his drinking. Desertion was certainly an act of escape, but the text is careful not to specify what Yves wants to escape from.

30 Again, in *Salammbô*, from which Viaud repeatedly drew chapter epithets in *My Brother Yves*, Flaubert had written of the mercenaries: 'They brought their need for tenderness to bear on a companion ... strange loves were formed – obscene unions as serious as marriages' (285–6).

31 Recall Halperin's comment, quoted in the Introduction, that during the nineteenth century 'political aspirations in women and (at least according to one expert writing as late as 1920) a fondness for cats in men were manifestations of a pathological condition, a kind of psychological hermaphroditism tellingly but not essentially expressed by the preference for a "normal" member of one's own sex as a sexual partner' (*One Hundred Years*, 15–16).

32 Loti at one point refers to the final stages of Barazère's venereal disease as 'this final impurity' (LXXXIX). On the other hand, he describes the sailors aboard the *Primauguet* as participating in 'a delirium of cleanliness' every morning as they wash down the ship (XCII). It is no surprise that they refuse to get near Barazère in the final stages of his illness (LXXXIX), but one also might wonder to what extent Loti is presenting heterosexual activity and/or women with whom it takes place as an uncleanliness foreign and even inimical to what appears to be natural man's immaculately clean world.

33 Wake wrote that in Viaud's works 'the handsome sailors themselves are oddly sexless' (*The Novels of Pierre Loti*, 44). What he meant by that it would be interesting to know. Are they sexless for Wake because they do not pursue women? Loti, who so often describes their physical attributes, would have disputed Wake's assertion.

34 To what extent this is an accurate depiction of the French navy in the 1880s and to what extent it is a projection of Viaud's fantasies it would be difficult to determine. One might, however, note Zeeland's comments in his study of homosexual activity in the modern American navy: 'It is an unsurprising reality that all male sailors tend to be sexually adventuresome' (*Sailors and Sexual Identity*, xix); 'young male sailors are more inclined to exercise sexual fluidity than their civilian counterparts' (10).

35 Wake's view of homosexuality is sad. He went on to explain that if Viaud linked his 'homosexual tendency' to Yves's alcoholism, it was because 'both

of them cause a deep-seated inability to adapt to the responsibilities of adult life which can only be overcome by a superhuman act of will' (*The Novels of Pierre Loti*, 99). Nowhere did he demonstrate that Viaud regarded homosexuality as a shirking of one's adult responsibilities. Nor, of course, does one change one's sexuality by an act of will – or even, unfortunately, one's alcoholism.

36 On 15 July 1878, several years before writing *My Brother Yves*, Viaud had written to Jousselin that his latest heterosexual affair involved 'being carried away by my senses, against which I can do nothing ... I let myself slide on a delicious and terrible slope that will end up in some black mud-pit' (*Private Diary 1878–1881*). In dedicating *My Brother Yves* to novelist Alphonse Daudet, Viaud wrote that 'they say that there was always too much disturbing love in my books,' and that his latest work did not contain any.

37 It is hard to understand Wake's assertion that Viaud was 'fascinated' by the handsome sailor's 'suppressed savagery' (*The Novels of Pierre Loti*, 103). When Loti recognizes Yves's deserter brother Goulven on the American whaler, he notes: 'And, with a wild [*sauvage*] movement, I saw him clench his fists, tighten his muscles, as if to resist anyway, in a hopeless fight' (LXXXV). This instinctual violence is not an aspect of these men that fascinates Loti, or, it would seem, Viaud.

6. Different Contexts, Different Sexualities

1 Lefèvre, *La vie inquiète de Pierre Loti*, 92.

2 Le Hir, 'Le soleil dans "Pêcheur d'Islande" de Pierre Loti,' 53.

3 On the cinematic adaptations, see Quella-Villéger, *Pierre Loti*, 486–7.

4 Wake, *The Novels of Pierre Loti*, 131.

5 The phrase 'they had once again become extremely gay at the idea of going down to sleep' (ils étaient redevenus tout à fait *gais* à l'idée de descendre dormir) is suggestive for modern readers but, as noted before, there is no evidence that the French adjective *gai* had its present meaning of homosexual in 1886 or for some time thereafter.

6 While in the navy, Sylvestre has letters from Yann, Gaud, and his grandmother (III:II), but not from his fiancée, Marie Gaos. This does not necessarily indicate anything about Sylvestre's feelings for Marie, however, or about his sexuality.

7 The one exception is when Sylvestre, in Indo-China, reads a letter from his grandmother 'in the middle of those groups of half-naked men, who were crowded together there, to read as well, in the unbreathable heat of that bat-

tery ...' (II:XIII). Significantly, Sylvestre's sojourn in Indo-China is the one part of the novel narrated by an 'I,' a French naval officer who must be Pierre Loti. In *From Lands of Exile* (1887), the work that Viaud published after *Iceland Fisherman*, Pierre Loti is once again the narrator, and once again there are many mentions of naked men, including two of Sylvestre and his shipmates ('From Lands of Exile,' VII, XIV).

8 See, for example, the conclusion of James Creech's study of *Adolphe*: 'Forged in Crisis.'

9 Poggenburg, 'The Dark Side of Loti's Exoticism,' 81.

10 Dupont, Préface, *Pêcheur d'Islande*, 31. See also Leguillon, 'Un aspect de l'amour chez Pierre Loti,' who wrote that 'Loti was wildly in love with this Gaud [the fisherman's daughter], who did not want him. The fisherman's daughter rejected the navy officer. We have the impression that Loti was indulging in rather disturbed feelings when he spent a long moment undressing this young woman whom he was not able to approach' (46), a reference to a scene in *Iceland Fisherman* where Gaud undresses for the night (I:V).

11 Viaud does not reveal the identity of the young woman in the published version of his diary. Local legend, as recounted to me one day in Ploubazlanec by her granddaughter, Annette Guilcher, has it that she was Celestine Floury, the sister of Guillaume Floury, a Pors Even fisherman whom Loti used as the model for Yann Gaos.

12 Poggenburg, 'The Dark Side of Noti's Exoticism,' 84.

13 Dupont, Préface, *Pêcheur d'Islande*, 33.

14 Ibid., 34.

15 Two years after his initial encounter with her, Viaud, back in Brittany, wrote to the then married fisherman's daughter, asking for a rendezvous. She denied his request (*Private Diary 1882–1885*, 170–8).

16 Quella-Villéger, *Pierre Loti*, 111.

17 Ibid., 112.

18 For that matter, Sylvestre, while in Indo-China, also resembles Viaud in one interesting respect. At the end of 1883, while serving in Indo-China, where he wrote much of *Iceland Fisherman*, Viaud published three articles in *Le Figaro* on the French capture of Thuan-an (Da-Nang). The French navy hierarchy read the last of the three as a criticism and recalled its author in disgrace. Viaud's voyage back to France, or at least the first part of it, is identical to Sylvestre's in the hospital ship after he has been mortally wounded by the 'Chinese,' suggesting that the author intended Sylvestre's shooting to be read, at least in part, as a critique of his 'ambush' by the French navy administration. Of course, to the extent that he identified with Sylvestre, there

could have been some vicarious wish fulfilment in Viaud's description of Yann's 'tenderness' for the younger sailor.

While he incorporated elements from various acquaintances into each of his literary characters, Viaud also seems, especially in this novel, to have parcelled out different parts of himself among his various characters. As he set about work on the novel, he wrote his publisher, Juliette Adam: 'I want my story, "At Sea" [the original title], to be very good; for that, it is essential that I not invent too much, that I not *fabricate* too much, that I live in the company of my characters.' Cited in Morin, 'De "Au large" à "Pêcheur d'Islande"'; original in *Lettres de Pierre Loti à Madame Juliette Adam (1880–1922)*, 100.

19 One might note that in the story 'An Old Man,' which Viaud penned while working on *Iceland Fisherman* and which he included in *From Lands of Exile*, the author depicted a woman's seduction by a sailor with 'white teeth' (VI) from the woman's point of view.

20 Barthou, *Pêcheur d'Islande de Pierre Loti*, 37.

21 Ibid., 38

22 Wake, *The Novels of Pierre Loti*, 86.

23 Ibid., 116.

24 Ibid., 142. One is reminded of the author's comment in his diary when his marriage proposal to the Breton fisherman's daughter was rejected: 'My last even somewhat respectable dream left with [the failure of this marriage]' (*Private Diary 1882–1885*, 5).

25 Wake, *The Novels of Pierre Loti*, 99.

26 Ibid., 117.

27 Ibid., 128.

28 Ibid., 127.

29 Is this just general worry, or are we to suspect that Gaud, well-educated and having lived in Paris, knew the well-publicized story, immortalized in his poetry, of the death by drowning of Victor Hugo's daughter of the same name in 1843?

30 The sea will be given all sorts of erotic connotations in *The Story of a Child* (1890), as we will see in chapter 8.

31 *From Lands of Exile*, the work Viaud published after *Iceland Fisherman*, also links Sylvestre and Yves. In it the narrator Pierre Loti remarks that 'the hut of [Sylvestre's] grandmother in Ploubazlanec ... is indeed very close to Plouherzel, Yves's village' ('From Lands of Exile,' XIV). When he offers to visit Sylvestre in his village, Loti also remarks that the latter 'worries suddenly about the welcome that he will have to offer me and says, lowering his head – exactly in the style of my brother Yves – "At our place, you know ..., there is a thatch roof."'

32 As we saw in previous chapters, 'brother' had taken on definite homoerotic connotations even before *My Brother Yves*, in *The Marriage of Loti* and 'Blossoms of Boredom.'

33 Buisine, *Tombeau de Loti*, 107.

34 Serban, *Pierre Loti*, 115.

35 Melchiori compared Viaud's descriptions in *Iceland Fisherman* to Turner ('Feelings about Aspects,' 187).

36 The exception is when Sylvestre goes to Asia (part III, chapters I–IV). There the colours, including frequent red, become vivid and violent, as if in a painting by Henri Rousseau, and Sylvestre dies.

37 Le Hir, 'Le soleil dans "Pêcheur d'Islande" de Pierre Loti,' 54. Barthou also remarked on the interesting use of colour in the novel (*Pêcheur d'Islande de Pierre Loti*, 298).

38 Henri Scepi considers a few examples of this in his promising but very short article, 'Rhétorique de l'incertain dans Pêcheur d'Islande.'

39 In his diary, Viaud compared the model for Yann, Guillaume Floury, to Mathô, the extremely masculine protagonist of Flaubert's *Salammbô* (*Private Diary 1882–1885*, 173), the novel that he had repeatedly cited in *My Brother Yves*. Flaubert's Mathô seems to have fixed himself in Viaud's mind as the epitome of powerful masculinity. In *Into Morocco* (1890), his account of his travels in that country, Viaud remarks that his Arab host, whom he describes as 'astonishingly handsome' (XXXI), also reminds him of Mathô.

40 Such fantasies were already being published in France at the turn of the century. Most notable among them were the 'primitive' novels of the two brothers who wrote under the pseudonym J.-H. Rosny the Elder, such as *The Quest for Fire* (*La Guerre du feu*), which first appeared in 1911 and which was the basis for the film of the same name.

41 In the first chapter, the text notes that Yann's eyes have 'a *sauvage* and proud expression.' When he throws Turc against a bulkhead, the narrative explains that 'his nature had remained a little *sauvage*' (I:I). Later Gaud remarks that he is a mixture 'of *sauvage* roughness and playful childishness' (I:V). At a more serious moment, Yann, cornered by Gaud in her father's house and pressed for an explanation of why he has been avoiding her, 'looks at her with a *sauvage* glance' (II:XIII). On their wedding night, as they prepare for bed, Yann 'felt himself return to being *sauvage*' (IV:VII). When he tells her that he will love her forever, the text describes Yann's lips as being 'somewhat *sauvages*' (IV:VIII).

42 Sylvestre, who in the navy serves as topman in the crowsnest, is repeatedly compared to a bird (II:IX, etc.), an animal generally linked to the feminine.

And, of course, to the extent that Viaud links Gaud to Loti in *My Brother Yves*, he undermines traditional gender differences with her as well.

43 For a survey of the work being done in those fields, see, for example, Marshall, *Configuring Gender.*

44 Maugere, *L'identité masculine.*

45 Ibid., 144.

46 Ibid., 73.

47 Again, on these early French studies of male homosexuality, see Rosario, 'Pointy Penises,' and Copley, *Sexual Moralities in France.*

48 Rosario, 'Pointy Penises,' 151.

49 Foucault, *The History of Sexuality*, 101.

50 Moon, 'Disseminating Whitman,' 260.

7. The Origin of Sexual Ambiguity in the Madame Butterfly Legend

1 Ono, *A Western Image of Japan*, 8.

2 Wake devotes only four pages to it, for example, in *The Novels of Pierre Loti.*

3 In his fine article, 'Lieutenant F.B. Pinkerton: Problems in the Genesis of an Operatic Hero,' Arthur Groos shows what elements of the opera Puccini and his librettists borrowed from Viaud's novel. There is also an opéra comique (opera with spoken dialogue) entitled *Madame Chrysanthemum*, with music by the once popular composer of French operettas, André Messager.

4 Readers of Viaud's previous novels will remember that Loti had made real efforts to learn Arabic so as to communicate with Aziyadé, and Tahitian so as to speak with Rarahu.

5 This line suggests almost a physical disgust at the idea of contact with Chrysanthemum. Commentators have been quick to point out the racism of the novel, and *pace* Viaud's few defenders on this point, the work is difficult to read today because of its definite bias on this issue. What does not seem to have occurred to any of the commentators, however, is that this is the first work that Viaud wrote after his marriage, which took place between his trip to Japan and the publication of *Madame Chrysanthemum*, and that some of the dislike and actual physical revulsion that Loti feels for Chrysanthemum may, in fact, be a reflection of the author's attitude toward the woman whom his family had chosen for his bed. Again, as with *The Story of a Spahi*, it is important not to confuse misogyny with racism, though in *Madame Chrysanthemum* as in that previous work the author does use the latter to reinforce the former. It is also true that, unlike in *The Story of a Spahi*, in *Madame Chrysanthemum* the native men are regularly disparaged as well.

6 Lerner, *Pierre Loti*, 72.

7 Blanch, *Pierre Loti*, 178.

8 Quella-Villéger, *Pierre Loti*, 124.

9 Szyliowicz wrote that 'Madame Chryanthème, Loti's "wife," provides a front for the hero's affection for his sailor friend, Yves' (*Pierre Loti and the Oriental Woman*, 84). Similarly, Damien Zanone wrote that 'Chrysanthemum is the screen used to mark the real destination of desire: Yves' ('Bretagne et Japon aux Antipodes,' 109). There is no front here, however; as we have seen, Viaud makes no attempt to suggest that Loti has any sort of interest in his Japanese consort. In that respect, *Madame Chrysanthemum* is very unlike *Aziyadé*.

10 It is interesting to note that Kikou San, Chrysanthemum's real Japanese name in the narrative, was in real life the name of Viaud's favourite driver, the model for 415, who, in the novel, has no actual name. Claude Farrère reported that Viaud had told him in 1904 that the Japanese woman who served as the model for Chrysanthemum was actually named Kanè and not Kikou (*Loti*, 73).

8. A Proustian Probing into Childhood and the Beginnings of Sexuality

1 Martin, Préface, *Voyages*, viii.

2 Bruno Vercier's edition of the French text gives one example of the extent to which Viaud altered autobiographical reality. In chapter XX the narrator, in the process of recounting 'my first love,' assures the reader that 'so that the narrative will be more faithful, I am letting my sister speak and, from the old notebook [in which she is described as having kept notes], I will simply copy.' In fact, as Vercier shows, the following passage in the novel is substantially different from the piece that Marie Viaud wrote (270–3).

3 Despite this, when Claude Martin paraphrased a scene from *The Story of a Child*, he wrote that 'little *Julien* climbed the stairs ...' (*Aziyadé* suivi de *Fantôme d'Orient*, 391). This shows the extent to which critics have insisted, despite the text itself, on reading this novel as pure autobiography and not distinguishing between the author and the created character.

4 There is a large body of criticism devoted to establishing the difference, if any, between autobiography and the novel. Some have argued that there is no essential difference, since both involve the arrangement of intentionally selected incidents. See, for example, Gusdorf, 'Conditions and Limits of Autobiography.' Others insist that there is a difference, that autobiography involves an effort to give an accurate account of past events. For this viewpoint, see Lejeune, *On Autobiography*. Since Viaud repeatedly altered events

in his childhood while writing the story/novel of young Pierre, *The Story of a Child* would qualify as autobiography only in Gusdorf's much looser sense.

5 Proust, *Correspondance*, vol. 1, 136. Two years earlier, in a passage that suggests *The Story of a Child*, Proust had told his mother how he took his copy of Viaud's *The Marriage of Loti* into the woods to read (108).

6 When Proust's novel first appeared, one French critic wrote that 'recollections of childhood that avoid arbitrary philosophizing and precocious senility are very rare. Once one has cited Tolstoy's *Recollections*, some chapters from Mr. Marcel Proust's autobiographical epic, and *The Story of a Child*, I believe that they have all been covered' (Proust, *Correspondance*, vol. 19, 243).

7 Vercier, 'Un papillon citron-aurore,' 40. Vercier pointed out certain important similarities between Viaud's novel and Proust's work.

8 See, for example, *From Lands of Exile* (1887): 'From Lands of Exile' IX, 'Mahé of India' III; *Madame Chrysanthemum* (1887) XXXII; *Autumn Japaneries* (1889) 169; etc.

9 In *The Book of Pity and of Death*, Viaud would write: 'I have never been able to talk about anything other than what I have seen well' ('The Work of Pen-Bron').

10 Brodin, comparing Viaud to Gide, wrote: 'Loti [Viaud], with more moderation, more puritan reserve, takes the reader as a confessor, like Gide. He entrusts him entirely with his doubts, his battles, his distress. He calls to him or her for help, he hides nothing from him or her ... This must be seen as an effort toward absolute, total sincerity' (*Loti*, 356). The passage from *The Story of a Child* just quoted, along with many other examples, makes clear that Brodin's claims for Viaud's total self-revelation are excessive, as does the beginning of Brodin's own statement.

11 The similarity between Viaud's aesthetic and that of the Impressionist painters, his contemporaries, already noted with regard to *Iceland Fisherman*, is once again very clear. As Dina Sonntag has remarked, for example, 'the mood of a moment, evoked by qualities of light, was of greater importance to [the Impressionists] than the precise development of details in service of an objective representation of things. For the Impressionists, the quickly captured impression of scenes and events was the highest truth expressible in painting' ('Prelude to Tahiti,' 87–8).

12 Cf. also his references to 'these notes' (V, IX, LXII).

13 The element of 'intensity' attached to these recollected impressions resembles Marcel's distinction between things remembered voluntarily and involuntarily, of which more shortly.

14 Vercier noted that, in this novel, Viaud was the 'precursor of both Proust and Freud' ('Un papillon citron-aurore,' 38).

15 Proust's narrator realizes from the beginning that there is a hidden aspect to his powerful aesthetic reactions that also needs to be explored. Referring to his pleasure at contemplating the Martinville church steeples, he writes:

> In noticing and registering the shape of their spires, their shifting lines, the sunny warmth of their surfaces, I felt that I was not penetrating to the core of my *impression*, that something more lay behind that mobility, that luminosity, something which they seemed at once to contain and to conceal. (*Swann's Way*, 254; emphasis added)

It will only be much later that Marcel realizes that the 'something more' resides in himself and not in the object. Could these steeples have had a homoerotic association for Marcel, as certain Breton steeples did for Loti in *My Brother Yves*? Could they have been meant to allude to Loti's steeples?

16 Melchiori noted that 'James ... had censured Loti for absence of composition,' writing: 'I am sure M. Loti has no views or theories as to what constitutes and does not constitute a plot' ('Feelings about Aspects,' 189). Years later critics would direct the same criticism against Proust's *Search*.

17 Already at the beginning of *Swann's Way* Marcel had written: 'The pictures which that kind of [voluntary] memory shows us preserve nothing of the past itself' (59).

18 In fact, Marcel claims that, as an adult and before his discovery of the power of involuntary memory, he can recall only one scene from his childhood (*Swann's Way*, 58). In reading Marcel's claim to have forgotten his childhood almost entirely and his elation over the discovery of a distancing and purifying involuntary memory, one might deduce a strong suggestion of guilt, shame, and disappointment that cannot deal with the self on more immediate terms. That coincides with what we know about Proust.

19 Marcel describes the object of his *Search* with the same depth imagery: 'Impressions such as those to which I wished to give permanence could not but vanish at the touch of a direct enjoyment which had been powerless to engender them. The only way to savour them more fully was to try to get to know them more completely in the medium in which they existed, that is to say within myself, to try to make them translucid even to their very *depths*' (*Time Regained*, 271; emphasis added). During the famous madeleine episode at the beginning of *Swann's Way* that constitutes Marcel's first realization of the importance of struggling to understand the glimpses of his past that involuntary memory provides, he describes how, after much effort to interpret what he experienced during such a moment, 'I felt something in me tremble, break loose, start to rise, something that had been detached at a great depth; I don't know what it is, but it is rising slowly' (81).

20 Earlier he had remarked on the fact that 'it is strange that my childhood, which was so tenderly coddled, has left me largely sad images' (XII). Marcel, in *Swann's Way*, does not find it strange that the only memory he retains of his childhood is his traumatic if momentary separation from his mother at bedtime (58).

21 A decade later, when describing his 1901 tour of China, Viaud would write that, after taking opium, 'we found, while speaking, groups of words, expressions, images that finally render the inexpressible, the underside [*l'en dessous*] of things, that which had never been able to be said' (*The Last Days of Peking*, 'Last Days of Peking,' IX).

22 Such epiphanic moments had evidently been confronting Loti, and perhaps his creator, for some time. In *Madame Chrysanthemum* (1887) he had, in one scene, mentioned that 'my ideas ... were almost clear at that instant of awakening' (XLVIII). In *The Book of Pity and of Death* (1891), he explained that things come out of memory at the edge of sleep ('Dream'). In *Notes of My Youth* (1923), he spoke of 'the anguish of awakening! ... Why always this strange lucidity that makes this moment something terrifying?' (26 March 1875). Ramuntcho will experience similar unpleasantness upon waking in the novel of that name, as we shall see in chapter 10.

23 Loti reports experiencing fear at what he saw in *Aziyadé* upon rereading it at the beginning of *Phantom from the East*. We will deal with that in the next chapter.

24 The dedication of *The Story of a Child* suggests that Viaud was not happy with some of what he had done since childhood: 'At least I will try to put in it what was best in me, at a time when there was nothing really bad yet,' but whether one should connect 'really bad' with sex is not specified.

25 Therapists find that children usually have an awareness of gender roles, distinctions, and expectations by the age of twelve.

26 Remember that Aziyadé, the embodiment of Loti's heterosexual involvements, had green eyes.

27 Viaud recalled having been as a child 'troubled ... by songs of sailors celebrating their return' in his next work, *The Book of Pity and of Death* ('Lives of Two Cats,' XX). As we have already seen, Loti mentions hearing such songs in *Blossoms of Boredom*. All this will colour one's reading of the erotic singing Pierre hears from shipboard in *The Marriage of Loti* and *The Story of a Spahi*, mentioned in the chapters devoted to those works.

28 Note the description of the sailors as being 'simpler' and 'freer,' recalling Viaud's fascination with the primitive in *My Brother Yves* and *Iceland Fisherman*.

29 Twenty-five years later, in a collection of pieces entitled *Some Aspects of the World's Madness* (1917), Viaud would write that, despite the differences in

their backgrounds, he had gotten along with common seamen when he entered the navy because of 'the common points of dreaming and childlike behaviour.' The homoerotic connotations of dreams and dreaming, suggested in *Iceland Fisherman* and *The Story of a Child*, will also be present in *Ramuntcho*.

30 Darkness (*le noir*) plays an important role in *The Story of a Child* from the beginning. In chapter II, Pierre recounts his early fear and yet fascination with the dark. In chapter IV, where he recalls his first encounter with the sea, he describes it as 'being of an almost black [*noir*] dark green' (IV).

31 Since the sea, as already noted, also gave him 'an impression of desolate loneliness, abandonment, exile' (IV), it is tempting to read the 'anticipated anguish' that it, or what it symbolizes, causes him as another expression of his anguish at the idea of the trouble that he feels his desire will produce for him. How much of this is hindsight, rather than the actual feelings of the then very young Pierre?

32 Readers of Proust will recall the young Marcel's strong ties to his mother – before he discovers the power of involuntary memory, the scene of his separation from her at bedtime is the only thing that he can remember from his childhood – but he does not seem to turn to her as a way of forgetting about desire. One reason many gay men feel a strong bond to their mothers is that she is the one woman with whom they can have an emotional relationship that is entirely in keeping with social expectations.

33 Michael Lerner wrote of Viaud's 'desire to stop time and retreat into the childhood situation of simplicity, stability, and vitality founded on family security, faith, and proximity to Nature' (*Pierre Loti*, 147) but suggested no causes. Remember the passage from *The Awakened* cited at the beginning of this chapter.

34 A passage in *Madame Chrysanthemum* from three years before is similar: 'I go back to my childhood much too often; in truth, I harp on it. But it seems to me that I only had impressions, feelings at that time' (XXXII).

35 This search for a lost intensity that would vitalize artistic creation can also be found in several of Viaud's distinguished literary contemporaries, such as Flaubert and Leconte de Lisle. Neither of them turned to their childhoods as a possible source, but they did both turn to the primitive, which, as we have seen, Viaud linked with childhood. In both cases, it is a question of returning to the origins of man.

Over a decade later, in *To Ispahan*, Viaud's account of his journey through Persia, the author would write: 'I probably indulge too much in returning to my childhood impressions; but it is because they were the most mysterious, as well as the most vivid' (Thursday, 3 May).

36 Keith G. Millward noted 'this terror of old age that will pursue him throughout his entire life' (*L'oeuvre de Pierre Loti*, 43). Gay men have been particularly
vulnerable to such a fear because society has made it difficult for them to
find partners, leaving a much higher percentage of them than their straight
counterparts to face the fear that they will lose their sensual, sexual attractiveness before they have attained the goal for which those powers are generally seen as mandatory.

37 Elsewhere Pierre, recalling his childhood attempt to hold on to every object
that he had collected while on the Isle of Oléron, speaks of 'this need to
carry everything off with me' (XX). A letter to one of Viaud's publishers,
Juliette Adam, suggests one reason why the author feared getting older: 'I
dream with a supreme terror of the moment when old age will come and
people won't love me anymore' (Lefèvre, *La vie inquiète de Pierre Loti*, 162).

38 Viaud's less altered autobiographical writings repeatedly demonstrate the
same preoccupation: he prefaced *First Youth* (1919) by explaining that he
had gathered together these recollections of his adolescence because 'I
wanted to stop time, reconstitute aspects that had been wiped away.'
Djénane's reasons for starting a diary in *The Awakened* will be discussed in
chapter 11.

39 In his published diary, Viaud wrote: 'My family had persuaded me that I was
frail and in need of being watched over like a delicate plant' (*Private Diary
1878–1881*, 101). Proust's Marcel, on the other hand, paints a generally negative picture of his family's efforts to alter his hypersensitivity (*Swann's
Way*, 50 and elsewhere). Both fictional children are forbidden to read Musset's poetry because of its potential effect on their nervous systems (*Swann's
Way*, 52–3; *The Story of a Child*, LXXVI).

40 In his published diary, Viaud recalled that as a child in Rochefort, 'I already
loved sailors; I felt myself drawn toward them, toward the life of seafolk,
toward adventures, independence and the unknown' (*Private Diary 1878–
1881*, 101). Again, Djénane's description in *The Awakened* of her captivity in a
harem from the age of thirteen will evoke a great deal of this.

41 Vercier offers an intriguing reading of the dream as a representation of
Viaud's feeling of loss at the marriage of his sister ('Un papillon citron-
aurore,' 40). This marriage is not mentioned in the novel itself, however.
Given the way Viaud leads into this dream, moreover, with the dissimulation
anecdote and the mention of the sailors singing as Pierre falls asleep, it
remains more likely that the referent of the dream figure, at least in the
novel, is Pierre's brother and not his sister.

For Viaud's own words on his affection for his brother and reaction to his
loss, see in particular *First Youth* X–XIII. As noted in the Introduction,

Buisine wrote that Viaud's homosexuality was an effort to find his lost brother (*Tombeau de Loti*, 351). Again, that would seem to be an inverted way of explaining the attraction apparently being described here.

42 In describing Mlle Vinteuil's scene with her lesbian lover, Marcel remarks:

Her sensitive and scrupulous heart was ignorant of the words that ought to flow spontaneously from her lips to match the scene for which her eager senses clamoured. She reached out as far as she could across the limitations of her true nature to find the language appropriate to the vicious young woman she longed to be thought. (*Swann's Way*, 227–8)

Mlle Vinteuil, unlike Viaud's non-heterosexual characters, buys in to society's evaluation of homosexuals as vicious/full of vice and seeks to use the defamatory language created to depict them.

43 Viaud would use the phrase 'unknown friends' to describe his readers again in *The Book of Pity and of Death* ('Notice from the author') and *Turkey in Agony*. In *Sleeping Beauty's Chateau* and *Supreme Visions of the East*, he would speak of 'my friends, known or unknown.' In *Jerusalem*, he altered the phrase, significantly, to 'my friends, my unknown brothers' (I). In *The Awakened*, as we shall see, he will speak of his 'unknown souls.'

44 Early in *Swann's Way*, Marcel explains:

I feel that there is much to be said for the Celtic belief that the souls of those whom we have lost are held captive in ... some inanimate object, and thus effectively lost to us until the day ... when we happen ... to obtain possession of the object which forms their prison. Then they start and tremble, they call us by our name, and as soon as we have recognized them the spell is broken. Delivered by us, they have overcome death and return to share our life. (59)

45 Proust attributes similar evocative powers to fiction. Cf., for example, *Swann's Way*, 118.

46 The biographical diary account that served as the basis for this episode can be found in *Private Diary 1878–1881*, 103–11. It is radically different, and the recollection of the cousin singing the song is entirely absent, proving again that *The Story of a Child* is a novel, however autobiographical.

47 The friends with whom the young Julien Viaud played while at his uncle's house in the Midi were named not Peyral, but Trassy (*Le roman d'un enfant*, ed. Vercier, 261).

48 Pointing out that the real-world model for the 'big cousin,' Armand Bon, was the man who married Viaud's sister Marie and took her away from the Viaud household, Vercier argued that Pierre's fascination with the butterfly-Boriessong association reflects Viaud's childhood desire to take the place of Bon

and recapture his lost sister ('Au papillon citron-aurore,' 39). One reading does not necessarily exclude the other, but since there is no mention in the novel of Marie marrying the nameless 'big cousin' I can accept Vercier's interpretation as a possible reading only of Viaud's life, and not of *The Story of a Child.*

49 In his next work, *The Book of Pity and of Death,* Viaud wrote that the memory of the dawn-yellow butterfly caused in him an 'undefined fear' ('Aunt Claire Leaves Us,' 5 December).

50 This association of the butterfly, Bories, and the big cousin also gives an interesting additional dimension to another, previous episode. Early in the novel, Pierre had recounted how, at the age of seven, he and his friend Antoinette used to pretend to be caterpillars that metamorphosed into butterflies (XV). Given Pierre's repeated dissatisfaction with his own appearance, the game suggests a desire to be transformed into a more physically attractive creature and perhaps, by extension, to become big like Pierre's cousin. There is also the notion that Pierre wanted to be able to transform himself into something that has, in Western society, feminine connotations. Viaud had already spoken of Jean Peyral's 'transformation' when referring to his experimentation with non-traditional relationships in *The Story of a Spahi* (I:I).

In the next chapter, Pierre explains that he also loved to collect butterflies as a child, but that 'those that flew into my courtyard, with the exception of a few strays that came from the countryside, were not very beautiful,' leading him to leave his house in search of more attractive specimens (XVI). Could this be read as a metaphorical explanation for why, at the end of the novel, he decides to leave his home and go to sea, that he wanted to find attractive men, in particular those open to a homosexual relationship, but had not been able to do so in Rochefort? It is worth noting that he pursues specimens of what he, himself, had wanted to become. It might also be mentioned that when Viaud had an acrobat's outfit designed for himself during his appearance with a circus, it had a large butterfly on the chest. The butterfly was clearly a significant symbol to Viaud.

All of this puts an amusing irony in David Belasco and Giacomo Puccini's alteration of Madame Chrysanthemum's name to Madame Butterfly.

51 In *Carmen Sylva and Sketches from the Orient,* Viaud would express his desire to have a specific language to describe his subject, Queen Elisabeth of Rumania ('Carmen Sylva').

52 In *Madame Chrysanthemum,* three years before, Loti had bemoaned the difficulty of finding language that not only described an object but also conveyed

the emotion that that object evoked. Speaking of his previous books, he had exclaimed: 'It seemed to me that the words never said as much as I would have liked. I struggled against my powerlessness to render the penetrating charm of things in a human language' (VIII). In *The Book of Pity and of Death*, Viaud bemoaned his failure to render the feelings of a scene ('Sorrow of an Old Prisoner'). This prefigures Proust's desire to convey what Marcel will call 'the truth' of experience, our reactions to it.

53 Vercier spoke of 'the ambiguity in which Loti's [autobiography] steeps' ('Le mythe du premier souvenir,' 1037) and wrote that the novel was couched in 'a discourse that is not supposed to show its object clearly' ('Un papillon citron-aurore,' 36).

54 Proust would suggest a negative version of such self-examination prompted by art when, at the beginning of the *Search*, he has Marcel remark that, having viewed the story of Golo in a series of projections on his wall, 'the crimes of Golo had driven me to a more than ordinarily scrupulous examination of my own conscience' (*Swann's Way*, 11–12).

55 As already noted, Viaud had made a similar complaint four years before in *Iceland Fisherman* (III:IX).

9. Works of Self-Doubt

1 Remember that in *Notes of My Youth*, Viaud would later describe his student days in Paris as 'an era of transition in my life' (June 1878).

2 While tracking down Aziyadé's grave, Loti had decided against chasing after Anaktar-Chiraz, who might know its whereabouts, and instead had gone to the café where he used to sit with Achmet (III).

3 Lerner, *Pierre Loti*, 81.

4 It is difficult not to see as part of her homophobia the fact that Blanch, in her section on *A Phantom from the East* (*Pierre Loti*, 190–4), discusses Loti's pursuit of Aziyadé to the exclusion of his inquiries about Achmet.

5 Viaud's diary entry for this period suggests that the person in the real-life incident that served as the source for this episode in *A Phantom from the East* was the Daniel on whom he had based Samuel. In the entry for 6 October 1887, Viaud gives his name as David, and in the corresponding passage in 'Short, dying sequel to *A Phantom from the East*,' a work that he never published, he mentions, as he does not in *A Phantom from the East*, that this David was in Salonika when the narrator first arrived there (Loti, 'Petite suite mourante à Fantôme d'Orient,' 212). In *Notes of My Youth*, Viaud had written on 2 March 1878 that 'Samuel has left for Salonika, where he has become once

more what he was in the past, a poor devil of a boatman, without a cent.'
There are too many coincidences not to suspect that the David Viaud met in
1887 was the same person whom he had known in Salonika and Constantinople in 1875–6 and turned into Samuel in *Aziyadé*.

It is interesting to note that in his diary entry for 22 November 1903,
Viaud, once again in Istanbul, would speak of visiting 'the house in Haskeuï!
That's where I had first received my dear little friend [Hakidjé], when she
returned from Salonika; there's where my poor Mehmet had worked so
much to arrange that room on the second floor' (*Istanbul*, 32; also Loti, *Cette
éternelle nostalgie*, 503). In *Aziyadé*, Viaud had depicted Samuel helping him
prepare his house in Istanbul (II:XX); in the novel Achmet did not appear
for the first time until after Aziyadé's arrival (III:VIII). Was Viaud misremem-
bering, or had he fictionalized that episode in his first novel?

6 Claude Martin cites some admirers of *A Phantom from the East* in the Preface
to his edition of *Aziyadé* and the other work (Préface, *Aziyadé* suivi de *Fantôme
d'Orient*, 23–4).

7 Wake, *The Novels of Pierre Loti*, 149.

8 Wake wrote that in *Sailor* Viaud 'tries to turn [escapism] into the poetry of
superior sensibility' (*The Novels of Pierre Loti*, 153).

9 Again, should one use these passages as interpretive tools for reading *A
Phantom from the East*? In that case, Aziyadé, in that text, would represent not
simply herself but Loti's entire first Middle East experience. This would have
an effect on how one interprets Loti's recurring dream of trying to return to
Aziyadé and its eventual disappearance.

10 A mother-son erotic relationship could be seen as a way of talking about
another socially unacceptable involvement, but there is never any hint that
Jean's mother's feelings for her son are anything other than maternal.

11 In his diary entry for 9 March 1891, Viaud mentioned 'that window [in his
office] where I spent so many hours dreaming with Léo.' Viaud's diary for
1891 was published by Pierre P. Loti-Viaud and Michel Desbruères as 'Journal intime inédit.'

12 Viaud's diary for 1891 makes continual reference to his sorrow at Léo
Thémèze's departure. See in particular the entries for 13, 14, and 19 April,
and 12 and 20 August.

13 Léo Thémèze, like Pierre Le Cor before him, got married suddenly, much to
Viaud's surprise. See Viaud's diary entry for 2 March 1891, in 'Journal
intime interdit.'

14 In Viaud's diary entry for 17 January 1891, he had noted: 'I cling, with a sort
of despair, to the least little fragile things that are mementos of those forever
finished years [the years that he had spent with Léo Thémèze].'

10. Creating the Allegorical Gay Novel

1 For what it is worth, Crucita, the Basque woman who served as one of the models for Gracieuse, evidently had her brother Ramoncho's eyes and smile. See André Moulis, 'Amours Basques,' 106, 109.

2 Besnier, ed., *Ramuntcho*, 272.

3 Moulis, 'Genèse de "Ramuntcho,"' 62–3.

4 Besnier's remark in the Preface to his edition of the French text that Viaud's description of the male companions in some of the earlier novels as 'brothers' bears witness to his 'essential affective immaturity' (16) suggests that Besnier has not understood all the connotations of that word in Viaud's texts. It also suggests that Besnier has a limited understanding of the nature of adult family relationships, regardless of sexuality.

5 In the corresponding scene in Viaud's diary, which he used as a model for this passage in the novel but in which he and his Basque friend, Otharré Borda, had simply paid a visit to Borda's sister with no plans of abducting her, the phrase 'in a singular tone of voice' has no equivalent. See Moulis, 'Genèse de "Ramuntcho,"' 76.

6 Moulis, 'Genèse de "Ramuntcho,"' 64.

7 André Moulis wrote that '*Ramuntcho* relates several imagined peripeteia, adventures that were not part of [Viaud's] personal life. For a change, Loti is not the constant hero of it. The novel therefore has a certain objective character' ('Genèse de "Ramuntcho,"' 55). As we shall see later, however, the novel has a considerable autobiographical element.

8 As noted in chapter 9, this feeling of being different from his companions had been new to the Viaud protagonist as of Jean Berny in *Sailor*. In that novel, however, the difference had been described as superiority and was not a function of heredity so much as of Jean's middle-class upbringing. The differences between Berny and Ramuntcho on this issue are both striking and significant.

9 In the Preface to his edition of the French text, Besnier, pointing out that Ramuntcho's desire to be elsewhere comes from his father, remarks: 'Heredity, in a word ... is what condemns Ramuntcho' (22). As we shall see, 'condemns' is too strong a verb to describe the attitude toward these desires presented in the novel.

10 Moulis quotes this passage in 'Genèse de "Ramuntcho,"' 75.

11 The phrase 'these innocent little cabarets' is meant to undercut the homo-erotic potential of this scene, much less any recollection of the ambiguous dives in *Aziyadé*, at least for some readers.

12 Moulis, 'Genèse de "Ramuntcho,"' 51.

13 It is interesting to note that Willa Cather, who, as John P. Anders has remarked, appreciated Viaud's novels for their coded expression of homosexual desire, also used primitive peoples, in her case Native Americans, as 'a site for homosexual projection' (Goldberg, 'Strange Brothers,' 481; see also 468).

14 Lerner, *Pierre Loti*, 99.

15 One of the standard words for homosexual men in turn-of-the-century France, the one that Proust's Marcel prefers, was 'invert' (Nye, *Masculinity*, 108). In the passage from *Ramuntcho* quoted above, Viaud used *renversé* rather than *inverti*, but it connotes the same idea.

16 Pierre Flottes pointed out that, in altering passages in his diary for insertion in the novel, 'Loti cast a sort of questionable, worrisome, and pallid light on the night work of the contraband runners' ('Sur un manuscrit de "Ramuntcho,"' 113). The atmosphere in *Ramuntcho* is not an accurate depiction of what Viaud saw while stationed in Hendaye, therefore, but rather an intentional alteration whose purpose we have the right to question.

17 Some years later, in *Corydon*, Gide would speak of 'the appearance of a contraband runner than you [society] force upon a uranist [homosexual]' (314).

18 We know that coded languages used exclusively by gay men existed in France during Viaud's lifetime. François Carlin, a French chief of police, mentioned the existence of 'a distinct queer subculture with its own language and its own dress code' in his anecdotal *Unnatural Prostitution* (1887). See Smith, 'Silence, Secrecy, and Scientific Discourse in the Nineteenth Century,' 99. Proust several times alludes to the existence of a separate gay language (*Sodom and Gomorrah*, 18, 28). According to Elaine Showalter, 'by the 1880s ... the Victorian homosexual world had evolved into a secret but active subculture, with its own language, styles, practices, and meeting places' (*Sexual Anarchy*, 106).

19 As the leader of a band of outlaws, he might remind some of Balzac's ambiguously portrayed Vautrin. As someone who searches out 'energetic, strong young men,' who 'was a good judge of thigh and shoulder muscles' (I:1), he might strike others as a precursor of Proust's Baron Charlus.

20 Ramuntcho is also twice compared to a cat (I:16, I:23) and Itchoua once (I:1).

21 Raymonde Lefèvre noted that the mountain on which Viaud based the Gizune, the Rhune, is only 900 metres tall, and expressed surprise that Viaud described its literary equivalent as enormous, crushing, dominating everything (*En marge de Loti*, 242). This only proves that the depictions of the Gizune are not simply landscape descriptions, but intentional efforts to convey something other than just settings.

22 Not surprisingly given the association of the contraband runners and what

they represent metaphorically with it, Spain's Arab flavour is mentioned in this novel: during one festival, 'two female singers,' performing while 'the wind from the south ... blows sweetly ... intone ... an old Spanish seguidilla, bringing to the Basque land the warm and slightly Arabic gaiety from beyond the near border' (I:4). Viaud's 'unknown friends' cannot help but make an association with *Aziyadé*, or even with the fact that several of the male objects of desire in subsequent novels, as we have seen, were described, often rather surprisingly, as having Arab traits.

23 The last words of the novel, the Latin prayer 'O crux, ave, spes unica!' (II:13), which seem to be spoken by the nuns inside the convent, have elicited various interpretations from different critics. For Quella-Villéger this line and its location constitute 'the ultimate vow of the novel' (*Pierre Loti l'incompris*, 167), a novel that, he asserts, is 'wise and pious,' and indeed 'Christian.' For Moulis, the novel shows Viaud's 'serious desire for faith' ('Genèse de "Ramuntcho,"' 50). One might argue, however, that since Ramuntcho leaves the convent behind, as he does his entire life in the Basque country, he is abandoning religion as well, especially after it has blocked his attempts to marry Gracieuse.

24 Note the description of the Basque men being 'of another essence than' Ramuntcho (II:4), again suggesting the idea of some fundamental distinction between the young player and most other men, a separate identity.

25 As a Basque, Ramuntcho does not have to declare a citizenship in France or Spain, and does so only when Gracieuse urges him (I:5). Not surprisingly, given the connotations of Spain in the novel, she wants him to become French.

26 Besnier, Préface, 15. Besnier sees running contraband to be like a game. This is not borne out by the novel where, as we have seen, it is generally depicted as an unpleasant and inglorious activity.

27 Remember Zeeland's remarks about the sexual experimentation that goes on in the navy (*Sailors and Sexual Identity*, xix, 10).

28 Besnier, Préface, 14–15.

29 Again, this is a change from the presentation of Jean Berny in *Sailor*, whose refined side had been presented largely as proof of his superiority over his fellow sailors.

30 In this sense, Ramuntcho has a great deal in common with the protagonist of Viaud's next and last novel, Djénane in *The Awakened*.

31 In this sense, Ramuntcho is different from both Loti in *Aziyadé*, who discovered the variety of life during his adolescence before he travelled abroad, and Djénane, in *The Awakened*, who will grow dissatisfied with her confined life not out of experience, but strictly through reading.

32 Again, notice the difference here between Ramuntcho and Jean Berny. The former becomes more different from the other contraband runners because of his efforts to get married; the latter, because of his birth and education. Wake described them both as 'the refined primitive' (*The Novels of Pierre Loti*, 167), but Ramuntcho is not refined so much as distanced by his different emotions.

33 Bergman, *Gaiety Transfigured*, 30–1.

34 Ignacio is first presented as unmarried and without children (I:20), so he might have been seen as someone who at least potentially could have shared and explained Ramuntcho's different desires. When he first hears from his uncle, the young man becomes 'troubled ... in a different way, by the thought of that uncle, enjoying the life of adventure over there' (I:9). Remember the connotations of 'adventure' noted earlier.

35 The existence of a community for the protagonist in Viaud's next and last novel, *The Awakened*, will be one of its most remarkable features.

36 Bergman, *Gaiety Transfigured*, 45.

37 Quella-Villéger, *Pierre Loti l'incompris*, 156.

38 Gide, *Si le grain ne meurt*, 290. Gide's subsequent description of Wilde as someone given to constant cleverness recalls Viaud's depiction of Ramuntcho's father as surrounding himself with 'refined men ... exchanging between themselves with light banter thoughts about the abyss' (I:1).

39 Bristow, *Effeminate England*, 2. Besnier claimed that Viaud wrote *Ramuntcho* during his trip through the Holy Land in 1894 (Préface, 19), Wake stated that he composed it in 1895 (*The Novels of Pierre Loti*, 161), and Quella-Villéger, who offers the most convincing evidence, that he created the novel in 1896 (*Pierre Loti l'incompris*, 167).

40 Nye, *Masculinity*, 120.

41 Cather also lambasted Wilde at the time of his trial, in what Jonathan Goldberg has described as 'gestures at once self-protective and self-hating' ('Strange Brothers,' 470).

42 Besnier, Préface, 19.

43 Near the end of Proust's novel, Marcel blames his bad health, which he in turn cites as the cause of his poor memory, on the time that his mother gave in to his nervousness and stayed up with him (*Time Regained*, 526).

44 Note that this 'desertion' happens while Ramuntcho is far away fulfilling his military obligation, just as in the cases of Jean Peyral and Jean Berny.

45 Viaud wrote *Ramuntcho* after his return from a trip to the Holy Land in 1894, but it is clear that he did not have a blind devotion to religion, much less, as a Protestant, to the Catholic church.

46 Quella-Villéger, *Pierre Loti l'incompris*, 167.

47 Wake, *The Novels of Pierre Loti*, 172.

48 Earlier, upon returning from military service and learning that Gracieuse had entered a convent, Ramuntcho had been willing to accept an existence in Etchézar that consisted of playing pelota and running contraband (II:8).

49 Quella-Villéger, *Pierre Loti l'incompris*, 169.

50 Besnier, Préface, 8.

51 Ibid., 9.

52 As we noted in chapter 1, he eventually fathered three with her, two of whom grew to adulthood, maintaining them in Rochefort, not far from the home that he shared with his wife, mother, and legitimate son.

53 Moulis, 'Genèse de "Ramuntcho,'' 55.

54 Ibid., 53.

55 Besnier, Préface, 22.

56 Ibid., 13.

57 Moulis, 'Amours basques,' 127.

58 Quella-Villéger, *Pierre Loti l'incompris*, 169.

59 Moulis, 'Amours basques,' 126.

60 Rivers, *Proust and the Art of Love*, 110.

61 Quella-Villéger, *Pierre Loti l'incompris*, 171.

62 Their circumstances are different, however. Ramuntcho is truly alone at his mother's death; Viaud had a wife, a mistress, children, friends, a career, etc.

63 Viaud's description in his diary of his mother's last days and his reaction to her death are extremely moving and also quite clearly composed, which is not to say either that it was not sincere or that it represented all of the author's feelings with regard to her. The pages in question, covering the period 10 October–13 November 1896, have been published in Pierre Loti, *Mort de ma mère*, ed. Fernand Lapland, but have not been translated into English.

11. A Defence of Homosexuals and a Consciousness Raising

1 *The Daughter of Heaven* does not touch on any of the themes examined in this study. As Claude Farrère, who served under Viaud on the *Vautour* when the latter completed the play and to whom Viaud gave the just finished work to read, wrote: 'I only find him here and there in this text in dialogue ... The "him" that I find here ... is, furthermore, not the Loti whom I have read, the Loti of his novels ... no: it is the Loti whom I know, the one who commands the *Vautour*' (*Loti*, 80). How much Viaud contributed to this play does not seem to be known.

2 Hélys, *Le Secret des 'Désenchantées*,' 69.

3 Martin, Préface, *Voyages*, viii.

4 For what it is worth, Farrère recalled that Viaud spoke to him about *Madame Prune* 'with a sort of visible disdain' (*Loti*, 57). But then, Viaud was reported as having spoken disparagingly about many of his works.

5 The novel's French title, *Les Désenchantées*, has no good English equivalent. André Lhéry, the character in the book who will write it, as Proust's Marcel will write the *Search*, and who gives it its title, explains that by *désenchantées* he means people who, after having had their minds put to sleep by 'traditions and dogmas,' awaken to the truth (XIV). If in English we had a noun to describe those whose have undergone a consciousness raising, that would be the best translation. *Those Who Have Had Their Consciousness Raised* is aesthetically unacceptable, however, and *The Disenchanted*, the title that has been used in the past on Clara Bell's English translation, does not immediately suggest this meaning. Viaud was careful to limit the use of *désenchanté* in the novel to the one meaning that he wanted it to have, moreover, cutting out a passage from one of Hélys's adapted letters that gave the word its more common sense of 'disillusioned' (compare *Secret*, 124, with *Awakened*, XIX). Since many of Viaud's other works have been published in English with various titles, I will use *The Awakened*, which is close to the spirit of the original. If the long-standing English title for Proust's work can be changed by modern publishers, so can this one.

6 Lefèvre, *Le vie inquiète de Pierre Loti*, 92.

7 Brodin, *Loti*, 290.

8 Szyliowicz, *Pierre Loti and the Oriental Woman*, 121.

9 Ibid., 94.

10 Hélys, *Secret*, vii.

11 Ibid., 117–18, 249, 272.

12 None of the critics who write on Viaud has taken Hélys to task for her deception, in part, I suspect, because older men duped by young women into thinking that they could be attractive have long been considered a safe target for ridicule in French culture (think of Molière's plays, for example), in part because Hélys's motives were so admirable: she wanted to help Turkish women, who really were suffering under the harem system (91–2), but realized that a book by her on the subject would not have had the impact of a book by Viaud (200). Why a novel that is the result of a collaboration should be unworthy of study is not clear, however. Scholars write on the works of the Goncourt brothers. If, as critics regularly repeat today, the function of literary criticism is no longer to evaluate literature but rather to analyse its content, the number of persons involved in creating a text should be irrelevant as long as there is interesting content.

13 Hélys, *Secret*, 274.

14 Ibid., 125.
15 Quella-Villéger, *Pierre Loti l'incompris*, 247.
16 On this, see chapter 3 of Raymonde Lefèvre's important monograph, *Les Désenchantées de Pierre Loti*.
17 Hélys recounts Neyr (Zeyneb in the novel) saying at one point: 'He cannot invent outside of himself' (194). In the novel, Viaud has Lhéry admit without any apparent regret: 'I can never talk about anything even half-way decently unless I have seen and lived it' (XIII). Lefèvre, for example, began her monograph by noting that 'the book ... was contrary to his own tendencies and his own convictions ... He was too conservative, too much taken by tradition, too opposed to "progress," to wish these mysterious, veiled women suddenly cast into reality' (*Les Désenchantées de Pierre Loti*, 15).
18 Did Hélys see this potential link when proposing her topic to Viaud? In one of her earlier letters she asked him: 'Has your soul always been at ease in its envelop and in its atmosphere?' (*Secret*, 94) What did she mean by this?
19 Wake, *The Novels of Pierre Loti*, 174.
20 Buisine, *Tombeau de Loti*, 146.
21 Hélys, *Secret*, 32.
22 It is interesting to recall that in *India* (1903), Viaud's account of his journey through that land in search of spiritual peace, he had three years previously come to an understanding of the idea of one universal soul when, seeing a young woman, he had thought to himself: 'She is I, I am she, and we are God' (*India*, VI:XIII).
23 The fact that so much of the Loti persona is embodied in Djénane may explain why Viaud chose not to name the French naval officer and author in the novel Pierre Loti.
24 Cf. Hélys, *Secret*, 236.
25 Viaud filled *The Awakened* with ironic reversals of situations in his previous novels, as we shall see.
26 Here *The Awakened* matches the text in *The Secret* exactly (237). Even if the episode was of her invention, however, Hélys would have known the corresponding incidents in *The Story of a Child* and may have been trying to make Leyla that much more sympathetic to Viaud. And, of course, Viaud chose to include the detail, though he was not obliged to.
27 Ramuntcho is not as involved with saving mementos of his past, but the text does mention that, before leaving the Basque region to do his military service, he plucked a blade of grass that he would 'save later with a saddened attachment' (I:25). Readers of chapter 9 will recall Jean Berny's mother's ambivalent relationship to the mementoes that she carries with her from lodging to lodging.

28 The passage in the corresponding letter in *The Secret of the 'Awakened'* shows that Hélys, knowing *The Story of a Child*, was making a clear play for Viaud's sympathy, or else was copying out of *The Awakened*: 'When my soul cries too much, the memories that haunt me like a regret, almost a remorse for my long forgetfulness, are my memories of childhood' (235).

29 Again, the corresponding passage in Hélys's text is almost identical: 'They return to me in an imperious fashion, coloured and brilliant. They show me a luminous land. I like to dream about this lost paradise to which I cannot, would not want to return' (235).

30 In a passage not included in even the latest version of the English translation of *The Captive*, Proust at one point describes the Baron de Charlus as wearing a mask over his real face. See Proust, *La Prisonnière*, 200. For the corresponding passage in the English translation, see *The Captive. The Fugitive*, 294.

31 It proves nothing, but twice Hélys remarked that, given his behaviour with them, she and her friends wondered if Viaud had ever really had any of the (heterosexual) romances that he described in his novels (*Secret*, 28, 75).

32 This part of the letter is not in Hélys's original (*Secret*, 106).

33 Louis Barthou wrote the same thing (*Pêcher d'Islande de Pierre Loti*, 281), as have other of Viaud's admirers.

34 There is also a link between *The Awakened* and Viaud. The verse from the Koran above the head of Djénane's bed, 'My sins are as large as the seas, but your pardon is larger still, Allah!' (III), which Viaud evidently chose out of several that Hélys had sent him (*Secret*, 251–2), reflects the author's continual concern with his salvation. (What he saw as his sins this line over Djénane's bed does not indicate.) Viaud was not religious. As he wrote in various places, he had lost his faith while still an adolescent. He was, however, hopeful that, as his mother and brother had believed, the elect would be reunited in heaven. Salvation would therefore give him the possibility of being joined through eternity with his loved ones, in particular his mother. This idea runs throughout his diaries; Viaud expressed it publicly at the end of *Galilee*, one of the three travelogues he published on his return from a trip to the Holy Land in 1894: '[Christ] said above all ... that there would be a union without end with the beloved, somewhere where one would be pardoned and pure forever' (VI).

35 Hélys, *Secret*, 14.

36 *Medjé* is the name of the novel by André Lhéry recounting his early love affair in the Middle East, and its principle female character. Just as Lhéry is meant to be seen as Viaud, so Medjé is Aziyadé.

37 Hélys, *Secret*, 192–3. In Viaud's diary for the period, he describes the three 'Turkish women' as 'raising their veils, showing their kind faces to the sky'

one day while he is out for a stroll with them (*Istanbul: Le regard de Pierre Loti*, 98). Hélys does not mention this in her book, and Viaud does not mention what colour eyes 'Leyla' had.

38 Hélys, *Secret*, 211–12. Viaud inserted this part of her letter almost verbatim into his text: 'Let all those shadows become mixed together, too: the beloved from before ... and these three other ones later ... Mix them all up, mix them up well and keep them together in your heart (it's not enough to have them in your memory)' (LII).

39 The idea that it is the people who love these individuals who make them suffer was Viaud's addition to Hélys's original, which read simply: 'May all of our tears, may my anguish at this hour fall upon those who oppress us' (*Secret*, 261).

40 As we noted in chapter 6, Djénane, faced with being married to Hamdi, writes in her diary: 'I feel like someone who has drowned' (IV), another instance where *The Awakened* seems to cast additional light on an earlier Viaud text. *Judith Renaudin*, Viaud's one original play, deals with a young Protestant woman who resists her father's pressure to marry Daniel Robert. The only link between the title character and the Loti persona, a slight one, is her remark that she will miss her garden when, along with other Protestants, she is forced into exile because of Louis XIV's revocation of the Edict of Nantes (II, iii). The play does not seem to have been translated into English.

41 Though André Lhéry is presented as experiencing no sexual attraction to men and having no traditionally feminine traits, the seldom-glimpsed Hamdi-Bey is described as having a 'sweet voice' and 'the slightly feline smile that he inherited from his mother' (IV).

42 Viaud took this passage verbatim from Hélys's corresponding letter (*Secret*, 122).

43 Chapter 1 contains several excerpts from Viaud's diary in which he spoke of having to play a role to hide his true self.

44 The term 'doubling' (*dédoublement*) is one that Hélys used often (*Secret*, 152, 177, etc.). Proust's Marcel at one point speaks of Albertine carrying on 'a double life' (*Fugitive*, 698) because of her sexual involvement with women.

45 This passage has no equivalent in Hélys's corresponding letter at that point (*Secret*, 144–5), though she mentions 'my dignity ... the best part of me' somewhat earlier (143).

46 Djénane's despair at being forced to be untrue to herself is presented in a way that was significant for Viaud himself. Faced with having to return to her husband after a short separation, the odalisque informs Lhéry that if Hamdi forces the issue, she will make use of the poison in the little silver flask that

she now carries with her at all times (XXII). (There is no mention of such a threat in Hélys's corresponding letter [*Secret*, 130–45].) As noted in chapter 1, Viaud had mentioned obtaining poison for suicide in a letter that discussed his family's efforts to get him married. When her cousins Mélek and Zeyneb ask her why she did not say no when her father mentioned the match with Hamdi, Djénane, her tears now flowing heavily, exclaims: 'Ah! I have already said "no" so many times! ... I was going to have to marry one of them, in the end!' (III). It would be easy to imagine Viaud, after years of pressure from his family to marry, having said the same thing, at least to himself.

47 Hélys's version: 'These hearts in which a young and generous sap boils, and to which action is forbidden, that can do nothing ... that are devoured or worn out by unrealizable dreams' (*Secret*, 155).

48 This line, linking 'dream' to unattainable love, suggests more erotic readings for some of the dreamers in Viaud's previous novels, such as Yann in *Iceland Fisherman* and the title character in *Ramuntcho*, especially when the former stands on deck at sea after having learned of Sylvestre's death and dreams about things that that text said could not be put into words (III:IX).

49 Hélys's version: 'Aziyadé is dead ... the little Circassian whom caprice or overwhelming desire threw into your arms is no more, and the time has come when ... instinctual love or love out of obeying has given way to love by choice' (*Secret*, 32–3).

50 Hélys, *Secret*, 261.

51 Ibid., 194.

52 The conception of and concern for community, what he calls 'solidarity,' is one of the three foci central to Paul Robinson's examination of gay autobiography in the twentieth century (*Gay Lives*, xvi–xix). He notes that of those who 'draw sharp lines between their own legitimate brand of homosexuality and the disreputable brand of others[,] Gide is the most striking example,' and that 'Julien Green's attitude toward homosexuality – his own and others' – is so hostile that it precludes any feeling of gay solidarity' (xvii). Even Genet he finds to be, as usual, self-contradictory on this point (xviii). The other two foci of his study, identity and concepts of masculinity (xiii), have also been central to our examination of the development of Viaud's novels.

53 The erotic connotations that 'intimacy' had had in earlier Viaud novels is absent here. The fact that, as part of modern gay slang, some gay men refer to their fellows as 'sisters' is an interesting coincidence but, I suspect, nothing more. Proust's Baron de Charlus does use 'sister' to refer to other gay men in *Time Regained* in a scene that takes place after the First World War (143), but there is a connotation of effeminacy that it is hard to imagine Viaud having wanted to evoke.

54 Remember also Ramuntcho's and Florentino's feelings of 'oppression' at not being able to express their feelings to each other (II:2). Proust, over a decade later, would repeatedly mention in his novel that one of the most difficult things that gays must face is not being able to talk about their love (*Sodom and Gomorrah*, 20, and elsewhere).

55 For what it is worth, Renaud was the name of a French sailor who had accompanied Viaud during part of his trip through China in 1901. See *The Last Days of Peking*, III.

One of the saddest moments in Blanch's study of Viaud and his writings is her comment: 'A feminine streak in Loti's [Viaud's] nature always made him crave a confidant to whom he could pour out his problems, hopes and griefs' (*Pierre Loti*, 265). What, one might ask, is feminine about wanting a confidant, and why should men deny themselves that very basic psychological need?

56 Lest Viaud be condemned for a negative portrayal of women with this episode, be it noted that he took it verbatim from one of Hélys's letters to him (*Secret*, 123).

57 Leo Bersani, in his very original reading of Proust, argued that 'he does sketch the outlines of a community grounded in a desire indifferent to the established sanctity of personhood' (*Homos*, 149), but this is a very different understanding of community, one in which 'relations would no longer be held hostage to demands for intimate knowledge of the other' (151). Michel in *The Immoralist*, as Bersani and others have shown, functions very much as a loner, and Jean Genet's protagonists usually have a love-hate relationship with other homosexual men. Paul Robinson noted that 'one searches the pages of [Julien Green's autobiographical writing] in vain for even the faintest hint of homosexual solidarity' (*Gay Lives*, 255).

58 We have already remarked on Viaud's use of the term in *The Story of a Child*. It had reappeared in *The Book of Pity and of Death* ('Notice from the author'), *Impressions* V, and would appear subsequently in *Turkey in Agony*. In *Sleeping Beauty's Chateau* and *Supreme Visions of the East*, he would speak of 'my friends, known or unknown.' He had altered the phrase, significantly, to 'my friends, my unknown brothers' in *Jerusalem* (I).

59 This is a refashioning of the same idea in Hélys's corresponding letter (*Secret*, 126).

60 Not surprisingly, given the final part about a man explaining a woman to herself, none of this passage has any equivalent in Hélys's corresponding letter (*Secret*, 106). Here Viaud was definitely presenting his own ideas about the function of literature in general, and perhaps his novels in particular.

61 Bergman, *Gaiety Transfigured*, 6–9.

62 Fernandez, *Le rapte de Ganymede*, 83.
63 Viaud changed Hélys's letter here, making it more assertive: 'The carefree and happy little girl has become a woman who has already cried a lot. Would she have been happier staying in her early life? Or did she *have* to leave it, did she *have* to become a thinking being? In short, did her life and yours not have to meet one day?' (*Secret*, 243) One can speculate on what Viaud may have meant when he changed Hélys's 'happy' (*heureuse*) to 'gay' (*gaie*), but again there does not seem to be any documentation indicating that *gai* meant homosexual in 1906.
64 Hélys, *Secret*, 157.
65 All of these ideas are in the corresponding Hélys letter (*Secret*, 260–1).
66 During a trip made to Istanbul three years after the initial publication of this novel, French writer Marcelle Tinayre met an older woman who complained that 'Loti's book caused dozens [of women] to blossom – Yes, many of these women learned that they were very unhappy. They didn't suspect it, before reading the novel' ('Notes d'une voyageuse en Turquie,' *La revue des deux mondes*, 1 November 1909, quoted in Lefèvre, *Les Désenchantées de Pierre Loti*, 118).
67 Hélys, *Secret*, 261.
68 Viaud took this phrase verbatim from one of Hélys's letters (*Secret*, 60). Could she have been thinking of the episode in the author's earlier novel when she wrote it?
69 It is true that near the end of the novel Viaud does indulge in some ego gratification, presenting Djénane as jealously in love with him (XXXVI, etc.), but Hélys contributed to this indulgence with her last letter, and perhaps with other things said before.

   Along these lines, there is never any physical description of Lhéry's young friend from the embassy, Jean Renaud, nor, for that matter, of several other men who are encountered briefly (XI, XVII, XXI, XXXIV, XLIII). Szyliowicz's comment, 'The Platonic association with the three women might provide a cover for Loti's [Viaud's or Lhéry's?] affiliation with the younger man' (*Pierre Loti and the Oriental Woman*, 87), is as gratuitous as it is undocumented. In the novel there is no suggestion that Lhéry has an erotic interest in Renaud, who is interested in a woman. One might also note, for what it is worth, that whereas Hakidjé/Aziyadé is recalled repeatedly in this novel, there is no mention of either Samuel/Daniel or Achmet/Mehmed. In short, André Lhéry is, rare for Viaud, a totally heterosexual male protagonist.

   Viaud's diary entries for the period are somewhat different. There he describes himself with Auguste-Laurent Masméjean, a mechanic from his ship who served as the model for Jean Renaud, and thinking repeatedly about 'my poor Mehmet.' (It might be remembered, as noted in chapter 9, that Viaud seemed to conflate Samuel/Daniel and Achmet/Mehmet in his memory as time went by.) Excerpts from Viaud's diary entries for the period 1903–5 can be found in *Istanbul: Le regard de Pierre Loti*.

70 Djénane complains that even though she can see Lhéry's eyes she cannot 'plumb their mystery,' and will therefore never know his 'exact thoughts' (LVI). Zeyneb spoke of Djénane's 'deep and serious eyes, where her soul appeared' (ibid.).

71 Hélys, *Secret*, 125.

72 In *First Youth* (1919), Viaud went back to referring to his sympathetic readers as 'unknown friends' (395).

73 Hélys, *Secret*, 69.

74 There is a corresponding passage in one of Hélys's letters to Viaud (*Secret*, 212–13). It is interesting to note that the term 'repressed' (*réprimé*) was Viaud's addition.

75 Hélys, *Secret*, 96; cf. *The Awakened*, XVI.

76 On this episode, see Rosario, 'Inversion's Histories | History's Inversions.

77 Hélys, *Secret*, 282.

Conclusion

1 The dramatization of *Ramuntcho*, because of the nature of its genre, retains none of the complex imagery used in the novel's descriptive passages. It also lacks any of the title character's reflections on his difference, any mention of the *irritzina* or his reaction to it, or any equivalent of the novel's descriptions of the various contraband episodes and pelota matches. Two important scenes from the novel that are included, the difficult last meeting of Ramuntcho and Florentino and Ramuntcho's burning of his father's picture, are substantially different and not gay suggestive in the play.

2 In one of her letters to André Lhéry in *The Awakened*, one that has no equivalent in *The Secret of 'The Awakened,'* Djénane wrote to the author: 'Once your book [on the plight of Turkish women] is finished, I would like you not to write anything else' (XXXVI). Whether this was Viaud's effort at justifying a return to novelistic silence I would not hazard to guess.

3 Several critics have argued homosexual elements in Proust's allegedly heterosexual protagonist, Marcel. Most, following the lead of Justin O'Brien, have concentrated on the fact that the major object of Marcel's affections, Albertine Simonet, is often based on a man, Alfred Agostinelli (see O'Brien, 'Albertine the Ambiguous'). While it is true that Proust made use of episodes in his own life with Agostinelli as the source for some of Marcel's interactions

with Albertine, I find nothing in *In Search of Lost Time* itself that indicates that one should view Albertine as a man, and everything to indicate that one should read the character as a woman. As Harry Levin observed years ago on this approach: 'A heavy burden of proof falls upon any critic who sets his word against the word of the writer he is discussing' ('Proust, Gide, and the Sexes,' 649).

This is very different from suggesting a transposition of sexes in *Iceland Fisherman*, for example, since, as we saw, Viaud filled that novel with references to *My Brother Yves* – which, obviously, was available to readers of the second novel – that linked Gaud to Pierre Loti in the preceding work and so allowed, indeed encouraged, the interested reader to view the second novel as a retelling of the first. The same is true, as we saw, of *The Awakened* and, to a lesser extent, *Sailor.*

Mark D. Guenette, on the other hand, working within the confines of Proust's work, has shown that Marcel exhibits definite, if only suggested, homosexual desire and love for his male friend Saint-Loup (see: 'Le loup et le narrateur'). Along these lines, see also Seiden, 'Proust's Marcel and Saint-Loup,' and Viti, 'Marcel and the Medusa.'

Bersani, taking a very original approach, accepts Marcel as heterosexual and then argues that 'Marcel Proust the homosexual had to submit to the tortures of being heterosexual for the sake of those "truths" that art enshrines' (*Homos,* 143).

4 Schehr, *Alcibiades at the Door,* 126. One might wonder if Schehr had read *Aziyadé, My Brother Yves,* or *Madame Chrysanthemum.*

5 Nye, *Masculinity,* 119.

6 Guenette, 'Le loup et le narrateur,' 245.

7 Meyers, *Homosexuality and Literature,* 60.

8 Robinson, *Scandal in the Ink,* 148.

9 Bersani, *Homos,* 161.

10 Robinson, *Gay Lives,* 258.

11 Recall Fernandez's description of the works on homosexuality that he was able to amass in the 1950s: 'The portrait that I could sketch of myself through the innumerable cases that I saw pass by in these texts was that of an inferior being condemned to suffer; "understood" sometimes, but always reviled; half way between a victim and a failure' (*Le rapte de Ganymede,* 83).

Works Cited

Works of Pierre Loti (Julien Viaud)

All of Viaud's novels and most of his other works are available in English. To aid those looking for translations of his works, I list first the English title that I used in this book followed by the original French, and then the various English titles under which translations of that work have been published. Since most of the translations have gone through different editions with different publishers, I have not provided publishing information for the various editions. For the works not available in English, I have indicated which French edition I used as my source.

Autumn Japaneries. Fr. *Japoneries d'automne.* Paris: Calmann-Lévy, n.d.
The Awakened. Fr. *Les Désenchantées*
   Disenchanted, trans. Clara Bell
Aziyadé. Fr. *Aziyadé*
   Aziyadé, trans. M. Laurie
   Constantinople, trans. Marjorie Laurie
Blossoms of Boredom. Fr. *Fleurs d'ennui.* Paris: Calmann-Lévy, 1893.
The Book of Pity and of Death. Fr. *Le Livre de la Pitié et de la Mort*
   The Book of Pity and of Death, trans. T.P. O'Connor
Carmen Sylva and Sketches from the Orient. Fr. *L'Exilée*
   Carmen Sylva and Sketches from the Orient, trans. Fred Rothwell
Cette éternelle nostalgie: Journal intime 1878–1911, ed. Bruno Vercier, Alain Quella-Villéger, and Guy Dugas. Paris: La Table ronde, 1997.
Correspondence inédite 1865–1904, ed. Nadine Duvigneau and N. Serban. Paris: Calmann-Lévy, 1929.
The Daughter of Heaven. Fr. *Fille du ciel*

The Daughter of Heaven, trans. Ruth Helen Davies

The Desert. Fr. *Le Désert*

    The Desert, trans. Jay Minn

Discours de réception de la Séance de l'Académie française du 7 avril 1892. Paris: Calmann-Lévy, 1892.

Egypt. Fr. *La mort de Philae*

    Egypt, trans. William Peter Baines

First Youth. Fr. *Prime jeunesse*. In *Le Roman d'un enfant, suivi de Prime jeunesse*, ed. Bruno Vercier. Paris: Gallimard, 1999.

From Lands of Exile. Fr. *Propos d'exil*

    From Lands of Exile, trans. Clara Bell

Galilee. Fr. *Galilée*. In *Voyages (1872–1913)*. By Loti. Ed. Claude Martin, 539–645. Paris: Laffont, 1991.

Iceland Fisherman. Fr. *Pêcheur d'Islande*

    An/The Iceland Fisherman, translations by William Peter Baines, Clara Cadiot, Helen James Bennett Dole, S. Guy Endore, Anna Farwell de Koven, H.A. Melcon

L'Ile de Pâques: Journal d'un aspirant de La Flore. N.p.: Pierre-Olivier Combelles, 1988.

Impressions. Fr. *Figures et choses qui passaient*

    Impressions, trans. unknown, with an introduction by Henry James

India. Fr. *L'Inde (sans les anglais)*

    India, trans. L. Werner Laurie

Into Morocco. Fr. *Au Maroc*

    Into Morocco, trans. E.P. Robbins

    Morocco, trans. William Peter Baines

Istanbul: Le Regard de Pierre Loti, ed. Alain Quella-Villéger. N.p.: Casterman, 1992.

Jerusalem. Fr. *Jérusalem*

    Jerusalem, translations by Marjorie Laurie, William Peter Baines

'Journal intime inédit,' ed. Michel Desbruères. In *Le Livre de la pitié et de la mort*. By Loti. Ed. Pierre P. Loti-Viaud and Michel Desbruères, 163–240. Paris: Pirot, 1991.

The Last Days of Peking. Fr. *Les derniers jours de Pékin*

    The Last Days of Peking, trans. Myrta Leonora Jones

Lettres de Pierre Loti à Madame Juliette Adam (1880–1922). Paris: Plon, 1924.

Madame Chrysanthemum. Fr. *Madame Chrysanthème*

    Japan, trans. Laura Ensor

    Madame Chrysantheme, translations by Laura Ensor, Hattie E. Miller, E.P. Robins

Madame Prune. Fr. *La Troisième jeunesse de Madame Prune*

    Madame Prune, trans. Samuel Richard Cobden Plimsoll

The Marriage of Loti. Fr. *Le Mariage de Loti*
   The Marriage of Loti, trans. Clara Bell
   Rarahu, trans. Clara Bell
   Tahiti, trans. Clara Bell
Mort de ma mère, ed. Fernand Lapland. Paris: La Nonpareille, 1989.
My Brother Yves. Fr. *Mon Frère Yves*
   My Brother Yves, trans. Mary P. Fletcher
   A Tale of Brittany, trans. William Peter Baines
Notes of My Youth. Fr. *Un jeune officier pauvre*
   Notes of My Youth, trans. Rose Ellen Stein
On Life's By-ways. Fr. *Reflets sur la sombre route*
   On Life's By-ways, trans. Fred Rothwell
'Petite suite mourante à Fantôme d'Orient,' ed. André Moulis. In *Galilée.* By
   Loti. Ed. Pierre P. Loti-Viaud and Michel Desbruières. Paris: Pirot, 1990.
A Phantom from the East. Fr. *Fantôme d'Orient*
   A Phantom from the East, trans. J.E. Gordon
A Pilgrimage to Angkor. Fr. *Pèlerin d'Ankor*
   A Pilgrimage to Angkor, trans. David McKay
   Siam, trans. David McKay
Private Diary 1878–1881. Fr. *Journal intime 1878–1881*, ed. Samuel Viaud. Paris:
   Calmann-Lévy, 1925.
Private Diary 1882–1885. Fr. *Journal intime 1882–1885*, ed. Samuel P. Loti-Viaud.
   Paris: Calmann-Lévy, 1929.
Ramuntcho. Fr. *Ramuntcho*
   Ramuntcho, trans. Henri Pène du Bois
   A Tale of the Pyrenees, trans. William Peter Baines
Sailor. Fr. *Matelot*
   Jean Berny, Sailor, trans. E.P. Robins
Sleeping Beauty's Chateau. Fr. *Le Château de la belle au bois dormant.* Paris: Calmann-
   Lévy, n.d.
Soldats bleus: Journal intime 1914–1918, ed. Alain Quella-Villéger, Bruno Vercier.
   Paris: La Table ronde, 1998.
Some Aspects of the World's Madness. Fr. *Quelques aspects du vertige mondial.* Paris:
   Calmann-Lévy, 1928.
The Story of a Child. Fr. *Le Roman d'un enfant*
   A Child's Romance, trans. Clara Bell
   The Romance of a Child, trans. Mary L. Watkins
   The Story of a Child, trans. Caroline F. Smith
The Story of a Spahi. Fr. *Le Roman d'un spahi*
   Between Two Opinions, trans. Mary Linsay Watkins

Love in the Desert, trans. unknown

The Romance of a Spahi, translations by William James Clark, G.F. Monkshood, Mary Linsay Watkins

The Sahara, trans. Marjorie Laurie

A Spahi's Love-Story, trans. unknown

Supreme Visions of the East. Fr. *Suprêmes visions d'Orient*. In *Voyages (1872–1913)*. By Loti. Ed. Claude Martin, 1353–1458. Paris: Laffont, 1991.

To Ispahan. Fr. *Vers Ispahan*. In *Voyages (1872–1913)*. By Loti. Ed. Claude Martin, 873–1019. Paris: Laffont, 1991.

Turkey in Agony. Fr. *La Turquie agonisante*

Turkey in Agony, trans. Bedwin Sands

Secondary Works

Anders, John P. 'Willa Cather, France, and Pierre Loti: A Spirit of Affiliation.' *Willa Cather Pioneer Memorial Newsletter* 38, 4 (1995): 15–18.

Balcou, Jean. 'La Vision bretonne de Loti.' *Revue Pierre Loti* 31 (1987): 153–64.

Barthes, Roland. 'Pierre Loti: *Aziyadé*.' In *New Critical Essays*, trans. Richard Howard, 105–121. New York: Hill and Wang, 1980.

– *The Pleasure of the Text*, trans. Richard Howard. New York: Hill and Wang, 1975.

Barthou, Louis. *Pêcheur d'Islande de Pierre Loti*. Paris: Mellottée, n.d.

Bergman, David. *Gaiety Transfigured: Gay Self-Representation in American Literature*. Madison: University of Wisconsin Press, 1991.

Berrong, Richard. '*Salammbô*: A Myth of the Origin of Languages.' *Modern Language Studies* 15, 4 (1985): 261–9.

Bersani, Leo. *Homos*. Cambridge, MA: Harvard University Press, 1995.

Besnier, Patrick, ed. *Ramuntcho*. By Pierre Loti. Paris: Gallimard, 1990.

Blanch, Lesley. *Pierre Loti: The Legendary Romantic*. New York: Harcourt Brace Jovanovich, 1983.

Bongie, Chris. *Exotic Memories: Literature, Colonialism, and the Fin de Siècle*. Stanford: Stanford University Press, 1991.

Bray, Alan. *Homosexuality in Renaissance England*. London: Gay Men's Press, 1982.

Bristow, Joseph. *Effeminate England*. New York: Columbia University Press, 1995.

– *Sexology*. London: Routledge, 1997.

Brodin, Pierre. *Loti*. Montreal: Parizeau, 1945.

Buisine, Alain. *Tombeau de Loti*. Paris: Amateurs de livres, 1988.

Cairns, Lucille. 'Homosexuality and Lesbianism in Proust's *Sodome et Gomorrhe*.' *French Studies* 51, 1 (1997): 43–57.

Camus, Renaud. 'Monsieur Ouin à Châteaudouble.' In *Chroniques achriennes*, 90–4. Paris: P.O.L., 1984.

Carter, William C. *Marcel Proust: A Life.* New Haven: Yale University Press, 2000.

Chauncey, George. *Gay New York: The Making of the Gay Male World, 1890–1940.* New York: Basic Books, 1994.

Cocteau, Jean. *Le livre blanc.* Paris: Passage du Marais, 1992.

Copley, Antony. *Sexual Moralities in France, 1790–1980: New Ideas on the Family, Divorce, and Homosexuality.* London and New York: Routledge, 1989.

Creech, James. *Closet Writing/Gay Reading: The Case of Melville's* Pierre. Chicago: University of Chicago Press, 1993.

– 'Forged in Crisis: Queer Beginnings of Modern Masculinity in a Canonical French Novel.' *Studies in the Novel* 28 (1996): 303–21.

Desbruères, Michel. Préface. *Mon Frère Yves.* By Pierre Loti. Paris: Christian Pirot, 1990.

Drake, Robert. *The Gay Canon: Great Books Every Gay Man Should Read.* New York: Anchor Books, 1998.

Dupont, Jacques. Préface. *Pêcheur d'Islande.* By Loti. Ed. Jacques Dupont. Paris: Gallimard, 1988.

Farrère, Claude. *Loti.* Paris: Excelsior, 1929.

Fernandez, Dominique. *Le rapte de Ganymede.* Paris: Grasset, 1989.

Flaubert, Gustave. *Salammbô.* Paris: Garnier-Flammarion, 1964.

Flottes, Pierre. 'Sur un manuscrit de "Ramuntcho."' *Revue d'histoire littéraire de la France* 42 (1935): 105–16.

Forster, E.M. *Maurice.* New York: W.W. Norton, 1971.

Foucault, Michel. *History of Sexuality.* Vol. 1, trans. Robert Hurley. New York: Vintage Books, 1990.

Genet, Christian, and Daniel Hervé. *Pierre Loti l'enchanteur.* Gemozac: C. Genet, 1988.

Gide, André. *Corydon.* In *Oeuvres complètes.* Vol. 9, ed. L. Martin-Chaffier. Paris: NRF, 1935.

– *Si le grain ne meurt.* Paris: Gallimard, 1955.

Girard, René. *Deceit, Desire, and the Novel.* Trans. Yvonne Freccero. Baltimore: The Johns Hopkins Press, 1965.

Goldberg, Jonathan. 'Strange Brothers.' In *Novel Gazing,* ed. Eve Kosofsky Sedgwick, 465–82. Durham: Duke University Press, 1997.

Goncourt, Edmond de, and Jules de Goncourt. *Journal,* ed. Robert Ricatte. 4 vols. Paris: Fasquelle and Flammarion, 1956.

Groos, Arthur. 'Lieutenant F.B. Pinkerton: Problems in the Genesis of an Operatic Hero.' *Italica* 64 (1987): 654–75.

Guenette, Mark D. 'Le loup et le narrateur: The Masking and Unmasking of Homosexuality in Proust's *A la recherche du temps perdu.*' *Romanic Review* 80, 2 (1989): 229–46.

Gundermann, Christian. 'Orientalism, Homophobia, Masochism: Transfers between Pierre Loti's *Aziyadé* and Gilles Deleuze's "Coldness and Cruelty."' *Diacritics* 24 (1994): 151–67.

Gusdorf, Georges. 'Conditions and Limits of Autobiography.' In *Autobiography: Essays Theoretical and Critical*, ed. James Olney, 28–48. Princeton: Princeton University Press, 1980.

Halperin, David M. 'How to Do the History of Male Homosexuality.' *GLQ: A Journal of Lesbian and Gay Studies* 6, 1 (2000): 87–123.

– *One Hundred Years of Homosexuality and Other Essays on Greek Love.* New York: Routledge, 1990.

Hanna, Martha. 'Natalism, Homosexuality, and the Controversy over *Corydon.*' In *Homosexuality in Modern France*, ed. Jeffrey Merrick and Bryant T. Ragan, Jr, 202–24. New York: Oxford University Press, 1996.

Hargreaves, Alex G. *The Colonial Experience in French Fiction.* London: Macmillan, 1981.

Hélys, Marc. *Le Secret des 'Désenchantées.'* Paris: Perrin, 1924.

Hwang, David Henry. *M. Butterfly.* New York: New American Library, 1988.

James, Henry. 'Pierre Loti.' In *Essays in London and Elsewhere*, 159–94. New York: Harper and Brothers, 1893.

Lefèvre, Raymonde. *Les Désenchantées de Pierre Loti.* Paris: Société française d'éditions littéraires et techniques, 1939.

– *En Marge de Loti.* Paris: Jean Renard, 1944.

– *Le Mariage de Loti.* Paris: Société française d'éditions littéraires et techniques, 1935.

– *La Vie inquiète de Pierre Loti.* Paris: Société française d'éditions littéraires et techniques, 1934.

Leguillon, Rolande. 'Un aspect de l'amour chez Pierre Loti.' *Rice University Studies* 59, 3 (1973): 43–53.

Le Hir, Yves. 'Le soleil dans "Pêcheur d'Islande" de Pierre Loti.' *Les Lettres romanes* 18 (1964): 53–8.

Lejeune, Philippe. *On Autobiography*, trans. Katherine Leary. Minneapolis: University of Minnesota Press, 1989.

Lerner, Michael G. *Pierre Loti.* New York: Twayne Publishers, 1974.

Levin, Harry. 'Proust, Gide, and the Sexes.' *PMLA* 65, 4 (1950): 648–52.

Magne, Bernard. 'Les figures zoomorphes dans "Le Roman d'un spahi."' *Annales de l'Université Marien Ngouabi. Série littératures, langues, sciences humaines* 1 (1989): 65–70.

Marshall, Barbara L. *Configuring Gender: Exploration in Theory and Politics.* Peterborough: Broadview, 2000.

Martel, Frédéric. *Le rose et le noir: Les homosexuels en France depuis 1968.* Paris: Seuil, 1996.

Martin, Claude. Préface. *Aziyadé* suivi de *Fantôme d'Orient.* By Pierre Loti. Ed. Claude Martin, 7–28. Paris: Gallimard, 1991.

– Préface. *Voyages.* By Pierre Loti. Ed. Claude Martin, vii–xvii. Paris: Laffont, 1995.

Martin, Robert K. 'Edward Carpenter and the Double Structure of *Maurice.*' *Journal of Homosexuality.* 8, 3–4 (1983): 35–46.

Maugère, Annelise. *L'identité masculine en crise au tournant du siècle 1871–1914.* Paris: Rivages, 1987.

Mayne, Xavier. *The Intersexes: A History of Similisexualism as a Problem in Social Life.* 1908. New York: Arno, 1975.

Melchiori, Barbara. 'Feelings About Aspects: Henry James on Pierre Loti.' *Studi americani* 15 (1969): 169–99.

Meyers, Jeffrey. *Homosexuality and Literature 1890–1930.* Montreal: McGill-Queen's University Press, 1977.

Millward, Keith G. *L'Oeuvre de Pierre Loti et l'Esprit 'fin de siècle.'* Paris: Nizet, 1955.

Moon, Michael. 'Disseminating Whitman.' *Displacing Homophobia.* Special issue of *The South Atlantic Quarterly,* ed. Ronald R. Butters, John M. Clum, and Michael Moon. 88, 1 (1989): 247–65.

Morin, Jeanne Elise. 'De "Au large" à "Pêcheur d'Islande."' *Revue Pierre Loti* 27 (1986): 49.

Moulis, André. 'Amours basques de Pierre Loti.' *Littératures* 2 (1980): 99–131.

– 'Genèse de "Ramuntcho."' *Littératures* 12 (1965): 49–78.

Muller, Marcel. 'Sodome I ou la naturalisation de Charlus.' *Poétique* 8 (1971): 470–8.

Mulvey, Laura. 'Visual Pleasure and Narrative Cinema.' *Screen* 16 (1975). Rprt. in *Issues in Feminist Film Criticism,* ed. Patricia Erens, 28–40. Bloomington: Indiana University Press, 1990.

Nye, Robert A. *Masculinity and Male Codes of Honor in Modern France.* New York: Oxford University Press, 1993.

O'Brien, Justin. 'Albertine the Ambiguous: Notes on Proust's Transposition of Sexes.' *PMLA* 64 (1949): 933–52.

Ono, Setsuko. *A Western Image of Japan.* Geneva: du Courrier, 1972.

Osaji, Debe. 'The African Image by a Non-African Novelist Dealing with Africa: A Case-Study of Le Roman d'un Spahi by Pierre Loti.' *Nigeria Magazine* 54, 3 (1986): 97–103.

Peniston, William A. 'Love and Death in Gay Paris.' In *Homosexuality in Modern*

France, ed. Jeffrey Merrick, Bryant T. Ragan, Jr, 128–45. New York: Oxford University Press, 1996.

Poggenburg, Helen Hart. 'The Dark Side of Loti's Exoticism: The Breton Novels.' In *Exoticism in French Literature*, 78–88. French Literature Series 13. Dept. of Foreign Language and Literatures. Columbia: University of South Carolina Press, 1986.

Press, Jacob. 'Same-Sex Unions in Modern Europe: *Daniel Deronda, Altneuland,* and the Homoerotics of Jewish Nationalism.' In *Novel Gazing*, ed. Eve Kosofsky Sedgwick, 299–329. Durham: Duke University Press, 1997.

Proust, Marcel. *The Captive. The Fugitive*, trans. C.K. Scott Montcrieff, Terence Kilmartin, rev. D.J. Enright. New York: Modern Library, 1993.

– *Correspondance*, ed. Philip Kolb. Paris: Plon, 1970–.

– *La prisonnière*, ed. Pierre-Edmond Robert. Paris: Gallimard, 1989.

– *Sodom and Gomorrah*, trans. C.K. Scott Montcrieff, Terence Kilmartin, rev. D.J. Enright. New York: Modern Library, 1993.

– *Swann's Way*, trans. C.K. Scott Montcrieff, Terence Kilmartin, rev. D.J. Enright. New York: Modern Library, 1992.

– *Time Regained*, trans. Andreas Mayor, Terence Kilmartin, rev. D.J. Enright. New York: Modern Library, 1993.

Quella-Villéger, Alain. *Pierre Loti: Le pèlerin de la planète*. Bordeaux: Aubéron, 1998.

– *Pierre Loti l'incompris*. Paris: Presses de la Renaissance, 1986.

– 'Sources et contextes.' In *Pasquala Ivanovitch et autres pages monténégrines*. By Loti. Ed. Alain Quella-Villéger, 127–35. Puiseaux: Pardès, 1991.

Rivers, J.E. *Proust and the Art of Love*. New York: Columbia University Press, 1980.

Robert, Louis de. *De Loti à Proust*. Paris: Flammarion, 1928.

Robinson, Christopher. *Scandal in the Ink*. New York: Cassell, 1995.

Robinson, Paul. *Gay Lives: Homosexual Autobiographies from John Addington Symonds to Paul Monette*. Chicago: University of Chicago Press, 1999.

Rosario, Vernon A. 'Inversion's Histories | History's Inversions: Novelizing Fin-de-Siècle Homosexuality.' In *Science and Homosexualities*, ed. Vernon A. Rosario, 89–107. New York: Routledge, 1997.

– 'Pointy Penises, Fashion Crimes, and Hysterical Mollies: The Pederasts' Inversions.' In *Homosexuality in Modern France*, ed. Jeffrey Merrick, Bryant T. Ragan, Jr, 146–76. New York: Oxford University Press, 1996.

Said, Edward. *Orientalism*. New York: Vintage, 1979.

Saint-Leger, Marie-Paule de. *Pierre Loti l'insaisissable*. Paris: L'Harmattan, 1996.

Scepi, Henri. 'Rhétorique de l'incertain dans Pêcheur d'Islande.' *Revue Pierre Loti* 27 (1986): 65–8.

Schehr, Lawrence R. *Alcibiades at the Door: Gay Discourses in French Literature.* Stanford: Stanford University Press, 1995.

Schultz, Gretchen. 'French Literature: Nineteenth Century.' In *The Gay and Lesbian Literary Heritage,* ed. Claude J. Summers, 293–8. New York: Henry Holt and Company, 1995.

Sedgwick, Eve Kosofsky. *Between Men: English Literature and Male Homosocial Desire.* New York: Columbia University Press, 1985.

– *Epistemology of the Closet.* Berkeley: University of California Press, 1990.

Seiden, Melvin. 'Proust's Marcel and Saint-Loup: Inversion Reconsidered.' *Contemporary Literature* 10 (1969): 220–40.

Serban, N. *Pierre Loti: Sa vie et son oeuvre.* Paris: Champion, 1920.

Sharpley-Whiting, T. Denean. *Black Venus: Sexualized Savages, Primal Fears, and Primitive Narratives in French.* Durham: Duke University Press, 1999.

Showalter, Elaine. *Sexual Anarchy.* New York: Viking, 1990.

Smith, Nigel E. 'Silence, Secrecy, and Scientific Discourse in the Nineteenth Century.' In *Articulations of Difference: Gender Studies and Writing in France,* ed. Dominique D. Fisher, Lawrence R. Schehr, 83–99. Stanford: Stanford University Press, 1997.

'Some in the media still insist upon using the "H" word.' *Gay People's Chronicle* 2 August 1996: 14.

Sonntag, Dina. 'Prelude to Tahiti: Gauguin in Paris, Brittany and Martinique.' In *Paul Gauguin: Tahiti,* ed. Christoph Becker, 85–106. N.p.: Gerd Hatje, 1998.

Stanton, Michael N. 'The Novel: Gay Male.' In *The Gay and Lesbian Literary Heritage,* ed. Claude J. Summers, 518–23. New York: Henry Holt and Company, 1995.

Summers, Claude J. 'Introduction.' In *The Gay and Lesbian Literary Heritage,* ed. Claude J. Summers, ix–xiv. New York: Henry Holt and Company, 1995.

Szyliowicz, Irene L. *Pierre Loti and the Oriental Woman.* New York: St Martin's Press, 1988.

Tapinc, Huseyin. 'Masculinity, Femininity, and the Turkish Male Homosexual.' In *Modern Homosexuality,* ed. Ken Plummer, 39–49. New York: Routledge, 1992.

Thompson, Victoria. 'Creating Boundaries: Homosexuality and the Changing Social Order in France, 1830–1870.' In, *Homosexuality in Modern France,* ed. Jeffrey Merrick, Bryant T. Ragan, Jr, 102–27. New York: Oxford University Press, 1996.

Troy, Robert de. *Pierre Loti.* Paris: Hachette, 1948.

Turner, William B. *A Genealogy of Queer Theory.* Philadelphia: Temple University Press, 2000.

Valence, Odette, and Samuel Pierre-Loti-Viaud. *La Famille de Pierre Loti; ou, l'éducation passionnée.* Paris: Calmann-Lévy, 1940.

Vedel, Émile. Préface. *Un jeune officier pauvre.* By Loti. Ed. Samuel Viaud, i–viii. Paris: Calmann-Lévy, 1923.

Vercier, Bruno. 'Le mythe du premier souvenir: Pierre Loti, Michel Lerris.' *Revue d'histoire littéraire de la France* 75 (1975): 1029–40.

– 'Un papillon citron-aurore.' *Revue des sciences humaines* 222 (1991): 35–40.

– Préface. *Aziyadé.* By Pierre Loti. Ed. Bruno Vercier, 7–30. Paris: Flammarion, 1989.

– Préface. *Le Mariage de Loti.* By Pierre Loti. Ed. Bruno Vercier, 9–38. Paris: Flammarion, 1991.

Vercier, Bruno, ed. *Le roman d'un enfant.* By Pierre Loti. Paris: Flammarion, 1988.

Vercier, Bruno, and Alain Quella-Villéger. *Aziyadé suivi de Fantôme d'Orient de Pierre Loti.* Paris: Gallimard, 2001.

Vercier, Bruno, Alain Quella-Villéger, and Guy Dugas. 'Du "Roman d'un enfant" au Journal d'un adulte.' In *Cette éternelle nostalgie: Journal intime 1878–1911.* By Loti. Ed. Bruno Vercier, Alain Quella-Villéger, Guy Dugas, 9–18. Paris: La Table Ronde, 1997.

Viti, Elizabeth Richardson. 'Marcel and the Medusa: The Narrator's Obfuscated Homosexuality in *A la recherche du temps perdu.*' *Dalhousie French Studies* 26 (1994): 61–8.

Wake, Clive. *The Novels of Pierre Loti.* The Hague: Mouton, 1974.

Woodress, James. *Willa Cather: A Literary Life.* Lincoln: University of Nebraska Press, 1987.

Woods, Gregory. *A History of Gay Literature: The Male Tradition.* New York: Yale University Press, 1998.

Zanone, Damien. 'Bretagne et Japon aux Antipodes, Les deux monuments d'un même roman d'amour pour Yves: Lecture de *Mon frère Yves* et *Madame Chrysanthème.*' In *Loti et son temps: Colloque de Paimpol 22, 23, 24, et 25 juillet,* ed. François Chappé, 97–110. Rennes: Presses Universitaires de Rennes, 1994.

Zeeland, Steven. *Sailors and Sexual Identity: Crossing the Line Between 'Straight' and 'Gay' in the U.S. Navy.* New York: Harrington Park Press, 1994.

Index